Cambridge Middle East Library

Women in nineteenth-century Egypt

Cambridge Middle East Library

Also in this series

Medicine and power in Tunisia, 1780–1900
NANCY ELIZABETH GALLAGHER

Urban notables and Arab nationalism: the politics of Damascus, 1860–1920
PHILIP S. KHOURY

The Palestinian Liberation Organization: people, power and politics
HELENA COBBAN

Egypt in the reign of Muhammad Ali
AFAF LUTFI AL-SAYYID MARSOT

Women in nineteenth-century Egypt

JUDITH E. TUCKER

The right of the University of Cambridge to print and sell all manner of books was granted by Henry VIII in 1534. The University has printed and published continuously since 1584.

CAMBRIDGE UNIVERSITY PRESS

CAMBRIDGE
LONDON NEW YORK NEW ROCHELLE
MELBOURNE SYDNEY

Published by the Press Syndicate of the University of Cambridge
The Pitt Building, Trumpington Street, Cambridge CB2 1RP
32 East 57th Street, New York, NY 10022, USA
10 Stamford Road, Oakleigh, Melbourne 3166, Australia

First published 1985

Printed in Great Britain at the University Press, Cambridge

British Library cataloguing in publication data

Tucker, Judith E.
Women in nineteenth-century Egypt.–
(Cambridge Middle East library)
1. Women–Egypt–Social conditions
I. Title
305.4'2'0962 HQ1793

Library of Congress cataloguing in publication data

Tucker, Judith E.
Women in nineteenth century Egypt.
(Cambridge Middle East library)
Bibliography: p.
Includes index.
1. Women–Egypt–Social conditions. 2. Egypt–
Economic conditions. 3. Egypt–Social conditions.
I. Title II. Series.
HQ1793.T83 1985 305.4'2'0962 85–5735

ISBN 0 521 30338 9

WV

For my parents,
RUTH H. and CHARLES A. TUCKER

Contents

Illustrations

All illustrations are reproduced by permission of the Library of Congress

Acknowledgments

I received invaluable assistance in the course of working on this book. The original core of research was accomplished with the aid of a Fulbright doctoral dissertation grant in 1976–1977, and two years of postdoctoral research and writing were made possible by fellowships from the Institute of Arab Studies in Belmont, Mass. (1981–1982), and the Social Science Research Council (1982–1983).

The archives of the maḥkamah sharʿīyah in Cairo yielded by far the most important primary materials for this study, and I thank the staff of the archives for their assistance. The late Mr Aḥmad al-Ḥīn of Cairo shared with me his extensive knowledge of the archives and of the conventions of nineteenth century legal records; I appreciated his help and regret that he will not see the fruits of his patient instruction. My research in Cairo also took me to the Dār al-Maḥfuẓāt and the Dār al-Kutub periodicals section, where the archival staffs were exceptionally kind and helpful. I spent several months in the Public Record Office and the British Museum in England and the Archives du ministère des affaires étrangères and Archives de la guerre in France, where I benefited from prompt and pleasant services.

The year I spent at the Institute of Arab Studies enabled me to write a good portion of the text, and I wish to thank Dr Khalil Nakhleh, Kim Watson, and Dixie Hallaj for providing a good working environment. I completed the text while a fellow at Harvard's Center for Middle Eastern Studies in 1982–1983. Dr Dennis Skiotis, Barbara Henson, Jacqueline Brown, Helen Ives, Pat Goad, and Catherine Jones gave their encouragement and, in some cases, concrete help in the final preparation of the manuscript; I thank them for their warmth and lasting friendship.

Teachers, friends, and family members assisted with ideas, criticism, counsel, and advice – I cannot hope to draw up a comprehensive list. Professor David S. Landes advised on my original dissertation on the subject, and his comments helped sharpen both theoretical approach and style. Mr Albert Hourani also advised on the dissertation and gave generously of his unparalleled knowledge of Middle Eastern history. Dr Roger Owen read the final manuscript and made several suggestions which saved me from error. While at work on the book, it has been my privilege and pleasure to serve on the editorial board of *MERIP Reports*. My fellow editors have been a formative influence on my thinking, as have the members of the Boston-area Alternative Middle East Studies Seminar, active in 1980–1982. Of the many individuals who lent ideas and succor, I wish to mention here Penny Johnson, Miriam Rosen, Najwa Makhoul, Irene Gendzier, Selma Botman, and Basim Musallam. My parents, Ruth and Charles Tucker, have been ever interested and supportive. Elizabeth Wetton and Patricia Carroll were meticulous and caring editors. Finally, my husband, Sharif S. Elmusa, helped in numerous ways. His sensitivity to the situation of his sisters, of blood and country, helped me avoid some of the pitfalls of projection, and his ability to turn every question on its head invariably forced me to reassess old interpretations and undertake new adventures.

JUDITH E. TUCKER

Georgetown University
October 1984

Abbreviations

BFAAPS:	British and Foreign Anti-Slavery and Aborigenes Protection Society
EI:	*Encyclopaedia of Islam*
FO:	Foreign Office, United Kingdom
I:	al-Iʿlanāt (court records)
IJMES:	*International Journal of Middle East Studies*
JESHME:	*Journal of the Economic and Social History of the Middle East*
MAE:	Ministère des affaires étrangères, France
MBA:	Maḥkamah Bāb al-ʿAlī (court records)
MM:	Maḥkamah Manṣūrah (court records)
P:	*Parliamentary Papers*, United Kingdom
PRO:	Public Record Office, United Kingdom
RRPE:	*Review of Radical Political Economics*
Vincennes:	Les archives de la guerre, France

Note on transliteration and dates

The Library of Congress transliteration system has been used throughout. Some place names familiar to the reader, such as Damietta, Rosetta, Khartoum, etc., have been written with their anglicized spellings; otherwise, the Arabic word or term is rendered in strict transliteration. In general, I have added "s" to the singular of Arabic words to form an anglicized plural. In a very few cases of frequently employed terms, i.e. *ʿulamāʾ*, the Arabic plural form is used.

Whenever the original source was dated by the hijrah calendar, I have retained the original date followed by an oblique stroke and the western calendar equivalent, i.e. 1266/1850 for 1266 AH and 1850 AD.

Introduction

She who trusts men, trusts a sieve to hold water.

Egyptian proverb (Aḥmad Taymūr, *al-Amthāl al-ʿāmmīyah*, 3095, p. 514)

I

The history of women in Egypt and the Middle East as a whole has been little studied. In part, such neglect reflects the general state of Middle East historiography: focus on visible political institutions, diplomatic events, and intellectual currents of the high, as opposed to popular, culture long confined the field of inquiry to upper class males at the expense of studying the role those of another class or gender played in the historical process. But even now, as a new generation of historians in the Middle East and West direct their attention to the social and economic history of the region and begin to write the history of social classes – peasants, urban craftsmen, casual laborers – whose history and culture remained obscure or irrelevant to the orientalist scholar, women are usually nowhere to be found, or receive only cursory mention.

Part of the problem surely springs from basic misconceptions about women's history and its relation to social and economic history as a whole, East or West. Women have always been numerically important in human populations, a sufficiently compelling reason perhaps to explore their past, but the full significance of the study of women lies elsewhere. The history of women demands an immediate awareness of a multitude of forces, institutions, and activities which elude analysis at the level of official political institutions, mainstream intellectual movements, or economic overviews; rather, the world of informal networks, popular culture, and the basic forces of production and reproduction define the arena of women's activities and therefore women's studies. The social and economic life of men, as well as women, of the peasantry and urban lower classes, who constituted the vast majority of the precapitalist and, at least in the Third World, capitalist population, was shaped by those activities and institutions in which women played a major and distinct role: without understanding the forms and dimensions of women's activities, we cannot grasp the contours of society as a whole.

Deeply rooted western attitudes further complicate the approach to Third World women's history. The nineteenth century equation of the West with progress and modernity, and the East with stagnation and tradition, still colors much of the discussion of women in Third World societies. While the most

1 "Dancing Girl," late nineteenth century

extreme versions propounded by our Victorian forebears – the enslaved woman as quintessential victim of the barbarous society of the conquered – no longer find broad acceptance, we still encounter the notion that "progress" for women was imported from the West and basically entailed a denial of indigenous tradition. Women's history, in the sense of linear progression, thus began with the penetration of western ideas which gradually permeated and transformed the receiving society; women's history in the Third World becomes the history of an intellectual elite acquainted with western thought who initiated the debate on women's role in society, a debate which eventually filtered down and took concrete legal and political form. Idealist and derivative, this line of analysis takes one small part of women's history for the whole, limits historical inquiry to the intellectual realm, and neglects indigenous economic and social structures and their development over time.

Women's history in the Middle East, while laboring under the burden of neglect of women's history in general as well as the special misconceptions surrounding Third World history, also exhibits a particular set of problems traceable to its orientalist connection. The orientalist heritage, described in some detail by Edward Said, bequeathed a specificially "Islamic" definition of history and culture, promoting an idealist epistemology in which much of Middle East history was perceived as the embodiment of the Islamic spirit, rather than the outcome of the complex interaction of material forces and ideological formations.[1] Faced with a dearth of information on the historical reality of women in the region, many writers simply revert to "Islam" for both description and cause of women's position.[2] "Islamic" customs, concepts, and sexual mores both dictate and define women's role in society. The argument is tautological and remarkably free of any process of verification: Muslim laws and customs reflect women's reality, that is, we can know how women lived and worked from a study of the rules, formal and informal, applicable to them; these same rules, however, also function as the main instrument of women's oppression, for they assign women an inferior position in society and limit their activities. The image of Islam as dictator of social life is further based on a set of assumptions that have not been subjected to historical or sociological investigation. As evidence of the diversity and complexity of women's roles in societies where Islam is the dominant religion multiplies, we make such assumptions only at the risk of confounding the normative and the real.

The focus on a monolithic Islam also suggests that women lived in a timeless privatized world untouched by historical change. The history of women in nineteenth century Egypt refutes this static version of the past, for women were affected by and, through their own actions, helped to shape the sweeping changes of the period. Between 1800 and 1914, the fundamental development which reverberated throughout society was the integration of Egypt into a European economic system and and the political subjugation which followed.

Although most of the Third World also succumbed to European imperial expansion, we will be concerned with the specificity of the Egyptian case. Everywhere colonialism meant a certain distortion of the economic base of the country as it was subordinated to an imperial center, a subordination which brought social and political transformation in its train. We must be fully conscious, however, of important differences among regions arising from at least four variable aspects of this process of integration.

First, the type and speed of economic integration influenced the extent of social change. In Egypt, economic change began early and proceeded rapidly: in the first half of the nineteenth century, as European penetration accelerated, large-scale plantation agriculture geared toward production for export came to dominate the countryside in place of a semi-subsistence family-based system, and imported manufactures replaced many of the locally produced crafts. Integration, while always somewhat uneven, was thorough and rapid: we can expect that it transformed the economy as a whole and touched the lives of all inhabitants.

Secondly, European penetration did not obliterate all pre-existing activities and institutions. The characteristics of indigenous society, the structures of production, reproduction, and ideology that predated the arrival of western economic interests, determined, in part, the outcome of the interaction of the West and local society. The particularities of early nineteenth century Egypt – its broad social formation – helped shape the course of western encroachment. Whether we label the dominant mode of production "oriental," "tributary," or "feudal," Egypt enjoyed, among other features, widespread activity in commodity production and a relatively centralized and powerful state formation, both of which influenced nineteenth century developments. While the ongoing process of class formation in the cauldron of capitalist growth owed much to the rhythm of the West, the economic, political, and social facts on the ground also played a real role. As we trace the impact of western penetration on women, we must be equally sensitive to the activities of, and attitudes toward, females in the period before Egypt felt the full impact of the West, as well as the ways in which these activities and attitudes interacted with the new demands of development.

Thirdly, imperialist penetration and colonial rule did not follow a single pattern. The strategies employed and institutions developed by the imperial power varied from one region to the next, and one epoch to another. The history of Egypt, especially in the second half of the nineteenth century, intersects with the historical development of British colonial strategies and policy. After 1882, British officials, as advisors to the Egyptian government, actually ruled the country: their decisions about the state budget – how much money to spend, for example, on irrigation systems or education – influenced the overall structure and growth of the State as well as the level and types of services it provided to the population. The history of the Egyptian state formation became, during the

1882 to 1914 period, largely the history of a colonial rule which sought to further the interests of the imperial country. While the individual aims or even personalities of colonial agents were not determinant in this process, the more general pattern of colonial strategy – reliance on the large landholding class, promotion of agriculture at the expense of other sectors, belief in the racial superiority of the West – permeated the views of those who ruled and had, through their concrete actions, a significant effect on Egyptian society. We need to look closely at colonial policy, especially at its impact on a basic economic and social level, in order to understand what the colonial experience held for women.

Lastly, the process of integration was influenced by Egyptians themselves, not only those of elite political circles but also by the men and women of the peasant and lower classes. The vision of popular or mass history as, first and foremost, the history of the oppressed, of the victims of the historical process, contains an element of truth yet neglects the very real role that people had in shaping that process. Women in particular, because of their sex, were subject to discrimination and constraints; at the same time, their ability to construct their own institutions or even take their struggle for certain rights to the streets contributed to the making of their history. The Egyptian population, male and female alike, did not witness nineteenth century transformations with passivity or docility: many women, for example, fought to protect the customs and forms of family relations that seemed to serve their interests. On the grand scale of mass revolt and the small stage of individual court battles, people resisted or accommodated change in ways which helped define the emerging society. The role of women in the construction of the modern history of Egypt forms a final and critical aspect of women's history of the period.

Not all women experienced these changes in the same fashion. The women of Egypt belonged to different classes and lived in diverse geographical settings; for a peasant of the Delta, a petty trader in Cairo, and a member of the palace *ḥarīm*, the bonds of womanhood undoubtedly paled before the vast separations, in experience and interest, created by class and environment. The following study concentrates on peasant and urban lower class women. Women of the provincial and urban elite appear only in passing when their experience helps to clarify the evolution of women's roles. Their world, the world of the Palace, the merchant elite, and the religious establishment, merits a separate study which would explore the lives of those associated with the wealthy and powerful.

II

How can we order and define the position of women in a discrete but rapidly changing period of Egyptian history? The book explores four interlocking dimensions of women's position and power in order to evaluate change in women's roles within the family and larger society: (1) women's access to property; (2) their position in the family unit; (3) their participation in social production; and (4) the prevailing ideological definitions of their roles. Each of these dimensions must be discussed against the backdrop of broad economic and social changes arising, in part, from the ongoing integration of Egypt into an economic system dominated by the West.

The first, women's access to property, that is, their rights to the use or control of certain portions of family or individually owned property, has been accorded a central place in the literature on women's position since the appearance of Engels' classic *The Origin of the Family, Private Property and the State*. The subjection of women to the control of male family members was linked to the emergence of private productive property (in land or animals) and the consequent male monopoly over the use and disposition of this property.[3] Although the relatively weaker claims of women to family property in most societies have been consistently noted, Engels' focus on private property has been revised on both theoretical and empirical grounds. The tracing of the oppression of women to private property in general without attention to the different meanings of property in different modes of production must be recognized as a major theoretical weakness. Some research suggests, furthermore, that access to property, while important, does not necessarily lead to the exercise of real power in the sphere of family relation.[4] In the case of Egyptian women, two questions about access to property will be raised. First, the formal rights, as embodied in legal rules and accepted customs, of women to property acquired through inheritance, the *mahr* (bridal gift), or their own labors, will be examined; male monopoly of family property cannot be presumed. Secondly, the ability of women to use these rights to attain economic independence and status, the degree to which formal rights held real meaning in the realm of economic relations, cannot simply be deduced but must be explored in the context of the actual participation of women in business affairs and productive activities, and their personal control over the fruits of their labor.

In chapter 1, women's relation to property will be explored in the context of the female role in agricultural production: to what extent did peasant women make critical contributions of agricultural labor and how did these activities affect their access to property and power? How did the major changes in the level and organization of agricultural production, most significantly the transition to an agriculture dominated by capitalist relations, influence their participation and therefore their hold on property? Chapter 2 poses similar questions about Egyptian women in trade, crafts, industry, and service occupations. Here we look to urban women and again consider the correspondence between their activities in the basic forms of production and their formal and actual rights to property.

Control of property, while related to the level of contribution to production, was often mediated through family arrangements, the second dimension. Access to property might strengthen a woman's position within the family power structure; on the other hand, family control of her person might negate any meaningful exercise of her property rights. At issue here is an understanding of the family as the product, primarily, of requirements of material production, or, alternately, as an institution which both reflects and structures material production and social life. Wolf, for example, has tended to relate the development of the peasant family to particular features of agricultural production: the availability of land, the intensity of cultivation, and the prevalence of wage labor all affected the division of labor and, thus, the numbers, roles, and power of various family members.[5] Others, however, stress that the contours of the family unit are shaped not only by its function of material production, but also by the wider functions of reproduction of the conditions of existence, including the care of children, the elderly or the infirm; the family, based on ties of kinship, redistributes the necessities of life to family producers and non-producers alike, binding them together in the basic economic unit of society. Women's position within the family is thus conditioned by the need for reproduction, in the broad sense, and the assignment of particular roles, especially the nurture of children, to women.[6] Just as family arrangements flow from the dual demands of production and reproduction, so does women's access to property depend on their role in these two, often intertwined, activities.

In chapters 1 and 2, the peasant and urban lower class family will be studied in its reciprocal relationship with society. The demands of production in rural and urban areas, the need to avoid parcelization of land through inheritance or the necessity of releasing the labor of some family members to satisfy demands from outside the family unit, for example, affected the size of, and division of labor and power within, the family. At the same time, however, the demands of reproduction, the tasks of childrearing and the provision of a multitude of necessary services entailed the allotment of roles based, often, on the sex and age of family members. Insofar as women's role in reproduction was generated and defined within the family unit, the family, as a basic social structure, also conditioned the processes of production and social relations in society at large. To understand women's position, we therefore need to study the Egyptian family not only as a unit of production, but also as a unit of reproduction in which constraints on women's rights and power arose as much from their role in reproduction as from their role in production. Marriage arrangements, inheritance practices, and obligations based ostensibly on kinship all reflected, and simultaneously influenced, the ways in which the family met its varied needs.

Thirdly, the extent to which women's role in social production, or work outside the context of shared family labor, reduces the economic and social control exercised by the family and thus enhances female independence and power has been the subject of considerable discussion. Engels again initated this line of inquiry by proposing that female emancipation depended on her participation in production "on a large social scale," impossible without the destruction of the monogamous family as an economic unit of society.[7] Although more recent writers also recognize the centrality of social production to women's condition, Engels' formulation has been greatly modified and expanded to encompass not only economic production, but also the participation of women in the sphere of politics and social relations outside the family. In this analysis, the historical formation of the State prompted the development of a "public" sphere clearly differentiated from the "private" domestic sphere; women, through their roles as childbearers and nurturers, were usually excluded from the public sphere of extrafamilial social relations and political power. The firmer the differentiation of these two spheres became, the more women were isolated from each other and placed under the authority of their male family members. Thus, even though women, in some societies, may have access to productive property and wield considerable power in the "private" sphere as a result, partial or total exclusion from the "public" sphere invariably acts to lower women's status and reduce their power.[8]

In studying the position of women within the Egyptian family, we proceed with careful attention to women's participation in the public sphere and its impact on family arrangements. In the period under discussion, economic activities not based on the family unit, such as corvée labor and wage work in agriculture and industry, were making new demands on the family. The role of women in this expanding sphere of public labor must be explored. In addition, the public life of precapitalist Egypt was based on a number of institutions, such as craft guilds, religious orders, and neighborhood associations. We first consider, in chapter 3, female participation in the institutions which organized and undergirded the social and political life of the city. Women's activities in institutions of male design, however, do not necessarily tell the whole story of female entrance into the public sphere. Women of the urban lower class also created, to a certain extent, a public world of their own; the structure of specifically female associations, and their impact on women's status within the family, add another dimension to the participation of women in the public sphere.

As the nineteenth century advanced, however, the growth of the State, first in its emerging absolutist form and later, after the British occupation, in its colonial form, enlarged the public sphere and encouraged official intervention in aspects of economic and social life. How did this extension of the public sphere and the entrance of the State into areas of life formerly reserved for family or corporate groups affect women? In chapter 3 we also investigate this process by reviewing developments in health and education in which state intervention was felt in the course of the century. The growth of the State also entailed the refurbishing of its repressive apparatus – the judiciary, police, and prison system – hastened along by the many revolts and acts of individual resistance to the central power. Chapter 4 looks at female participation in the public sphere of the urban and rural uprisings of the century, and examines the ways in which state repression subsequently dealt with women.

While control of property, family relations, and participation in the public sphere remain fundamental to an appreciation of women's roles and status, the fourth dimension, that of ideological definitions of women's roles, cannot be overlooked. The ascription of particular, and often negative, character traits to women and the assignment of females to the status of a second sex is undoubtedly rooted in past material conditions, obscured by the passage of time, and elaborated by an ongoing organization of production and reproduction which entails female subordination. Although social views of women thus arise out of social needs, the set of legal rules, customs, and popular perceptions defining the roles and status of women may, in certain historical periods, appear relatively autonomous and play a real part in determining the position of women. Indeed, the idealization of women and their role may have its greatest impact in moments when the objective situation of women is changing rapidly, and the search for stability and continuity lends ideology more force. The variety of expression of such views, which often appear in the myths and folktales of popular culture in a form quite distinct from official political or religious pronouncements, gives them an elusive quality responsible, no doubt, for a tendency in the literature to ignore this dimension altogether, or focus exclusively on the views of women amongst literate officialdom or the dictates of a monolithic "Islam."

In trying to ascertain the views of women prevailing in nineteenth century Egypt, we are limited to written documents and inferences drawn from the known course of events. Written materials, be they chronicles, official statements, or legal documents, overrepresent the views of upper class male culture; we draw primarily on the minutes of religious court proceedings which, insofar as they record the voices of litigants from varied social backgrounds, reveal, in considerable detail, the perceptions of men and women alike. The affairs of the *maḥkamah al-shar ʿīyyah*, of course, were colored by the precepts of the Muslim religious law, the *sharīʿah*. An evaluation of attitudes toward women based on court records must therefore distinguish between the definitions of women's roles as embodied in the law *per se*, and the interpretations and subtle modifications of the law as it evolved in response to social conditions. Furthermore, and particularly in a period of rapid economic and social change, the definitions of women's roles based on religious law might influence the material situation of women: the very existence of female rights to property, for example, lent legitimacy and power to those women who could exercise them. The constellation of cultural attitudes, including those explicitly expressed in the *sharīʿah*, was not the only determinant of women's position but was modified by, and in turn modified, women's family life and labor.

The ideological structures and cultural attitudes surrounding and defining women's roles acquire a clarity and starkness when we focus on the margins of society. Women who inhabited the social netherworld of unacceptable behavior – prostitutes – or of absolute legal impediment – slaves – stood stripped of the usual protections and identities afforded by family connections. Their activities in production and reproduction tended to be insignificant or distorted, for their economic and social roles lay elsewhere. Bereft of family relations that so often helped define the rights and obligations of others, these women lived outside the network of kin and confronted society without the usual supports and protections. We therefore can observe how the ideological dimension, in an unadulterated form, defined the role of women in an environment divorced from basic economic processes and social structures. The prostitutes studied in chapter 4, and the women slaves in chapter 5, constituted a very small proportion of Egyptian women and their lives were in no way representative of their sex. Yet, precisely because of their marginality and the unidimensionality of their social existence, they help us understand the set of attitudes which shaped the position of all women in Egypt.

III

The study of lower class women and their activities on their own behalf has dictated extensive use of the *sharīʿah* court records. The religious courts, the *maḥkamah al-sharʿīyyah*, constituted the single institution with extant records to which women of all classes had access, and where they could tell their stories and lodge their complaints. Although the records from Muslim courts have been used to great advantage to shed light on the world of women in seventeenth century Anatolia, the Egyptian nineteenth century records have been neglected.[9] André Raymond's signal work on Cairo tapped the information available in successions recorded in the religious courts in the very early part of the century, but the wealth of cases touching family and business affairs of all kinds has yet to be fully explored, much less utilized.[10] The paucity of our knowledge about the actual functioning of the courts, their personnel, and their evolution over time may well explain this phenomenon.

The Egyptian *sharīʿah* courts, which adhered to the Ḥanafī *madhhab* from 1805 on, changed in function and influence over the course of the nineteenth century. The procedures, independence, and weight of the decisions had much to do with the growth of state power and its impact on the judicial system. The jurisdiction and organization of the *sharīʿah* courts had long been influenced by a history of conflict and cooperation between the state power and the judicial system. When the civil power flourished, the religious court system sometimes functioned as a lever of political control, buttressing state policy and implementing state directives; with the waning of central control and authority, the *sharī'ah* courts could assert a tenuous independence and even acquire some of the State's political prerogatives.[11] Throughout most of history, however, the courts proved obedient to political authority and served the goals and interests of the rulers without hesitation.

The nineteenth century in Egypt, however, witnessed an intensified struggle for control of the judicial system between the *'ulamā'* and the State. During the period of Ottoman rule, from 1517 to the rise of Muḥammad 'Alī, the staff of the *sharī'ah* courts was, in theory, appointed by and responsible to Istanbul. Sultān Sulaymān initially placed a Turkish *qāḍī l-'askar* (literally a "military judge") at the apex of the Egyptian judicial system. With the aid of four lieutenant judges, his task was to oversee the administration of *sharī'ah* justice. Egypt was divided into 36 court districts, and the district *qāḍīs* were appointed to their posts by the *qāḍī l-'askar* of Anatolia. The *qāḍī l-'askar* in Cairo and the provincial *qāḍīs* were recruited from the ranks of Turkish-speaking *qāḍīs* serving elsewhere in the Ottoman Empire. In the course of the eighteenth century, the waning of Istanbul's direct control over the judicial system weakened the *qāḍīs*' role in the Ottoman administrative system. The courts were gradually Egyptianized: by 1798, in the then 36 judicial districts in Egypt, only six *qāḍīs*, including the *qāḍī l-'askar*, were drawn from the Turkish-speaking *'ulamā'*; the majority of judges were recruited from the Egyptian *'ulamā'*.[12] The religious courts were no longer headed by Turkish judges whose judicial roles were intertwined with administrative tasks on behalf of the Empire: judges with allegiance to the imperial power were replaced by judges with local ties and interests. The courts, like other administrative structures of the period, had attained a certain independence with the faltering of Ottoman rule in Egypt.

After a brief and abortive attempt by the French occupation forces to exercise control over the *sharī'ah* court system at the very end of the eighteenth century, the nineteenth century State moved with more caution yet more thoroughness in pursuit of control of the judicial system. While nominally respecting the independence of the *sharī'ah* courts, the civil authority gradually asserted control over the court's personnel and further limited its jurisdiction. The chief *qāḍī* of Cairo, still appointed from Istanbul by imperial *firmān*, recruited *qāḍīs* for all local courts with the exception of Alexandria. Although the Empire thus retained, in theory, its direct hold on the *sharī'ah* courts, the Sultān's appointee was not always able to assume his post, especially when the Egyptian State was in open conflict with Istanbul. *Sharī'ah* court judges, drawn from the ranks of the Cairene and provincial *'ulamā'*, while thus freer of interference from Istanbul, were undoubtedly more subject to pressure from political authorities in Cairo and the provinces. The State refrained, however, from any overt regulation of procedure in the *sharīʿah* courts until 1856, when Saʿīd reached an agreement with Istanbul to the effect that all *qāḍīs* in Egypt, except the chief *qāḍī* of Cairo, would be appointed and paid a fixed salary by the Egyptian government; procedural rules were also promulgated for the courts and the elaborate witness system was abolished. In the second half of the century, court personnel were brought further under state control: the 1880 Regulations for *sharīʿah* courts gave the Egyptian Khedive power of appointment of all *qāḍīs*, including the *qāḍī* of Cairo, and new laws in 1908 and 1911 extended state control over religious education and the certification of members of the *ʿulamāʾ* for admission to the ranks of the *qāḍīs*.[13]

During the same period, the State made inroads on the jurisdictional territory of the *sharīʿah* courts. A series of new law codes, particularly the *qanūn al-fallāhah* in 1830, the *qanūn al-siyāsah al-malakīyyah* in 1837, the *qanūn ʿamm* in 1849, and the new penal code of 1863, represented official declarations by the civil authority on the scope and limitations of the *sharīʿah* courts. By acknowledging the fact that most penal matters would be dealt with by members of the civil administration and that all punishment, even for matters reserved to the *qāḍī's* judgment, would be meted out by secular authorities, these *qanūns* clearly and officially established the role of the State in the judicial process.

The development of civil laws and codes was accompanied by the establishment of civil councils and courts which gradually assumed jurisdiction over legal matters formerly reserved for *sharīʿah* courts. Although the State had long exercised extraordinary jurisdiction over penal and administrative matters, the official creation of standing judicial bodies with well defined authority deepened and systematized the State's control of the administration of justice. In the 1820s and 1830s, the State established a number of new *dīwāns* (ministries) with judicial powers extending to criminal matters, property disputes, and even *waqf* affairs. A civil high court, the *majlis al-aḥkām*, was established in the late 1840s and, a few years later, similar judicial councils were set up in four provinces. Staffed by representatives from the military and civilian administrations along with members of the *ʿulamāʾ*, the councils administered the newly codified land laws. Finally, in the period between 1876 and 1883, new civil courts, the Mixed Tribunals and the National (Native) Courts, were charged with the administration of most civil law; the *sharīʿah* system was expressly limited to questions of personal status: marriage, divorce, inheritance, paternity, guardianship, and *awqāf*.[14]

Although the various civil codes and courts had no official jurisdiction over questions of family law, the very presence of systems of civil justice invariably led to trespass on this *sharīʿah* preserve. State officials with judicial powers could act, in some cases, as a court of appeal upon unfavorable *sharīʿah* judgments, having the advantage of means of enforcement at their disposal. One *ḥākim siyāsī* (civil judge) granted a judicial decree of divorce to a woman whose case would surely have been dismissed by the *sharīʿah* court: her husband had left her well provided for during a brief absence.[15] The civil official *cum* judge might directly challenge the authority of the religious law, as reported in an opinion of the *muftī* in Cairo:

Question: There is a man incapable of supporting his wife and she demanded [support] from him numerous times in the presence of the *'ahl al-ʿilm* [*ʿulamā'*] and he could not, so she demanded [support] from him in the presence of the *ḥākim siyāsī* [civil judge] and he ordered him to provide support and he did not have that which supported himself, so he ordered him to divorce [her], and he threatened him with beating and frightened him, and he said to her "you are divorced" in the presence of the *ḥākim* and a group of Muslims, and after his return from the *ḥākim* he admitted that. And if her waiting period ended and she wanted to marry another, is that permissible? And cannot her divorced husband prevent her from doing so on the grounds that a divorce under coercion is not valid?

Answer: Divorce under coercion is a reality among us and God is exalted in knowledge.[16]

Here the civil judge interfered in an affair clearly within the competence of the *sharīʿah* court, and even employed means (coercion) which were anathema to the *sharīʿah* process. The *muftī* himself, in a brief but pointed response, recognized that the *sharīʿah* courts were hardly in a position to contest the power of the State, even when it chose to intervene in spheres reserved to the religious courts.

Although the State thus could and did assert control over the personnel, procedure and jurisdiction of the *sharīʿah* court, the religious court system still preserved a certain autonomy and integrity through most of the century. While occasionally accused of corruption, as in the state prosecution in 1832 of *wukalā'* (agents) who employed questionable practices in pursuing their functions as expediters, the *sharīʿah* court retained an identity sufficiently separate from the central government, as well as enough of a reputation for justice, to maintain it as a popular institution.[17] The sheer number of cases preserved in the court archives (see Appendix) stands as convincing proof that many Egyptians viewed it as their institution, as a place to which they could go for redress. Lower class women, for example, many of whom were illiterate and ill-informed as to the niceties of court procedure, came, often on their own, to plead their case before the local *qāḍī*. Despite the sometimes onerous financial burden of fees and bribes, the court remained a locus of popular appeal. We can assume, therefore, that the procedure and substance of court deliberations were familiar and comfortable enough to encourage the non-elite to view the court as their institution. That the enterprise of Islamic law, in its arcane scholarly dimension, remained the province of a small intellectual elite cannot be questioned. Yet, in the *sharīʿah* courts of the nineteenth century, aspects of elite culture intersected with the cultural traditions and social arrangements of the peasant and urban lower classes. The judge bridged two cultural traditions: the application of Islamic precepts was tempered by recognition of social reality. Widespread recourse to the religious courts on the part of a disparate population testifies to the success of this marriage of two worlds.

The actual impact of *sharīʿah* decisions is more difficult to assess. Court documents yield little information on the method of enforcement of the *qāḍī's* verdict. A few isolated cases demonstrate that the religious courts could not, especially in the face of a countervailing judgment by political authorities, enforce their ruling. We can infer, nevertheless, that the religious court was far from being a forum for hollow rhetoric: the widespread practice of bringing disputes and grievances to the *qāḍī* would certainly have fallen off if the court had been rendered totally ineffectual. We cannot know with certainty, however, whether any given decision was implemented. Nor do court decisions in themselves paint an accurate picture of society, for they blended ideological concerns with the exigencies of daily life.

The outcome of a court case is thus of less interest to the social historian than the overall information offered. Court documents provide valuable insights into family and property relations as the litigants are identified by their family ties, and property holdings are often described in some detail. Situated in historical context, court records of the nineteenth century also tell the vital story of a society in formation. Imbued with "Islamic" values and sensitive to local custom, religious courts appear to have championed a way of life that was fast being supplanted as Egypt was drawn into the European orbit under the aegis of the renovated State. The *ʿulamāʾ* who staffed the *sharīʿah* courts were both agents and adversaries of the new state formation: in the latter capacity, they upheld customary rights and obligations against state encroachment and social dislocation. Coming to the court with their claims and complaints, the peasantry and urban poor of Egypt were hardly passive spectators in this process. By examining their use of the court to defend their former rights and social arrangements, a picture of resistance begins to emerge. The religious court constituted a crucial forum for the development of strategies to minimize state intervention and the consequences of capitalist penetration.

In the following study of women in the nineteenth century, court records are a valuable contemporary source. Minutes of cases and collections of *fatāwā* (legal opinions) lend information on women's property holding, labor, family relations, and general response to a situation of stress and change. Women of all social backgrounds brought their business to court. The elite seldom made a personal appearance, preferring to entrust their affairs to a *wakīl* (agent). Peasant and lower class urban women, however, usually presented their own cases before the *qāḍī*. Buying and selling property, pursuing thieves and debtors, seeking familial support and divorce, they used the court to help conduct their business and personal affairs. Court proceedings, then, record not only the economic activities of women but also their own perceptions of their rights under the law.

The court records and the *muftī's fatāwā*, however, constitute a main source only in the first part of the century. With the narrowing of the jurisdiction of the *sharīʿah* court, and its gradual loss of autonomy to the central power, the records of the religious courts come less and less to reflect the wide range of economic and social activities: by the 1870s, these courts were effectively dealing only with questions of personal status. The many changes in court structure, procedure, and personnel also render comparisons across time of incidence of cases, changes in verdicts, etc. relatively meaningless. Indeed, in the later part of the century, the development of civil courts and the growth of the state apparatus circumscribed the activities of "traditional" institutions like the *sharīʿah* courts, and spread their functions amongst a number of new institutions. While the court records come to contain less information on social and economic life in this period, other sources of information appear as the State begins to survey and record the activities of the population with increased vigor. As the century progresses, then, we rely more and more on material generated within the state apparatus rather than the religious court system. Implicit in this approach is the assumption that the State, especially in its colonial form, was coming to have more of an impact on its population, and that official policy had begun to play a significant role in the lives of both women and men.

Chapter 1

Ploughs and shares: women, agricultural productions, and property

Women are crooked like scythes, but were it not for its crookedness, the scythe would not mow.

Egyptian proverb (Taymūr, 2940, p. 489)

A calf raised by a woman will never plough.

Egyptian proverb (Taymūr, 1961, p. 332)

Throughout the nineteenth century, Egypt remained a predominantly agrarian society: most of the country's wealth was produced, and the majority of its people lived, in the countryside. While the population multiplied over threefold between 1800 and 1900, from roughly 3,800,000 to 11,000,000, the percentage of the population inhabiting cities or large towns increased more modestly, from 10 to 14–15 per cent during the same period.[1] The vast majority of Egyptians continued to live in the many small villages found along the banks of the Nile and throughout the fertile Delta where they worked the land for their own subsistence and for production of the agricultural surplus which constituted the bulk of the country's earnings abroad as well as the livelihood of its citizens at home. During the century, as new crops and technology, changes in land tenure patterns, increased state intervention, and, above all, accelerated integration into a world economy transformed the face of the Egyptian countryside, the peasant family endured as the basic social and economic unit.

It was this family, more than the State or corporative unit, which assigned work roles and regulated most aspects of its members' lives. The peasant family was producer, reproducer, and consumer; its internal logic was not, however, that of the capitalist enterprise. As Chayanov pointed out, the peasant producer strove not toward maximization of profit, but rather the achievement of a "labor–consumer balance" where an equilibrium is struck between meeting family demands for consumption and the drudgery of the labor required for additional consumption.[2] The peasant family integrated and balanced the demands of production – the actual agricultural labor – with the demands of the reproduction of the conditions of existence – care for the young, old, and ill, shelter and sustenance – bonding together those who worked and consumed and those whose age or health limited them to consumption only. As an ideal type, the peasant family knew no division between home and workplace; the house

2 "Women and Child," late nineteenth century

and the land constituted a single field of activity and the distinctions among production, reproduction, and consumption were blurred.

Although the peasant family in nineteenth century Egypt formed such a discrete unit of production and consumption with an internal logic and control of its own, it was but part of a wider economic system. The prevalence of internally regulated, partly self-sufficient, although almost never autarkic, peasant family producers cannot itself define this system. The mode of expropriation of peasant produce and labor, above that needed for subsistence, by a dominant class influenced and transformed the structure of the peasant household. The production of goods for exchange in a local market similarly altered any internal family balance of labor and consumption struck purely in response to family needs. The many incursions of a State and world market which promoted certain crops and methods of farming had repercussions felt by the most isolated of peasant households. The models of a "peasant economy" or a "domestic mode of production," in their exclusive focus on the workings of the family itself, fail to situate the peasant producer within a wider context, thus suggesting that the peasant unit remained static and unchanging, to be bypassed eventually or annihilated totally by the rise of capitalism.[3]

Certainly in nineteenth century Egypt, the internal organization of the family was influenced by the demands of the State made in the form of taxes on agricultural production, the lifeblood of a ruling class existing primarily on an agricultural surplus. A portion of family labor time was simultaneously channeled into the production of agricultural and artisanal goods for the local market. Thus, while the peasant family might maintain control of the organization of its production and consumption, the level of production, over and above that of its own needs, would not remain simply a question of whether or not to increase the level of family consumption. To meet the demands of the State and its officials, as well as landlords, and to orient at least a portion of its production for exchange, the peasant family organized its labor with an eye to considerations external to family need. Peasant labor above that required for subsistence was also expropriated in the form of corvée labor on state irrigation projects and the land of state officials as well as labor service on large estates. But beyond these demands for surplus produce and extra labor, the State and landlords had little interest in the regulation of peasant households. The family remained the basic economic unit, working together to produce goods for subsistence, exchange, and taxes. While the peasant family was thus by no means a self-contained unit, it still retained a certain autonomy in the organization of its own production and consumption.

The peasant woman was first and foremost a producing member of this family: her activities in agricultural and craft production were performed in the context of the peasant family; her roles also reflected, however, the varied functions of the family group. As agricultural laborer, artisan, trader, processor of food, childbearer, and caretaker of young and old, her life wove together the many strands of family existence. Her world, like that of her menfolk, was molded not only by the requirements of material production but also by the social and legal structures undergirding the family unit. She was both actor in and subject to the customs, traditions, and judicial rules governing the relations of property, kinship, and sexuality within the family as well as between family groups. In exploring the role of the rural woman, we find her within a "domestic economy," that is, within the family production and consumption group, the basic unit in society. The peasant family in turn must be viewed within the context of the patterns of agricultural production that shaped its economic role as well as the established social customs and legal rules that regulated its activities.

The family was certainly not left unchanged by the events of the nineteenth century: the labor and leisure of rural women were profoundly affected by the gradual evolution of Egyptian agriculture. The crops grown, the pattern of landholding, and the legal definitions and political force which influenced social relations in the countryside touched all social institutions, including the family. In order to understand the experience of the peasant woman, we need, therefore, to survey the history of nineteenth century agriculture, particularly the changes in land tenure and labor utilization that formed the background to the transformation of the peasant family.

Egyptian agriculture in the nineteenth century

The characterization of Egyptian agriculture and, indeed, Egyptian economy and society as a whole during the nineteenth century remains a subject of debate. The ongoing integration of the Egyptian economy into a global system in this period is acknowledged by most writers, but there is little agreement on the nature and pace of this integration or its effects on society in general, and the relations of production in agriculture in particular. On the one hand, despite such integration, Egyptian society is perceived as basically static and unchanging: social institutions and the vast majority of the population were left untouched and intact throughout the course of the century, a phenomenon "connected with the fact that during that period Egypt was not transformed from an agrarian into an industrial society."[4] Here social change of a far reaching sort can only be the product of industrialization; integration into the world economy, through the growth of an export-oriented sector, failed to transform the basic character of society.

A divergent view perceives the rise of an export-oriented economy, revolving around the cultivation and export of cotton, as the motor force of social change; its broad strokes sweep clean the social slate. Issawi asserts that: "The transition from a subsistence to an export-oriented economy is accompanied by the breakdown of traditional feudal, communal, or tribal structures. The ties binding the individual to the village or tribe are gradually loosened or violently snapped, and labor becomes a mobile marketable commodity."[5]

Although the idea that integration into the world economy involved internal change of some magnitude rings true, Issawi's interpretation remains incomplete in several respects. First, his discussion of the "export-oriented economy" lacks a description of the precise nature of capitalist penetration. In his account, Egypt developed and retained an export-oriented economy by virtue of the local rulers' narrowness of vision coupled with the lack of political autonomy and, of course, the political and economic domination of the West. Without an analysis of the actual dynamic of capitalist penetration as it came into contact with internal realities (beyond the political response of the ruling class), the resulting social transformation merely "accompanied" economic change. Lack of attention to the specific character of capitalist penetration in Egypt also assumes a certain passivity on the part of Egyptian society. Social transformations were wrought willy-nilly by economic developments; Egyptian social classes, especially the *fallāḥīn* (peasants), apparently succumbed to the new order with barely a whimper. The idea that internal class structure and even *fallāḥ* resistance might have shaped the history of capitalist penetration is neglected.

Other writers have turned their attention to the question of capitalist penetration and, more specifically, to its impact on indigenous society. The move toward cotton cultivation for export, beginning in the 1840s, invariably affected rural society. But what were the dominant features of the emerging system of agricultural production? The nineteenth century saw the growing commercialization of Egyptian agriculture, increasing differentiation among the peasantry according to the amount of land they controlled, and the rise of a wage labor class, all of which suggest capitalist organization. On the other hand, certain peculiarities of this capitalist development, most notably that this was a "capitalism without local agricultural capitalists,"[6] have led to the characterization of Egyptian agriculture as "backward colonial capitalism."[7] The role of the State in the early process of capital accumulation and direct state intervention in relations of production in the countryside, which entailed primarily political rather than economic coercion, distinguished this sort of "retarded" capitalism. Capitalism, having penetrated with the cultivation of cotton for sale in the world market, transformed the precapitalist relations of production in the countryside, but the central role of the State and the persistence of many precapitalist forms of exploitation inhibited the transition to a fully capitalist system.

This process can usefully be divided into four periods of distinct, but not discontinuous, development primarily on the basis of patterns of land tenure and external demand for peasant labor, both of which reflected the evolution of crops and technology that accompanied a fairly steady conversion to cash crop agriculture.[8] In the first period (1800–1820), on the eve of the rise of large-scale commercial agriculture, the peasant family tended to control the land it cultivated and the labor it employed: small family plots remained the rule and corvée labor, while practiced, was usually performed locally so that family life and work was not disrupted by the absence of able-bodied members. During the second period (1820–1850), the rise of a powerful unified State under Muḥammad ʿAlī and the beginning of significant cotton cultivation entailed a number of government policies which weakened peasant tenure and, above all, exposed the peasant family to a debilitating level of corvée labor and military recruitment which often robbed the family of its most productive members. While the power of the State was on the wane by 1850, the third period (1850–1882) witnessed the strengthening of an elite of large landholders, also at the expense of the peasantry, who made further inroads on peasant land and energy in the form of labor service; the cotton boom of the 1860s and 1870s accelerated these trends as the demand for land and labor grew insatiable. The British occupation of 1882, which inaugurated the fourth period (1882–1914), ushered in a colonial regime which did not tamper much with patterns of land tenure, accepting ongoing peasant land loss as a necessary feature of its own alliance with the landed elite; it did abolish the corvée, but many of its functions had already been assumed by labor service on large estates. With a colonial administration at the helm, *de facto* if not *de jure*, the State systematically intervened in Egyptian agriculture, particularly in the promotion and improvement of infrastructure critical to the cotton crop which continued to occupy a central place in the Egyptian economy.

Although some of the events separating these periods – the rise of Muḥammad ʿAlī, the British invasion, etc. – heralded dramatic changes in the political structures of the country, on an economic and social level the four periods are best viewed as evolutionary phases, not as historical disjunctures. Cuno's argument against viewing the 1858 land law as the watershed event for private property in Egypt[9] can be expanded to include most features of Egyptian agriculture: the introduction of new crops and techniques, the changes in land tenure, and the waxing and waning of external demand for peasant labor all reflected ongoing development of Nile Valley agriculture in rhythm with the exigencies of a world market. The particularities of Egyptian agrarian history, however, owe much as well to indigenous features; the laws and customs that governed agricultural exploitation, the structure of the peasant family, and a long period of resistance and rebellion on the part of the peasantry also shaped nineteenth century rural history.

1800–1820: Agriculture and rural industry before Muḥammad ʿAlī

In the period preceding the rise of extensive cotton cultivation, the peasant family grew a mix of crops geared for subsistence, the payment of taxes, and the local market. Utilizing a basin system of irrigation, most agricultural land lay along the Nile and depended on a series of dikes and canals to channel the annual flood. Many crops sown after the flood, in November and December, required relatively little fertilizer or labor: the arduous task of lifting water from the Nile was demanded primarily by summer crops. Family subsistence was based on the winter crops of beans, lentils, chickpeas, and onions, grown from December to March, and the flood season corn crop, grown from August to November. Alongside the crops marked for family consumption, winter wheat and barley were cultivated for the payment of taxes and, whenever the rate of taxation permitted, for sale on the local market. Flax and tobacco, winter crops which need completely flooded land and therefore irrigation, were also grown and fueled local industry.[10] The peasant family thus balanced its crop mix to meet the varying demands of its own consumption, of taxes, and of a modest production for the local market. Winter and flood time crops, grown from August to March, freed family members for other kinds of labor in the summer off-season. Some of this labor was siphoned off by the *multazims* (tax-farmers) who used the corvée or forms of economic coercion to recruit workers for crops which grew in the dry pre-flood months.[11] Cotton, rice, indigo, and sugar cane needed irrigation during their summer growing season. The labor requirements when the Nile was low were staggering: while winter crops might require anywhere from 8 to 86 man-days per *faddān*, cotton inputs of labor could rise to 500 man-days per *faddān*.[12] Summer crops were geared primarily for industry and export: cotton and sugar cane were locally processed, often in enterprises run by the *multazims* themselves, and most rice and indigo were exported abroad.[13] The limited cultivation of summer crops was clearly a source of profit to the *multazims*.

Although the peasant family could organize its labor and production as it wished to insure family subsistence and to meet tax obligations, political incursions and the whims of nature might combine to render rational calculation useless. Between 1780 and 1798, a succession of poor harvests brought scarcity and even famine to the countryside.[14] When the Nile was low and land became uncultivable, peasant families left their homes for other villages or for Cairo.[15] Political turmoil also placed heavy burdens on peasant resources: warring Mamluke houses imposed extraordinary levies in the form of taxes and billeting costs in the late eighteenth century, sometimes causing a desperate peasantry to flee their exactions. Even in the best of times, when outright political warfare was not disrupting agricultural production and transport, the absence of effective state control left its mark on the countryside. By the end of the eighteenth century, for example, many dams had fallen into poor repair. The State was, in theory, responsible for the upkeep of the *sulṭānīyah* dams while the villages tended the *baladīyah* dams, but government neglect of its responsibilities had placed the burden of all dam upkeep on the villages. The organization of irrigation had grown more disordered and decentralized, and village feuds over water rights were commonplace.[16] Subject to such ineffectual state power, political strife, and the vagaries of nature, the peasant family was far from constituting an isolated economic unit.

Systems of land tenure also conditioned peasant production. The title to all agricultural land was vested in the State; the *taṣarruf* (right of usufruct) was divided between the *multazims* and the *fallāḥīn*. The *multazims* were responsible for collecting and delivering the *mīrī* (land tax) to the central government from the *iltizām* (tax farm) land under their control. Their own income came from the *fā'iz*, the difference between what they could extract from the *fallāhīn* and the *mīrī* they owed to the State. In addition, they were assigned a certain portion of the *iltizām*, the *ʿarḍ al-wasīyah* (*usyah* land) for cultivation on their own account which they could lease or exploit directly using corvée or wage labor.[17] By the early nineteenth century, they were, by and large, a class of absentee landlords, numbering some 6,000 who depended on local *shaykhs* and other retainers to watch over peasant production. *Iltizām* land, formerly held for a year or two, had become heritable and alienable property, and the *multazims* formed a distinct group with considerable political power.[18] In lower Egypt, the peasant-held land (*ʿarḍ al-fallāḥ*) in the *iltizām* was divided into fixed portions (*athār*), farmed and passed down within the family group. In Upper Egypt, where uneven flooding changed the area of cultivable land from one year to the next, each family received a certain proportion of the available land each year.[19] The role of the village *shaykh* and the community remained central in both cases: the village as a whole was held responsible for its assigned taxes and corvée labor was allocated by the local *shaykhs*.

Most *fallāḥīn* held usufructory rights to a portion of the *ʿarḍ al-fallāḥ*. On these plots the peasant family exercised total control over production from ploughing to harvest; decisions about crop mix and input of labor time were governed by the demands of subsistence and the variety of taxes owed to the *multazim*, usually paid in wheat or barley. Many members of the family also labored on *usyah* land as leaseholders, sharecroppers, or corvée and wage laborers. In the cases of leases held outright, the peasant producer acquired rights to a piece of land for one year or longer and could exercise crop decisions. Also common was the practice of sharecropping (*muzāraʿah*) on *usyah* land either leased to the *shaykh* or *ʿumdah* (village head) or sharecropped directly under the *multazim*. The *multazim* or *shaykh* provided the land and the seed; at harvest, the seed was collected and the peasant received from one third to one quarter of the crop.[20] Some *usyah* land was directly exploited by the *multazim* whose lieutenant (*qāʾimmaqām*) lived on the *ʿarḍ al-wasīyah* and supervised production using wage or corvée labor recruited by the local *shaykh* or the unpaid labor of peasants dependent upon him.[21] Since most peasant families controlled a portion of the *ʿarḍ al-fallāh* on which they grew subsistence crops, the labor demands of *usyah* land undoubtedly removed able-bodied family members from the family plot. Summer labor on *usyah* land cropped in cotton, rice, or indigo fell in the off-season for subsistence crops, but the *fallāḥīn* could be drafted for winter labor as well. Whether as paid or unpaid laborers and corvée workers, or as sharecroppers, a part of family labor time was spent growing crops destined for industry or export to the profit of the *multazim*.

Trade and industry, dependent on the production of the countryside, linked the peasant family to an economic system far more complex than that of its own subsistence. A portion of family labor time was devoted to the production of commodities directed toward the local market or export. In the eighteenth century, rice was the leading export of Egyptian origin to Istanbul and Syria. Given that half of all Egyptian exports remained within the Ottoman Empire, the rice trade with the East was crucial to the Egyptian economy.[22] Second in importance, excluding the lucrative transit trade in coffee and spices, was linen cloth destined for Istanbul, Syria, the Maghreb, Africa, and Arabia. Rough cotton cloth was also exported to Arabia, the Maghreb, Africa, and Europe, although by the second half of the eighteenth century European cloth imports were replacing locally produced textiles. By importing fine cloth from Europe, Syria, and Istanbul, and exporting the locally made rougher stuff, Egyptian exports and imports of cloth still remained in balance throughout the eighteenth century. Export trade depended heavily on local market fairs, especially the yearly *maulids* held throughout the Egyptian provinces. Combining religious and trade functions, the *maulids* of Sayyid Aḥmad al-Bedawī in Ṭanṭah, Sīdī Ibrahīm al-Desūqī in Desūq, Sayyid Aḥmad al-Fargalī in Abī Tīg, ʿAbd al-Rahīm al-Qanāʿī in Qīnah, Sīdī Ibrahīm al-Shalqāmī in Shalqām, and al-Qadīsah Dimyānah near Balqās served as the centers for the purchase of agricultural and artisanal goods produced in the countryside.[23] Traders attended from all over Egypt and especially from Cairo to buy foodstuffs and cloth for urban consumption and export.[24]

Much rural trade was directed exclusively toward the local market. Many villages held weekly markets, staggered with the market days of their neighbors, so that trade within and among villages flourished. In the province of Asyūṭ, for example, cloth, oil, and pottery produced in the principal town found their way to the markets of neighboring villages which might boast a population of only 200 to 300 houses.[25] While most types of rural industry could be found throughout the countryside, some villages specialized in certain wares, producing for the Cairo market as well as rural consumption. The villages of Banūd and Balās in Upper Egypt manufactured clay jugs (*qulal*), much sought after by Cairo merchants. Maʿsūrah, Sanūras, Tanīyah, and Minūf were known for their woven mats, while villages in Fayyūm supplied distilled rose water to Cairo.[26] Palm-leaf baskets from the Rosetta area were in demand for transport and storage.[27] The major part of the rural industry, however, was probably for local use: most villages manufactured dried brick, rugs, copper items, and oil for everyday needs.[28]

Textile production occupied the primary place in rural industry. Again production revealed a dual orientation: part of the woven cotton and linen was directed toward Cairo and the export market and the rest was reserved for local consumption. The export market relied on the weavers of major rural textile centers, principally Maḥallah, Rosetta, Damietta, Minūf, and Shibīn in the Delta, and Madīnah al-Fayyūm, Banī Suwayf, Asyūṭ, and Manfalūt in Middle and Upper Egypt.[29] Weavers clustered in these centers: some 500 people worked in the cotton industry in Maḥallah, and Damietta boasted over 300 weavers of linen and silk.[30] The peasant family played an important role in this textile production: most of the preliminary operations, including carding and spinning, were performed in rural homes. Villages surrounding the textile centers also produced their own cloth and the many small villages surrounding Damietta were known for high quality table and ceremonial cloths.[31] Wool, the principal stuff of local clothing, was spun and woven on a small scale throughout rural areas.[32]

The political and economic disruptions of the late eighteenth and early nineteenth centuries undoubtedly affected rural industry. Mamluke warfare and Bedouin incursions rendered transport and communications insecure and a weak central government was unable to regulate prices or improve chronic transportation problems. Although rural industry geared to consumption in the immediate vicinity suffered less from the disruption of internal trade routes, overall impoverization of the peasantry reduced the demand for local manufactures and poor harvests limited the supply of raw materials.[33] The textile industry faced an additional challenge as European-made textile imports increased. While the prices of raw textile materials soared in the late eighteenth century, the price of finished textile products of local manufacture remained steady. Raymond has suggested that the influx of imported textiles depressed the price of local textiles and may have ruined many of the local artisans.[34]

Despite the dislocations of the period, ameliorated to some extent after Muḥammad ʿAlī assumed effective control and instituted state monopolies in agriculture and industry in the late 1810s and 1820s, rural industry and agricultural commodity production were a crucial part of the economy of the countryside. Through a network of markets and trade routes, goods of rural origin were sold both locally and abroad. The peasant family, oriented primarily toward the production of crops and artisanal goods for its own use, also spent an important part of its labor time on non-subsistence crops and other products destined for the market. Levies of labor and taxes by state and local officials and the existence of production for exchange modify the vision of an isolated peasant family engaged in subsistence activities. The "domestic economy" based on the peasant family was clearly shaped and influenced by forces exterior to the peasant household.

1820–1850: Agriculture and rural industry in the time of Muḥammad ʿAlī

The role of the State in the transformation of the Egyptian countryside really commenced under Muḥammad ʿAlī. The peasant family unit gradually lost control over the organization of its production and consumption as the central government interfered directly in peasant life through a system of agricultural monopolies, corvée labor, military impressment, and the confiscation of peasant land. State incursions and land loss shaped the internal transformation of society as well as resistance to external control on the part of the *fallāḥīn*.

Muḥammad ʿAlī officially became *wālī* (viceroy) of Egypt in 1805, and, having managed to annihilate his political opponents by 1812, he embarked on an ambitious program of increasing state revenue to the end of gaining strength and independence for Egypt, still *de jure* under the suzereignty of the Ottoman Empire.[35] European demand for agricultural produce, stimulated by the disruptions of the Napoleonic Wars, led him to seize direct control of Egypt's grain production. In 1812, the entire grain crop of Upper Egypt was appropriated by the State; the *fallāḥīn* were prohibited from selling any of their grain directly to merchants, and the crop was shipped to Lower Egypt for state sale to European traders. The rice crop of Lower Egypt was similarly monopolized and by 1816 flax, sesame, safflower, safflower seeds, indigo, cotton, beans, and barley came under total state control. The government advanced seeds and animals to the *fallāḥīn* who in turn had to cultivate and transport the crop to a local depot. The State assigned crop prices and, after the deduction of advances and employees' salaries, the *fallāḥ* received a voucher for the balance. The *fallāḥīn* thus lost all control over the marketing of their produce. They were forced to sell their crops to the State at a low fixed price; the State then charged greatly increased prices to foreign and local traders. Since the *fallāḥīn* were forbidden to hold back any produce, they suffered the additional burden of buying back grain, at higher prices than they had sold it, for their own consumption.[36]

The State also asserted control over cultivation. Through the provincial administration, it dictated to each *shaykh al-balad* (village head) the required amount and mix of crops, seeking not only to control the export trade, but also to be able to respond to foreign demands for increased exports of certain crops, particularly cotton. Muḥammad ʿAlī sought political and economic leverage through the reorganization of Egypt as his private farm. In a conversation with the British consul in 1830, he estimated the year's cotton crop at 200,000 quintals, adding: "I did not think it proper this year to plant more but if England and I went hand in hand, and in the event of an American war, she should call on me for a quantity sufficient to supply all her manufactories; She should have it *exclusively*. Mention that."[37]

Bravado soon changed to chagrin as agricultural production faltered in the mid-1830s and food and labor shortages plagued the countryside. The various monopolies were gradually dismantled and control of agricultural production was decentralized. It seems unlikely, however, that the *fallāḥīn* were able to reassert their control over production. Although they were allowed to sell their wheat, corn, beans, and barley on the local market in 1831, the government still designated the crops to be grown and fixed prices. While agricultural trade was demonopolized in the late 1830s, the State first reserved the right to fix prices, and then insisted that the peasants pay their taxes in kind or sell their produce at government prices.[38] The State did cede direct management of the crop mix, although certain areas near the Nile, which included some of the best agricultural land, were reserved for the cultivation of cotton, indigo, opium, and flax, which remained state monopolies until 1842.[39]

In the face of declining revenue and pressure from the European community, codified in the Anglo-Turkish Convention of 1838, the Egyptian government had thus revised its monopoly system. At the same time, however, Muḥammed ʿAlī's redistribution of land preserved state control of production through indirect means. By 1844, nearly half of the agricultural land, and certainly the best land, had been granted by the State to royal family members, Turkish officials, and village *shaykhs*.[40] The cultivation and sale of produce were directed by the new grantees under strong state influence. The French consul noted that such land grants constituted a total evasion of the free trade stipulations of the

1838 Convention, and made little difference in the actual organization of production in the countryside:

> if the Pasha had executed the treaty of 1838 to the letter, the fellah, thanks to the suppression pure and simple of the monopolies, would produce and sell, and the traders would enter into direct communication with the peasants; this, one sees, is not the current situation; by virtue of his total power, the Pasha, while abolishing the monopolies, gave the land to landholders . . . and he has created, thus, an intermediary class between agriculture and the trader, few in number, foreign to the mass of the population, but to which he has given free disposition of the crops, and which, therefore, on the one hand is by itself in a singular relationship with the fellah concerning all that pertains to the cultivation of the land, and, at the same time, on the other hand, is likewise in a singular relationship with European trade for the sale of the products.[41]

The central bureaucracy no longer told the peasant family what to produce, but state officials *cum* landlords controlled peasant activity on their estates; the erosion of peasant control of production continued.

Incursions of the State also affected peasant control of their labor power. The policies of Muḥammad ʿAlī in this period necessitated the widespread use of corvée labor for public works and agriculture, as well as military impressment. The introduction of long-staple cotton, sought after by European industry, required the building of extensive irrigation works: the new canals and dams essential for summer cultivation. While corvée labor had been used on irrigation projects before the appearance of long-staple cotton, the scope and duration of forced labor now increased dramatically. As many as 400,000 peasants could be called to work each year for an average period of four months.[42] The Maḥūdīyah canal was built by the forced labor of approximately 315,000 peasants who were supplied by village *shaykhs* from seven different provinces. Peasants had to supply their own food and shelter during an enforced period of absence from home. Anywhere from 12,000 to 23,000 men, women, and children, laboring without proper food, lodging, or tools, died on the project in a ten month period in 1819.[43] Corvée labor on irrigation projects occupied some 300,000 men in 1841.[44] In the late 1840s, conditions were improved slightly in an attempt to correct the acute shortage of agricultural labor. A levy of 58,000 men to excavate three large canals in Lower Egypt was subject to new conditions: "they are only to be compelled to work 100 days at the excavations, the said period to commence as soon as possible after the harvest is completed, and to terminate at the autumnal season for sowing and preparing winter crops."[45] Ironically enough, most of these state irrigation projects brought no benefit to peasant lands, but rather enabled the large estates to undertake cotton cultivation.

Military recruitment also drained the peasant family of labor. Muḥammad ʿAlī's political ambitions dictated the fielding of a sizeable army. After various attempts to raise an army of slave and Sudanese recruits failed, he started a massive program of peasant recruitment.[46] By 1830, after he had directed provincial and village officials to supply set quotas of men, the Egyptian standing army and navy numbered from 54,000 to upwards of 75,000 troops, supplemented by from 15,000 to 24,000 Bedouin irregulars.[47] In the same year, however, the supply of able-bodied men was drying up; that year's levy "produced such a small number of men suitable for military service that one is tempted to believe that it is the last the exhausted population can supply."[48] The following year's recruits included boys of twelve and thirteen years, for "men are needed at any price, and children become improvised soldiers."[49] When the countryside could no longer satisfy recruitment needs, the State turned to Cairo itself, levying some 10,000 men in 1832, most of whom were reportedly Nubians or menial workers of other origins.[50]

When the *hatt-i sherif* of 1841 insisted on the reduction of the Egyptian army to 18,000 men, the peasant–soldiers were not demobilized but rather sent to work on irrigation projects or landed estates.[51] Never fully released from military service, the peasant population was subjected to a new round of levies during Ibrāhīm Pāshā's brief reign in 1848. Soldiers and sailors who had formed the backbone of the labor force in the Nile dam project were returned to active military service and new corvée levies dragooned *fallāḥīn* to take their places; 14,000 new soldiers were also conscripted from the provinces.[52] The overall effect of military conscription was to remove vast numbers of *fallāḥīn* from their lands and villages for a period of service that might last a lifetime, thus cutting their ties to the land and transforming family and village society.

If not caught in the net of corvée labor for irrigation projects or military service, the *fallāḥ* was still subject to forced labor in state industries and mines. Muḥammad ʿAlī's industrialization scheme created some 100,000 factory workers, but it is not clear how many of these were *fallāḥīn* as opposed to displaced craftsmen.[53] The closing of many factories in the 1830s did not spell the end of forced labor in industry: in 1842, for example, approximately 1,000 men were drafted for work in the state arsenal and dockyard.[54] State mines utilized forced *fallāḥ* labor, condemning unwilling workers to be "bereaved of their wives and children, compelled to severe labor and food such as might be eaten during periods of dearth."[55] Mine workers were paid 40 *parahs* per day, reduced to 16 to 29 *parahs* after deductions for food, out of which they often had to pay their land tax.[56]

Exemption from all these forms of forced labor and impressment was granted to peasants working on the large estates controlled by Muḥammad ʿAlī, his family members, and officials. Observers noted that corvée levies often bypassed estate lands, so that agricultural work could proceed uninterrupted.[57] The recruitment of peasant inhabitants from the villages near the estate for work on the estate's property seems scarcely distinguishable from other forms of corvée labor: peasants were coerced, and often received no pay for their labor. Wages, such as they were, were usually in arrears and sometimes paid in unmarketable products. Ibrāhīm Pāshā, for example, was said to have paid all workers on one of his estates in molasses produced by his sugar factory in Upper Egypt.[58]

The policies of forced labor and military impressment created a severe labor shortage in the countryside when there were few hands left to till and harvest. Agricultural production suffered in Upper and Lower Egypt in the 1830s as the rural village population came to be composed chiefly of women, children, and the old and infirm.[59] Bowring estimated the entire Egyptian population in 1830 at 2,000,000 to 2,500,000, a substantial undercount; he also reported, however, a disproportionately high number of females, officially figured at 135 females to every 100 males, but, in his opinion, probably much higher.[60] The observations of foreign residents are confirmed by letters from *khuṭṭ* (district) *shaykhs* to the State's official gazette in 1829–1830, reporting critical labor shortages in the lower and middle Egyptian areas of Fūwwah, Kafr al-Shaykh, Ṭanṭā, and Fayyūm.[61] At mid-century, the situation had apparently been ameliorated, and the theme of rural desolation was not so prevalent, but labor shortages could still arise at harvest time.[62] The increased appropriation of peasant labor time by outside forces, whether the state bureaucracy or local officials and landlords, the physical removal of the most productive family members from peasant-held land, and the fact that peasant families often had to sustain members in the State's service was to have a grave impact on the structures and functions of the peasant family.

The family was also affected by loss of control over the land itself as the formation of large estates and the dispossession of peasant land proceeded apace in the first half of the nineteenth century. During Muḥammad ʿAlī's reign, state policies and the rise of cotton cultivation initiated two distinct trends in patterns of land tenure: first, the central government increased its direct control of the land; and secondly, when this policy failed, the State promoted the rise to power of local officials and a new landed class.

State intervention in agriculture and trade, as described above, formed part of the State's attempt to mobilize agricultural resources to the political end of generating revenues for building a strong military force. To gain direct and immediate control of the agricultural surplus, Muḥammad ʿAlī first had to weaken, and then eliminate, the *multazims*, the holders of *iltizām* land. They deprived the State of the revenues from their *usyah* land, and of the amount of the *fa'iẓ*; furthermore, they obstructed direct state intervention into production. Alongside *iltizām* land, some 600,000 *faddāns* in Upper Egypt and the Cairo vicinity were held as agricultural *waqf* land (*al-rizāq al-aḥbasīyah*), created by land grants by former sultans or *multazims* out of their *usyah* holdings. This *waqf* land, free of land tax in the seventeenth and eighteenth centuries, was taxed at very low rates in the early nineteenth century.[63]

Between 1806 and 1815, Muḥammad ʿAlī moved to wrest control of the land and tax collection from the *multazims* and *nāẓirs* (trustees) of *waqf* land. The State first demanded half of the *fāʾiẓ* and raised taxes on *usyah* land. In 1811, a cadastral survey in Upper Egypt resulted in the confiscation of all *iltizām* land with tax arrears or no positive proof of title. An 1814 survey of Lower Egypt followed, with the result that most *multazims* in the country were removed from their holdings with or without compensation. *Waqf* land was similarly taken over by the State: it was first subject to the same tax as *iltizām* land and then confiscated if found in excess of, or without, valid title.[64] By 1815, then, the State had assumed substantial control over the agricultural land in the country.[65] Under the old system, the role of the village *shaykh* and community remained central: the village as a whole was responsible for its assigned taxes and corvée labor was allocated by the local *shaykhs*.[66] Under the new *iḥtikār* or state monopoly system, although most of the land remained in the possession of peasant families and the power of the village *shaykh* was enhanced, taxes were collected directly by state officials who also told the *fallāḥīn* what and when to plant. An intricate hierarchy of central and regional officials exercised broad powers which included the direct supervision of agricultural organization and production.[67]

In the 1830s, however, the combination of economic crisis and foreign pressure ushered in changes in policy: the Egyptian State abandoned most of its monopoly practices and tempered its direct control of agriculture. Muḥammad ʿAlī's land grants to various officials and royal family members took the form of *ʿuhdahs*, *abʿadīyahs* and *chifliks*. *ʿUhdah* grants resembled the old *iltizām* insofar as the holders (*mutaʿahhids*) were responsible for tax collection; the amount of the *mīrī*, however, had to equal the total amount collected from the peasantry. The holders were, like the *multazims*, entitled to a certain portion of the land which they might farm on their own account by employing day labor or a system of sharecropping.[68] Two important features appear to differentiate the *ʿuhdah* from the *iltizām*: the grantee had to deliver the estate's produce to the State at fixed prices and heed the State's guidelines on land use. *ʿUhdah* grantees were thus, of necessity, directly involved in the day to day agricultural work, prompting some to observe that the *ʿuhdah*'s *fallāḥīn* were little more than agricultural laborers working for the estate's holder.[69] The peasants, however, retained their *athār* land. While they might be called upon for more labor service, there is little to suggest that their legal rights of usufruct were being undermined in this period. On the contrary, peasants bought and sold, pledged, rented, and inherited the usufruct with a freedom bespeaking full ownership.[70]

Abʿadīyah grants of uncultivated land were tax free on the condition that it be brought into cultivation, but because the land had not been previously cultivated, the grantees had to encourage peasants to come and settle from other regions to work as wage laborers or sharecroppers. *Chifliks* enjoyed advantages not available to *ab'adīyah* estates in that control was centralized and the connection to the State was close enough to assure first access to state irrigation works and financing. The peasants on *chifliks* lost all rights to the usufruct and were reduced to day laborers working for a percentage of the cereal harvest. They might be given, in addition, a small plot for subsistence cultivation. Peasant flight posed the problem of labor shortage: *chiflik* managers were known to commandeer *'uhdah* peasants for work on their estates.[71]

Between 1820 and 1844, the area of cultivated land held in various forms of estate grants rose from 10 to 44 per cent of all cultivable land, and, by mid-century, the best Delta land had passed in its entirety into the hands of the new grantees.[72] Peasant families never regained their former level of control as the area of *athār* land decreased and they were subject to the intervention and directives of the State and the new grant holders. While their legal rights to the land they managed to retain remained strong and secure, they were actually losing a good part of their holdings. The State still concerned itself with agricultural production: in 1835, the governors and *shaykhs* of the provinces of al-Sharqīyah, al-Gharbīyah, al-Daqhalīyyah, and al-Minūfīyah were instructed on how much cotton to plant and four "ordonnateurs généraux" were assigned to the provinces to supervise production.[73] State policies of taxation, which fixed taxes on peasant land above taxes on estate land, further hastened peasant dispossession through flight and bankruptcy.[74] Peasant land loss through state seizure for land grants, failure to pay taxes, foreclosures for non-payment of private debts, and flight to escape the corvée and conscription had transformed the face of the Egyptian countryside by 1850. The Egyptian peasant family, formerly a semi-autonomous producer with usufructory land rights and substantial control of labor time and production, was increasingly supervised and subject to widespread expropriation of its land and labor.

1850–1882: Agriculture during the cotton boom

Such pressures on peasant family arrangements were further intensified by the spread of cotton cultivation, particularly during the 1860s. Egyptian peasants had long been encouraged to pay at least part of their land taxes in cash, and thus were accustomed to growing marketable crops; up through the 1850s, however, grains, particularly wheat, probably remained the leading cash crop.[75] While the long-staple cotton so much in demand by European, and particularly English, textile industry had been introduced in the time of Muḥammad 'Alī, it was grown in fairly modest amounts until the American Civil War triggered the cotton boom of the early 1860s. As prices soared, both large landholders and small proprietors planted cotton: some one half to one third of Delta land was given over to the crop once every two years. As described by Owen, the highly commercialized character of the crop (it was almost entirely exported) prompted new institutional arrangements: merchants, ginners, and usurers, whose roles often overlapped, operated throughout cotton areas, buying, selling, and processing the crop, loaning the peasants money, and, not uncommonly, acquiring land themselves via debt foreclosure. By 1882, a number of private enterprises were occupied with the business of agricultural land deals; the large land mortgage companies, such as the Crédit Foncier Egyptien and the Land and Mortgage Company, proved highly successful ventures.[76]

The growing problem of peasant dispossession for debt was exacerbated by state policies of taxation. Onerous taxes were exacted on the land classified as *kharājīyah*, which included most land held by small peasants; tax rates actually rose in the early 1870s when the price of cotton, and therefore peasant income, plummeted.[77] In 1867, government taxation was already spreading misery in non-cotton regions: Lady Duff Gordon reported that taxes on land, people, animals, and crops when harvested and again when sold, as well as special duties on a host of goods such as charcoal, butter, and salt, had reduced the peasants to a diet of barley gruel and forced many to sell their draught animals.[78] Official British circles commonly held that the Egyptian *fallāḥ* fell into debt primarily because of his love of festivities and spendthrift ways, seizing pleasure today without thought of the bill to be paid tomorrow. A British investigator reported quite the contrary after questioning peasants in Asyūṭ about their debts in early 1883:

Q: Have the people not borrowed to buy new wives?
A: Some have. Only the rich have more than one wife.
Q: Is not this the cause of much debt?
A: (vehemently) No! no! no! It is the taxes of Ismail Pasha. We are too poor, we find it too hard to live to think of divorces and marriages and new wives.[79]

While the small peasantry struggled under tax burdens, large landholders, most of whose land was classified as *ʿushūrīyah*, paid land taxes at far more favorable rates, sometimes as little as one quarter of the peasants' rate.[80] The State did make some halfhearted efforts to raise revenues from the landed elite by undertaking a program of land reclassification in the 1860s, and through the law of *muqabalah* in 1871 which promised long-term tax relief to any landholder who paid six years of taxes in advance. In general, however, large landholders managed, during this period, to get more, not less, of their land classified as *ʿushūrīyah*, and actually reduced their tax burden through the advantages offered by the *muqabalah* law.[81]

The State did not simply milk the agricultural sector; ambitious irrigation projects, particularly canal construction under Khedive Ismāʿīl (1863–1879) helped to expand the area of cultivated land from 4,200,000 to 4,800,000 *faddāns* as more water became available; more intensive cropping, new types of seed, labor-saving investment, and improved transport all contributed as well to a rise in the productivity of Egyptian agriculture, enabling it to keep pace with a growing population and rising demand for exports of grain and cotton.[82] Much of the labor which expanded the irrigation and transport systems was secured by recourse to the corvée which continued to decimate the peasant labor force. Duff Gordon reported appalling losses of labor in Upper Egypt in the 1860s when more than half of the adult male population were taken from their fields for 60 days during May and June, the time of the corn harvest.[83] The canals and railways undoubtedly demanded the most labor, but peasants were also drafted for work in mines, sugar factories, and agricultural labor on private estates. When the State embarked on joint venture projects with foreign companies, it often undertook to supply the drafted labor of its subjects. The contract between the Terranova Society and the Egyptian government for joint exploitation of sulfur mines in Upper Egypt included clauses stipulating that the State would furnish all manual workers.[84] Egyptian participation in the Suez Canal project involved the provision of *fallāḥ* labor at a rate of 20,000 men each month, drafted throughout Egypt; they were paid at the end of their stint on a piece-work basis, but were required to reimburse the Suez Canal Company for all food it had supplied.[85] The state sugar plantations and factories of Upper Egypt also bled *fallāḥ* labor, and peasants of the region complained bitterly in 1882 that they were forced to neglect their own farms as a result.[86] The large landed estates of the Khedive and his allies also continued to make labor demands. Hekekyan reported from a village near Manṣūrah in 1855 that: "The Sheikh Abd il-Rahman Bortos, a good looking old man – informed me that the villages were ruined by the incessant demands for men to work at the palaces, public works and farms of the Viceroy; that men were paid nothing except at the works of Sitti Zeinab and that the village had to maintain them with bread."[87] Forced labor on landed estates may have allowed the *fallāḥīn* to remain in their own villages, but it deprived peasant holdings of their labor just as surely as the public works corvée.

Although some claimed that the corvée had been much reformed and workers began to receive food and regular pay in the 1850s, there is much evidence of abuses persisting throughout the period.[88] The workers still might receive no pay, and continued to be responsible for their own food, shelter, and tools; they were often sent a considerable distance from their home village and forced to work long hours.[89] Villiers Stewart's investigations turned up the following statement, made in 1882, by peasants from Upper Egypt:

> We are taken by force to work on the sugar estates and in the factories. Not one of us would go willingly. We would all leave tomorrow if we could. Many have farms of their own; they are taken away from them, and the farms are neglected. Nominally we are paid P.T. 1½ to P.T. 2 per day, but it passes through the hands of the Sheikhs, and they stop most of it on different pretexts, arrears of taxes, and what not.
>
> Those of us who work inside the factory are kept there day and night. Each man works six hours at a time, and then is relieved, but he is not allowed to leave the factory lest he

should run away. The work is carried on day and night for three months. The men off duty must sleep on the stone pavement of the factory, amid the noise and heat. Each man works twelve hours out of the twenty-four, in alternate shifts of six hours.[90]

The peasantry was still subject to a military draft in addition, but the small standing army usually did not require many conscripts. Occasional waves of conscription, particularly under Ismāʿīl when the army reached almost 50,000 men, continued to be a source of grievance; the level of panic produced by Muḥammad ʿAlī's levies was not, however, reached again.[91]

In theory, new laws introduced during the period should have expanded peasant land rights. Land laws promulgated by Saʿīd's regime in 1855 and 1858 supposedly systematized and regularized peasant acquisition of the usufruct, and guaranteed peasant tenure and the rights to inherit, rent, sell, and mortgage the land.[92] Actually, as we have seen above, the peasantry had long enjoyed all these rights in practice; the court records confirm that recourse to legal titles to prove possession of the usufruct, systematic practices of inheritance, and full latitude to alienate *mīrī* land characterized peasant landholding both before and after passage of these laws.[93] While the new land laws may have influenced, upon occasion, relations within a given peasant household, peasant security and access to land were not particularly promoted by a set of laws which simply acknowledged existing practices.

Nor did these laws slow the inexorable erosion of peasant holdings to the benefit of large landholders. While most of the individuals who acquired large properties under Muḥammad ʿAlī lost them under ʿAbbās, the consolidation of land soon recommenced. Ismāʿīl and other members of the royal family owned some 900,000 *faddāns* in the 1870's, or roughly one fifth of all cultivated land in the country; by the 1890s, 42.5 per cent of all registered land was held in properties of over 50 *faddāns*.[94] The cotton boom period witnessed a clear net loss of peasant-held land: peasant holders, whose land was still classified as *kharājīyah*, lost some 300,000 *faddāns* to large *ʿushūrīyah* holders between 1863 and 1880.[95] Debt was the most prevalent cause of loss. The cycle of small peasant debt has been amply illustrated: forced to borrow at high rates of interest in order to get the seed and animals necessary for sowing and paying monthly installments on their taxes, the peasants then had to repay these loans, often in kind, at harvest time when crop prices were lowest. The fall in the market price of cotton in the late 1870s erased the margin of profit of small holders altogether, making repayment of loans impossible, and foreclosure often ensued.[96]

The very largest royal estates created during the period, which might be 10,000 *faddāns* in size, were often rented out, at least in great part, to tenants on a cash or sharecropping basis; since few peasants possessed ready cash, we can assume that some form of sharecropping was most common. Arrangements undoubtedly varied. Villiers Stewart reported on several from Upper Egypt: in one village, the peasants rented land for one third of the crop and payment of the land tax of 125 piasters; elsewhere they paid 200 piasters per *faddān* plus 1½ *ardabbs* of produce, which could consume the entire first crop of corn and, thereafter, the landlord took 77 piasters and 1½ *ardabbs* on the second crop of barley. Such rack rents had reduced these tenants to penury, and only exemption from the corvée through the offices of their landlord allowed them to stay afloat.[97]

A second, and increasingly common, method of exploitation of large estates, especially in the more commercially oriented Delta, used service tenants on what came to be called *ʿizbahs*. Although precise arrangements and conditions again varied, the basic idea was the permanent installation of tenants on an estate and the use of their labor in exchange for housing and a subsistence plot. Different *ʿizbahs* employed different practices: the amount of labor exacted, the payment of wages for additional work, the shares of crops, the provision of livestock, etc. did not conform to any given model, but the system overall enabled large landholders to get dependable workers at low rates of pay.[98] On one medium-sized estate of 150 *faddāns*, for example, a peasant received, in return for his labor, a share of the estate's produce, the milk from a water buffalo he tended, and half the produce of the piece of land he was given to cultivate in his spare time; his wife and children also earned cash wages for field labor during the harvest season. On other estates, the peasant might be paid in cash or kind for each day worked on the estate.[99]

The number of peasants who worked on others' lands, whether as renters, sharecroppers, or permanent laborers, certainly increased between 1850 and 1882 as the agricultural sector came to be dominated by large-scale farming and landlessness grew more common.[100] The absolute majority of the Egyptian peasantry, however, remained small peasant proprietors farming family plots while battling swings in market prices, burdensome taxes, rapacious debt collectors, and draining corvée duties. The dispossession of peasant land, previously a product primarily of state policies, now proceeded apace as a result of market mechanisms, particularly the interaction of price and debt on the individual peasant, which were but the immediate symptoms of a longer-term transition in Egyptian agriculture.

1882–1914: Egyptian agriculture under British colonialism

The attention paid by the nineteenth century Egyptian State to the agricultural sector waned temporarily during the final days of Ismāʿīl's rule (1863–1879) and the early period of Tawfīq's (1879–1892). State bankruptcy, a proto-nationalist revolt led by Aḥmad ʿUrābī, and massive foreign intervention, first economic and then military, more than occupied the minds of Egypt's administrators.

Only with *de facto* British rule firmly in place by the mid-1880s did the State again focus on the development of agriculture by addressing problems of technology, pest control, tax burdens, and peasant indebtedness.

The British well understood that repayment of Egypt's foreign debts, the overweening responsibility of the colonial "advisors," depended upon the vitality and expansion of the agricultural sector. A stable and secure countryside, which only measures minimizing peasant hardship, and thus social tension, could provide, remained an equally important goal of their policy.[101] On a secondary and rather more mundane level, the immediate interests of many English at home as well as colonial administrators lay in the countryside, specifically in the cotton crop. The long recognized interest of textile manufacturers in access to long-staple Egyptian cotton was supplemented by growing European involvement in local marketing arrangements. Harry Boyle, faithful secretary to Lord Cromer, wrote to his mother of "the most appalling cotton speculation" in which officials such as Major Brown, the sub-head of the Irrigation Department, "made £400,000 by rigging the market with information he had," and Lord Cromer himself realized "a colossal fortune."[102] Concern for the overall solvency and stability of the country thus converged with the material interests of Lancashire and local officials to focus attention and effort on the promotion of agriculture.

The colonial administration first tackled the irrigation system, repairing and expanding dikes, dams, and canals. Three important barrages were also completed between 1890 and 1902: Nile water was now held up at the apex of the Delta (just south of Cairo), Asyūṭ, and Aswān. With the extension of feeder canals, summer water became available throughout the Delta and much of Middle Egypt. The spread of perennial irrigation enabled many peasants to cultivate cotton and encouraged them to switch from a three year rotation scheme to a two year one characterized by an increase in cotton planting but a reduction of fallow and bean production. By the early 1900s, the resulting rise in the water table, soil deterioration, and increased insect attacks had led to a decline in cotton yields; although many of these problems might have been solved by a vigorous drainage program, British officials apparently lacked the money and long-term perspective for a sustained effort.[103] Officials did recognize losses due to soil exhaustion and pest invasion, particularly of the cotton worm, but their response was limited to the relatively inexpensive expedient of creating a Department of Agriculture in 1911 charged with agricultural extension services, specifically the promotion of better seed, a three year crop rotation, and energetic cotton worm control by the peasants themselves.[104]

The problem, as Richards has described it, was not one that could be solved by information alone. The Egyptian peasantry were ruining their land by overcropping and overwatering, not out of ignorance but out of a desperate indebtedness: they were forced to maximize their incomes every year, even at the expense of the future, in order to pay the moneylender.[105] British administrators confronted the problem of peasant debt primarily by a program of tax reform: the abolition of most extraordinary levies and a reduction of the land tax were supposed to ease the peasant burden. Not all efforts bore immediate fruit: although the disparity between the *ʿushūrīyah* and *kharājīyah* tax rates was recognized as highly discriminatory, taxes were not finally equalized in all districts until 1912 because of the political influence wielded by large landholders. The peasantry continued to have difficulty meeting their tax obligations throughout the period as taxes and the fluctuating price of cotton forced them to turn, year after year, to the usurious moneylender of the countryside while the State abdicated all responsibility for their plight.[106] As late as 1912, official ideology still placed the blame for peasant debt on peasant extravagance: "The Egyptian peasant has had from time immemorial an ingrained habit of spending more money than he can afford on ceremonies, such as marriage, etc., and moreover he willingly ruins himself in litigation rather than make terms with his adversary."[107] Pursuing this logic, Kitchener then noted that the peasant, if only he would live temperately, had no need of credit. Indeed, the "Law of Five Feddans," passed in 1912, which protected the small cultivator's land, house, and tools from foreclosure, effectively barred him or her from the money market since he or she now possessed no security of any kind. Kitchener acknowledged that all state lending facilities benefited larger owners but, so the argument ran, the only land which needed major investment was owned by large holders with access to credit.

While state policies thus tended to further harm the small holder, the more extensive and intensive cultivation made possible by expanded irrigation had created a "second cotton boom" from the early 1890s onward; cotton composed more than 90 per cent of Egypt's total exports by 1914, and brought the country greater purchasing power and more investment capital than ever before.[108] The profits and burdens of the boom, however, were not very evenly shared: the peasantry continued to suffer from drains on its labor and loss of land throughout the British reform period.

The demands of the corvée, on the other hand, were greatly lightened under British administration. Colonel Scott Moncrieff, one of the key British officials in the Egyptian Public Works Department and an avid opponent of the corvée, thought that engineering advances coupled with wisely used paid labor could eliminate the need for forced labor altogether. Although Moncrieff's position was strongly supported by Nūbar Pāshā, then Egyptian Prime Minister, Cromer tended to demur on fiscal grounds: the budget could not cover the necessary expenditure. After privately tendering his resignation in early 1887 in protest, Moncrieff was convinced to stay on in his post and cooperate in a program of gradual reduction.[109] Estimated figures for corvée labor vary widely during the 1870s and 1880s, from 50,000 to 200,000 people for 100 days per year, but the trend is clear: the number drafted for work on the irrigation system was gradually cut back from 1884 to 1888, the last year when corvée labor was used for the heavy work of dredging canals.[110] Peasants were still liable to be drafted as watchmen on the river and canal banks and, in time of emergency, such as a breach in the dam walls when the Nile was unusually high as in 1892 and 1894, the number called up could suddenly increase.[111] In general, however, Moncrieff's position that the corvée was uneconomic, unwise, and immoral had won out.

Military recruitment was also less draining during the final years of the century. While the army had reached some 50,000 men under Ismāʿīl, it was drastically reduced under the British, stabilizing at some 13,000 officers and men in the early 1890s, of which five battalions were composed of blacks who had enlisted voluntarily.[112] Although British administrators had held out the hope that they could make the entire army a volunteer force and thereby earn some much needed popularity, the most they accomplished was a more systematic and regularized form of conscription. A new recruiting law introduced in 1885 specified exemptions for students, only sons, and those who could pay an exemption fee; punishment for draft evasion was shifted from the village *shaykh* to the family in 1887, and finally to the individual evader alone in 1902. Military commissions rather than local officials and notables were charged with running the recruitment, and roughly half of all eligible draftees obtained some form of exemption. Finally, the age of recruitment was fixed at 19 to 27, and the term of service at four years, although many soldiers were apparently kept longer.[113] All in all, there is every reason to believe that military impressment no longer weighed as heavily on the peasant family.

If peasants were able to exercise more control over their labor in this period, their situation on the land was less promising. The trend toward consolidation of land in the hands of large holders continued at the expense of the small and middle peasant proprietor. Despite Cromer's assurances that the policy of the Egyptian government under his tutelage was directed toward maintaining small holders in possession and preventing their ouster in favor of Europeans, the land tenure records he presented, comparing the situation in 1896 with that of 1906, showed a significant increase in large holders and a gain of 10 per cent in land held by Europeans. As population growth of 1.3 to 1.5 per cent a year outstripped the expansion of land in the rural areas, average plot size fell and the number of landless grew: by 1907, only 9 per cent of rural families owned 5 *faddāns* or more. Meanwhile, the area of large holdings was increasing, from 42.5 per cent of cultivable land in 1894 to 44.2 per cent in 1913.[114] Peasant indebtedness and the combination of high rents and low produce prices in the 1890s visibly swelled the ranks of a new class of landless laborers with no rental arrangements who hired out for a daily wage of 2 to 3 piasters.[115]

The *ʿizbah* system continued to absorb a good number of these peasants. The majority of large estates came to be managed, in this period, as *ʿizbahs* employing *tamalīyyah* workers (service tenants). The arrangements for *tamalīyyah* workers continued to vary. In some cases, the tenant paid a reduced rent for his small plot and received a monthly cash wage in exchange for his services: one typical *tamalīyyah* worker paid 505 piasters in an annual reduced rent in 1903 for 1½ *faddāns* while receiving 300 piasters in wages. His plot therefore provided not only subsistence, but also a cash income from cotton which enabled him to meet rental payments and other expenses.[116] Although the *ʿizbah* system gave the *tamalīyyah* worker access to the land he needed to feed his family and livestock, tenure remained insecure: a change of proprietor might spell an abrupt termination of the arrangement. In 1883, for example, 49 families of *tamalīyyah* workers, who had cultivated their plots since the days of Muḥammad ʿAlī, were summarily displaced when new owners arrived with their own workers.[117] Still, service tenants enjoyed a far more stable existence than the *tarahīl* workers usually employed on a daily basis for the seasonal tasks of harvesting, pest control, and irrigation upkeep. Often imported from the *Saʿīd* where a basin system of irrigation and a dense population had produced rural unemployment, *tarahīl* workers journeyed northwards for two to six months each year to work the labor-intensive summer crops as wage laborers. Their presence brought both flexibility and economy to the *ʿizbah* system: they were hired only as needed, provided their own transport and housing, and were not granted any land.

Many of these *ʿizbah* employees, both *tamalīyyah* and *tarahīl*, sharecropped or rented land as well. Sharecropping was still practiced on a limited scale, particularly on medium-sized properties. Sharecroppers might get as little as one quarter to one fifth of a cotton crop, although arrangements differed by region and even by crop. In general, however, the period witnessed a shift from sharecropping to cash rents as peasants acquired greater access to cash from growing cotton and the system proved less risky for the landowners.[118] Land rents were expensive enough to necessitate cultivation of a high return crop like cotton. One family, for example, paid 670 piasters a *faddān* in 1903; while they could produce corn worth 490 piasters or wheat worth 630 piasters on one *faddān*, the same area could support cotton with a market value of 2,340 piasters.[119] With all the other expenses of seed, tools, food, fuel, and clothing to consider, most peasants must have been forced to crop as much cotton as possible to cover their rents.

The small peasant proprietor also tended to overcrop. Some 20 to 25 per cent of cultivated land remained in the hands of small peasant landholders who might work it with family hands, seasonal hired labor, or a partner brought in on a sharecropping basis. Although the extra water of the post-1882 period benefited small plots, and peasant yields rose, indebtedness continued to encourage intensive cultivation and therefore soil deterioration which led, after 1900, to a discernible fall in peasant yields. Although legally secure on the land, the poverty of debt prevented the peasant from utilizing chemical fertilizers or effectively fighting a growth in insect infestation caused by new cropping patterns.[120] In practice, the peasant family's hold on the land had never been more tenuous. Improvements in infrastructure, particularly irrigation, had proved a double-edged sword for the small peasantry: without reasonable credit arrangements to enable them to emerge from the cycle of debt, the more intensive cropping led to greater land loss.

Women and the land

How did women experience the vicissitudes of the Egyptian peasantry in the nineteenth century? We must look first at their activities in agricultural production as well as the social and legal arrangements governing their access and claims to land.

Women as agricultural laborers

The Egyptian peasant woman has always worked long and hard in the fields. Members of the French Expedition remarked upon the large number of peasant women actually toiling on the land.[121] That women were thought perfectly fit for heavy manual labor was made abundantly clear by the early nineteenth century policy of subjecting them to corvée labor: women and children formed an important segment of the labor force in cotton and rice cultivation, especially at harvest time.[122] The employment or drafting of female and child labor for work on *usyah* land at times of peak demand implies that females were viewed primarily, however, as adjunct workers in agricultural production, whether on the family plot or on the *multazim*'s holding. Sporadic and seasonal recruitment of women at harvest and pest-control time could proceed without undue disruption of production on peasant holdings where men supplied most labor in the fields. Women thus formed a pool of surplus labor early on in agriculture, to be utilized on the family plot and on *usyah* land, lending cohesion and flexibility to a dual land tenure system. The scope and form of a woman's agricultural labor may have been influenced by existing property relations: care of the house, tools, and livestock over which she had partial proprietary rights would constitute one natural role, and free her for intensive seasonal labor on *usyah* land.

When rural labor shortages arose during the Muḥammad ʿAlī period, women's labor came to be central, not only to agricultural production but also to the building of the country's rural infrastructure. Most contemporary observers remarked, often with horror, on the numbers of women and children engaged in forced labor on irrigation projects, carrying away the earth dug up by the men.[123] ʿAbbās Pāshā, in a conversation with Hekekyan, recalled his opposition to Muḥammad ʿAlī's policy of utilizing forced female labor:

> One day in Shoobra His Highness [Muḥammad ʿAlī] said to me, "Abbas, we must make the women work," and I replied boldly, for I could not contain myself – "I have seen women delivered on the dykes and forced the following day to recommence their work of carrying earth and mud clods. The men are made to work by us – without remuneration – who will cook for them and make their bread?"[124]

After he assumed power, ʿAbbās indeed issued a decree in 1851 forbidding the corvée recruitment of pregnant women or those with children less than three years old, children under age eight, men and women over age seventy, and anyone with a dangerous infirmity. Stiff penalties were prescribed for any *shaykh* or official who recruited peasants from one of the forbidden categories.[125] Although some of the excesses of the corvée may have been eliminated, women and children still worked long hours on public projects at little or no pay in the early 1850s.[126]

Most observers suggest that whole families were recruited for corvée labor. In work on the Maḥmūdīyah Canal, peasant families were brought together to live and work as a unit, camping on the canal banks.[127] Hekekyan described the process of recruitment in one village, where the *shaykhs* organized a body of 600 men, women, and children for work on a transverse dike, opting to recruit families and leave behind able-bodied men.[128] A French overseer claimed that his canal project utilized family labor primarily at the request of the husbands and fathers themselves, who did not want to leave their families unattended at home.[129] Thus the pattern of shared family labor continued under the corvée. But while they might strive to keep the family physically together, peasants still objected to changes in the traditional assignment of tasks. Workers on one *chiflik* in Manṣūrah protested against the employment of women because their wives would not have time to prepare food.[130]

By the 1880s, however, as the overall demands of the corvée lessened, women and families were less often found in corvée labor. The newly systematized corvée required each landholder to come in person, or send a designated substitute, to do a two or three month stint on the canals. Lord Dufferin estimated that 100,000 to 130,000 men spent from 60 to 120 days each year performing corvée labor.[131] A *shaykh al-balad* from the province of al-Baḥrīyyah thought the system essentially fair, "but it is an unnecessary aggravation that the men are sent away to other parts of the province instead of working in their own neighborhoods where their wives could bring them food." Peasants from the province complained more forcefully:

> The forced labor is very onerous; it goes on from four to six months in the year. One-eighth of our population are taken away for it. Some pay substitutes, others go themselves; they have to go to any part of the Mudirieh [province] they are ordered to away from their wives and families; that makes it worse, it is so much more difficult to send them food and other necessaries.[132]

As long as corvée demands were high, joint family work under the corvée had served the interests of the *fallāḥīn* and the State. The tasks of nurture and protection could be carried on even when the family was temporarily displaced from the land. The corvée formerly appropriated family labor as a unit; the family continued to live and work together, producing for its own subsistence in the periods of relief from forced labor. Long stints of toil on the corvée impoverished the family but did not sever the bonds of shared production and consumption. It fell to the family to provide for its non-producing members, even during absence from home, for the State played no role in insuring the reproduction of conditions of existence. Corvée labor could be extracted by the State precisely because the family remained more or less intact, carrying on the functions of production for subsistence, provision of shelter, care for the young, old, and sick, and social regulation. Peasant protests against excessive use of female labor, and state reform of the corvée system, both spoke to the need to preserve family structure in lieu of any real assumption by the State of the family's diverse functions.

As the corvée was systematized and its burden reduced, it made less use of female labor: women and children, no longer recruited as a general rule, remained in the home village. Their labor could be mobilized by the State in times of special need: in 1909, when the cotton worm threatened Egypt's most valuable crop, the government activated a cotton worm control program which included 110,000 children recruited to pick the contaminated leaves in areas where labor was scarce.[133] Over the course of the nineteenth century, however, the practice of recruiting family labor was abandoned in favor of an all-male corvée. Women and children might work just as hard on the family plot, or be occasionally pressed into service in times of emergency, but they played a greatly reduced role in state-organized public labor.

We find more continuity in women's agricultural labor within the family unit. Given the heavy labor demands of irrigated agriculture, all hands were important to survival. Divisions of labor along sexual lines were not uncommon: men, for example, operated the *shadūf*; some six men from different households would cooperate in order to irrigate a *faddān* or two during the dry season in Upper Egypt.[134] In times of labor shortage, however, such divisions could break down. As the heavy military draft of the Muḥammad ʿAlī period drained the villages of men, the women who remained assumed new roles in agriculture as production for family subsistence became solely their responsibility. Tasks previously reserved for men, such as operating the *shadūf* or climbing date palms to pollinate the flowers, became women's work. The shortage of draught animals even led women to harness themselves in place of water buffaloes to turn millstones.[135]

In more normal times, women were still commonly found doing field labor: in the modest peasant family, be they owners or renters, the number of hands the family could muster to the field determined the presence or absence of profit; the labor of wives, daughters, and daughters-in-law figured prominently in a family's survival. Service tenants depended upon female labor for the care of the family plot while the men worked the *ʿizbah*'s land. With the tenant's reduced work days on the family's land, it was small wonder that the wife usually reigned supreme there: "In this, and most similar cases, the wife directs the household, concludes the bargains for the sale and purchase of produce, and does the greater portion of the field labour."[136] In addition to labor on family-held land, women and children might also earn an extra cash wage of about half the man's for field work in harvest or pest-control time on the *ʿizbah*.[137]

Women's labor in agricultural production, essential to the family plot, was thus used only as an occasional supplement on *ʿizbah* lands. As the *ʿizbah* system came more and more to dominate Egyptian agriculture over the course of the nineteenth century, and the family corvée was replaced by an all-male draft, sexual divisions of labor grew more pronounced. Men filled the ranks of day laborers, whether as service tenants or hired wage workers, while women tended the family plot. While the importance of peasant women to agricultural production was by no means diminished, women were excluded, more or less, from the more socialized forms of this labor on large estates.

Women as property holders

The woman's relationship to the land was influenced by her ability to make legal land claims. In the early part of the century, most women worked on the family plot without enjoying title to the usufruct of the *mīrī* land. Although Islamic laws of succession gave females rights to set portions of their relatives' estates, *mīrī* land belonged to the State and thus succession was not governed by religious law. Cases recording peasant succession in the Manṣūrah courts therefore remain silent on the disposition of *mīrī* land because such land was not the property, in the legal sense of full ownership, of an individual. In theory, the usufruct was conferred by the State on whomsoever it wished; in practice, the sons or other male relatives of the deceased usually acquired the usufruct of his portion of the *ʿarḍ al-fallāḥ*. Peasant plots thus passed from father to son; women rarely established usufruct claims.

Customary disposal of *mīrī* land reflected and sustained the structure of the peasant family. Daughters were only temporary members of their father's household; upon marriage they joined their husband's family unit. *Sharīʿah* court records of property sales in Manṣūrah suggest that the functional family unit was usually composed of a man and wife and their children, or grown sons presumably with wives and children of their own, who remained in economic association before and after their parents' death. Within the extended family unit, few children survived their parents. Out of fourteen families in the Manṣūrah records for which we have full household information, twelve couples had three or less children at the time of the death of one of the parents.[138] High infant mortality, the grim product of famine and plague, limited family size. Economic association among peasant family members most commonly bound only one or two male children to their parents and each other. Court records dealt primarily with heritable property, that is, buildings, town land, livestock, tools, and other goods, but patterns of joint ownership of such property probably reflect ongoing family association on the land as well. In an arbitrary sample of some 38 purchases of peasant property made between 1801 and 1820, six of the purchases were made jointly: three by a man and wife, two by brothers, and one by a man and his mother.[139] Women were associated with husbands and sons, not with their own parents or siblings.

Islamic succession law, by giving women a share in their parents' movable property, did not always buttress the predominant family form: legal heirs often were not members of the same functional family. If co-heirs lived in different family units, they might sell their jointly inherited property. Among the same 38 property transactions, we find another six cases involving joint sellers: in four instances, relatives jointly sold their inherited property to an outsider. To counteract inheritance laws which tended to fragment family property, sales and purchases were also made among the heirs in order to keep the estate intact and in the hands of a functional family unit. Ten out of the 38 cases involved such transactions: people bought property from relatives who were co-sharers in family estates. Despite the lack of access to *mīrī* land, women could be important property holders in their husbands' or sons' households. Transfers of property among heirs often consolidated property in the hands of women: six of the ten purchases directed toward unification of family property were made by women. In buying property from a brother, father, father's wife, uncle, or son by a divorced husband, women consolidated the inheritance they brought to the family entered through marriage.

Indeed, a peasant woman could possess a significant amount of cash or valuables, acquired with part of her *mahr* (bridal gift) or through inheritance and her own labor. One case of theft, recorded in Manṣūrah, demonstrates the economic power a woman could yield. Bedawīyah, a peasant woman, accused her neighbor Maryam of stealing from her during a visit. The list of missing items included six silver *riyāls*, four French *riyāls*, two Venetian sequins, seven Egyptian gold pieces, gold brocade worth four Venetian sequins, a silver plate, and a silver necklace – a handsome horde by all accounts. This property was Bedawīyah's alone, and she assiduously pursued her neighbor to regain her lost goods. Eschewing reliance on any male relative, she personally brought her case before the village *qā'immaqām* and then resorted to the *sharī'ah* court.[140]

The laws and customs regulating disposal of the *mahr*, paid by the husband, help explain this sort of economic independence. One part of the *mahr*, paid by the husband, was usually spent by the new couple to acquire household items or agricultural tools; the remainder constituted a reserve which reverted to the wife in the case of divorce or widowhood. A wife thus retained a claim on her husband or his heirs, a practice probably calculated to avert female destitution and discourage the frequent severing of family ties. The *mahr* and debts owed to a wife formed, on occasion, a significant portion of a man's estate, indicating the economic power a woman might possess through her control over goods and cash placed at the service of the family. Upon the husband's death, repayment of the wife took precedence over any inheritance claims.

In two such cases in the early nineteenth century, peasant widows immediately laid claim to 24 per cent and 58 per cent of the total value of their husbands' respective estates, excluding their legal shares of the inheritance.[141] In both instances, a distinction was made between what was owed the wife as the balance of her *mahr*, and what was owed as accumulated debt. Clearly the material contributions the women made to their husbands' households had not become part of the husbands' property; wives retained distinct legal claims not only to repayment of the *mahr*, but also to repayment of the value of any specie or goods they had inherited or earned. If the estate proved insufficient for reimbursement, the principal heir, usually the husband's son, was required to make payment. Such obligations were taken seriously: the court named the heir responsible for paying the wife's debt and witnessed the eventual repayment of the woman.[142] The documented ability of women to assert such claims and gain the support of the court must have softened the economic blows which could follow the dissolution of family ties.

The rights of the peasant woman to her individual property were recognized throughout the nineteenth century. The protection afforded by the right to payment of the balance of her *mahr*, her share in successions, and any debts owed her by her husband at the time of his death continued to provide a certain economic security. Women used the court to collect any outstanding obligations: one peasant woman took a debtor of her deceased husband to the Manṣūrah court and obtained a judgment that he pay her monthly installments; another, when her husband's estate failed to cover the debts he owed her, pressed for payment from the husband's nephew who had taken control of the land formerly cultivated by her husband.[143]

Sometimes, the husband paid his debts over the course of the marriage. In the case of the woman Zahrah, a review of economic bonds conjured up an atmosphere of precision bookkeeping rather than the joys of matrimonial union:

> the esteemed Aḥmad Maḥmūd, naval lieutenant from the ninth battalion of Ḥasan Aghā bin Bāshī gave legal testimony . . . that he possessed and he owed by legal right and observed legal practice to his wife, the *ḥurmah* Zahrah, the woman, daughter of the esteemed Haj Aḥmad al-Fāris, the Egyptian, the sum of 7,000 *nisf fiḍḍah*: 6,000 *nisf fiḍḍah* from the balance of her bridal gift (*ṣadāq*) and 1,000 *nisf fiḍḍah* from a debt to her, and he had paid her three copper plates and a dipper worth 49 *ghrūsh rūmī*, an Arab *kilīm* (rug) worth 40 *ghrūsh rūmī*, the sum of this being 80 *ghrūsh rūmī* that he has paid to her, or 3,200 *nisf fiḍḍah* and he undertakes its legal discharge. Of this, 3,000 *nisf fiḍḍah* is from the balance of her bridal gift and the rest is from his debt.[144]

Zahrah, a relatively wealthy woman, was amply protected in the case of death or divorce. Even among the poorer peasantry, women owned certain things, usually household goods or jewelry, which were independent private property. In one family of rentors, the wife's jewelry alone was valued at some 15 per cent of the family's yearly income; in an even poorer family of day laborers, the wife possessed jewelry worth over 20 per cent of the family's combined annual wage.[145]

While the *sharī'ah* court consistently upheld the peasant woman's rights to this property, the drive for consolidation of family property sometimes resulted in the illegal disinheriting of women. Family disputes over the divsion of estates in the Manṣūrah region often involved women whose relatives had deprived them of legal shares. One peasant woman, 'Iz, accused her deceased husband's brother, 'Alī, of cheating her and her children out of shares in her husband's property.[146] The content of the estate suggests that the deceased worked in economic association with 'Alī and perhaps other brothers, for the disputed property included one half of a camel, one third of a water buffalo and its calf, one half of a horse, one third of a mill, a plough and a gun, several *ardabbs* of wheat, beans and flax, and a few articles of clothing. The court agreed that this property, or its cash equivalent, must go to 'Iz and her children; 'Alī promised to pay them as soon as he sold the grain. The case underlines the vulnerability of the peasant woman, especially after the death of her husband. Inheritance laws notwithstanding, the temptation to disinherit female in-laws must have been great.

The plight of 'Iz also brings the peasant family into sharper focus. Here the functional family consisted of brothers, together with their wives and children, who probably farmed a portion of *mīrī* land. 'Iz, while she may have owned jewelry, clothing, tools, and livestock inherited or acquired on her own, could only assert a claim to the fruits of family labor through her husband. Even though she was a productive member of a household, her position in the family was mediated by her husband: the division of his estate after his death suggests that 'Iz and her children would now form their own household.

The court's reference to the legal concept of *sharikah* (association) to define the rights and obligations of a family could effectively strip women of their rights. In a household association composed of a father, his sons, and their wives, the daughters-in-law occupied a very precarious legal position. If one of the sons should die before his father, the daughter-in-law often found herself left with nothing. The *muftī* repeatedly ruled that as long as a son was living and working with his father, all family property was vested in the father. Women sometimes asked their fathers-in-law, upon the death of their husbands, for payment of the balance of the *mahr* and a share in their husband's inheritance; if the woman had been living with her husband's family, her request was invariably denied by the court.[147]

A husband's absence, particularly common in eras of heavy military recruitment, could also jeopardize his wife's position in the extended family. Many cases from the Muḥammad ʿAlī period involved peasants living and working in a unit of brothers, with their wives and children, who shared the goods, livestock, and land left by their father. The brothers, viewed under Islamic law as a *sharikah*, a legally defined economic association involving reciprocal obligations, contributed more or less equal amounts of labor time to family production and held equal shares of the inheritance. The absence of one, however, might lead to dispute over the proper division of the fruits of family production and the assignment of family responsibilities.

A peasant family quarreled bitterly in 1849 over the division of their joint property when the time came, perhaps when the children were of age, to divide the patrimony and establish separate households. One of the brothers had served in the army, faithfully sending home his pay for the support of his wife and children, residing with his brothers and their families. The quarrel revolved around what precisely should be considered part of the shared inheritance, and thus divided among them, and what belonged to each individual brother. The *muftī* ruled that the inheritance of the father and its increase should be divided equally, but what each brother earned during the others' absence "through his own work and effort is his alone." The money sent home by the soldier had been earmarked for the support of his wife and children and thus formed no part of the inheritance; indeed, if the other brothers had used part of it for other purposes, they must refund this sum.[148] It appears that even though the soldier's wife and children remained part of the wider family economic unit, the fact of the husband's absence modified the pattern of joint production and consumption. The wife and children only formed a part of the peasant household through their relationship with their husband and father. If the soldier had not sent home his pay, they might well have had to leave the family hearth.

Thus the peasant woman, as agricultural laborer on the family plot, could make but a tenuous claim to control of family agricultural production: death or divorce could sever her relationship to the family unit and the land it worked. Her position was improved, however, by her strong legal claim to a share in buildings, livestock, and movable property. As she moved from one family group to another, propelled by marriage, divorce, or death, she carried along her rights to the tools of agricultural production. Her property was her own: fathers, brothers, husbands, and sons had no right of guardianship over females in their majority.

While the legal basis of female claims to *mīrī* land and other property did not change during the Muḥammad ʿAlī period, we do find that women were often actively pressing claims to the land. As the power of the State grew, one of its local representatives, the *ḥākim*, acquired some powers of appointment of the usufruct. The courts at mid-century asserted two sometimes contradictory principles for the disposal of *mīrī* land upon the death of the usufruct holder: first, the sons or male relatives of the deceased, if capable of farming the land and paying the taxes, should inherit the usufruct; and secondly, local officials had the right to invest whomsoever they wished.[149] Daughters, wives, and sisters came to ask for a share of *mīrī* land as part of their inheritance. Daughters were told by the courts that the usufruct goes solely to the sons as long as they are working the land and paying the taxes.[150] When a man died, leaving only his sister and his brother's sons, the court refused to consider the sister's request for a share in *mīrī* land.[151] In the case of a *fallāḥ* survived by his sister, two daughters, and a nephew, the usufruct in its entirety passed to the nephew.[152] Although female heirs rarely succeeded in overriding the customary male right to *mīrī* land, they were probably emboldened to contest male claims in court because of the extension of the *ḥākim*'s powers of decision and the weakening of customary rights.

Under certain circumstances, women could obtain usufruct rights. If a father ceded part of his land to his daughter during his lifetime, the daughter had a strong claim to retention of the land. In one case, the *muftī* forbade the dead man's sons to take *mīrī* land away from their sisters on the grounds that the women had cultivated it for a number of years before and after their father's death.[153] In the absence of male children, daughters sometimes managed to acquire rights at the expense of other male heirs. In the case of a widow, left with two young daughters, who had continued to cultivate her husband's *mīrī* land for five years after his death, the court denied the husband's brothers all rights to the land.[154]

The most common female claim rested on the initial consent of male heirs. If male relatives ceded part of the land to female heirs upon the death of the holder, any of their later claims were void. They often had a change of heart, it seems, and attempted to wrest the land from their female relatives by pressing their rights as males. The court denied their requests: the fact that they had waived their rights deserved mention in most decisions, but the past performance of the women in meeting their tax responsibilities carried equal weight. The court was also quick to remind all parties that the final right belonged to whomsoever the *ḥākim* invested, although there was some question as to what powers of discretion the *ḥākim* could exercise in the presence of surviving male children.[155]

Rights to *mīrī* land thus came to rest partly on custom and partly on the will of local officials. *Mīrī* land usually remained intact in the hands of one or more sons. There were seldom more than a few claimants to the land, for peasant families remained small: all seven families in the Manṣūrah records of 1829 to 1846 for which we have full household data had three or fewer children at the time of one of the parents' deaths.[156] Nevertheless, women rarely inherited the usufruct unless their male relatives specifically allowed them to do so.

Women also continued to encounter male resistance to their claims to movable property. One woman, in a case referred to the *muftī*, complained to the court that her father-in-law had denied her a share in her husband's inheritance.[157] Elsewhere, sons of the deceased simply divided the father's inheritable property among themselves with no regard for the rights of their mother and sisters.[158] The *muftī*, in such cases, strongly upheld the rules of Islamic inheritance, insisting that the widow is entitled to one eighth of her husband's estate, and the female children to one half that of the males' share. We can understand why a father might attempt to protect his daughters' rights and future by dividing his property before his death; in one such instance, the eldest son tried to prevent the division, claiming that part of the property had been acquired by his personal effort and should be his alone.[159]

Men were expectedly loath to see family property pass into female hands given the kinship nature of the family productive unit. Many peasant households, as *sharikahs*, were based on brothers who shared the *mīrī* land left by their father. Their sisters, who married into other households, removed their shares of the heritable property from the paternal household. Evidence exists that sisters, upon the death of their father, often ceded their share of property to their brothers for a consideration.[160] A voluntary waiver of inheritance rights was binding on all heirs: the husbands of two women who attempted to claim, after the death of their wives, what their wives had ceded to their brothers, were told by the court that such grants were irreversible unless the women themselves had demanded return during their lifetimes.[161]

The legal division of inheritable property often took place some time after the father's death. The determination of whether or not the female heirs should share in any augmentation was apparently related to the position of women within the family productive unit. As long as the sisters and brothers remained under the same roof, working together, they formed an association or *sharikah*. The sisters could make legal claim to share in any buildings, livestock, or other goods and money the household acquired after, as well as before, the death of the father. When the sisters did not remain in the paternal household, they were not considered part of the brother's *sharikah* and were entitled to a share of the property only as it stood at the time of the death of their father.[162]

Quarrels, arising over the division of the heritable property, often pitted women against their brothers. A woman might claim that her brother had purchased goods as the father's agent and therefore they formed part of the father's estate: one sister battled with her brother for a share in his water buffalo on these grounds. Sometimes the sisters' heirs pressed a claim: one man, upon the death of his wife, asserted that some jewels, a copper vessel, and a water buffalo, which had been in his wife's possession, formed part of her estate. The court ruled that the goods had only been loaned to the woman by her mother and brother and should therefore revert to their household.[163]

The overall trend in the division of inheritable property was to limit the female share to the minimum required by Islamic law or even to subvert legal injunctions by denying women part of their inheritance. These tactics strengthened the family productive unit at the expense of females who married outside the household. Women were forced to appeal to the court, which sided with them in cases of flagrant flouting of Islamic law, but may not have been able to insure implementation of its decisions. In a household composed of brothers in economic association, the wife of any one brother had a strong claim to inherit her legal share of her husband's property. Brothers-in-law might simply seize property, however, with no regard for the rights of the widow. One woman, Rabīyah, complained to the Manṣurah court that her brother-in-law had ignored the legal division of her husband's estate and grabbed her daughter's share for himself.[164] Women also testified that their rights were whittled away by false claims of association on the part of their brothers-in-law. One woman reported that her husband's brother had taken her water buffalo, claiming that he had shared it with her husband. The court noted that the animal, bought by the woman and her sister-in-law after her husband's death, could hardly be considered the brother's joint property. Elsewhere a woman and her children protested similar false claims of association on the part of the brother-in-law.[165]

On the other hand, women or children might base property claims on an association denied by the husband's or father's brothers. The children of a blind man, who had been living with their father's brother, asked for a share in their uncle's inheritance on the grounds that he had been their father's associate. The decision of the court, denying their claim, suggests that a non-productive household member and his dependants could not establish property rights over the fruits of household production. Even when the man was a productive member of the *sharikah*, his wife and children were only entitled to their share in his portion of the property exactly as it stood at the time of his death. Any additions made after that time belong exclusively to the other brothers.[166]

Peasant families sometimes protected themselves from disinheritance and acrimonious dispute by naming, in court, the principal legal heirs. Beginning in the early 1840s, cases testifying to the legitimacy of children and the health and whereabouts of principal heirs, normally wives and children, make an appearance. In some instances, the male head of the family came to court before his death to name his legitimate heirs; elsewhere, wives and children prevailed upon witnesses to testify to their existence, and thus, by implication, their rights of succession after the death of the *paterfamilias*.[167]

The system in which women held weak claim to the *taṣarruf* of the family plot, and thus to full partnership in the family *sharikah*, was challenged, at least in theory, by the Land Law of 1858. According to the letter of the law, all *kharājīyah* land became subject to Islamic rules of succession and women, therefore, were to inherit shares of land just as they inherited movable property. At first blush, the new law might have dramatically altered patterns of land tenure. It seemed to reverse a clear pattern: during the 1850s, while the *ḥākim*'s power of choice receded into the background in the court's arguments, the right of a son or sons to exclusive control of *mīrī* land was often reiterated.[168] At the same time, however, the right of other male relatives to supersede a holder's wife or daughters was not usually championed by the courts. If there were no surviving sons, any evidence that the *taṣarruf* holder had desired to alienate the land to his wife or daughters seemed sufficient to erode the claims of more distant male relatives.[169] The drive to leave the land within the functional family unit, the *sharikah* of parents and children, had already proved stronger than the stated official preference for male heirs to *mīrī* land.

Ironically enough, in some cases the new law diminished the female share: when a man left a wife and brother, the wife could lay claim to only one quarter of the land, her portion under Islamic rules of succession, so that automatically the brother took the lion's share.[170] In general, however, there is no evidence that the law transformed patterns of peasant tenure: while Islamic law was now to be applied to *mīrī* succession, the practice of land inheritance was little changed. Sisters commonly allowed the eldest son to hold the *taṣarruf*; the new law appeared to benefit them directly only insofar as it lent additional legal backing to their claims to the fruits of the *sharikah*'s production as long as they remained under the family roof.[171] Once they married, they apparently departed without their land: the peasant *sharikahs* of the second half of the century were usually associations of brothers.[172]

Before and after 1858, then, patterns are consistent: some peasant women did hold the usufruct to *kharājīyah* land and thus were, for all intents and purposes, small landholders. These women sold and mortgaged land to which they clearly enjoyed uncontested rights of usufruct.[173] They had usually acquired the land in one of two ways: in the absence of male children, daughters could gain control of the land at their father's death, or male relatives, especially a father, ceded the usufruct to women as a form, no doubt, of material provision.[174] The majority of peasant women, however, did not possess land during the nineteenth century;

as long as the peasant household contained adult males, men retained control of the land, a control only partially counterbalanced by the woman's contributions to production and successful claims to movable property.

Peasant women and the family

The world of the peasant woman in Egypt was molded by contradictory forces which undermined and strengthened her position within the family. On the one hand, her lack of claim to family-held land and her tenuous ties to a given family unit, liable as they were to be severed by divorce or her husband's death, testify to the pronounced patriarchal and patrilocal character of peasant society and the basic insecurity of female status and position. Conversely, the very active role women played in agricultural production on the family plot promoted female independence and power within the family setting. The peasant woman's primary identity was that of a family member; her ability to overcome the impediments to power and security in the family context is therefore key to assessing her position in society as a whole.

The rights and obligations of family members were defined by Islamic laws, more precisely by the Ḥanafī *madhab* applied in the Egyptian courts of the nineteenth century. The voluminous records of the *sharīʿah* courts demonstrate the frequency with which peasants used the court to clarify family relations or deal with family problems. The proceedings also reveal the extent to which peasant women managed, within the framework of law and the judicial system, to assert the rights or privileges allotted them or, conversely, to minimize disabilities. Marriage arrangements, divorce proceedings, issues of child custody, guardianship, and familial support affected the lives of women very directly, shaping the latitude of independent action and control they could achieve within the family. Although Islam provided the legal underpinnings for family relations through its detailed regulation of family life, law in theory was not always law in practice. The power of custom and the ways in which women themselves could influence their situation impinged upon legal practice and contributed to a fluid and ongoing evolution of women's status in the family.

First, the right of a woman to choose or refuse a husband partially defines the position she will enjoy in marriage. Under Islamic law, a woman in her majority has the capacity to contract her own marriage without the interference of a marriage guardian or *wālī*.[175] Egyptian peasant women actualized this capacity: young women could choose their husbands and arrange their own marriages as long as the groom was "suitable," that is, of similar social standing, and offered a *mahr* appropriate to the bride's social status and personal qualities. Despite the occasional bid by a relative to block a woman's choice, the courts invariably recognized her ability to marry without the permission, or good offices, of her family.[176] The tested ability to arrange her own marriage if necessary was matched by her right to refuse a match. The high-handedness of one *shaykh al-balad*, who forced a peasant woman to marry the man of his choice, was denounced by the *muftī*: such coercion renders a marriage void (*bāṭil*).[177] Before reaching her majority, however, a girl could be legally married off by her father or grandfather without her permission. The Egyptian courts saw many cases of this kind, suggesting that fathers often married their daughters at a young age before they could exercise the rights of choice or refusal.

Once married, a woman's position within a marital household could be threatened by the male right of polygamy. The male prerogative of marrying up to four wives, on the condition that he treat them equally, had the potential of undermining the women. With the arrival of a second wife, a woman's control over present family resources diminished, and her future shares in her husband's estate were cut in half. Children born to the second wife established claims which competed directly with those of her children. Unlike a divorce (*ṭalāq*), second marriages did not involve compensation to the first wife: the balance of her *mahr* remained in her husband's keeping. In a monogamous marriage, the mere threat of a second wife, which would reduce the first wife's status and material claims, could act as a powerful disciplinary tool enforcing female submission. The Manṣūrah records of 1800 to 1820 suggest, however, that polygamy was by no means widespread among peasant families in the early nineteenth century. In the 14 families for which we have full data, for example, we find only one case of polygamy, one man with two wives.[178] A century later, in-depth household studies of six "typical" peasant families still yielded only one with more than one wife: a fairly wealthy peasant owner and overseer of a large estate who had married two women.[179] Such low occurrence may be a product of material conditions, the scarce resources of the peasant family not permitting the luxury of a second wife. Women themselves may have successfully resisted the introduction of co-wives, although information is lacking. In any event, neither the actuality nor the threat of polygamy was a salient feature of the peasant woman's life.

If polygamy remained rare throughout the nineteenth century, divorce was commonplace. Of the three recognized types of divorce in Islamic law, two – *faskh* (*tafrīq*) and *khulʿ* – are generally ratified in court. *Faskh*, a judicial decree of separation usually granted at the request of the wife, appears most favorable to the woman insofar as she obtains a wanted divorce but yet retains her claim to the balance of the *mahr* and support during her waiting period (*ʿiddah*). *Khulʿ*, divorce by mutual agreement, is essentially an arrangement whereby a woman can ransom herself from an unwanted marriage through payment of a compensation, often by surrendering her claims on her *mahr*. While both *faskh* and *khulʿ* were usually female-initiated, the most prevalent form of divorce was surely *ṭalāq*, unilateral repudiation of a wife by a husband, pronounced outside the courtroom.

Peasant women rarely succeeded in obtaining a decree of *faskh* from a *qāḍī*; we did not find a single request in the Manṣūrah records. The *muftī* occasionally dealt with cases in which extreme impediments provided the grounds for *faskh*: a woman whose husband proved impotent could obtain a decree of *faskh*, and a Christian woman who converted to Islam might be separated from her husband at her request unless he converted also.[180] Although not theoretically permitted in Ḥanafī law, women did at times persuade their local *qāḍī* to grant a decree of *faskh* on the grounds that a husband was providing insufficient material support and companionship. As military and corvée recruitment during the Muḥammad ʿAlī period drained the villages of men, many women found themselves legally married but without husbands. In order to remarry, they sometimes prevailed upon the court to issue a divorce decree on the grounds of lack of material support or even the "loneliness of the marriage bed."[181] In general, however, women were discouraged from seeking the form of divorce most beneficial to them.

On the other hand, the *khulʿ* form of divorce was frequently used by women. It commonly entailed discharging the husband from his financial obligation to pay the balance (*muakhkhar*) of her *mahr*, a portion usually held in escrow for the woman until the marriage was terminated by death or divorce. While *khulʿ* represented one form of divorce that the woman could initiate, it often proved very costly indeed. One Bedouin woman obtained her divorce by cancelling her husband's debts to her, forfeiting all claim to support during her *ʿiddah*, and returning a *mahr* of most handsome proportions: five silver bracelets, fifteen camels, two cows, and four woolen blankets.[182] While some women managed to obtain their freedom through the sacrifice of their *mahr* alone, others gave up material support during the *ʿiddah* and child support payments as well.[183] Although *khulʿ* did enable peasant women to leave an unsatisfactory marriage, the economic losses entailed must often have been difficult to sustain and therefore acted as a brake on recourse to *khulʿ* proceedings. Still, some women did barter their rights to a portion of family property in order to break their marriage bonds.

Ṭalāq, unilateral repudiation of a wife, was probably the most common form of divorce. Although *ṭalāq* as such was never recorded in court records, cases concerning property matters, particularly successions, sometimes mention a divorced woman (*muṭalāqah*). The male right to divorce his wife without cause or court process was limited, in practice, by economic relations within the family. A woman divorced by *ṭalāq* retained full rights to the property she had brought to the marriage, including the balance of her *mahr* and support during the *ʿiddah*. Divorce did not necessarily mean destitution or eviction from the shared home. In one case, a divorced woman bought a house from her former husband, using her independent means to gain full ownership of what had probably been their marital domicile. If the woman already held legal title to the family house, she might choose to retain it or sell it to her husband: one divorcée sold her house in Manṣūrah to her former husband.[184] In both these transactions, the effects of divorce were mitigated by the woman's claim to possession of money or property legally distinct from that of her husband. Because a woman's withdrawal of her property from the family unit could cause economic disruption, especially when her legal property constituted a sizeable portion of family resources, *ṭalāq* was not to be pronounced lightly; it involved the severing of economic bonds which might prove detrimental to the family.

Repudiation could harm a woman's economic standing insofar as it cancelled her inheritance claims on her husband. Once divorced, a wife no longer inherited her husband and thus lost her major claim on family property should the head of the family die. A woman might thus go to some lengths to prove that she had been divorced during her husband's fatal illness, the one circumstance in which she could still inherit; if the judge were convinced, however, that the husband had actually recovered and later died from another illness or accident, the divorced woman lost her bid for a share of the estate.[185]

Recognizing, on balance, the material advantages of *ṭalāq*, many women who wanted a divorce preferred that their husbands repudiate them. One peasant woman took her husband before the *nā'ib* (assistant) to the local *qāḍī*, claiming that he had divorced her according to the *ṭalāq* formula but now refused to honor the divorce. After she had produced two male witnesses, the *nā'ib* agreed that a divorce had occurred and instructed the husband to accept the consequences of his action. If a woman could not produce witnesses, however, she was less likely to be able to prove a *ṭalāq* had taken place as long as her husband denied it. One man returned home after a long absence to find that his wife had married someone else, claiming that he had divorced her before he left the village; when he contested the claim and she failed to present any evidence, her second marriage was annulled and she was "returned" to her first husband.[186]

Other peasant women tried to force their husbands, one way or the other, to divorce them. Having enlisted the cooperation of the local *shaykh al-balad*, one woman managed to bully her husband into pronouncing a divorce. Another used blackmail: she threatened to take her husband to court and claim that he had stolen her jewelry unless he divorced her; so she "frightened him" and he indeed complied with a repudiation. In such cases, however, the courts usually ruled the divorce invalid if any coercion of the husband were proved.[187] Still, despite divorce laws which seemed to give the male near total control, peasant women sometimes managed to leave marriages when and how they wished, a testament to the power they could wield in the family.

Women experienced greater difficulty when children were involved. Child custody rules in the case of divorce prejudice the woman's position by depriving her of the material and emotional benefits her children offer. The patriarchal character of Islamic law is especially pronounced in the matter of regulations pertaining to custody and guardianship of the children of a divorced couple. While a mother enjoys the right of *ḥiḍānah* (custody) in Ḥanafī law of male children up to the age of seven and female children until they reach puberty, she does not normally exercise the right of *walāyah* (guardianship). The father, as *wālī* (guardian), retains the power to act on behalf of his minor children in property transactions and marriage arrangements, a right transferred to other paternal male relatives in the event of a father's death.[188] Children, then, are legally part of the father's line; the mother's custody is limited in time and scope, for she is but the temporary caretaker of young children.

A case from Manṣūrah demonstrates the paternal family's prerogative of guardianship after the father's death. The family of one Ḥasan al-Shāb came to the court to demand payment of the *diyah* (blood money) from the *shaykhs* of the village of al-Badālah where Ḥasan had met a violent death. Ḥasan's two daughters, his only children, were the issue of two different wives, one divorced and one his widow, both of whom survived him; legal guardianship of the daughters, however, was vested in Ḥasan's cousin Aḥmad. Aḥmad claimed the daughters' share of the *diyah* on their behalf, while Ḥasan's widow claimed her own share: children whose mothers were alive and well still came under the legal guardianship of distant relatives on the father's side, regardless of whether their mothers were divorced or widowed.[189]

In some circumstances women could acquire the status of *wālī* of their children by a deceased husband. Mubārakah, a divorced wife whose former husband had died, sold a house Manṣūrah in her capacity as legal guardian for her minor daughter.[190] Barring the unlikely possibility that all male paternal relatives were dead, Mubārakah had gained rights based on very tenuous legal ground. Her case suggests that a woman might establish a right of guardianship if her husband's family did not insist on claiming the child, and that, in any event, children did not always become the wards of their father's relatives. The documented expansion of legally sanctioned rights of *ḥiḍānah* into rights of *walāyah* counters the impression left by attention to legal rules alone; divorced or widowed women were not always deprived of their children.

After the exodus of menfolk from the villages commenced in the reign of Muḥammad ʿAlī, male *wālīs*, essential for the arrangement of minors' marriages as well as many other legal transactions, could be in short supply. The Ḥanafī *muftī* reviewed a case which posed problems arising when the entire male line had left the village. A maternal grandmother wanted to marry her ten-year-old granddaughter to a man of equal social standing who offered a "fair" *mahr*, but the girl's father had been missing for some time and her uncle, the father's brother, was serving in the military in Alexandria. The *muftī* ruled that the mother or grandmother could give the girl in marriage when adult males were absent only if the suitor and the *mahr* were indeed proper. Marriage arrangements made by the women or the mother's family alone would, in any other circumstances, be of questionable legality. Thus, although female relatives did not, in the absence of males, acquire identical powers as *wālīs*, they were often empowered by the court to assume the role as long as the proper male *wālīs* were unavailable.[191]

Women did retain their special rights to the custody of young children, but the divorcée or widow lost such rights as soon as a boy reached seven or a girl attained puberty. The courts consistently enforced this rule despite women's frequent attempts to keep their children beyond the legal age. When faced with a woman's request, the judge's reply was brief and to the point:

In a legal presentation, *saʿādat bāshā*, the *mudīr* of al-Daqhalīyah . . . submitted a petition on behalf of the *ḥurmah* Zahrah, the divorced wife of Muḥammad the blacksmith, which testified that she has with her a son by him [Muḥammad] and she wants to keep him with her, and so a legal ruling was given that the Ḥanafī master has given a formal legal opinion that a son, when he has attained the age of seven, belongs with his father; this boy is over ten years old and he should be with his father. Such is the imperative legal decision given on the ninth of Rabīʿ II, 1261.[192]

A woman still might resort to evasion of the law in her struggle to keep her children in her care. One father, coming to court to ask for compensation for the death of his son, alluded to such a custody conflict:

The esteemed ʿAlī ʿAṭā Allāh from al-Jamalīyyah in the wilayet of al-Daqhalīyyah accused the esteemed Muhḥammad Abū ʿAlī Idrāsī from the same locale [saying] that he [ʿAlī] had previously divorced his wife, the *ḥurmah* Fātimah, the woman, daughter of Sayyid al-Ahl from Sibāt on the small river, and he had a son by her, Aḥmad, eight years old and weaned. Prior to this time, she hid him [Aḥmad] with the above-mentioned accused without the permission of his father. And he [Muḥammad] sent him [Aḥmad] to water a horse and he [Aḥmad] was killed in an accident. The accused was questioned about this and he replied that he [Aḥmad] had taken the horse without the permission of its owner and he [Muḥammad] had not commissioned him to water it; the horse had thrown him into a canal in the above-mentioned place and he did not know anything further about what had befallen him; and so he regretted receiving this legal accusation. So our lord *effendī* [the judge] ruled that no payment be made under any circumstances.[193]

Whether Fātimah had taken her son to the house of a relative or employer is not stated, but her intent to retain custody of the child through stealth beyond the legal age limit seems clear. As long as she remained in her husband's village, her attempt appeared doomed to failure if her husband were to insist on his paternal rights. Still, her extralegal maneuver suggests that women might resort to subterfuge or flight to avoid the loss of their children.

Women's rights to the custody (*ḥiḍānah*) of young children could, however, come under attack. Court decisions evinced little sympathy for the plight of the divorced or widowed woman who, in the absence of maintenance from her own family, was forced to work outside the family unit to support her children. In the nineteenth century, many court cases involved disputes over child custody, particularly when the woman, having lost her position in her husband's household, had not been reintegrated into her parents' household. The woman lost her rights to *ḥiḍānah* if she had no means of support. The divorced husband could be asked to pay a certain sum (*ijrah*) toward the support of the child, but should he plead poverty, he had the right, in lieu of payment, to entrust the care of the child to another female relative. A widow, left nothing by her impecunious husband, could lose her custody rights in favor of her husband's family.[194]

If a woman, stripped of her role in the peasant household, turned to outside work to support herself and her children, she ran the risk of being declared an unfit mother. One woman, having obtained a *khulʿ* divorce by agreeing to waive her rights to return of the balance of her *mahr*, was left with no means of support except a monthly payment from her husband for the care of their three-year-old son. Unable to maintain her own household, she went to work as a servant in her sister's house. The child's father could then claim that she, by working, neglected the child and negated her claim to monthly support payments and child custody. The *muftī* agreed: the mother could keep her son only if she left her sister's employ. Another woman, caught in the same dilemma, lost custody of her three young girls by taking a job as a domestic servant in a nearby village.[195]

Peasant women who engaged in petty production and trade to support their children could also be deprived of custody. By accusing his divorced wife of buying and selling goods in the local market, a man won custody of their six-year-old daughter. A woman who earned her living by making pancakes at home and selling them in the market was likewise declared unfit. Husbands and other relatives were also wont to deprive women of custody by accusing them of indecent behavior and prostitution.[196] Many women remarried promptly, thereby reintegrating themselves into a family. Young children were forbidden by law, however, to live in the same household as a "foreigner" (*ajnabī*), that is, a person who was not a close relative of the child. The Egyptian courts enforced this rule, and because the new husband would most probably have *ajnabī* status, the mother lost custody upon remarriage.[197]

While many peasant women lost custody of their young children, basic material ties between mother and child could persist. Children by a former marriage remained a woman's legal heirs: the husband and children from her family at the time of her death were co-heirs with children from previous marriages. Her property, inherited from a former husband, might devolve on children by a subsequent marriage. Rights to inheritance shares on the part of half-brothers and half-sisters spun ever more intricate webs of property relations, linking parents and children of different marriages.[198] Women could thus be bound to their children of previous marriages not only by blood, but also by complex economic relations. The case of Ṣalāḥah, a woman from Manṣūrah, illustrates these complexities. She had married twice and borne a child by each husband: a son, ʿAlī, by her first husband, and a daughter by her second husband. Upon the death of her second husband, she and her daughter inherited shares in his property; with the death of her daughter, part of the daughter's share went to her half-brother ʿAlī so that he acquired a portion of his mother's second husband's property. Ṣalāḥah bought out ʿAlī's share of a house in Manṣūrah, thereby consolidating her second husband's property under her control.[199] If, on the other hand, ʿAlī had predeceased her, she might have acquired claims to some of her first husband's property through her son.

Ṣalāḥah's purchase demonstrates the complexity of property relations and the countervailing tendency to avoid excessive fragmentation of estates. When succession arrangements rendered mothers and their children co-owners of property, some women possessed the means to purchase their children's shares. When children from several marriages inherited from their mother, close relatives of the mother might attempt to reunite the property. A woman whose dead sister had two sons by different men bought their shares of their mother's inheritance to add to what she had inherited from her father, the sons' maternal grandfather.[200] Such exchanges indicate that a woman's children by a first husband were not ordinarily part of her household or her relatives' household after her remarriage. Nevertheless, a multiplicity of present and potential (to be activated upon death and succession) property relations united mothers to all their children.

Although women were legally disadvantaged in the sphere of child custody and guardianship, their claims to property and their status as independent economic producers counterbalanced, in part, the loss arising from their displacement from a household in the wake of divorce or a husband's death. Court records indicate that women, in some circumstances, retained custody and effective guardianship of their children through legal and extralegal means. Even when children remained part of their fathers' households, the material bonds between mother and child were not totally severed. Succession laws strengthened the maternal relationship: mother and child were reciprocal heirs. Women, utilizing their legal inheritance rights and their control over property, need not forfeit all material benefits from children. The bare outlines of custody law, suggesting, as they do, complete physical and emotional dispossession, do not accurately reflect a woman's position after her departure from a family. Women in nineteenth century Egypt, through inheritance, purchase, and sale, managed to mitigate some of the negative consequences of prejudicial custody law and to retain their hold on portions of property despite the loss of their children to another household. As the century wore on, however, the court, by basing its judgments of what constituted a fit mother on an ideal type, the peasant woman whose primary identity was as a member of the production/consumption family unit, refused to come to terms with a changing reality. By reaffirming the traditional family structure, it prejudiced the case of those who, by the erosion of that structure, had been deprived of former networks of support. Many of the more painful custody cases, where women were deprived of custody because they were independent working mothers, reflect the social stress that followed economic change in the countryside.

One casualty of economic upheaval was certainly the coherence of the peasant family that had provided unquestioned support for all members. By mid-century, we begin to encounter a number of cases in which peasant women turn to the court to invoke their rights to *nafaqah* (maintenance) by male relatives. One woman came on behalf of her two young daughters, pleading dire poverty and requesting the court to order the father of her dead husband to support his grandchildren. Another woman, incapable of supporting herself, demanded *nafaqah* from her brother.[201] Others told grim tales of marital treachery: one woman related how her husband had taken her jewelry and used it as the *mahr* to marry a second wife; when she complained, he beat her and sent her back to her family. She then took her complaint to the local *qāḍī* who ruled that her husband must pay her a specified monthly support (*nafaqah*), but her husband had failed to do so.[202] The *muftī* generally responded favorably to such requests, stressing the responsibility of male relatives to support any females in need, and that of husbands to support their wives. But the very fact that women had recourse to the court with such matters seems to underline the breakdown of support patterns based on the rules governing the *mahr*, marital debt, and the female rights to *nafaqah*.

The regulation of these types of family relations in the *sharīʿah* courts reflected the power of women in the family. Islamic family law defined a woman's family role in often contradictory terms. The patriarchal flavor of the law was pronounced in matters of divorce and child custody, reinforcing a patriarchal and patrilocal family structure: women, upon marriage, became members of their husband's family; their children belonged to the paternal line; wives could be cut loose from the household simply by their husband's decision to divorce them. Conversely, a woman's legal *persona* was far from that of chattel: she inherited and held property in her own right and her male relations through birth or marriage enjoyed no special claim over her possessions. In nineteenth century rural Egypt, women were often in a position to utilize property claims to establish a certain independence and control in the family setting. That women actively pressed these claims, managing their own affairs in ways which counterbalanced legal and social impediments, testifies to the power and status they had attained within the family. The court, by upholding family rights and obligations, gave peasant women a forum in which they could demand maintenance of family systems of care and mutual support. Despite the vicissitudes of rural life in the period, peasant women, as long as they remained part of the family unit, asserted their rights to customary support and so helped maintain the family as social regulator and economic unit.

Conclusion

The world of the peasant woman in the nineteenth century was shaped by a complex set of interlocking economic, structural, and ideological realities. Woman's roles in economic production, the internal structure of the family and its relation to the larger society, and the customs and social ideals embodied in Islamic law all contributed to the delineation of her position in society. Women themselves, through the manipulation of contradictory definitions of their roles and status, achieved considerable power and control in a fundamentally patriarchal setting.

In rural Egypt of the early nineteenth century, the family remained the basic economic unit. In the context of shared family labor in agriculture, spheres of production and reproduction were not rigidly divided. The peasant woman, while undoubtedly assuming primary responsibility for the care of non-productive family members, found herself part of a cooperative family unit. Joint family labor in the cultivation and processing of agricultural products established joint claims to the fruits of production. Although women generally did not enjoy rights of usufruct to the land, tools of production, livestock, and implements often formed part of their individually held property. The hearth and the field of the peasant family were not sexually segregated domains: with only two or three children in her care, a woman worked in the home and field alongside her male relatives, although less of her labor time went into the family plot. The minimal nature of state or corporate intervention strengthened cooperative family bonds. State demands for produce and labor were made on the family as a whole; although taxes may have strained family resources and the corvée siphoned off able-bodied workers, forced recruitment of the peasantry for long-term corvée labor or military service did not begin until the Muḥammad ʿAlī period. Peasant families thus exercised considerable control over the organization of their time and labor, so that sexual divisions within the family developed more in response to immediate family need than imposed demands from the outside.

By the end of the nineteenth century, state policies formulated in concert with the demands of capitalist penetration had produced economic dislocation in the Egyptian countryside by creating an agricultural wage labor force and dispossessing the peasant family of land. Population movements, land loss, and impoverishment weakened the ability of the peasant family to continue producing as a unit and supporting its non-productive members. Although all members of the family owed their status and security to their position in the household unit of production and consumption, women, in a patriarchal society, were more vulnerable, subject to greater limitation of their rights and privileges as the family unit faltered.

State intervention and the commercialization of agriculture did not, however, immediately divide economic life into "public" and "private" spheres. The family was still very much a cooperative unit which assumed major responsibility for the welfare and regulation of its members. But the decreased ability of the family to organize its labor time as it wished and the growing tendency for menfolk to join the wage labor force while women remained on the family plot weakened cooperative arrangements. As scarcity of land and capital and the demands of the economy tightened the family belt, women found themselves in a disadvantaged position. Usually excluded from title to land, their claims to the fruits of agricultural production were mediated through male relations. As long as women exercised effective control over other parts of family property, and were recognized as full members of the cooperative family unit, they were in a position to mitigate the more injurious effects of their tenuous connection to the land. But lack of land title, combined with the tendency to define the family cooperative association (*sharikah*) in ways prejudicial to women, eroded many female rights and claims. Attempts to consolidate and strengthen family holdings and ties were often undertaken at the expense, rather than to the advantage, of sisters and wives.

The patriarchal character of peasant family structure manifested itself most clearly in a woman's tenuous position in any given family. Patrilocal marriage made her a temporary member of her natal family, while death or divorce could sever her connection with her husband's family. Her lack of access to land, a social necessity as long as she remained *en passage*, further weakened her position. Yet, by virtue of her rights to movable property, this transience was also her strength: her marriages and divorces involved the disposition of property; as a carrier of property claims, her departure from a family could bring economic disaster in its train. Thus divorce was not to be pronounced lightly, and she could actually ransom herself from an unwanted marriage. Her access to property further allowed her to mitigate the negative effects of divorce. Claims to inheritance and the legal capacity to buy and sell property made it possible for her to avoid, in most instances, complete dispossession and destitution.

To realize the power and security that abstract property rights afforded, however, peasant women needed both knowledge and a forum. The role of the religious court system was contradictory, for while it often championed female property rights and the principle of support for women, it also bowed to the dispossession of women upon occasion and actually abetted the process through its strict application of the *sharikah* concept and its willingness to interpret female rights in a narrow fashion. Peasant women still viewed the court, however, as an institution that they could turn to in order to protect their position. They continued to bring their problems, large and small, before the *qāḍī*, thus testifying to their own belief in the efficacy of the court and the power of Islamic justice.

As the nineteenth century brought sweeping change to the Egyptian countryside, peasant families, especially women, used the court to cling to former patterns of economic and social sharing. The drive for consolidation of family property, however, often took place at the expense of those members whose legal and customary rights were weakest. Women, acting to protect their rights, were sometimes able to impede, but not arrest, the inroads made on their domain. Their activities undoubtedly contributed to the maintenance of family bonds: the family still constituted an important refuge and source of security in a period of dislocation.

Chapter 2

Spindles and songs: women in urban occupations

They married off the beggarwoman to reform her, so she hid the bread on the shelf and said: "Oh mistress, do a good deed" [i.e. returned to begging].

Egyptian proverb (Taymūr, 998, p. 169)

Had it not been for chiseling and sawing, women would have learned carpentry.

Egyptian proverb (Taymūr, 2571, p. 429)

The economic contributions of nineteenth century Egyptian women were by no means confined to agricultural labor; over the course of the century, women worked as petty traders and merchants, as craftswomen, as industrial wage laborers, as property and business managers, and as service workers. Unlike female labor in the agricultural sector, which was usually performed on family-held land, women in trade, crafts, industry, and service usually worked on the margins of the family unit of production. Their labor did not generally form part of a family-based enterprise, and the tools of their trade were, very likely, their own personal property. Such women could undoubtedly aspire to more independence than the peasant woman tied to a family plot, but, as in the peasant family, their independence in the sphere of economic production did not necessarily always loosen the family bonds of shared consumption. Still, as we shall see below, women with direct and individual links to the market economy could elude, to varying degrees, some of the more stringent forms of family control.

The distinction between the peasant woman and her sister in trade and crafts should not, however, be too finely drawn. As we have already seen, rural Egypt, througout the nineteenth century, produced for the market: the petty trade of the early part of the century was gradually overshadowed by the rise of large-scale agricultural enterprises supplying a capitalist world market; it is difficult to locate, at any time in the century, a "pure peasant" who stood entirely outside of the market system. In addition, many of the women who lived in rural areas and worked, at least part of the time, in agricultural production also made important contributions to trade and crafts by carrying agricultural goods to market or working in the network of rural craft production, particularly in textiles. But a peasant woman pursued trade and crafts as an adjunct to her and her family's labor on the land. In urban areas, especially in Cairo, a woman was

3 "Egyptian Lady," late nineteenth century

far more likely to practice her trade full time, thereby heightening its importance to her income as well as her habits of thought.

The difference in family arrangements in urban areas surely played a role: although urban families, especially those residing in the peripheral areas of the city, might cultivate a small parcel of land or, in denser quarters, supplement the family diet by raising poultry and vegetables, the bulk of material production involved trade, artisanal, and service activities which connected family members as individuals to the urban economy. For the greater part of the century, however, the organization of urban trades did allow for some family cooperation. The modest size of shops and workshops as well as the absence of differentiation between the two – many workshops doubled as retail outlets for the goods produced – encouraged joint family labor. The tendency of occupations to be passed down from parents to children suggests, indeed, that the family group cohered in the sphere of production. On the other hand, women and men often practiced distinct trades and forged links to the market based on individual, not familial, production. The greater and more direct dominance of the market in urban areas probably tended to reduce the number of affective family ties, loosening at least somewhat the bonds of kinship.

In both settings, women's presence in socialized, as opposed to familial, forms of economic production could not but increase her contacts with, and knowledge of, the world outside the household. The benefits of increased income were supplemented by the benefits of worldly experience: as producers, buyers, and sellers in the public sphere, women gained knowledge of business transactions and developed the ability to operate successfully in the marketplace. The importance of these skills, and of society's recognition that women possessed them, cannot be overstated: female savvy and self-confidence, acquired through connection to the market, were often the strongest means of protection of a woman's property and other rights.

Women's participation in the trade, crafts, and industry of the period can only be understood in the context of overall Egyptian economic development. As in agriculture, the lives of Egyptian women, like men, were profoundly affected by the transformation of Egypt's economy; in the case of trade and industry, however, the effects were even more cataclysmic. The extraordinary developments in nineteenth century Egyptian trade and industry provide the backdrop to the history of women's work in these sectors.

Trade, crafts, and industry in the nineteenth century

The trade, crafts, and industrial sectors developed, as did agriculture, in the context of Egypt's integration into an economic system dominated by Europe. Substantial agreement exists on the major contours of this development. First, trading patterns reflected such integration both quantitatively and qualitatively. Over the course of the century, the value of Egyptian import and export trade increased some forty- to sixtyfold, convincing proof of the rapidity with which the country was harnessed to an international economy. At the same time, Egyptian trade patterns shifted from an import/export trade oriented primarily to regions south and east of the country – Sudan, the Arabian peninsula, the Far East – to an almost exclusive trading relationship with Europe in which Egypt exported cotton and imported manufactured consumer goods. Secondly, local crafts increasingly faced competition from these manufactured items; while many were able to survive and even flourish despite European imports, some crafts shrank in volume and a few, such as textiles and glass, may have been eliminated altogether. Thirdly, the failure of a concerted effort during the Muḥammad ʿAlī period to establish modern industry in Egypt was followed by a few, more modest attempts in the period up to 1882; thereafter, British colonial policy effectively discouraged most local industrializaton, and Egypt became dependent on the importation of manufactured items.[1]

While the path of transition to colonial capitalism can be traced on a factual level, difference in interpretation and emphasis color the history of trade and industry. At the heart of the disagreement lie fundamental questions about the evolution of class structure and the impact of European penetration on class development. Why did the Egypt of the nineteenth century not spawn an indigenous capitalism? Some writers have argued that entrepreneurial failure, such as the dearth of both skill and interest in industrial enterprise, severely impeded independent capitalist development: for a variety of social and historical reasons, Egypt did not produce the capitalist middle class that could take charge of trade and industry.[2] The failure of statist industrialization has often been linked, on the other hand, to European sabotage: blame for Muḥammad ʿAlī's denouement is laid squarely at the feet of the Anglo-Turkish Convention of 1838 which fixed tariffs and prohibited monopolies.[3] Neither approach is totally convincing because of the failure to situate the problem of industrialization simultaneously within the context of internal social structures and world market forces. Egyptian industry suffered from both internal constraints and European opposition. Further study is necessary, however, to clarify the resistance to industrialization on the part of various social classes in Egypt, be they potential entrepreneurs or wage workers, as well as the barriers mounted by a world economic system which already entailed divisions of labor and disparities in power.

The following discussion of trade, crafts, and industry takes both internal specifics and world market structure into account. Nineteenth century development can usefully be divided once again into four periods: 1800–1820, 1820–1850, 1850–1882, and 1882–1914. In the first period, 1800–1820, trade was oriented primarily toward the region. International trade, particularly transit trade in coffee and spices, continued to be an important source of revenue for some of the wealthier Cairene merchants, and trade with Europe remained clearly secondary to transit and grain trade within the Ottoman Empire. Internal markets generated the bulk of demand for craft production which was carried out, in most cases, in small-scale workshops in urban areas or in family homes in the countryside. From 1820 to 1850, the policies of the Egyptian State under Muḥammad ʿAlī and the quickening pace of integration into a European-dominated economic system changed trade patterns: imports of manufactured items and exports of raw materials, largely grains and cotton, were increasingly directed toward western Europe. At the same time, the State's ambitions to control the export trade and establish modern domestic industry disrupted former trade networks and the organization of labor in many crafts, but did not succeed in the permanent implantation of a modern industrial sector.

In the third period, 1850–1882, the process of economic integration continued apace, as ever more extensive trade ties were supplemented by direct European investments, primarily in trade and land ventures, and large loans of European capital to the Egyptian State itself. The State still took an interest in industry, investing in infrastructure and some limited industrial projects, but the enormous debts to foreign lenders precipitated economic and political crisis. Overall, the conversion to an economy dominated by one cash crop, cotton, was completed in this period with all the attendant dislocations produced by growing landlessness among peasants and the channeling of investment capital almost exclusively to cotton-related activities. Under the British occupation, from 1882 to 1914, these economic trends continued and were institutionalized as state policy. The British-controlled colonial government strongly endorsed free trade, which meant continued dependence on cotton export and the import of most manufactured goods. Former state initiatives in the field of industry were all but abandoned, and Egypt was categorized as an agricultural country without a significant industrial future; the British occupation thus sealed the course of Egyptian economic development up to the eve of World War I.

1800–1820: Trade and crafts before the rise of Muḥammad ʿAlī

Although Egypt, and particularly Cairo, retained much of its former reputation as a regional center of trade, crafts, and culture at the beginning of the nineteenth century, events in Europe were already impinging on its internal development and changing the relative weight and nature of trade and crafts in its economy. The lucrative coffee trade had suffered a severe blow from competition with European island coffee.[4] At the same time, the quickening pace of the industrial revolution in Europe had given rise to demand there for raw materials to be processed, such as cotton, jute, metals, and foodstuffs. The growth of exports to Europe coincided with the rise of a strong commercial orientation among the ruling elite of the Mamluke beylicate: the commercial sector flourished under their control but the position of merchants in transit trade slowly deteriorated as exports of raw materials and the importation of European textiles gradually acquired a greater share of the market.[5]

Cairo retained its position as the center of Egypt's Mediterranean, African, Red Sea, and Maghreb trade, and its markets still bustled with the buying and selling of Arabic gum, ivory, incense, coffee, and textiles of all kinds.[6] The economic tide, however, was slowly turning against certain types of trade. The elite of the trading community, that is, those with the largest operations and fortunes who controlled the coffee and spice trade from the East, were overwhelmingly of Turkish and Maghrebi origin. Similarly, the Maghreb trade was monopolized by merchants from North Africa, either resident in tightly knit Maghrebi communities in Cairo or based in their home countries, and much of the African caravan trade was conducted by people from the caravans' places of origin. As the importance of Europe in Mediterranean trade increased, western merchants, usually dealing with local minorities as intermediaries, dominated the import of manufactured cloth and the export of grains. It was the members of these groups involved in international trade and resident in Cairo who formed the majority of prosperous merchants.[7]

The participation of merchants of Egyptian origin in international trade was minimal. Many traders of Egyptian provincial origin were involved, however, in local trade. Merchants from the major textile centers of Asyūṭ, Fayyūm, Maḥallah, and Taḥtah brought processed cloth to their markets in Cairo. Although their fortunes rarely rivaled those of the spice and coffee merchants, the cloth trade and its spin-offs employed more people in the city than any other activity except the processing and distribution of food. The cloth trade guilds were highly specialized: some twelve to fifteen guilds organized cloth traders on the basis of the precise quality and origin of the cloth they sold. The textile trade shared common features with other kinds of local trade such as the lack of competition, the small-scale nature of most operations, the absence of an efficient credit system, and a specialization which reflected national and local origin. It was also tightly tied to the demands of the local market: activity peaked in the month of Ramaḍān when people tended to refurbish their homes and wardrobes, and just before the departure of the caravan for Mecca. Despite such drawbacks, a minority of Egyptian cloth merchants left sizeable estates, which secured them a place, following Raymond's categorization, among the ranks of the commercial elite.[8]

In the latter part of the eighteenth century, the penetration of European manufactured goods began to make clear inroads on local craft production. Trade with Europe in the period from 1776 to 1781 already displayed the imbalance that was to characterize trading patterns throughout the nineteenth and into the twentieth centuries: roughly 60 per cent of exports to Europe consisted of raw materials while 58 per cent of imports were manufactured items including cloth and paper.[9] By the early nineteenth century, cloth imports included not only finer French stuffs geared for luxury consumption but also the cloth of daily wear:

> The manufactured article most widely consumed in Egypt is the cotton cloth called "indienne" which the Egyptians use for their vests, their turbans, and for their furnishings. The texture, colors, taste, and low price of this cloth has made these people adopt it and the preference for it above all cloth of their country has hurt their manufactures. Many of their factories have ceased all production.[10]

Yet, around 1800, artisanal activity occupied, directly or indirectly, the majority of the active urban population. Crafts were still organized, however, along traditional lines which posed structural limitations to growth and adaptability. The lack of division between production and distribution, with many craftsmen selling their wares in small shops, meant small-scale enterprise and limited accumulation of capital among the artisan class. Most private enterprises probably employed only two or three workers with the exception of sugar mills, rug weaving establishments, and tanneries. Artisanal production was very much the province of the artisans themselves, for the more affluent merchants and beys invested their earnings from trade in additional trading ventures or land. Crafts were also highly specialized. As Raymond notes, in 1801 Cairo had six guilds of iron crafts, each one specializing in a different product, such as nails or needles. Specialization also extended to religious and ethnic groups: Jews, Copts, Armenians, and Greeks monopolized certain sectors of the jewelry crafts as well as weaving, tailoring and embroidery. Such specialization can be seen as a voluntary limit on competition which, in combination with the hereditary nature of most crafts and their tightly knit coresidential character, acted to diminish conflict. The development of crafts further suffered from geography: indigenous supplies of metals, coal, and wood were either meager or non-existent.[11]

Structural limits to the growth of large-scale enterprise and the accumulation of capital in the crafts sector were exacerbated by political attitudes toward crafts production. The State, under the commercially oriented beys, viewed crafts production solely as a source of tax revenues and extraordinary levies in time of need. Outside of two state workshops, the mint and the shop which manufactured the *kiswah* (covering) sent yearly to the *ka'bah* in Mecca, the State showed no interest in production processes, in marked contrast to other Middle Eastern cities, some of which boasted large numbers of state-sponsored workshops.[12] The beys and their merchant allies concentrated their attention on, and invested their capital in, higher status and more lucrative commercial activities or land.

Despite structural weakness and lack of political support for crafts, Cairo remained an artisanal city. Because the majority of the active population were linked to craft production, the economic and social roles of most men and women rested, in part, on their participation in actual production and related activities. Not all crafts, however, enjoyed equal status or remuneration. In 1800, textile crafts still held a signal position in the urban economy, both in terms of the number of people employed and of production. In Raymond's study, one third of all artisanal successions were those of textile artisans who were, by and large, wealthier than other craftsmen. Next in importance came the leather crafts, with a few big tanneries alongside a number of small shops whose artisans were relatively poor. Food-related crafts and wood and metal crafts were also important but, with the exception of large oil presses and sugar refineries, tended to be very small-scale operations which yielded only a modest income.[13]

Although a significant portion of the cloth marketed in Cairo originated in the major textile towns of Upper and Lower Egypt, city artisans were also engaged in most textile operations. Raw cotton and flax were carded, combed, and spun in shops concentrated in the north of the city close to the cloth markets, and then woven in one of the many small weaving shops scattered throughout the city. The stages of urban cotton and linen processing bore a marked resemblance to rural industry, for many of the preliminary operations, including carding, bleaching, combing, and spinning, were performed in households and the processed yarn was then sold to weavers. The spinning and weaving of silk was a Cairene specialty and some 30 to 35 silk spinning workshops were still functioning in the late eighteenth century.[14] Although urban crafts were more likely than rural crafts to be practiced in workshops under some form of guild supervision, family industry did play a role, especially in the textile and food sectors.

The organization of both trade and crafts in this period was clearly precapitalist: most production and exchange were controlled by small individual or family businesses and geared toward a local market. Although European competition, arising out of the explosion of its trading activity and the expansion of its industrial capacity, was beginning to be felt, particularly in the large merchant community, the traditional organization of economic life still held sway. Most people engaged in trade and crafts production had been little affected by European expansion, and the Egyptian State took almost no interest, other than for tax purposes, in the regulation or promotion of the urban productive sector. The dramatic changes accompanying the rise of a powerful and centralized State under Muḥammad ʿAlī were still in an incipient stage.

1820–1850: Trade and industry under Muḥammad ʿAlī

Muḥammad ʿAlī's economic policies, designed to increase state revenue and bolster Egypt's military might and independence, reverberated throughout the trade and crafts sectors of society. Through a system of monopolies, the State gradually assumed direct supervision of external and internal trade and the better part of craft production. The export of agricultural products first became a state monopoly in the 1810s, much to the dismay of European business interests in Egypt. European agents and consuls, imbued with the free trade ideology of the day and concerned about the fate of their own and their fellow countrymen's commercial interests, later decried the monopolies as contrary, in letter and in spirit, to the Anglo-Turkish Tariff of 1820. When questioned on the state and quantity of trade with Egypt, the British consul, for instance, replied with vehemence:

If However by Trade are intended – Imports of which perhaps nine tenths are for account of government – and Exports that are effected by a few favoured agencies, originating in the compulsory labours of a decaying peasantry, and tainted with a Monopoly, as unparalleled in Commercial history, as it is anomalous in Political Economy, and contrary to the spirit and letter of the only Treaty, which legalizes the Trade of His Majesty's subjects with Egypt, Then that Trade must be considered as having increased.[15]

Despite European grumblings and much unsolicited advice to the contrary, monopolization of agricultural trade was swiftly followed by state attempts to control the craft production of textiles, the largest industry in rural and urban Egypt. In 1821, all private weaving was prohibited; weavers were required to use raw materials provided by the government and return all finished cloth to government stores.[16] In workshops, the State owned the tools of the trade, set prices, and paid spinners and weavers a fixed salary or a piece-rate. An Administration of Spinning and Weaving oversaw other forms of textile production through a market monopoly: the smallest home spinner could only buy raw materials and sell finished products under government auspices. One unsympathetic observer was struck by the thoroughness of such state intervention:

He [Muḥammad ʿAlī] makes himself sole proprietor of everything and has brought down the natives to work as his slaves. He will not permit them to sell a bit of cotton twill, hemp, or cloth, a bit of wool, or even a mat though worked by themselves to any person but himself and that at his own price, not even to keep an article for their own use but first to sell it to him at a reduced price and when the Government mark is put upon it to buy it back again at an advanced price for wear.[17]

Peasant producers who had previously relied on small-scale home textile production for a supplementary cash income were particularly squeezed. Their yarn and cloth fetched low prices at the government stores, and, although textile products were accepted in payment of the land tax, they were assessed at as little as one third of the current market price.[18]

State monopolies of internal trade and crafts were not to endure, however, for much over a decade. By 1831, grain and vegetables were again allowed to circulate freely within the country although the government still retained control of all external trade: export crops such as cotton, flax, rice, indigo, and silk remained a state monopoly along with transit goods like coffee and ivory.[19] In 1834, producers of yarn, cloth, and mats were freed from their obligation to deal solely with the government; they could buy and sell their articles as they pleased as long as they paid a set tax to the State. Artisanal goods and agricultural produce could once again be freely traded in local rural markets and urban centers.[20] While declining production in agriculture and crafts had thus forced the State to reassess its monopoly scheme on the internal level, export monopolies continued to be a source of friction between the Egyptian government and European interests throughout Muḥammad ʿAlī's reign.

State monopoly practices were but one cause of deep transformations in the nature and scope of indigenous trade and crafts production: state industrial schemes reorganized textile production and trade in ways that were to have effects long after the industries themselves had been dismantled. Beginning in 1818, Muḥammad ʿAlī set out to industrialize the textile sector. Two cotton spinning and weaving factories were soon established in Cairo, one in Khurūnfīsh and one in Būlāq, and equipped with European-made jennies, carding machines, and looms. At the height of the industrialization program in the 1830s, Egypt boasted some thirty factories for the spinning and weaving of cotton.[21] The size of the factories varied greatly, but the largest, that at Khurūnfīsh, housed 370 carding machines, 100 mule-jennies, and 300 looms.[22] Although figures for domestic use of raw cotton lack precision in this period, the factory system greatly increased indigenous demand. Local needs for industry probably tripled or quadrupled, from some 20,000 quintals in 1820 to 60,000 to 70,000 quintals in 1834.[23]

Other textile production, that of linen, wool, and silk, was industrialized on a lesser scale. Flax spinning establishments were erected in several provinces in Lower Egypt, but the approximately 3,000 linen weavers generally remained scattered throughout the country. Woolen cloth production was more centralized: three factories supplied the needs of the army for uniform material. The factory in Būlāq, the largest of the three, included shearing, dyeing, fulling, spinning, and weaving operations. A *ṭarbūsh* factory in Fūwwah met army demands for headgear by producing some sixty hats a day. Spinners and weavers of wool, however, were still to be found throughout the countryside. In the silk industry, both the raw materials and craft skills had to be imported because Egypt lacked indigenous sources. In the silk factory at Birket al-Fīl, Armenians from Istanbul wove Syrian thread.[24]

Although factories for the production of sugar, indigo, paper, glass, gunpowder, and arms were also established, it was the textile sector that most disquieted foreign observers. As early as 1817, the French consul in Cairo was predicting that Muḥammad ʿAlī's silk factories would deal a mortal blow to

French silk exports.[25] During the 1820s, a more sanguine view seemed to prevail. The French consul in Alexandria assured his government that the new textile factories would not harm French commercial interests, and added that, in any case, the importation of French machinery more than compensated for any commercial loss. The new French consul in Cairo echoed this view, pointing to the poor materials, unskilled workers, and low quality of the final product as insurance against undue competition with French exports.[26] According to the British consul, English exports of cotton goods had yet to suffer from local competition and probably would not sensibly decline; Egyptian industries, in any event, would "disappear" eventually.[27]

As the number and overall production of the textile factories increased in the 1830s, a tone of alarm resurfaced; the British consul remarked that:

> Some of the Manufactories of the Pacha are prejudicial to the sale of English Cotton stuffs. The consumption of those stuffs has sensibly diminished – as the Inhabitants use the manufactures in this country which are even exported to Syria, to Hedjas and to Turkey.
>
> Experience has however shewn that Egypt is essentially an agricultural country and cannot be a Manufacturing one.[28]

The French consul voiced similar concerns, noting that Egyptian factories furnished at least one third of all locally consumed cotton goods and almost all calico cloth, while local *ṭarbūsh* factories had totally destroyed French *ṭarbūsh* exports.[29] Fears of further inroads on the Egyptian textile market were gradually assuaged, however, as the industrialization program faltered in the 1840s. By 1845, Egypt was again importing *ṭarbūshes*; the French consul reported in 1849 that the textile industry was almost completely shut down and cotton cloth imports had revived.[30] One lone textile factory survived into the 1850s, but the challenge once mounted to European market interests was no longer a concern.

The size of the new industrial labor force at its height remains a matter of some dispute. Gross figures offered by Rivlin (40,000) and Fahmy (260,000) are probably equally wide of the mark.[31] Part of the disparity stems from Fahmy's inclusion of spinners and weavers working at home or in small shops, as well as construction workers, in his total. If we are concerned with all workers whose organization of labor was transformed by the institution of a factory system, such a broad definition of the new working class makes a good deal of sense. Even so, some of Fahmy's numbers appear inflated: his total of 110,000 weavers and spinners seems an exaggeration.[32] His estimates of laborers in various factories, however, jibe well with those of contemporary observers or even appear somewhat conservative. He estimates workers in cotton factories, for example, at 15,000, some 5,000 to 15,000 less than Hekekyan and Bowring.[33] His figures for the arsenals match those of the British consul.[34] The rough estimate of some 100,000 workers in various factories thus seems credible, but the number of construction workers, spinners and weavers dispersed throughout the countryside is more difficult to determine since these categories included many seasonal, part-time, and corvée workers.

Workers in the new labor force, in the narrow sense of those employed in recently established factories, were drawn from disparate sectors of the population and from abroad. In the early stages of industrialization in the silk industry, for example, the dearth of skilled labor in Egypt led to the importation of silk spinners from Livourne and Istanbul.[35] Employment of European workers could bring troubles in its train. Although protected from Egyptian justice by the Capitulations, European workers were implicated in so many disputes and "disorders" that the Egyptian government insisted in 1826 that foreign workers must obey Egyptian law and be subject to the authority of the local police. The decision was quickly rescinded, however, in the face of the workers' threat to leave the country.[36] While skilled workers from Europe and parts of the Ottoman Empire were free to leave the factories if conditions were not satisfactory, others from territories controlled by Egypt were pressed into service. Some sixty residents of Bethlehem, for instance, accused of participating in a revolt against the Egyptian occupation forces in Palestine, were rounded up and shipped to Egypt for forced labor in the arsenal in Alexandria.[37]

Foreign workers, whether recruited for their special skills or impressed as a punitive measure, undoubtedly formed a very small proportion of the labor force. After a short-lived experiment in using black slaves from Sudan in the textile factories, the State turned to its own population to supply the bulk of labor needs.[38] Peasants, artisans, and shopkeepers were forced to enter the factory as the government launched irregular levies of workers in Cairo and the countryside.[39] Provincial factories drew on the surrounding agricultural areas: fallāḥīn were forcibly recruited from the fields to labor in nearby mills. In Cairo, the *shaykhs* of eight quarters in Cairo proper, and another two in Miṣr al-Qadīmah and Būlāq, were responsible for furnishing workpeople for local state factories along with their other duties.[40] Most accounts thus suggest that the labor force was recruited locally: peasants manned the factories in the countryside while urban industries employed city dwellers. Exceptions were made, however, when forced labor was used as punishment for recalcitrant subjects. In 1833, for example, some 1,000 *fallāḥīn* from various provinces, who had maimed themselves to avoid the military draft, were sent to work in the arsenal in Alexandria.[41]

Wages inside the factories made forced recruitment a necessity. *Fallāḥīn* could earn as much if not more by remaining on the land, while artisans appear to have taken a definite cut in pay. According to the available information on wages, unskilled laborers, usually of *fallāḥ* origin, were paid from 1 to 2 piasters (40 to 80 *parahs*) per day, a wage which might fall to half a piaster (20 *parahs*) if food were provided. Skilled weavers, working on a piece-rate system, might earn up to 4 piasters a day, and carpenters, blacksmiths, and other artisans in industrial service were paid anything from 2½ to 5 piasters.[42] Disregarding for a moment the cash income a peasant might gain through the sale of produce from his own land or from leisure-time artisanal activities, and the other material and psychological benefits of working at home, employment in the factory still held no material advantage over agricultural wage labor. In the mid-1820s, before the shortage of labor in the countryside became acute, an agricultural worker was paid about 1 piaster a day. As the demand for rural labor rose in the 1830s, *fallāḥīn* with the potential of earning 3 to 5 piasters as agricultural laborers were forced instead to work in cotton factories for 1 piaster. Although official directives pegged artisanal wages at 8 piasters a day, that is, at about the going rate for employment outside the factories, the actual pay received was far lower.[43] Thus artisans, while better paid than unskilled workers, also found factory labor a financial burden. The fact that the wages of all categories of workers were often up to a year in arrears greatly increased the material deprivation that accompanied entrance into the factory labor force.[44]

Contemporary European critics of Muḥammad ʿAlī's industrialization program painted a grim picture of factory life: virtual prisoners in the workplace, poorly fed and subject to frequent flogging, the unwilling workers soon grew malcontent and ill.[45] Overt hostility to the project of industrialization certainly colored such accounts, but even a staunch supporter of Muḥammad ʿAlī's policies is forced to concede that hours were long and conditions harsh.[46] The purely political, as opposed to economic, coercion of the new labor force – the status of workers as impressed laborers in government service – meant that industrial workers enjoyed no more choice of place or type of occupation than their fellows drafted for corvée labor or the military. Indeed, Muḥammad ʿAlī, when strapped for additional troops in 1840, proposed the creation of several new regiments of workers from state factories in Alexandria, Cairo, and Maḥallah: the new labor force was thoroughly subject to the demands and exigencies of the state apparatus.[47]

Although many of the policies in trade and industry proved temporary, the integration of Egypt into the European economic system was surely hastened by the State's promotion of the export trade, particularly in cotton. Ironically enough, the policy of industrialization had the long-term effect of opening the Egyptian market ever wider to European manufactured goods: the disruption of certain crafts, particularly textiles, lessened their ability to compete with imports while, at the same time, new demands for manufactured goods had been created. The price of thwarted industrialization was to prove high. The economic dislocation and adjustments of the Muḥammad ʿAlī period did not find compensation in the full development of a modern industrial sector; on the contrary, they helped encourage a European interest and involvement in

Egyptian economic affairs that led to near total western economic domination in the second half of the century.

1850–1882: The web of debt
After the failure of broad industrialization, the Egyptian economy developed around the cultivation and export of cotton, and the import of European industrial goods. The total value of foreign trade skyrocketed from £E3.7 million in 1850 to £E21.8 million in 1880, and consisted, primarily, of the exchange of cotton for manufactured consumer goods. As the demand for cotton grew, and prices rose astronomically during the American Civil War and the cotton blockade of the early 1860s, the financing, transport, trading, and processing of the cotton crop dominated economic activity.[48] Foreign merchants and financiers flocked to Egypt, attracted by the flourishing trade of the cotton boom, opportunities in land speculation, and the fabulous rates of interest that could be charged on loans to businesses and the government: some 80,000 foreigners arrived in Egypt in 1865 alone.[49]

The Egyptian State, under the Khedives ʿAbbās, Saʿīd, and Ismāʿīl, continued the tradition of state responsibility for the country's infrastructure. Most new projects were geared toward the cash crop: the government laid railways and erected telegraph lines, improved canals and bridges, participated in the Suez Canal venture, built lighthouses, and enlarged ports, all of which benefited cotton producers and marketers.[50] Although the vast majority of factories founded under Muḥammad ʿAlī had been sold, sat idle, or were razed, the cotton boom of the 1860s prompted the State to establish a number of ginning factories in ports and towns in cotton growing regions: by the early 1870s, the State was operating about a hundred ginning establishments and two weaving factories in Būlāq. The Khedive Ismāʿīl pursued a conscious course of industrialization: one mission he sent to Europe returned to build a paper factory in Būlāq which employed 220 workers; the government also ran munitions and arms factories, a brickyard, and some seventeen sugar factories. Many of Ismāʿīl's attempts to industrialize were foiled, however, in 1875 when fiscal pressures forced the State to liquidate the majority of its industrial enterprises. While the State retained control of some ginning and sugar factories, the few modern plants operating in the late 1870s and early 1880s were mostly privately owned enterprises engaged in the processing of agricultural products – gins, mills, and presses – or in the production of light consumer goods – glass, leather, and cigarettes.[51]

State enterprises continued to depend upon the forced recruitment of labor. A government sugar factory in Upper Egypt, for example, obtained its work force through the *shaykhs al-balad* of neighboring villages who supplied the names of men suited for factory labor. Workers received a wage of $1\frac{1}{2}$ to 3 piasters a day, and labored 12 out of the daily 24 hours in alternate shifts of 6 hours. Local people were also liable to be recruited for unpaid labor in the sugar fields.[52] Although one *shaykh al-balad* claimed that peasant-held land did not suffer as a result, labor still had to be impressed and workers kept in the factory by force; a free market in labor had yet to be created.

The availability of displaced craftspeople for factory labor remains a subject of some disagreement. Some contemporary observers, such as Stanley Lane-Poole, reported that very few crafts survived the influx of European manufactures: in the country towns, a set of residual crafts requiring minimum skills – "tanning, dyeing, rude carpentry and tannery, weaving, tinkering, and pottery" – were all that survived.[53] Certain crafts may well have disappeared, but overall this decline appears to have been exaggerated. As Owen points out, in the period leading up to the British occupation, European imports catered primarily to new demands and tastes among Europeans and the upper class in Egypt; most articles of local consumption were still being produced by local craftspeople. Indeed, in the early 1870s, some 28,000 textile workers, three times the estimated number of the eighteenth century, plied their trade in Egypt. While certain branches of the textile crafts were adversely affected, craftspeople also proved resourceful in the development of new types of products which could hold their own against European imports. Significant decline in the crafts industry may well belong to a later time.[54]

The 1850 to 1882 period can be seen, in general, as a time of transition for trade and industry. The dramatic development of the Muḥammad ʿAlī period gave way to the gradual, but inexorable, harnessing of Egyptian trade and industry to an economic system controlled by Europe. Many elements of the organization of the indigenous economy endured, particularly in petty trade and crafts production, but the penetration of European goods and finance capital was steadily transforming the economy; the full effects of this process were to be felt after the British occupation in 1882.

1882–1914: Colonial policy in trade and industry

British military occupation in 1882 ushered in the age of the veiled protectorate: British officials effectively directed the government while preserving the fiction of an independent Egyptian State.[55] The official British view, as expressed by Lord Northbrook, was that "The interest which England has in Egypt is derived from the necessity of securing the safety of the Suez Canal, through which the trade of Her Majesty's Eastern Empire passes," and short of rescuing Egypt from the threat of anarchy or occupation by a foreign power, England would not intervene in Egyptian affairs more "than is necessary to secure these objects." The same report, however, included proposals for the reform of the corvée, tariffs, and taxation, all of which apparently fell within the boundaries of this legitimate intervention.[56] In fact, British officials, and particularly the

British Consul-General Lord Cromer, ran the country from 1882 to 1914, making all basic decisions concerning trade and industry.

Trade policy was governed by free trade ideology, strongly reinforced by the British industrial interest in protecting the Egyptian market for its own products and maintaining its near monopoly over Egypt's cotton crop. To these ends, British officials steadfastly refused any increase in the external tariff while maintaining countervailing duties on local production. Such policies further solidified the prevailing pattern: in general, Egypt imported manufactured goods and exported raw materials, the absolute majority of which went to Great Britain. The State played no direct role in trade, whether external or internal, contrary to its traditional patterns of involvement. Indeed, private companies were encouraged to enter commerce through the granting of profitable concessions, and the central government eschewed all interference in trade, exercising control over neither the money supply nor interest rates.[57]

Such policies could not but inhibit the development of industry. Although the country enjoyed certain advantages, including a solid infrastructure, a sizeable local market, and an indigenous supply of capital, industrial development on a significant scale required protective tariffs. Not only did British officials refuse this form of protection, they also insisted that two new cotton spinning and weaving factories established at the turn of the century pay a duty of 8 per cent on all their products, thus depriving them of even the slim protection provided by the 8 per cent external tariff. Still, some investments were made in industry, particularly in the primary processing of raw materials or the production of perishable or bulky goods. By 1911, Egypt housed 37 manufacturing companies, including cotton ginning and pressing, processing of foodstuffs, and the production of cigarettes and cement. Factory closings, however, were common: an Alexandrian glass factory founded in 1885, the Egyptian Cotton Mills Ltd founded in Cairo in 1899, and five of the seven sugar companies established in the 1890s had failed by 1907. In some cases, however, growing political pressure from nationalist groups seems to have convinced British officials to give limited support to local industry: the Egyptian government did give small, but critical, tariff advantages to a few companies between 1906 and 1908.[58] By 1914, while a small modern industrial sector had been established in Egypt, most factories still operated on the margins of economic survival, without the forms of protection and encouragement needed to expand production.

Industrialization, such as it was, gave rise to a modern working class: in 1916, modern factories employed some 30,000 to 35,000 workers from peasant, artisanal, and, in the case of skilled workers, European backgrounds.[59] Conditions were severe and pay was low: unskilled cotton ginners, for example, worked up to 17 hours a day for 1 to 1½ *ghūrsh*.[60] Nor were safety measures in force: the English capitalist Charles Galloway, chairman of Galloways Ltd in

Manchester, complained to Cromer about the "extremely lax manner in which the steam boilers of the various manufactories, which are now becoming so numerous in Egypt, are being worked and supervised and owing to which many lives are sacrificed." One of his directors had recently toured Egypt and returned "shocked" by unsafe practices, including the stopping up of safety valves and the operation of boilers at dangerously high pressure. Galloway suggested that Egypt needed some safety regulations and regular inspections, but Cromer parried his complaint by citing the difficulties of dealing with both the Egyptian government and private business interests.[61]

The State having abdicated all responsibility for regulating working conditions, labor actions and organizations tended to focus on conditions and pay. Between 1899 and 1907, at least seven workers' associations were formed, and a number of strikes were organized among cigarette wrappers, warehouse and port workers, and railway and spinning factory employees. The nascent working class movement received considerable support from the Nationalist Party, founded in 1907: for the rest of the prewar period, the fate of working class movements was bound up with that of the Nationalist Party which set up schools in working class areas and assisted unions with publicity and legal counsel during strikes. Both the unions and the nationalist movement were severely repressed by the government between 1910 and 1914.[62]

The modern industrial sector, despite the importance of the political activities of its new working class, remained marginal to the Egyptian economy both in terms of its contributions to production and the number of workers it employed. The Egyptian census of 1907 records some 380,000 workers in "industries"; if a maximum of 35,000 were employed in modern factories, at least 345,000 workers remained in traditional crafts, still a substantial undercount because part-time and home-based producers were probably not listed.[63] There is little question that European manufactured goods made substantial inroads on certain crafts, but Cromer's oft-quoted version of the near total destruction of many traditional crafts, including "spinning, weaving, braiding, tassle making, dyeing, tent-making, embroidering, slipper making, gold and silver working, spice crushing, copper beating, water skin making, saddle making, sieve making, wooden bolt making, lock making etc." seems an overstatement.[64] In the late nineteenth and early twentieth centuries, observers reported finding high quality crafts throughout the country, including basket work, pottery, and textile and rug weaving.[65] W. de Morgan, a pottery expert sent from England to assess the level of the craft, praised the skill of Egyptian potters in no uncertain terms: "nothing can be added by instruction to the skill of the Egyptian throwers, already greatly in advance of the Europeans."[66] The State itself took an interest in encouraging the development of crafts through the establishment of trades schools which instructed students in new techniques and styles calculated to compete with European imports. De Morgan, for example, was charged with ascertaining whether Egyptian clays, dyes, and labor could be used to produce glazed pottery of the quality of Italian or Greek imports, and whether the necessary skills could be taught in the new trades schools. Such projects could, however, have the unanticipated effect of actually suppressing local crafts: Persian rug patterns taught at the Asyūṭ trades school displaced the local *kilīms*, and European weaving patterns introduced in Sohag led to the disappearance of the traditional weaving of Akhnim a few miles away.[67] Nevertheless, there is little question that many crafts and significant numbers of craftspeople survived during this period and continued to supply the local demand for relatively simple items of daily use such as pottery, baskets, and cloth.

The policies of the British occupation crystallized prior trends in the development of trade and industry. The tying of Egyptian trade and production to European, and particularly British, economic needs proceeded apace through official promotion of free trade and free enterprise at the expense of state protection, or even state regulation, of commerce and industry. Large amounts of capital, accumulated through the cultivation and sale of cotton, coupled with the potential large local market did, nevertheless, encourage the establishment of modest modern industry; it continued to suffer, however, from certain structural problems such as shortages of fuel and the unwillingness of the State to lend it support. As a result, the number of people absorbed into the modern working class remained small; most Egyptians pursued their trades outside the modern factory setting. Women's contribution to economic production was directly affected by the forms of organization, and level of industrial development, in Egypt: women worked in trade, crafts, modern industry, and services alongside men, and their labor, as well as their rewards, was defined and molded by nineteenth century changes.

Women in trade, crafts, and industry

Throughout the nineteenth century, rural and urban Egyptian women participated in petty trade, an activity well suited to a woman's situation insofar as a trader could fix her own hours and conduct her business close to home or keep her younger children by her side. In the major market towns of Upper and Lower Egypt, women and girls dominated the market, selling vegetables, eggs, bread, utensils, and cloth.[68] Some became businesswomen with substantial assets whose dealings with other women and men entailed large amounts of money and goods. Women borrowed weighty sums from each other, using the court to settle claims and counterclaims surrounding the holding of securities and the terms of the transaction.[69] The scope of the business could be truly vast: one woman owed 7,436 piasters to a male merchant, the price of soap and tobacco which she had received from him, presumably for resale.[70] The majority of women in trade, however, operated on a more modest, if not desperate, level. If divorced and working to support children, trading, like some other activities, might render them unfit mothers in the eyes of the court: a woman who sold pancakes lost custody of her daughter in favor of the girl's father. Trading was not, however, always an absolute impediment. A man who questioned his divorced wife's fitness for custody of a child because of her trading activities could be denied permission to take the child unless he could prove that the mother's work had disastrous effects.[71]

Cairene women were particularly prominent in the peddling of foodstuffs. The more humble itinerant sellers did not have business problems that necessitated court action so that the records generally remain silent concerning their activities. Observers commented, however, that many peddlers, as opposed to shopkeepers, were women, and certain items, including bread, fruit, vegetables, and dairy products, were sold almost exclusively by female peddlers. Men peddled pastries, sherbet, and textile goods, while sugar cane and water might be sold by either sex.[72] Such observations jibe well with a later list of women's professions in Cairo which included greengrocers, bakers, and sellers of milk.[73]

Cairo and the major provincial towns also supported the activities of a rather more affluent class of women traders, the *dallālahs* (female peddlers), who supplied goods to secluded women of the upper classes. Among the wealthy elite of Turkish or Egyptian origin, the institution of the *ḥarīm* dictated an almost absolute seclusion of wives and concubines; women of this class, rarely leaving the women's quarters, could not frequent the local market. Their purchases of clothing, jewelry, and other personal needs were conducted through the offices of *dallālahs*, women of lower class origin who purveyed luxury goods to inhabitants of various *ḥarīms*.[74] A Manṣūrah court case, recording the payment of a debt owed to such a peddler, illuminates the structure of these transactions. Um Rizk, a woman of peasant origin, collected 110 *ghūrsh rūmī* (Ottoman piasters)[75] from her client, Sitt Khadījah, the white slave of a Turkish official, as payment for two veils of white cloth.[76] The case suggests that Um Rizk conducted her business as an independent peddler rather than as a broker for a textile merchant; the debt was owed directly to her, not to a merchant or manufacturer. Other *dallālahs* might act as intermediaries between male merchants and *ḥarīm* clients. Business quarrels were sometimes brought to court for settlement: in one case, a woman in the jewelry trade argued with her client over the price paid for her wares. Elsewhere, a male cloth merchant attempted repossession of his goods from such a female intermediary.[77] As a small businesswoman, a *dallālah* used the court to pursue her debtors and protect her investments; such activity shows that some women engaged in petty trade were cognizant of their legal rights and ready to press their business claims in court if necessary.

Although women were far more likely to be found in itinerant trade, some women did own, and presumably operate, small shops. One woman agreed to purchase a shop from its male owner, paid half of the price, and then tried to bargain the seller down on the balance; after the owner cancelled the sale and sold the shop to another woman, the would-be purchaser pursued the matter in court. Another woman, on her deathbed, sold her shop to her daughter in a vain attempt to evade a son's claims to the property. But women shopkeepers, unlike women peddlers, appear relatively rarely in the Cairo commercial network; as often as not, a woman would sell the shop she acquired, for example, upon the death of her husband.[78]

Of far greater importance to Egyptian trade was female participation in bourgeois trading circles. Wealthy women joined commercial associations under their own names and using their own capital. Many women invested their money in a "silent partnership" (*muḍārabah*) in which the other partner would conduct the business and then share the profits in pre-specified proportions; in some cases, the partner was a male relative, but women were more likely to invest their money in business ventures with unrelated men. As the silent partner, women often grew vociferous in insuring that they received the proper return on their investment. One woman in Gīzah had invested 1,150 *ghūrsh* with which her partner bought rope; after the sale, however, he used her share of the profit to buy onions which rotted before shipment, resulting in a net loss of money. She demanded, in court, full payment of her share of profit from the sale of rope, since the onion venture had been undertaken without her knowledge or permission.[79] Women also lodged complaints in court if their partners were late in payment, or had died before the sharing of the profits, leaving their estate in debt to the partner.[80] Females were not always the silent partner; men might invest their money in a commercial association in which a woman conducted the trade. If an active partner incurred losses in the normal conduct of business, the silent partner could not insist on the return of his or her money. Accordingly, when one ill-starred woman merchant shipped the association's wheat on a boat which sank with all its cargo, her partner lost his entire investment.[81]

Female involvement in the eastern and African oriented trade of the Muslim merchant elite is well documented in the early nineteenth century court records: women invested in the sea trade of spices and the caravan slave trade.[82] The fate of these elite women traders was linked, however, to the shifts in Egyptian trade patterns: we find fewer traces of women's participation in large-scale trade in the later court records when, in any case, most important commercial transactions tend to take place outside the *maḥkamah* in newly created commercial courts. We cannot be sure whether or not some women managed to transfer their activities to the expanding European trade, but it seems highly likely that they, like the elite Muslim merchant class of which they formed part, were replaced by Europeans or members of ethnic minorities associated with Europe.

The lower class trader did not suffer the same fate, for petty trade in agricultural produce was left to the local, casually organized market in which women played a dominant role.

The involvement of rural and urban women in petty trade followed logically from their role in agricultural and craft production. Women played a crucial role in early nineteenth century rural textile industry as employees in textile workshops, spinners in cottage industry, and own-account producers of textiles for home use and exchange. In the large provincial textile centers, women formed a part of the labor force drawn from the surrounding rural areas. Workshops employed both men and women, utilizing their labor during slow agricultural months. Cotton and linen workshops in Maḥallah, for example, employed 800 to 1,000 workers of both sexes and all ages.[83]

Most textile operations, however, were performed in the home. Home industry was organized in at least three different ways: traders or weavers parceled out cleaning and spinning to peasants; peasants themselves bought raw cotton or linen and later resold the spun product to weavers; the family cleaned, spun, and wove raw materials, especially wool, for its own use and local sale. Women and children provided much of this labor in the home. Under the putting-out system, traders bought both local and Syrian cotton for distribution to female spinners; after the payment of a set piece-rate, the spun material was then transferred to weaving workshops controlled by the trader. Weavers also played an entrepreneurial role: in many instances a weaver had his cotton spun by female spinners working at home. Much cotton and linen processing depended on a market chain rather than the organizing hand of one weaver. Peasant women came to the village market to buy flax and raw cotton which they spun and bleached at home, and then resold the spun product to weavers in the marketplace. The finished cloth made a final journey to the local market where traders purchased it from the weavers, often for export.[84]

Women thus participated, either as workers in the putting-out system or as petty commodity producers, in the key rural industry. Their labor in linen and cotton processing was not tied to family agricultural production: since the family plot rarely produced sizeable quantities of flax or cotton, women depended on the market for raw materials for their craft. Part of their labor linked them directly to a world outside the sway of the family unit: buying and selling on the market, they were probably more active in the realm of petty commodity production, and contributed more to the family cash income, than their male relatives. The significance of this activity for the economy as a whole cannot be underestimated. French observers, concerned with the promotion of French exports to Egypt in the late eighteenth century, stressed the centrality of rural female labor to the production of linen and cotton cloth for export to the East.[85]

Wool processing was geared for a far different market. As the primary material of local wear, woolen cloth, often spun and woven by the peasant family, was destined for family use or for sale on a limited scale. Observers noted that the family as a whole processed wool in their spare time; spun wool was then woven at home or sold to local weavers.[86] Little sexual differentiation appears in the division of tasks: men, women, and children washed, cleaned, and spun woolen yarn. Production of woolen cloth was closely linked to family agricultural activities, for family members were processing the produce of their own flocks rather than purchasing raw materials. Joint family labor in wool production reflected joint family labor in agriculture. Here women functioned as members of the family economic unit, producing for use and exchange; the familial character of the work is striking. In contrast, Bedouin women of the time assumed total control of wool production as they cleaned, spun, and wove the cloth used for clothing and tents.[87] As caretaker of all livestock, the Bedouin woman naturally assumed responsibility for the processing of animal products, including wool. Responsibility in the peasant family was assigned far less rigidly, with the family as a whole sharing in the processing of joint produce.

In Cairo, women artisans also worked at home and in shops in most of the major crafts. Patterns of employment in urban textile crafts appear similar to those in rural industry: much of the cotton and linen thread destined for weaving workshops was carded and spun by women working at home. Accounts of urban weavers, however, never mention women, thus suggesting that they were effectively barred from that occupation.[88] While women's work in textiles was concentrated in operations performed at home, either in own-account family industry or in a putting-out system, and women were therefore absent from the more public branch of the trade, their role in spinning tied them, like their rural sisters, to the market economy. The exclusion of women from weaving cannot, however, be explained solely on the basis that the work was performed in workshops, exposing women to public view and violating an ideal of seclusion. On the contrary, the court records give evidence that women did labor in crafts with public contact, especially in the food processing sector: women ran small bakeries and oil presses where their own labor could be supplemented by that of female employees. Other women are mentioned as small shop owners, although it is not clear from the cases whether or not the shops were craft as well as retail operations.[89]

The policies of the Muḥammad ʿAlī period, particularly state intervention in home-based industry, eroded the craftswoman's control over her work. Women, who had formerly worked autonomously at home, spinning and weaving for family consumption and for sale on the local market, became government employees. In the state-controlled cottage industry of the 1820s and 1830s, local *shaykhs* distributed flax and cotton to women to spin into yarn. Working with quotas and for a set wage, these women lost the control they had once exercised over the pace of their labor and the sale of their product.[90] As detrimental as such a change must have been to the smooth integration of home crafts and family duties, and to actual earning power, it was short-lived: the government monopoly of textile crafts was lifted in the mid-1830s.

Home textile production did not, however, automatically regain a position of primacy in the local economy. The fate of male weavers, more visible because many worked outside the home in large and small shops and were guild members, illustrates the irreversible nature of change in textile crafts. Before the institution of monopoly, women, working at home, had spun flax and cotton into yarn and sold it to male weavers. State control of weaving at first concentrated many of the weavers in factories and workshops where yarn was supplied from the State's own spinning factories or cottage industry; even in the less industrialized linen production, weavers were employees of the State, forbidden to use looms privately even though they remained dispersed throughout the country.[91] Upon lifting the textile monopoly in 1834, the government imposed, in its place, a fixed head tax on each weaver regardless of how much cloth, if any, he had produced. Many weavers evaded the tax by permanently fleeing their villages, leaving their fellow villagers responsible for payment. The havoc wrought in the organization of the weaving industry by government regulation and taxation was reflected in the disappearance of weavers' guilds in various parts of the country. Although most artisanal guilds survived this first wave of industrialization more or less intact, the weavers never regained their former levels of organizational strength.[92] Rising imports of European-made textiles combined with government policies to damage, irrevocably, the organization and output of the textile crafts. The fate of the many female cotton spinners who had worked at home was tied to the fate of the weavers they supplied. Although women continued to spin and weave wool for family consumption, their major productive link with the local market was greatly weakened.

The policies of the Muḥammad ʿAlī period and growth in the imports of competing European goods had far less impact on female crafts which were based on special skills and geared to local tastes. Embroidery and dressmaking, for example, continued to be important and remunerative occupations. Working at home, an urban woman could make a good independent living as an embroiderer of women's jackets or of other luxury items destined for use by the wealthy; some successful women might also employ young girls to help them with the work. Girls in their teens served periods of apprenticeship at low wages before becoming full-fledged seamstresses who worked out of their homes or in a dressmaker's shop.[93] So employed, a woman could aspire to be the major cash earner of her family circle, a reality accepted by the courts when the issue of family support arose. The *muftī* was quick to point out that a man's legal responsibility for a female relative's support did not extend to cases where she but not he earned a handsome living:

Question: There is a rich woman, and there is clear proof of that, who works as a seamstress, and she has a son who is poor and in debt from whom she wants daily support (*nafaqah*). And if her affluence is proven with legal evidence, is she not allowed to demand anything from her son since she is rich and the son is poor and has debts, and she is capable of remarriage and still attractive?

Answer: The wealthy are required to give support to the poor even if they are capable of earning . . . but if her son is not wealthy nor has a livelihood, whether she be rich or poor it is not incumbent upon him to provide her support, and God is exalted in knowledge.[94]

Social perceptions of the conflict between work and family responsibilities, especially that of child care, continued to plague women who worked outside the home. One craftswomen (*ṣāḥibah al-ṣanāʿi*) lost custody of her young daughter to her divorced husband who claimed that the girl was neglected because her mother worked in the marketplace.[95] Another woman also forfeited custody of her son because she "was out of the house most of the time, making dough and baking for a wage."[96] Here, two divorcées, dependent upon their own earnings for their and their children's livelihood, were penalized for working outside the home. Although women could find craft employment other than in home textile production, the lack of flexibility in location and hours could be a major disadvantage. Even if not gainfully employed outside the home, female crafts could still form an important part of domestic labor. In working class families studied by Vallet in the early twentieth century, women invariably made clothing for themselves and their children out of cheap cotton cloth they purchased in the market; although these women were not likely to spin their own yarn or weave their own cloth, they were all amateur seamstresses.[97]

The presence of women in textile crafts undoubtedly encouraged their employment in the textile industry, in the factories of the Muḥammad ʿAlī period and later in the more modest enterprises of the turn of the century. During the Muḥammad ʿAlī era, women and children worked alongside men in many of the factories. Nevertheless, certain divisions of labor along the lines of sex and age seemed to prevail in most workplaces. Some of the new industries were almost exclusively female. The *ṭarbūsh* factory at Fūwwah, for example, was initially established with the aid of Tunisian women workers, imported for the purpose, who instructed Egyptian women in the arts of spinning and netting wool. Although the factory employed workers of both sexes in the 1830s, the bulk of the labor was performed by women who carded and spun the wool which was then netted into *ṭarbūshes* by young girls.[98] Coarse woolen cloaks for military wear were also manufactured at Fūwwah with women playing an equally important role, so that when Muḥammad ʿAlī undertook to establish a cloak factory in Syria to supply the Egyptian occupation forces, the twelve workers dispatched for the purpose included eight women.[99] The dominant position of female workers in the *ṭarbūsh* industry is something of an anomaly, for most of the other new factories employed females in more limited numbers. As a new industry in Egypt, the various processes in *ṭarbūsh* manufacture had not previously been the domain of a given sex and thus the recruitment of women did not trespass on any customary division of labor. More importantly, the absence of large machinery and mechanized operations, generally staffed by male workers in other factories, encouraged female employment.

In cotton and linen factories, on the other hand, women and children worked at the tasks which had formerly been their province in home and cottage industry spinning and weaving. A cotton cleaning establishment near Manṣūrah employed girls to feed some 32 roller gins driven by oxen.[100] Women and children were also present in significant numbers in cotton spinning: in factories in Esneh and Damietta women and girls labored alongside the more numerous men.[101] In flax cleaning, the pattern appears similar: women scutched flax in cattle-driven mills. When steam power was utilized in a factory, however, women were less likely to be employed. In the Manṣūrah flax mill, run by steam, all the scutchers were men, while a neighboring mill, operated by animal power, still employed some women.[102] Men also tended to operate the larger and more sophisticated machinery: in the oxen-powered Būlāq factory, mules with 216 spindles were run by two men assisted by children; indeed, most mule-jennies and power looms were run by male workers regardless of the factory's power source.[103] In the textile industry, then, female and child labor was more heavily used in animal-powered factories, on smaller machines, and in less mechanized and auxiliary tasks.

Children lacked the physical strength required to operate some of the heavier machinery but, for women, the logic seems different. At a time when women in the countryside were harnessing themselves to turn water pumps and mills in the place of their requisitioned animals, the exclusion of women as machine operators undoubtedly had a rationale other than that of physical strength. Women were noticeably absent in the workplaces with more sophisticated equipment.[104] In these showpiece factories, established and run on the European model and often overseen by European managers, the absence of women may well have reflected growing opposition among reformers in Europe to widespread employment of women in industry. It seems likely that members of missions sent by Muḥammad ʿAlī to Europe would have imbibed attitudes antagonistic to such female labor and transferred them to Egypt.

Male advantage in the realm of unskilled labor became male monopoly in skilled work. Artisans employed in various textile factories were almost exclusively male; lists of carpenters, blacksmiths, and turners, better paid and treated than the bulk of the labor force, did not include any females.[105] Insofar as skilled workmen were recruited from the ranks of preindustrial artisans, the dearth of women in many of these trades explains their subsequent absence in skilled positions in the factories. State training policies also assigned skilled labor to men. Training programs, planned to supply fitters, pattern makers, spindle and fly makers, and file cutters, enlisted only "a certain number of young men"; the training of women was apparently limited to *ṭarbūsh* production.[106] The factory system did not introduce this particular division of labor but it did institutionalize it in textile production where discrepancies between the sexes in skill and remuneration had not previously been so striking.

Consistent with such divisions of labor, recruitment often brought entire families into the factory where men, women, and children could specialize in certain tasks. Some observers applauded the use of family labor as an opportunity for all members to contribute to family production and security. One European traveler thought the factories had "considerably alleviated the condition of the lower orders, by giving employment to many (children as well as adults) who formerly depended on a precarious agriculture for their subsistence."[107] Others went further to divine conscious benevolence in the factory scheme: "we again remark that the intention of their [the factories'] creator was to ameliorate the existence of his people, by providing them with work, by occupying children who ordinarily would be a burden for the family, by providing work for men, and for women ill-suited for cultivation."[108] Enlisting entire families in factory service did indeed allow for the earning of a family wage, for the sharing of costs of family subsistence among all members. Given that the very meager pay was often late in coming, however, and that such recruitment, by removing all members simultaneously from agriculture and other pursuits, cancelled other contributions to the family budget, such policies could have disastrous effects. The industries did not survive long enough, however, to require a reassessment of the policy of using family labor.

Women's role in the more limited industrialization of the late nineteenth century exhibited many of the same patterns. Women typically worked at particular tasks which came to be thought of as their province. In cotton ginning factories, women and children sorted the incoming cotton while men tended the ginning machines. Women also picked over tobacco leaves in cigarette factories while men rolled, cut, and packed the cigarettes. On many construction sites, women functioned as assistants to male workers: bearing baskets on their heads, women hauled bricks and sand from the ground to skilled workers on the upper floors. In many cases the joint family labor of the Muḥammad ʿAlī period persisted: many cotton ginning factories, for example, recruited peasant families – men, women, and children – from the rural areas surrounding the factory for the five month ginning season. Concentrated in adjunct positions defined as "women's work," female workers received less pay: in the ginning factories, a woman received 2 to 4 piasters a day to the man's 6 to 8; in the more highly paid cigarette industry, women sorters earned 7 piasters a day, while male cutters and packers took home 10 piasters. Despite the fact that male and female unskilled laborers in the construction trade performed the same tasks, women were commonly paid a daily wage of 4 piasters, 2 piasters less than their male counterparts. Finally, the skilled trades, in industry and construction, remained closed to women; with a very few exceptions, all the mechanics, carpenters, masons, and even machine operators were men.[109]

Although women thus shared in the onerous conditions of the later nineteenth century work force, including a 10 to 15 hour day six or seven days a week, we encounter official blindness to women's work. Vallet's personal investigations repeatedly belied the results of the 1907 Census. The Census listed three women as construction workers and contractors consistently denied that they ever employed females, but Vallet counted 27 women working on just one site he visited at random. Similarly, while the Census reported that the cigarette industry employed a total of 1,804 men and 13 women, Vallet counted 20 women workers in a single one of the 37 functioning cigarette factories.[110] Anglo-Egyptian officials tended to impose their version of the family economy, man as wage-earner and woman as housekeeper, on the Egyptian reality. In a memorandum on combating the plague, Pinching, Director-General of the Sanitary Department, described the government's quarantine measures in Alexandria: all suspected contacts were placed in quarantine for seven days but only males, age 16 and over, were paid compensation "for wages lost in quarantine." In Port Said, under a modified isolation system, women and children were confined to the home but "wage earners," all presumed to be men, could go out, Ironically enough, the first case of plague in Alexandria in the 1900 epidemic had appeared in a "wage earner" of another kind, a female rag-picker.[111]

Official obliviousness to the composition of the labor force and the strong laissez-faire attitudes of Cromer and his colleagues continued to forestall any state regulation of female labor, despite the sensitivity to women's working conditions that had developed in England in the course of the nineteenth century. Indeed, up to 1914, the Egyptian government did not attempt to intervene in the labor process at all, with the singular exception of a child labor law passed in 1909 which addressed the particularly brutal conditions in many of the ginning factories: children under nine years old were prohibited from work in ginning, and children between the ages of nine and thirteen could not work more than eight hours a day and were forbidden night and dangerous work.[112] Women's work in the industrial sector, however, undervalued and underpaid, was not recognized, much less regulated.

As many of the crafts that had traditionally occupied women and provided them with an independent income were being eroded by foreign competition, women's role in the embryonic Egyptian industry was primarily that of adjunct worker. To a great extent, the decline of women's productive activities simply mirrored an overall decline in the productive capacities of the country as a whole. The sexual division of labor, however, also developed new sectoral division: by the end of the nineteenth century, women entered modern industry only as marginal and unskilled workers. The erratic course of industrialization had had a chilling effect on women's participation in industry.

Women in service occupations

Service occupations had long occupied a significant number of women: only women could perform certain services for other females because of special knowledge or the demands of propriety. Domestic service, midwifery, and soothsaying comprised the chief occupations which took women into the home territory of others to minister to personal need.[113] Public baths, usually reserved for women on set days, also employed a number of female bath attendants who apparently could earn enough to become small property holders.[114] Only an older woman, with complete access to the intimate world of the family, could act as marriage broker (*khāṭibah*), passing along information on the attributes and expected *mahr* of prospective brides to the family of an interested groom.[115] Many such services were central to the organization and cohesion of the community: women provided the social glue because of their ability to move in all circles.

Not all women in services were confined to women's space: women might work as weighers in the public market or as drummers hired for weddings and other festive occasions, amassing tidy sums of money in the process.[116] Although female musicians, dancers, and singers could be well remunerated and many achieved a certain economic independence, the issue of respectability could arise. The *ʿawālim*, the aristocracy of female entertainers, were not initially tinged with the least shadow of impropriety. The occupational title of *ʿālimah* used the word signifying woman scholar to designate an accomplished female singer. Talent and training combined to win these women high standing, as Savary, a French traveller, observed in the 1770s:

> They are called *almé* (savantes). A more painstaking education than other women has earned them this name. They form a celebrated community within the country. In order to join, one must have a beautiful voice, a good possession of the language, a knowledge of the rules of poetry and an ability to spontaneously compose and sing couplets adapted to the circumstances. The *almés* know all the new songs by heart. Their memory is furnished with the most beautiful *moals* [*mawwāls*: musical poems] and the prettiest stories. There is no fete without them; no festival where they do not provide the ornamentation.[117]

Lane cautioned against confusing this class of entertainer with public dancers or prostitutes. The *ʿawālim* were hired to perform in the *ḥarīm* in front of women, often in a special apartment overlooking the open court of the household so that men could listen without seeing them. They were handsomely remunerated for accomplished singing and musicianship, and seemed to enjoy an uncompromised social position.[118]

The art of the *ʿawālim* endured during the nineteenth century. Lady Duff Gordon, attending a christening in 1862, encountered one of the most renowned of that era:

> Sakna, the Arab Grisi, is fifty-five – an ugly face, I am told (she was veiled and one only saw the eyes and glimpses of her mouth when she drank water), but the figure of a leopard, all grace and beauty, and a splendid voice of its kind, harsh but thrilling like Malibran's . . . The eight younger *Halmeh* . . . were ugly and screeched. Sakna was treated with great consideration by the Armenian ladies with whom she talked between her songs. She is a Muslimeh and very rich and charitable; she gets £50 for a night's singing at least.[119]

The *ʿawālim*, respected artists, must be distinguished from other female entertainers, particularly dancing girls, whose reputation, as we shall see in chapter 4, shaded into that of prostitutes.

Domestic service, on the other hand, was tainted with ambiguities in status and a particular kind of vulnerability. In the early part of the century, Egyptian women who worked in the wealthier Turkish, Egyptian, or European households were subject to the importunate demands of their employers as well as a measure of social opprobrium. Although the upper classes in the time of Muḥammad ʿAlıi reportedly preferred slave domestics to free-born servants, some women did find work in the *ḥarīms*. The plans of one mistress to marry her servant to one of her male slaves, against the wishes of the woman and her family, suggest high-handed treatment within *ḥarīm* quarters.[120] Although many European households employed local women, a certain uneasiness in the arrangement could erupt into scandal. An English bachelor, accused of "living with" his servant by her irate husband, created one such incident which rocked local society.[121] Galvanized perhaps by this event, and the need to assuage opposition to the foreign presence which was often cloaked in religious sentiments, Muḥammad ʿAlī moved to limit the employment of Muslim domestics:

> The Pasha, advised by those around him or not, had issued out an ordinance through the new chief of Police, that no Musselman woman or girl is in future to enter the service of any family of the Coptic, Greek, Syrian, Armenian and European Christians in Cairo under pain of being seized by police agents, hurried to the Nile, sacked and thrown in the river to be drowned.[122]

Whatever the effect of this measure, it was not uncommon for European households to employ French, Maltese, and Greek domestics rather than Egyptians.[123]

Despite the air of disrepute attached to domestic service, as craft and industrial opportunities shrank, women might find no other way of earning a living; domestic service was one of the few clearly expanding female occupations. Sometimes the price of employment came high: divorced women, working as servants to support themselves, lost their children just as surely as craftswomen, should their husbands contest their rights. The *muftī* ruled in one case that even a widow's employment in service cancelled her claims to the care of her children.[124] However prejudicial such work proved to be to the status of the divorced or widowed, single women might parlay the economic independence gained through service into a new-found autonomy. In one unusual case presented to the *muftī*, a young woman from the countryside, employed as a servant in Cairo, refused to marry the man her father had selected from her natal village; the *muftī* conceded that, under Ḥanafī law, a girl of legal age could not be forced to marry against her will.[125] Such defiance of parental authority suggests that domestic service, despite its lowly status, could enhance a woman's situation within her family by providing independent means and a separate abode.

Domestic servants suffered greatly, however, from the dearth of regulation and organization of the occupation. Like many of the overwhelmingly female trades, domestic service was poorly served by the guild corporations; the emergence of cooperative associations among maids was required to protect and support women in an occupation which, by definition, tended to isolate employees. As the number of domestic servants swelled during the nineteenth century, however, there is little evidence that maids formed protective networks. The seduction, rape, beating, and forced marriage of maids by male employees, as reported in court records, illustrates the vulnerability and powerlessness experienced by women in service.[126] The dearth of parallel cases of complaints of abuse from women who labored in crafts or petty trade emphasizes the special problems faced by maids. The reputation of domestic service, ambiguous at best, undoubtedly encouraged such abuse, but recourse to the court also reflected the absence of voluntary organizations among servants which could provide a refuge for maltreated maids or impose informal sanctions on abusive employers.

Testimonies to female competence: multazimahs and nāẓirahs

That society considered its women eminently suited for the management of property and other business was a perception arising naturally from the very active role of women in the chain of economic production and distribution. Female competence was strongly affirmed by the many *multazimahs* and *nāẓirahs*, female holders of *iltizāms* and female managers of *waqf* property. Often, although not always, women in these positions came from families of affluence and social standing, and were managing very sizeable amounts of property indeed; women thus controlled a not insignificant portion of society's wealth.

The holders of *iltizām* land, *multazims*, were originally drawn from the ruling class *per se*, that is, from the ranks of the beys and members of the Mamluke households. Over the course of the eighteenth century, however, the revenues from *iltizām* land gradually came to form an increasingly significant portion of the estates of many members of the commercial elite who acquired *iltizām* titles either through direct purchase or loan default. Title to a particular *iltizām*, whether comprising the rights to tax collection on a piece of agricultural land or similar rights to the collection of taxes on certain occupations, also tended to remain within the same family, coming, in practice although never in theory, to form part of a family's inheritable property.[127] Because *iltizāms* were not private property (*mulk*) under law, Islamic rules of succession did not apply to *iltizām* holdings in the same way that peasant tenure on the *'arḍ al-fallāḥ* was not subject to Islamic laws of division. In the peasant economy, as we have seen, the usufruct usually passed to male descendants, effectively barring women from a share in the family's land. Although elite women from *multazim* families may have been less favored than their male relatives for succession to *iltizām* title, a Cairo court sample of 1801 to 1822, with sixteen instances of *multazimahs*, demonstrates that women could and did come to control *iltizāms*.[128] Women of the elite probably acquired title to *iltizām* land more often than peasant women obtained the *mīrī* usufruct.

Information in the court records is too fragmentary to allow for a definitive explanation of the female *multazim*, but the phenomenon may well reflect the nature of family relations and women's economic roles among the elite. Within those families with large fortunes, female legal claims to inheritable property rendered women important carriers of sizeable portions of the family wealth. Instead of constituting solely a drain on a family's material standing, a woman's potential or actual ownership of family property provided the key to forging family links and alliances essential to elite society. The beys and Mamluke retainers, the commercial elite, and some members of the *'ulamā'* solidified their ties and promoted mutual economic interests through careful control of marriage arrangements. Since elite marriage drew on women's property rights to cement existing family links or create new family alliances, it guaranteed that female inheritance would not be reduced to a legal fiction: such alliances must rest on the woman's actual access to wealth. Women as wealthy traders and *multazimahs*, exercising control not only over inherited property but also other forms of wealth, were enjoying the fruits of their legal position buttressed by social perceptions of their abilities and the uses to which they could be put.

State abolition of the *iltizām* system may have had a detrimental, albeit unplanned, effect on the elite woman's role in the economy. After the dismantling of *iltizāms* in the second decade of the nineteenth century, women *multazims*, along with their male counterparts, became an extinct breed. Such state intervention narrowed the field of upper class women's activities: under the state monopoly system, agricultural land formerly held in *iltizāms* and urban tax collection were shifted to the control of state bureaucrats whose ranks, by all accounts, did not include women. The eventual rise of a new landholding class did enable women, as members of landholding families, to reacquire some control of landed property. We find ample instances of women inheriting, buying, mortgaging, and managing sizeable pieces of land at mid-century and later.[129] After the exile of military officers and some of their allies from Egyptian notable families as punishment for participation in the ʿUrābī Revolt of 1880–1882, the resources of their wives left in Egypt were scrutinized and found substantial. The wife of Muḥammad Sāmī Pāshā al-Burūdī, from an aristocratic family, personally owned 1,400 *faddāns* in the provinces of Baḥrīyyah and al-Daqhalīyyah, in addition to three buildings in Cairo. The other women, wives of officers from humbler, usually Egyptian provincial, backgrounds, were less well off but tended to control at least some property: the wife of ʿAlī Faḥmī owned 31 *faddāns*, and Aḥmad ʿUrābī's wife was planning to purchase 52 *faddāns*.[130]

Women were also much in evidence in the various arrangements governing *waqf* property. During the nineteenth century, many of the shops, warehouses, and residences of Cairo and some agricultural land were held as *waqf* properties. Once endowed by the original owner as a pious act, a *waqf* property could not be sold or mortgaged, and its revenues were earmarked for the immediate or eventual benefit of a religious or charitable cause. Since the founder could assign part of the *waqf*'s income to his descendants or, in some cases, the total income until the family line was extinguished, and *waqf* property was protected from most forms of taxation and confiscation, such alienation of property might actually work to secure the descendants' enjoyment of and hold over family property.[131] In the original deed of endowment (*waqfīyah*), the founder appointed an administrator (*nāẓir*), often from among his descendants, who received about 10 per cent of the income and was charged with the maintenance of the property and the distribution of revenues as specified in the *waqfīyah*.

Women appear as founders, beneficiaries, and administrators of *waqf* property in the court records. They established *waqfs* on the property they owned, whether buildings, shops, or land, to benefit religious institutions or individuals.[132] In one exceptional case, a woman with substantial wealth in buildings, palm trees, fishing grounds, and land utilized the *waqf* to promote a limited form of matrilineal inheritance: the income of the *waqf* she founded was to accrue to her daughter's children through the generations and then, upon the extinction of the daughter's line, to the women of the *ashrāf*, the descendants of the Prophet.[133] Many founders of *waqfs*, both male and female, appear to have used the institution, in part, to provide specifically for female heirs whose claims on the inheritance would normally be weaker than those of men. Ismāʿīl Pāshā, for example, established two *waqfs*, one to benefit each of his wives; in converting part of their property to *waqf*, other men provided for their wives, concubines, and daughters.[134] Although women might directly profit from the establishment of a *waqf* on family property, sometimes the terms of the *waqfīyah* served to disinherit them. One founder specified the income for "his children, and his children's children, and his children's children's children, and his children's children's children's children, and their children and their descendants . . . the male and never the female"; in this and other similar cases, such an exclusion was ruled legally permissible.[135]

Women not infrequently administered both charitable and family *waqfs* as official *nāẓirahs*. They might be selected by the founder, or inherit the position in a line of family succession; once appointed, however, a woman could not be dismissed as long as she fulfilled the duties of the post. *Nāẓirahs* managed to use the court forum with success to protest any infringement of their rights of administration.[136] In her position as *nāẓirah*, a woman could exercise considerable control over the property and often gained material advantage over her fellow descendants. In one *waqf* transfer (*istibdāl*), Fāṭimah, the *nāẓirah* for a *waqf* established by her grandfather, received 50 per cent of the price paid for a *wakālah* (caravanserai) while three other descendants, including a man, received one fifth or less.[137] *Waqf* administration involved a number of possible business transactions, including the keeping up or renting of *waqf* property, the overseeing of the income, the supervising of repairs to the endowed mosque or school, etc. Widespread social recognition of a woman's suitability for the position of *nāẓirah*, entailing as it did responsibility for all these transactions, further testifies to the perception of women as independent legal actors with requisite skills and knowledge. Although most *waqfs* were endowed by members of the ruling and commercial elite, women of the artisanal class also administered a number of more modest *waqf* properties.

Caution is called for, however, in assuming that these roles automatically enhanced the elite woman's independence and freedom of action in all spheres. Although access to wealth undoubtedly promoted a woman's power, control over her marriage, which involved the disposition of family property, would be of crucial importance to her family. The seclusion of an elite woman and her absence from much of public life speaks to substantial social control of her movements. In the court setting, for example, an elite woman rarely appeared in person, for her court business was conducted through the offices of an agent (*wakīl*), usually her husband or a close male relative, in contrast to the woman of the artisanal or lower classes who almost always presented her case in person.

Businesswomen and the family

While women often conducted their business as individuals, they also might operate in family economic association. In at least one aspect of their business-related activities, property sales and purchases, a woman's primary economic relationship of a familial character was generally forged with her husband: patrilocal marriage removed her to the groom's hearth and home where she entered into a new domestic economy based on the marital relationship. The pattern of joint sales and purchases of property among family members in Cairo from 1800 to 1860 (Table 1) highlights the material bonds between husband and wife: transfers of property between a married couple accounted for 25 of the 75 cases of property transfer among relatives. Transfers between sisters and brothers, mothers and sons, and mothers and daughters were of secondary significance and can be explained as the means of consolidating inherited property in the hands of a single heir. Husbands and wives, however, were co-heirs only in the relatively unlikely event that one of their children had inherited property from a more distant relative and then predeceased them both, so that the predominance of husband–wife exchange suggests that marriage did indeed entail economic association.

Table 1. *Property transfers and joint sales and purchases*

Female associations with relatives	Woman sells to	Woman buys from	Total	Woman, joint purchase with	Woman, joint sale with	Total
Husband	7	18	25	11	12	23
Brother	2	11	13	3	6	9
Daughter	0	2	2	9	3	12
Son	5	6	11	4	4	8
Mother	0	8	8	8	0	0
Father	0	1	1	1	0	1
Sister	0	5	5	11	9	20
Cousin	1	1	2	0	0	0
Uncle	0	2	2	1	0	1
Aunt	0	2	2	2	0	0
Nephew	1	0	1	1	0	1
Niece	0	1	1	0	0	0
Father-in-law	1	0	1	0	0	0
Grandmother	0	1	1	0	0	0
			75			75

Source: Maḥkamah Bāb al-ʿĀlī, s. 323, 345, 366, 370, 387, 388, 413, 440, 476, 1216–1276/1801–1860.

Husbands and wives also made joint sales and purchases: 11 of the 41 joint purchases and 12 of the 34 joint sales made by relatives were cooperative husband–wife transactions. Since marriage did not automatically bring the legal consolidation of a couple's property, evidence of joint holdings demonstrates the tendency of married couples to acquire property and goods together, that is, to form an economic unit based on a voluntary, at least in a legal sense, pooling of income and property.

Although the marital bond remained strong, by mid-century we find that sisters were as likely to make joint sales and purchases as were spouses. Joint sales might represent the liquidation of inherited property, but joint purchases by sisters, most of which were made after 1840 and accounted for 11 of the 41 cases of joint purchase, point to ongoing economic association. While women continued to marry their economic affairs to those of their husbands, they increasingly conducted business in concert with a sister or sisters as well. The growth in sororal economic relations seems surprising, especially in view of the fact that we have no evidence of a decline in the practice of patrilocal marriage, which removed a woman from her family, inhibiting the development of economic relations with members of the household of birth, be they parents, brothers, or sisters. The tendency of sisters to band together, to retain joint control of property and undertake shared economic transactions, may have arisen out of the pressures of the time. First, state policies of recruitment for military and industrial service, which drew on urban as well as rural dwellers, could deprive a woman of her primary economic partner, her husband, and thus encourage her to seek cooperation with other members of her family. Association among sisters, whose status as co-heirs may have offset the divisive effects of marriage into different households, constituted an alternate alliance, undoubtedly preferable to the thorny path of association with a husband's brothers who all too frequently displayed a penchant for limiting or even negating their sister-in-law's rights. Secondly, the economic dislocations of the period could hold particularly severe consequences for women; cooperation among sisters may have developed in response to a general need to shore up their situation and reassert economic independence within the family. In league with their sisters, women could pool small amounts of capital and purchase property without depending on a husband, who might be absent, or male relatives, who might ride roughshod over female rights.

As in the countryside, urban women commonly resorted to the court to protest abrogation of their rights through disinheritance. During the first part of the century, disputes over successions multiplied, with women appearing most frequently as plaintiffs.[138] Although women, upon occasion, were swindled out of lawful shares in their father's property by their brothers, the most common complaint was that members of a husband's family negated the claims of a wife and children, or the children by a divorced wife.[139] Women, either on their own account or as guardians of their children, went to court to protest exclusion from the division of the husband's estate. Whether a woman had been divorced or not, her children by a deceased husband were clearly entitled to a share in his property. As long as the children were part of her household, their claims were of signal importance to her well being and her ability to maintain an independent hearth. Women's protests in this period suggest that they, and their children, were sometimes treated as interlopers by other members of their husbands' families, such as the husbands' brothers, second wives, or children by second wives, and denied rightful shares of property.

Abrogation of women's inheritance rights and high-handed treatment in general were discouraged, however, by the multitude of economic ties that bound husband and wife. Urban women, like their rural sisters, could be the debt-holders as well as the wives of their husbands. Familial debts were not a casual affair, for they entailed formal obligations under the law. One *ḥurmah* (title of lower class woman), for example, came to the court in Cairo to press a claim against her husband, ʿAlī. Two years previously, ʿAlī had borrowed ten *riyāls* from her under a legal agreement with a fixed repayment schedule. Not only had he failed to repay her, but his debt to her had increased with a loan of seven cushions and a rug (*kilīm*). Despite ʿAlī's testimony that he had already repaid four *riyāls* and sold the rug with her permission, the judge, noting that he lacked legal evidence of any payment or permission, ruled that he must pay his wife ten *riyāls* and the price of the rug, and return the seven cushions.[140] The woman's financial claims on her husband and her willingness to take him to court for default highlight the financial power she could wield in her relationship with her husband which could surely be used to safeguard her position within the marital family.

Emboldened by their familiarity with the law and their experience in business transactions of various kinds, Cairene women proved willing and able to further protect their position in the family by insisting, when necessary, on payment of material support owed them by their husbands. Fāṭimah, the *khātūn* (upper class title), brought one such case to court, testifying that:

> the above-named, her husband, the defendant, left her in his house on the Samakīn road in Ḥaṭṭ al-Salībah along with his second wife, his slave by the name of Nasrah, daughter of ʿAbd Allāh al-Sōdā [the Black], and fled at the time that the French "smiths" of infidel faith invaded Cairo, and he was absent from them for a period of one year and three months without giving legal support. And a few days after his flight, the aforementioned woman took her claim on the first day of Ṣafar 1214 to the *sharīʿah* court and asked for a decision in her favor for support from her aforementioned husband . . . and the court ruled that he should give her 30 *nisf fiḍḍah* each day . . . and she now claims the payment of support adjudged to her from him from the beginning of the above-mentioned month

> of Ṣafar to the end of the month of Rajab of the year noted below . . . that makes 293 Egyptian *riyāls* (calculating each *riyāl* as 90 *nisf fiḍḍah*) which she is entitled to in legal opinion.
>
> And the defendant, when asked for a response to the claim . . . said that before his flight he had buried in his house chests which contained a quantity of *dirhems*, jewels, and household goods which was shared by his legal wife and his slave . . . and an explanation was requested from the aforementioned woman and she recalled that a few days after the arrival of the French in Cairo she and the slave were dislodged from the aforementioned house . . . and she had not returned to the house since, and she was not cognizant of the fact that the chests were hidden there . . .
>
> and he [the defendant] must provide her [the plaintiff] the complete sum required for the stated support, and he is ordered to pay it to his aforementioned wife in its entirety . . . 6 Shaʿbān 1216.[141]

The weighty sum required by the decision and Fāṭimah's perseverance in collecting her due reveal a woman's ability to enforce her rights to support of considerable magnitude. The Cairo court records demonstrate that many women continued to press their claims to marital support (*nafaqah*), especially that owed by husbands in the wake of divorce.

Conclusion

The developed market economy of nineteenth century Egypt in which women participated as producers and traders lent women economic independence and habits of dealing with the world outside the household. By buying, selling, and offering their services in the market, women became well acquainted with currencies and principles of economic transactions; they also developed a sense of themselves as independent economic producers and amassers of small capital. Thus equipped, women could turn to the *sharīʿah* courts with some confidence to defend their property and inheritance rights. The simple existence of such rights did not, of course, insure that they would not be ignored or abrogated, but the higher sanction of the religious law and the presence of courts to enforce it were of critical importance. The law, while it did not legislate women's position within the family and society, provided legal rights and a context in which women could protest and struggle on their own behalf. As the law itself evolved in rhythm with social and economic developments, women, bringing their problems to court, were part of that evolution. Through the court records, we clearly witness the role women played in nearly all aspects of the Egyptian economy, from petty trade to *waqf* and *iltizām* administration.

Although women often pursued their trade or conducted their business as individuals, we also find them in family association, most commonly with their husbands. It was the small nuclear family, the husband and wife unit, that formed the basis for much business and property holding, not the larger extended family of received wisdom and inheritance law logic. Women did, by mid-century, appear to be diversifying their economic associations by joining with sisters, but their ties with their husbands remained strong and complex, bonding them through shared property, joint business ventures, and carefully recorded debts. We can be sure that the male temptation to exercise his legal and social prerogatives to mistreat or even dispense with his wife was tempered, in practice, by his keen awareness of her economic clout.

The major economic development of the nineteenth century affected women's activities in production, distribution, and services. The erosion of some branches of textile crafts and their replacement by indigenous factory production in the Muḥammad ʿAlī period and, later, by imports of European-made articles, displaced women crafts workers. Women were not then hired on an equal basis in workshops and industry: although the factories of Muḥammad ʿAlī utilized some family labor, all skilled work went to men. Later in the century, when modest industries were established to process the cotton crop, women were again confined to a few of the most menial and unskilled operations. Female petty traders, involved in an activity less subject to state regulation or competition from Europe, continued to sell their wares, particularly foodstuffs; the more affluent women merchants, however, shared the fate of their male counterparts and were gradually pushed aside by European companies and their local agents. Only in services, particularly services rendered to other women, did the opportunities for women clearly expand. Rapid urbanization in the second half of the century increased the demand for household maids and all matter of women who performed special services, such as seamstresses, hairdressers, tattooers, musicians, etc. As the female role in production in the urban economy contracted, service activities multiplied: by the end of the nineteenth century, working women were concentrated in this world of casual services and informal networks.

Chapter 3

Private and public life: women and the growth of the State

My lover and I are content, so why, judge, are you concerned?

Egyptian proverb (Taymūr, 556, p. 91)

What frees women is the distance of men.

Egyptian proverb (Taymūr, 728, p. 121)

The State in eighteenth century Egypt was centralized and fairly adept at collecting the agricultural surplus in the form of land taxes despite the bitter infighting of the beys and friction between Cairo and Istanbul. The ruling beys aspired to the relatively modest goals of protecting state revenues through the imposition of an order sufficiently strict to avoid a slide into anarchy; while parts of the countryside, particularly in Upper Egypt, did elude the control of the central government from time to time, Egypt overall exhibited a high degree of political unity in a period when regional trends had veered strongly toward decentralization and the emergence of many small power centers, such as in Syria, Palestine, and Iraq. That the State managed to retain control over most of its hinterland was due rather more to fortuitous geography – the Nile Valley forming a natural and eminently accessible political unit – than to secrets of statecraft. The State's activities stopped far short of active intervention into the lives of its subjects: as long as the land was cultivated and the taxes were paid, the organization and quality of life in the country lay outside the concern of the government.

One of the dramatic changes of the nineteenth century was the gradual emergence of a more active and interventionist State under Muḥammad ʿAlī and his successors. State regulation of production through introduction of new agricultural and trade policies had an unintended impact on the organization of social life: many of the systems undergirding social welfare – the mechanisms for provision of material support for those in need, care for the old and ill, and nurture and training of the young – depended on family arrangements and, particularly in urban areas, on voluntary corporative associations. As the State began to regulate agriculture, trade, and crafts production, and the pace of capitalist penetration quickened, both the family and corporative institutions were weakened without, necessarily, the concurrent development of substitute forms of social support. Over the course of the century, we see only a few

4 "Carette transportant des femmes arabes" (cart carrying Arab women), late nineteenth century

embryonic state social institutions evolving, primarily in response to a dire need for assistance which grew as traditional forms of mutual aid faltered. The emergence of a modern state formation invariably entailed the erosion of traditional corporative institutions; rarely, however, has it meant the total annihilation of these institutions which commonly survive, albeit in a changed or truncated form. The lives of all members of Egyptian society were touched by the extent to which groups and networks of regulation and support were dismantled by socio-economic developments, and whether the State did or did not step in to fill the breach.

Although all members of society were affected, women, holding primary and direct responsibility for the provision of food, shelter, and sustenance, felt the transformation deeply. As the old social bonds were loosened, many women found that the organizations and institutions which had absorbed the greater part of their energies and had given them, in return, critical assistance, were in a state of disarray: in their neighborhoods, trades, and religious groups, women faced the disruption, although not the dissolution, of intricate networks of exchange and support. Excluded from the institutions of male design, the world of women, even more than that of men, had been structured and undergirded by informal and "traditional" arrangements, and women, therefore, experienced these changes in a more immediate fashion.

In the following chapter, we sketch the traditional forms of social organization of family, quarter, guild, and religious group that prevailed among women at the beginning of the nineteenth century, and then explore the degree to which these institutions were modified or eliminated by nineteenth century developments. The role of the State, in the first instance, was limited to intervention in economic affairs which indirectly affected social organization. In the latter part of the century, however, the State took a more active interest in the living conditions of the population, especially in the fields of health and education. The erosion of former institutions and the rise of an interventionist State, however modest in its aims, was to prove a double-edged sword for women.

Women and "traditional" institutions

In the early nineteenth century, women's social existence, particularly in urban areas, was lived in and through a number of "traditional" institutions, the family being among the foremost. Neighbors, members of the same professions, ethnic groups, or religious orders were also organized in formal and informal groupings which cut across family lines. To the extent that women belonged to such communal organizations, and the organizations took upon themselves some tasks of economic and social regulation, the family monopoly over economic and social life was modified. Guilds might, in a limited fashion, interfere in the organization of labor; religious orders and charitable endowments (*waqfs*) might assume the burden of caring for the old and ill. While Cairo boasted numerous social institutions, however, the weakness of the state formation in the period preceding the rise of a strong bureaucratic State under Muḥammad ʿAlī set firm limits on such involvement in social affairs. Without systematic state intervention in the health, training, housing, and feeding of the population, the very partial and piecemeal services offered by charitable institutions and communal organizations left the family very much at the center of social life. Most of the present functions performed by the peasant family were likewise the province of the urban family: the regulation of sexuality, and provision of shelter, training, and nurture were not assumed in any thoroughgoing fashion by external institutions. Thus, while coherence of the family based on shared production was somewhat diminished in the city and alternative institutions concerned themselves with the well being of family members, the family still played a role as prime arbiter of social existence.

Any inroads on family control by the greater number of independent economic activities or membership in extrafamilial social organizations may have been counterbalanced by the stronger hold of ideological definitions of women and the family in the city. First, Cairo housed the religious establishment of the country which represented and interpreted dominant ideology. The *'ulamā'* (religious leaders) were by no means a monolithic group: they belonged to different schools of law and *ṣūfī* orders, and enjoyed close economic and social ties to diverse elements of the population. Nevertheless, their weight in the city undoubtedly heightened awareness of, and adherence to, a Muslim law and tradition less diluted by social practices than in the countryside. Regardless of the actual content of dominant ideology *vis-à-vis* women, the greater probability of conscious appeal to religious precepts could result in tighter social control, particularly within the family. Secondly, the size and diversity of the city could act to make such control a more crucial requirement of family life; contacts with strangers and associations that transcended family boundaries potentially imperiled the family's monopoly over regulation of its members' behavior. One possible response would be closer and more diligent attention to the task of social regulation, often at the expense of women. The ideology surrounding women's role in the family thus intersected with the scope and nature of their material production and their participation in cooperative groups to define their status and power in the city. Although the "domestic economy" resting on joint family production was weaker than in the rural areas, the family still remained a basic social and economic unit which both determined and reflected the position of women.

At the same time, women in Cairo were very much part of the institutions basic to early nineteenth century urban life. The social and economic existence of most Cairenes was organized around three overlapping institutions: quarters or districts (*ḥarah*, pl. *ḥarāt*), guilds (*ṭā'ifah*, pl. *ṭawā'if*), and *ṣūfī* brotherhoods (*ṭarīqah*, pl. *ṭuruq*). In 1800, the city was divided into 53 administrative districts, each headed by a *shaykh al-ḥarah* who exercised police powers in his district as a representative of the chief of police. Each *ḥarah* contained several alleyways (*durūb*) around which clustered buildings with shops and dwellings; the gate to the alleyway could be closed and locked at night.[1] Internal solidarity within the *ḥarah* undoubtedly arose more from shared use of space and the many economic bonds among the quarter's residents than from administrative definition. The records of property sales in Cairo courts always included specific information on rights of access to shared wells, gates, and courtyards that accompanied the purchase of a given shop or house. The specialization of quarters in certain crafts and trading activities meant that many neighbors were also bound by shared interests in the production, transport, or sale of particular items.

In these quarters, where family, social, and economic life revolved around clusters of houses, women were certainly active in the reciprocal arrangements and petty quarrels that marked the life of the neighborhood. In one court case from a popular peripheral quarter, al-ʿUtūf, lying to the northeast of the Azhar and Khan al-Khalīlī, we glimpse the sometimes turbulent relations among the women:

> five days previously, the aforementioned *sharīfah* Fāṭimah assailed the aforementioned *ḥurmah* Rabīʿah (represented by proxy), and she [Rabīʿah] had been carrying a child in her womb by her aforementioned husband for a period of two months, and she [Fāṭimah] struck her a fierce blow on her stomach with her hand, causing the blood to flow, and so she miscarried. And the aforementioned agent [Rabīʿah's husband] makes claims against her [Fāṭimah] for what befell her . . . And the aforementioned defendant [Fāṭimah] was asked for an explanation and she states that the minor daughter of the plaintiff by his aforementioned wife was playing with the minor son of the aforementioned defendant on the aforementioned date in the quarter known as al-ʿUtūf where they all live. And the daughter of the aforementioned woman assaulted the son of the aforementioned and struck him painfully, and so he went to his mother and complained to her. And then the aforementioned woman [Fāṭimah] left her house to investigate the assault on her son and she found the girl and her mother . . . and she argued with her and the aforementioned woman [Rabīʿah] assaulted the *shaīfah* Fāṭimah with insults and rebukes, and the argument and the fight intensified . . . and they decided that the aforementioned *sharīfah* Fāṭimah pay the honorable ʿAbd Allāh, the porter, compensation for the miscarriage and his rights and the rights of his wife . . . And so the agent received on behalf of his aforementioned wife from the honorable Hāj ʿAlī husband of the aforementioned woman [Fāṭimah] the amount specified to her, the agreed sum of reconciliation of two Egyptian *riyāls* in one payment which is equal to 181 *nisf fiḍḍah*, legally received in the aforementioned legal session . . . 12 Shaʿbān 1216.[2]

Rabīʿah and Fāṭimah's public brawling stands in striking contrast to the image of the sheltered urban woman barred from public space. Despite the negative character of the case, the quarrel illustrates the intensity of relationships in the quarter as well as the social intercourse of women in the neighborhood. Women, coming and going in the streets and alleyways near their homes, formed links and, as we have seen, engaged in volatile confrontations.

Many gainfully employed Cairenes also belonged to guilds organized around the production and trade of certain commodities or the provision of services which might overlap with quarter networks. The workshops, small stores, and houses crowding the heart of the medieval city lodged a largely Muslim population of Egyptian background who made a living from local trade and artisanal production. Raymond divided this population into two classes on the basis of income and activity. The wealthier group was composed of local traders, master craftsmen of the more prosperous guilds who owned workshops and stores, and *shaykhs* of many of the city's guilds. Although they did not amass the large fortunes of the commercial elite, some acquired the trappings of upper class life, including the possession of mamlukes and *iltizāms*. As employers of labor and owners of sizeable trading and industrial establishments, they formed a local bourgeoisie that lacked, however, the international connections and direct access to power of those in alliance with the beys. They are easily distinguished from most of their neighbors in the medieval quarter: artisans involved in the less prosperous trades, like food processing, textiles, and leather, or owners of small retail shops made up the vast majority of the population who both lived and worked in the area. The remainder of Cairo's active population was composed of those who lacked the ownership of any tools of production: itinerant sellers, water carriers, animal drivers, domestic servants, and day laborers of various kinds inhabited the peripheral areas of the city. Their life bore the stamp of the urban poor: basic food, shelter, and clothing with few luxuries.[3]

The importance of guild organization to many of these trades was clearly reflected in the numerical strength of the guilds: working with the definition of a guild as a "group of individuals exercising in one city the same professional activity under the authority of a *shaykh*," Raymond estimates that Cairene guilds numbered 230 to 240 at the turn of the century. He divides the French list of 193 guilds into 38.3 per cent artisanal guilds, 33.7 per cent commercial guilds, 20.2 per cent service guilds, and 5.7 per cent entertainment guilds.[4] The members of any one guild were usually found in a particular quarter of the city; if the same profession were exercised in different quarters, several guilds operated in the trade, although a few guilds did have members spread throughout the city. Most guilds displayed religious and ethnic homogeneity because occupations were monopolized by one group, or different ethnic groups were organized, with some exceptions, in different guilds.[5]

The guilds served as a social, economic, and administrative organization for much of the active population during Mamluke and Ottoman times, except for members of the higher bureaucracy, the army, and the *ʿulamāʾ*.[6] Government control of guild *shaykhs*, however, was probably stronger than the internal coherence of guild structure as early as the seventeenth century; by the late eighteenth century, the independence and social weight of guild traditions and structures were questionable in many cases. As relative decline in artisanal production and growth in the commercial sector swelled the numbers of employed in skilled and unskilled service occupations, neither the government nor the guilds provided adequate regulation and security for the working population. Many guild ceremonies and hierarchical ranking of membership had fallen into disuse and private protection societies appeared to assume some guild functions.[7] The very fluidity of the guild structure, yet to be well studied for the period, may have assured the survival of the institution during the nineteenth century; new crafts and occupations could develop, at least initially, outside the guild system without meeting guild resistance, or they could be organized within very loose putative guild corporations. The number of guilds decreased only slightly: in the 1870s, ʿAlī Mubārak listed 198 Cairene guilds, a decline of only some 30 to 40 over the turbulent course of the century.[8]

Aside from guilds of women prostitutes and singers and dancers, the eighteenth century sources fail to mention female corporations or women's participation in male corporations. The ceremonies of initiation that accompanied entrance into the more established guilds were apparently not open to women. A later nineteenth century list of "women's guilds" (*ṭa'ifāt al-ḥarīmāt*) cited by Baer, which included many of the common female occupations, probably merely recorded recognized women's professions. Many of the more frequently cited women's professions fell into the category of low-status occupations which were not organized into real guilds or guilds of valid pedigree. Although groups of entertainers, prostitutes, and beggars might march at the end of guild processions, they formed units drawn together for the purposes of taxation rather than actual corporations. Other trades which women commonly practiced, such as cooking and baking, were organized in guilds which lacked either the authority of a *shaykh* or a proper lineage.[9] Women's tenuous connection to the guilds may have arisen out of a combination of ideological bias which excluded women from corporative institutions, and the clustering of women in low-status service occupations. As the service trades, many of which were poorly remunerated and lacked the status associated with a long guild heritage, grew to embrace a greater proportion of the urban population in the nineteenth century, many women service workers found themselves outside the guild structure, organized in "guilds" which were primarily administrative structures rather than true corporative units.

The working world of women was not completely atomized. Within service occupations, the majority of women's social and business contacts among themselves were probably cultivated through informal associations unattached to the dominant male institutions. The fountains and markets of the quarter served as meeting places and frequent home visits allowed time for discussion of mutual interests. Business could also be conducted at the public bath, a social institution of great importance for women. Most contemporary accounts mention the numerous baths which served all classes of women with the exception of the most wealthy, who could afford a bath at home. The several hours needed for a thorough scrubbing, soaking, depilation, and a period of repose afforded ample time for visiting and conversation in a totally female environment.[10] Professional women bath attendants and female owners of some baths constituted a corps of female personnel who could function as a clearing house for information and contacts. Travellers' accounts and elite chronicles of male authorship cannot provide, of course, any window on the intricacies and purposes of bath visiting, but it figured prominently in the urban woman's activities and gave her both the opportunity and setting for discussion of marriage arrangements, business transactions, family disputes, and the numerous other arrangements undergirding social and economic life. The bath serves as an example of the sort of informal institution of the woman's world that existed parallel to, and in isolation from, the formal guild of masculine design.

Finally, for the middle class of merchants and artisans and the urban poor, the growth and increasing vitality of a number of *ṣūfī* brotherhoods supplemented guild organization. While the membership of some elite brotherhoods, most notably the Bakrīyah-Khalwatīyah and the Sadāt al-Wafa'īyah, was drawn largely from the upper class and wealthier merchants, other brotherhoods, many of which were based in Cairo, counted artisans and the urban poor among their followers.[11] Sometimes we find an overlap in membership and function between these brotherhoods and the guilds. The Bayyūmīyah order, for example, claimed the majority of water carriers among its adherents and even attempted, later in the nineteenth century, to appoint the *shaykh* of the water carriers' guild. The Rifa ʿīyyah order had acquired so many members from among the ranks of acrobats, jugglers, and snake charmers that Muḥammad ʿAlī charged the order with the usual guild function of collecting the head-tax (*firḍah*) from those engaged in such occupations.[12]

A substantial proportion of the non-elite segment of the urban population was drawn to the "popular" orders whose practices and doctrines often offended middle class sensibilities. Al-Jabārtī, representative of established religious opinion, railed against the "fallacious" orders and those "possessing unlawful instruments," probably in reference to the use of swords, snakes, broken glass, and various other props for self-flagellation or impressive physical feats. Such antagonism, which took more concrete form later in the century when many "popular" practices were outlawed, suggests a heightened division of orders along class lines. Although the *ṭarīqah* took its place, in some instances, among the institutions of elite culture, it also provided a forum for lower class cultural expression which could, under certain circumstances, take the form of outright opposition to theological trends championed by established *shaykhs* as well as the temporal power and influence of the upper levels of the religious hierarchy inside and outside the state administration.[13]

The activities of many of the orders were open to women. Lower class women, still engaged in contemporary times in many of the popular religious traditions such as cemetery visits and *dhikrs*, were very much part of the popular religious celebrations scorned by the elite.[14] In the circular of 1881 issued by the Shaykh al-Bakrī to the chiefs of the *ṭarīqahs*, the participation of women in the orders' ceremonies and processions appears to be a source of special irritation to the religious establishment. The circular instructs cemetery keepers to prohibit men and women from meeting in the cemetery during Friday visits and to fix separate hours for sexes. Furthermore, the orders are forbidden to beat drums at *dhikrs* when women are in attendance.[15] Women clearly participated alongside men in the rituals and practices of the *ṭarīqahs* so that we may assume that they partook, as well, of the social ties, benefits, and solidarity that accompanied *ṭarīqah* affiliation. Women were also enthusiastic participants in the *maulids*, or popular celebrations of a holy person's birthday; according to al-Jabārtī, during their occupation of Egypt the French actually encouraged *maulid* rituals in order to get women out of their houses and onto the streets where they could have access to them.[16]

Women also benefited from the varied services offered by the more staid religious establishment of the mosque and al-Azhar. Elite women received religious education and might study with the leading *ʿulamāʾ* of the day.[17] Although we lack information for the earlier part of the century, we know that many *kuttābs*, primary schools attached to mosques, were open to girls in the late nineteenth century, and nowhere is this held to be an innovation.[18] The social life of the neighborhood mosque was shared by men and women of all classes; even in the heartland of religious orthodoxy, women were not strangers to public religious life. As one observer noted after a visit to the al-Azhar mosque: "Contrary to the ideas commonly prevailing in Europe, a large portion of the votaries consisted of ladies, who were walking to and fro without the slightest restraints, conversing with each other, and mingling freely among the men."[19] Thus, although women's presence in various religious circles was not always greeted with enthusiasm or good grace, urban women continued to participate in social life of an ostensibly religious character.

Women did participate in traditional social groups based on ties of neighborhood, occupation, or religious practice, but at a level which generally reflected the male orientation of public society. While public contact, material support, and education, at least basic literacy skills, were made available to many urban women by institutions of local and traditional allegiance, the evidence suggests that on balance craft guilds and *ṣūfī* orders remained of marginal importance to most women. Female economic and social ties were more likely to be formed in the context of associations of female design – in the streets and around the fountains of the quarter, in the public baths, in the small fruit and vegetable markets dominated by women traders. Lacking the formal organization and official recognition accorded other institutions, women's associations of the nineteenth century have left only occasional traces; they enabled the urban woman, however, to play significant social and economic roles despite her exclusion from many male social institutions.

The growth of the State and traditional institutions

Women's participation in the urban social institutions of quarter, guild, *ṣūfī* order, and informal association was affected, to varying degrees, by the changes in women's economic roles and by independent developments within these institutions, many of which were subject to increases in state control. The reform of urban government and the physical renovation of Cairo seemed relatively low priorities during Muḥammad ʿAlī's reign; extensive city planning

Hausmann style emerged only in the second half of the century. Nevertheless, Muḥammad ʿAlī did tackle the issues of urban security, sanitation, and, to a limited extent, circulation. Private quarter guards were supplemented by military patrols, thereby transferring the traditional quarter responsibility for its own defense to the state apparatus. The urban police system was streamlined and centralized as the power of the chief of police (*zābit*) was consolidated and increased. In the 1830s, the government launched a sanitation campaign, imposing new regulations on householders, including the task of cleaning the streets and alleyways of the quarter. The following decade saw more direct interference in quarter life as the State required the opening of all streets by removing the platforms (*masṭabāt*) which extended from many shops into the roads and alleyways of the city. Some building regulations, designed to promote quasi-European architectural styles, trespassed on the territory of social *mores*: in the 1840s the government outlawed the use of carved wooden lattices covering windows (*mashrabīyah*), which had served to protect women of the household from the gaze of passers-by. Plans for the construction of two major thoroughfares, one of which would cut through the densely populated areas near the citadel, were drawn up and the work of razing begun.[20]

In the second half of the century, the pace of municipal reform quickened. Strongly influenced by European models of city planning as celebrated in the Paris Universal Exposition of 1867, and intent on showing the best possible face of Cairo to important European visitors expected for the formal opening of the Suez Canal in 1869, the Khedive Ismāʿīl embarked on an ambitious program of urban development in the late 1860s. Although the master plan for Cairo included renovation of the older sections of the city, actual work centered on the development of a modern European-style sector to the west of the old city. In the "traditional" quarters, plans for the penetration of the old city, patterned on Hausmann's approach to old Paris, envisioned a number of open squares (*maydāns*) and wide straight boulevards which would cut through the old *ḥarāt*. The plans soon hit multiple snags caused by the complexity of property arrangements and quarter relationships: difficulties in surveying holdings and settling on compensation slowed the work of acquisition and demolition. In the 1870s, the State managed to complete the building of two *maydāns* and two boulevards planned in Muḥammad ʿAlī's time, the only ones to be built in the old city during the entire nineteenth century. The Boulevard Muḥammad ʿAlī took a sizeable toll: its 2 kilometers required the demolition of 400 large houses, 300 smaller houses, mills, bakeries, baths, and several mosques.[21] It was, however, an exception: the juridical and customary ties which bound the neighbors of the quarter proved an effective barrier to further state intervention of the kind. Most of the government's efforts, under the Khedives of the 1860s and 1870s, and then under the British in the latter part of the century, were directed toward the establishment and development of the new section of the city to the west, different enough in style and function to suggest the emergence of a new and distinct city. The British continued to improve and enlarge the new city where they lived and worked, while the traditional city remained very much the same; municipal services, such as water, gas, and sanitation, were contracted out to private companies and made available only in the modern city of the west. Demographic explosion and the development of some official responsibility for services to the entire city were to come only in the twentieth century.[22]

However piecemeal and embryonic, many of these reforms suggest an attempt on the part of the State to assert its authority over the social life of the city. The novelty of the central power's involvement in municipal affairs should not be overplayed; in the seventeenth century, for example, the rulers of Egypt enlarged Cairo streets and oversaw whitewashing and restoration projects.[23] Starting with Muḥammad ʿAlī, security and sanitation were no longer left entirely to the devices of the quarter's inhabitants as in the eighteenth century, however, and street cleaning as well as plans for major new roads undoubtedly reflected the State's ambitions in the sphere of popular control: the unruly urban mobs which had filled the streets in the first two decades of the century were still a recent memory. On balance, the intervention of the State in the life of the older quarters remained modest, and not dissimilar to that of the seventeenth century, effectively limited to matters of security; neighborly ties still underlay most social organization.

Women still played a central role in neighborhood economic life. Even with a decline in crafts industry, women, buying and selling in the market, retained an active role in the family economic unit. Their trips to and from the quarter market continued to provide a context for substantial contact with neighbors and local tradespeople. Petty commercial exchanges exposed women not only to public view, but also to public altercations which could degenerate into minor street brawls. In one infamous incident at mid-century, reported by both the British and French consuls in Cairo, a woman "of the people" quarreled with a Greek grocer over a small debt; the argument climaxed in a chase through the quarter and a struggle during which the grocer boxed the woman on the ears. Summary justice was meted out swiftly and harshly, for the Greek was arrested, taken to the citadel, and condemned to 660 blows of the bastinado.[24]

The details of the case testify to the active public presence of the woman, and the willingness of the State to intervene with alacrity in social conflicts which threatened to disturb public order. Rather than allow the conflict to be resolved by the inhabitants of the quarter or the religious courts, the State stepped in as arbiter of conflict, dispensor of justice, and defender of the woman's honor. Although women were still active in the economic affairs of the neighborhood, state intervention in such a petty dispute does suggest that women's public role and the problems it produced were a matter for state concern and regulation. Official interference in neighborhood affairs, even on a restricted level and in response to a particular crisis, speaks to nascent state involvement in social regulation formerly reserved to families and corporative groups, as well as a subtle decline in quarter responsibility for the resolution of internal conflicts.

The impact of state policies on the guild structure was probably equally subtle. It has been argued that statist industrialization under Muḥammad ʿAlī entailed restrictions on some guilds and the outright suppression of others, thereby creating a new labor force largely free of corporative ties.[25] Although internal guild solidarity and traditions were certainly far from robust, the weakness of corporative structures predated the Muḥammad ʿAlī period. Most government enterprises, in any case, were established in new branches of production, especially military supplies, which interfered little with most crafts; the number of guild members drafted for government industry was probably too low, as well, to cause significant harm to an already weak guild structure. The notable exception lay in the policies surrounding textile crafts: here, as government monopolies took over the distribution of raw materials and the handling of the yarn and cloth at each stage of production, the corporative organizations of spinners and weavers tended to disappear.[26]

Although the recruitment of women into newly established textile industry, such as *ṭarbūsh* production, undoubtedly was facilitated by the absence of guild organization, it seems unlikely that guild decline *per se* had a dramatic effect on women's participation in craft industry in general. Many textile processes, like combing and spinning, which had employed women before the industrialization program, had not been under corporative organization in any case so that women continued their labors outside the guild system. It was the absolute decline in textile crafts, rather than any decline in the guild structure, that struck at female participation in the urban economy. Women continued, as we have seen, to practice various professions, especially in petty trade and food crafts, while their role in textile production shrank. Because women had never been fully integrated into the guilds, however, changes in the numbers or fortunes of these organizations had little real effect on the female role in the urban economy.

Increased state regulation of the *ṣūfī* brotherhoods (*ṭarīqas*) first emerged under the Muḥammad ʿAlī regime. A *firmān* issued in 1812 invested a new *shaykh al-sajjādah al-Bakrīyyah* and conferred extended powers on him: this *shaykh* now exercised authority over most of the orders in Egypt, including many which had not previously been subject to control by any central authority. The *firmān* did not have real effect, however, until the 1840s when governmental agencies became active in support of the *shaykh*'s expanded powers and the rival office of the *shaykh al-Azhar* was excluded from interference in the affairs of the orders. The State's interest in extending the *shaykh al-sajjādah*'s powers may well have been to weaken the power of the *ʿulamāʾ* as a whole by placing the "respectable" middle class Azhar-connected orders under the same authority as the popular orders they so despised, thereby depriving some of the Azhar *shaykhs* of their power base and exacerbating tensions and conflicts between the two groups. This administrative reform may, indeed, have helped to promote a division between the "orthodoxy" of the established Azhar scholars and the mysticism of the orders, an estrangement which was to grow over time into outright opposition and animosity between the two groups in the next generation.[27]

Tighter regulation may also have arisen in response to the State's concern with the insurrectionary flavor of some of the popular orders. An 1881 Circular, issued by the *shaykh al-sajjādah*, was a clear demonstration of the use of his administrative powers to forbid many of the popular practices which disquieted authorities. The various articles required the order to obtain permission from the *shaykh al-sajjādah* before holding fairs or ceremonies, forbade religious assemblies in public thoroughfares, and banned rowdiness, disorder, and unorthodox practices of all kinds.[28] The popular orders, after their involvement in political strife in the period preceding Muḥammad ʿAlī's consolidation of power, had been, it is argued, relatively quiescent in the first half of the nineteenth century: an orientation toward ecstacy and escape replaced the emphasis on social doctrine.[29] Nevertheless, the move to centralize control of the orders and the later ban on all activities which, when conditions were ripe, might provide a forum for popular dissent or revolt, suggests that the State did not overlook the dangers inherent in unbridled expressions of popular culture.

Part of the regulatory effort was directed at limiting the role of women in order ceremonies. The 1881 Circular, by forbidding the use of drums when women were present and insisting on sexual segregation during cemetery visits, underscored the State's role as enforcer of the dominant ideology defining women's position and relations between the sexes. The central authorities had assumed, to a certain extent, the previously self-appointed task of Azhar-connected *shaykhs* of policing popular religious culture and eliminating practices and traditions that came into conflict with upper class religious culture. The 1881 Circular, however, suggests that little progress had actually been made, and many of the more irritating practices, including the active participation of women, continued unabated. Indeed, the obvious presence of women in contemporary times at *sūfī dhikrs* demonstrates that women maintained their place in these practices, and attempts to limit their role in popular religious practice met, ultimately, with failure.

The nineteenth century State tampered with traditional forms of social organization only in a modest fashion. Most of the urban social institutions, particularly quarters and *sūfī* orders, were not amenable to state regulation: undergirded by law, custom, and a heritage of self-government, popular institutions proved relatively impervious to change through official will or edict. State intervention did not fundamentally alter women's participation in these institutions; certain economic developments – the erosion of textile crafts and some forms of trade, the expansion of the service sector – had a far greater impact than governmental decisions. The gradual expansion of state prerogatives played only a secondary role in the disruption of traditional arrangements.

Wary of entanglement in existing institutions, the nineteenth century State tended to develop its social programs through the establishment of new institutions rather than the reform of the old. Here, official plans and decisions shaped a set of embryonic social organizations which came to serve as the basis for many twentieth century institutions. As the nineteenth century State began to take an interest in the health and training of its population, for example, it developed limited medical and educational programs, thus intervening in areas traditionally reserved to the independent initiative of informal networks and religious institutions. Official attitudes toward women came directly into play: the extent to which the State allowed or encouraged female participation in these newly created sectors was to influence women's position in present, and future, institutions of official design.

Health care and the State

The State addressed the question of the health of its population early on in the nineteenth century. Shortages of labor and depopulation in the countryside called the attention of government officials to health problems, particularly those of epidemics and the consequently high infant mortality which so greatly affected population growth. The epidemic of bubonic plague which struck in 1835, for example, killed an estimated 150,000 people, of whom some half lived in Cairo.[30] Smallpox was thought to be responsible for the deaths of anywhere from one third to one half of all children under age five during the 1820s.[31] While smallpox was apparently brought under control in the late 1830s, minor outbreaks of plague recurred into the twentieth century: in 1907 and 1908, for instance, we find 2,764 recorded cases of plague.[32] Egypt was also a port of call for the cholera pandemics of the nineteenth century: in the 1883 cholera epidemic, 58,369 deaths were registered, although observers thought the actual number closer to 80,000 to 100,000; another epidemic in 1896, which affected some 703 villages, resulted in an official death toll of 18,105, also considered a substantial undercount.[33]

These peaks in Egypt's death rate were accompanied by a fairly constant high rate of infant mortality. While we lack reliable figures, observers in the nineteenth century generally agreed that throughout the greater part of the period, roughly half of Egyptian children did not survive age five. Indeed, as late as the year 1910, infant mortality in Cairo was estimated at 376 per thousand: over one third of those born were not to outlive childhood.[34] Children were particularly likely to die from cholera and were also susceptible to measles, diphtheria, and gastro-enteritis, all of which could prove fatal. One measles epidemic in Cairo in 1904 left 750 children dead; during the summer of 1909, the city's children were dying at the rate of 600 to 700 each week, probably primarily from dehydration caused by cholera and gastro-enteritis.[35]

Faced with such morbidity, not unusual in industrializing cities, the State in Egypt concerned itself, in the first instance, with the survival of its population. Under Muḥammad ʿAlī, efforts in the field of health focused on the arrest and prevention of fatal disease. Beginning in the 1830s, the government tackled the problems of sanitation in Cairo, cleaning streets, developing a trash disposal system, and filling in some of the stagnant ponds; visitors noted marked improvement in the hygienic conditions of the city.[36] It may well be, however, that these rather limited efforts marked the apogee of state involvement in the improvement of sanitary conditions during the nineteenth century. From 1850 to 1882, Egyptian rulers turned their attention almost exclusively to the building and improving of the new section of Cairo, while the older quarters, there as well as in Alexandria, were ignored. Studies of sanitary conditions in 1883 reflected this period of neglect: in Cairo, we find open sewers and contaminated drinking water; in Alexandria, canals into which refuse from tanneries and cemeteries drained were actually a source of drinking water. In both cities, stagnant ponds and poor drainage threatened the health of the population.[37]

Ten years later, the British occupation had not brought any improvement. Cromer himself was of the opinion that sanitary conditions in the country as a whole were little better than in 1883: the Nile and canals were polluted by drainage from residences, slaughterhouses, and tanneries; stagnant ponds still abounded; the absence of public latrines and sewers endangered public health. A deplorable situation but, Cromer intimated, an unavoidable one, for "sanitary reform is expensive."[38] Although an official Sanitary Department had been established, its budget was small: a plan to sanitate the city of Cairo requiring an expenditure of £E1.25 million in the mid-1890s had to be dropped for lack of funds.[39] The lack of state involvement in sanitation was a philosophical as well as financial matter: Cromer clearly thought that the burden of responsibility for the health and sanitation of the population should not be borne by the State. In this spirit, Sir Colin Moncrieff, head of the Public Works Ministry, reported that:

> The Public Works ministry has been for years trying to find capitalists willing to establish water-works in the native cities of Egypt, where the absence of good drinking water is a very fruitful source of disease. At last, in 1891, a beginning has been made. A contract has been entered on with a Water Company already established as Assiout for the creation of thirty taps in the streets, from which filtered water may be freely drawn for two hours each day.[40]

The problem of infant mortality was the object of slightly greater state solicitude in the course of the nineteenth century. In 1836, the government undertook a country-wide immunization program against smallpox, reaching both urban and rural areas through a network of locally recruited paramedical workers. The results were highly successful: smallpox, a major child killer, was virtually eliminated in Egypt.[41] As we have seen above, however, the lack of adequate sanitation and the persistence of epidemic and endemic disease in the nineteenth century brought little relief from high rates of infant mortality, a problem no doubt exacerbated by the economic crises of the latter part of the century which brought increased landlessness, urbanization, and poverty, all breeders of high mortality rates.

In the early 1900s, criticism of these rates focused the attention of British officials on the problem: the Consul-General's annual report began, in 1904, to include a separate section on infant mortality. State health initiatives were bound to be limited, however, as long as official policies laid the blame on the irresponsibility and ignorance of parents rather than the absence of public health initiatives and the chronic poverty of much of the population. In response to a report on increased infant mortality in Cairo in 1909, two years after he had left Egypt, Cromer offered his own analysis of the problem:

> I have no doubt that the real reason is that Egyptian mothers do not in the least understand how to look after their children. You are probably aware that infant mortality in England and Wales is about 132 per thousand births, but that the rate is much higher, going up to as much as 208 per thousand, in the manufacturing towns where women are largely employed in the factories. Moreover, it is rather a remarkable fact, which is not generally known, that when a strike takes place, and the women are therefore obliged to stay in their homes, the infant mortality at once decreases.[42]

The remedy lay, happily enough, in the sphere of private initiative: Cromer looked to the dispensaries established in Cairo and elsewhere by "charitable ladies" for instruction of Egyptians in the care of their children.[43] These views persisted after Cromer's departure. Discussion of infant mortality in 1909 focused on the need to educate mothers in habits of care and cleanliness and the "rational upbringing of children": the Lady Cromer Dispensaries and the Société protectrice de l'Enfance, established by princesses from the Khedivial family, were to launch the attack on infant mortality by providing instruction to the poor.[44] Only two years later, however, officials had apparently decided that more active measures were required: the 1911 Annual Report called for the training of village barbers and midwives in pharmacology so that they might provide initial treatment for sick children who lacked a doctor's services, programs strongly reminiscent of the Muḥammad ʿAlī period, and cited the role of poor village sanitation, particularly the presence of stagnant ponds, in infant mortality.[45]

In a variety of other ways, the Egyptian government in the early twentieth century began to take responsibility for the health of the population, very much as it had done in the time of Muḥammad ʿAlī. For British officials, programs of state-sponsored medicine marked a departure from past policy. Although the British had overseen the foundation of a Service Sanitaire shortly after the occupation began, its meager budget (some £E69,000 per year in the 1880s – less than the costs of a single hospital in London) circumscribed its activities. In response to the Egyptian army commander's request in 1886 that the government open a pharmacy in Aswān, where the army had found itself the sole source of medicines for the local population, the Inspector General of the Service Sanitaire replied that he had not the budget for free medicine, and, in any event, it was not his responsibility: "In no country in the world is such a task undertaken by the State: if people want doctors and medicine they must procure them themselves and pay for them."[46] True to form, during the next decade activity in the field of public health focused, in general, on the control of epidemic disease through the establishment of cordons sanitaires around affected towns and the quarantine of suspected carriers, particularly from the pilgrimage traffic.[47] While the State also undertook vaccination programs and attempted to systematize the collection of birth and death statistics, the extension of health services remained very limited.

By the early 1900s, faced with mortality rates suggesting a real crisis in public health, the government began to take a more active interest in the regulation of conditions directly deleterious to health. In 1904, for example, a new law gave the State powers to intervene in "établissements insalubres"; officials could now insist upon proper ventilation and sanitation in industrial enterprises. Similarly, the Pharmacy Law of the same year set up the first system to license pharmacists and inspect their shops.[48] The State also made forays into health extension services by recruiting village barbers into state service. The government under Muḥammad ʿAlī had used barbers to good effect in its vaccination programs, and the barbers had continued, throughout the nineteenth century, to perform vaccinations and minor operations, and pass information on births and deaths along to the central government. In 1908, the State began to pay one barber in each village a small salary in return for which he was asked to collect specific information of various diseases. In succeeding years, barbers were legally authorized, after passing an examination, to vaccinate, circumcize, and apply leeches, cups, and simple dressings. The one "sanitary" barber in each village was finally made an official representative of the Public Health Department (formerly the Service Sanitaire); he was instructed to insure that all children were vaccinated, examine the deceased, issue certificates of death and burial permits, and report any deaths from infectious disease and suspicious illness. The government sponsored programs, ranging from a three week series of lectures to three months of hospital training in first aid, to equip some of the barbers with semi-professional training. At the same time, the State encouraged local provincial councils to open dispensaries for children: in 1913, those run by local boards were functioning in Manṣūrah, Ṭanṭah, Zaqāzīq, Minūf, Benī Suef, Minyah, Asyūṭ and Fayyūm, with others planned for Gīzah and Damanhūr.[49]

We cannot be sure how many people were actually served by these programs, although the village barber system had the potential of bringing rudimentary health services to the majority of the population. The information we have concerning hospitals, however, suggests that health services continued to reach relatively few people. The State, in the person of its ruler, had funded and operated hospitals at least since the Mamluke period. When Muḥammad ʿAlī expanded the hospital system for soldiers and civilians alike, he followed a clear, if unstated, precedent of ruling class charity toward the poor and ill. This government hospital system, as distinct from hospitals operated by private benevolent or religious societies, continued to function throughout the nineteenth century. Its early promise under Muḥammad ʿAlī gave way to the grim reality of hospitals as unhygienic and understaffed dumping grounds for the indigent or outcast ill. By the 1880s, a visitor to Maḥallah al-Kūbrā could report: "the hospital so-called was one of the dirtiest filthiest buildings I have visited in Egypt or elsewhere. There were no patients. The native doctors at Mahalla confessed to never having visited a single poor patient – one reason for this being that the Fellaheen class prefer to die where attacked and never come to the hospitals."[50] In Manṣūrah, the same situation prevailed and no doctors saw, much less treated, patients. The women's ward in the hospital at Port Said housed six women in a room fit for two, probably all of whom were prostitutes: five of the six were suffering from venereal disease. Only the "poorest classes" allowed members of their families to be admitted to the "lunatic asylum," and everywhere most hospital personnel were illiterate and untrained.[51]

In the 1890s, the Public Health Department addressed these deficiencies by reequiping and enlarging some of the old hospitals, and building new ones. By 1908, there were 21 general hospitals in Egypt with a total of 2,153 beds; 33,241 patients were treated, more than double the number admitted in the year 1891 but still only 0.3 per cent of the population. Grave problems persisted: in 1906, for example, the Abbassīyah Asylum, with a capacity of 877 patients, housed over 1,000; the Foundling Hospital in Cairo lost 95 of the 112 babies it received that year – a hospital mortality rate of 85 per hundred. The Department ran these institutions on a shoestring: private donors and public subscription campaigns were needed to supplement the monies allocated by the government.[52]

Lack of hygiene and trained personnel made hospitals dangerous places for the ailing; popular resistance to this form of institutionalized medicine was based, at least in part, on realistic assessments of the patient's chances of survival in such an environment. Government officials realized that some of their policies had encouraged people to hide outbreaks of disease, for "To report a case means to have the Government agents down upon the village, whitewashing, disinfecting, and whisking away each patient to the dreaded hospital."[53] Fear of the hospital and the strong desire to keep ill family members at home could also lead, at times, to violence. Public health officials constantly asked for police protection, and a riot actually broke out in Miṣr al-Qadīmah in protest at disinfecting measures taken during the 1894–1897 cholera epidemic. After students at al-Azhar resisted attempts to disinfect their quarters during the same epidemic, and "rather roughly handled the Public Health people," the police charged the barricaded door to their lodgings and fired on stone-throwing students, killing one and wounding another.[54] During the 1900 outbreak of plague in Port Said, popular objection to the Health Department's insistence on hospitalizing and isolating patients led to "riotous conduct and a certain amount of damage being done to Government property, and in some cases even personal injury."[55] As long as state concern for the health of the population was expressed in extreme and dramatic measures taken to combat epidemic disease, government health institutions remained firmly associated, in the public mind, with the disastrous death toll and inadequate resources of periods of epidemic, and the heavy handed intervention of officials not present during more normal times.

As the primary nurturers and caretakers of ill family members, women as a group could be particularly affected by state intervention in health care. Outside of control of major epidemics, most state intervention was limited, however, to minor reforms of existing health institutions. A notable exception lay in repeated official attempts to control and professionalize the occupation of midwife, a central activity in the community life of women. In the early part of the century, Clot-Bey, a French doctor in Muḥammad ʿAlī's employ, was authorized to establish a midwifery school near the new medical school in Cairo. The first pupils, ten Abyssinian and Sudanese slaves, were later joined by up to a hundred Egyptian women, orphans and daughters of soldiers. The curriculum stressed basic literacy skills as well as minor surgery, the care of disease, and deliveries. Upon graduation after a four to six year program, many of these women went to staff official health services in Cairo, Alexandria, and other major towns.[56] As part of the State's effort to combat the plague in the 1840s, graduates of the school, members of the newly constituted health teams, were assigned to visit ill women and inspect the dead in Cairo and Alexandria.[57] The school continued to play a role in the governmental health system throughout the century: official midwives, graduated from the school, were responsible for inspecting the dead and disinfecting their homes during the 1883 epidemic. As of 1885, the State employed 139 nurses and midwives authorized to perform obstetrical services.[58]

In the 1880s, however, graduates of the school were losing some of their professional status. As the scope of training and professional title of *ḥakīmah* (woman doctor) implied, graduates were actually more like trained doctors, specializing in obstetrics and female diseases, but instructed in hygiene and minor surgery as well.[59] With the organization of the Sanitary Service in 1884, they were officially titled "sages-femmes" and confined to the practice of legitimate obstetrics. Being trained graduates, they were distinguished from the majority of midwives, labeled "accoucheuses" by the Sanitary Service, who lacked professional training altogether. While a sage-femme might be called upon to testify to the competence of a lay midwife or accoucheuse, her responsibility for general health care was curtailed and her status in the state health services had clearly been lowered.[60] The Midwifery School limped along under these conditions, surviving into the 1900s: in 1904, for example, the school graduated only five students.[61] As the duties and status of the graduate sage-femme became little different from those of the untrained village midwife, incentive to enter the school was lost.

Official concern with high infant mortality did focus attention on the training of midwives in the 1910s. Because Egyptian midwives' "complete want of knowledge of their trade" was held responsible, along with "the lamentable ignorance and carelessness of the mothers," for the high rates of mortality, the government encouraged a program designed to raise the skill levels of village midwives. Under the direction of the Central Ladies' Committee of Cairo, the older model of education, as embodied in the Midwifery School's broad curriculum, was abandoned in favor of a number of maternity schools in Cairo and provincial towns where midwives underwent a short period of training under "a qualified English matron." After returning to her village, each midwife was to be visited regularly by a staff member from the closest maternity school.[62] Insofar as the direction and staff of the system were almost exclusively European, the establishment of these schools signaled the complete domination of midwifery education by western models and personnel. The scope, however, was narrow: the majority of midwives practiced their trade without the benefit of attendance at one of the new schools. While official interest in the village midwife had thus led to some rudimentary training of traditional health workers, the new programs neither built on indigenous institutions nor penetrated the poor urban quarters and numerous villages of the countryside.

As the graduates of the *ḥakīmah* school gradually became identified as solely midwives, the country lacked facilities for the training of female doctors. In the 1880s, a substantial number of women doctors were still available for government service: medical teams sent out in the 1883 epidemic routinely included female doctors, and a list of Egyptian officials published in the 1880s named 43 women doctors out of a total of 142 physicians in state service.[63] While the Cairo government hospital undertook the training of Egyptian nurses in the 1890s to supplement the nursing staff, which was composed primarily of English nurses, little was done for the training of female doctors. Up to at least 1913, the School of Medicine in Cairo admitted men only, and British officials were slow to acknowledge the need to educate women in the medical profession.[64] Despite the fact that women had been trained and active in medical service in Egypt for the better part of the nineteenth century, Cromer, for example, could see little call for women doctors. He found complaints about quarantine practices, particularly the examination of women by male doctors, to be couched in "very exaggerated language," for "I am aware that in exceptional cases women like to be attended by female doctors, but I conceive that throughout the civilized world, attendance by medical men is still the rule."[65] And, indeed, with the downgrading of the Midwifery School and the restriction of medical education to men only, it became impossible for women to acquire medical education in Egypt outside the spheres of nursing and midwifery.

State intervention into health care in the first part of the century had involved the training of women as doctors and public health workers in order to help control the epidemic diseases which disrupted the country. Government officials held, and acted on, the belief that the female sector of the population could only be reached through the use of female personnel: women were trained and employed as health workers as part of a broader attempt by the State to control disease. British officials in the latter part of the century, however, while paying lip service to the need to reach the broadest section of the population possible, tended in practice to encourage the development of European-inspired health care systems which restricted women's roles and remained, in any case, chronically strapped for funds. The earlier emphasis on paramedical health care personnel did persist in the form of programs for the training of village barbers and midwives alongside the more predictable approach of constructing new hospitals and educating male doctors and female nurses. We see, however, a lack of integration of the "modern" medical institutions – hospitals staffed by trained professionals – and the traditional ones – village midwifery and family care. Women, and women's main health problems, were by and large left to the marginal sphere of the untrained paraprofessional and private charity.

Education and the State

The nineteenth century Egyptian State also took a direct, although sporadic, interest in the development of education. As part of the drive toward the building of a State and population strong enough to resist European encroachment, Muḥammad ʿAlī founded a number of schools modeled on the European system. The Council of Public Instruction, established in 1836, supervised 54 state-run primary and secondary schools throughout Egypt during the latter part of Muḥammad ʿAlī's reign. Not surprisingly, given the emphasis on reforms calculated to promote technological transformation, other new educational institutions focused on military, professional, and technical training geared to introduce European practices. Between 1824 and 1839, schools were established in the fields of military sciences, medicine and pharmacy, midwifery, veterinary medicine, applied chemistry, mines, civil administration and accounting, languages and translation, crafts, and technology. This new education system functioned alongside the older system of elementary schools attached to mosques (*kuttābs*), and the advanced religious and classical education offered by al-Azhar.[66]

Under Muḥammad ʿAlī's successors, the Khedives ʿAbbās and Saʿīd, the fortunes of the new educational system waned: ʿAbbās closed many of the schools but retained a Ministry of Public Instruction, while Saʿīd dismantled the Ministry but reopened a number of the schools. When Ismāʿīl came to power in 1863, the state-run school system consisted of one primary school, one secondary school, one military school, and one school of medicine, pharmacy, and midwifery in Cairo, in addition to a naval institution in Alexandria. In the early years of his reign, Ismāʿīl founded a number of new schools, including a primary, a preparatory, a military, a polytechnical, and a medical school, all located in ʿAbāssīyah. Later, he revived many of the professional schools originally established under Muḥammad ʿAlī, including schools of administration, languages, crafts, and teachers' training. As the fiscal crisis of the 1870s loomed ever larger, however, many of the state-run schools were closed down yet again.[67]

British rule did not bring revival. Indeed, during the first decade of British control, the Egyptian government almost completely neglected education. In 1892, the entire state-run school system consisted of 33 primary schools, 2 secondary schools, training schools for teachers and military and police officers, and schools of law, medicine, and engineering. The lion's share of schooling in the country, that provided by some 8,000 *kuttābs*, enjoyed neither state financing nor supervision. During the 1890s, the government did acquire jurisdiction from the *waqf* administration over some *kuttābs*, and developed a system of grants-in-aid in return for privileges of inspection over others. By 1900, however, only 483 or some 6 per cent of the existing *kuttābs* were under government inspection. In education, as elsewhere, British officials tended to denigrate the role of the State and place their hopes in private initiative: private societies to establish and run *kuttābs* and technical schools were lauded as the solution to educational problems.[68] The absence of a commitment, either moral or financial, to public education impeded the operation of the Department of Public Instruction whose advisor, Douglas Dunlop, was considered one of the more difficult of the Anglo-Egyptian officials. As described by one of his English colleagues: "He was an industrious organizer and a strict disciplinarian but he had little experience of the world at large, his outlook was limited and he had little sympathy with the Egyptians and their idiosyncracies while he never in his long service of some 30 years acquired even a rudimentary knowledge of the Arabic language."[69]

The personnel and policies of the Department of Public Instruction were soon singled out for criticism by Egyptian nationalists and their sympathizers among the British intelligentsia.[70] While attacks on British policy did help to bring incremental increases in the Department's budget and the expansion of the primary and secondary systems, educational policy continued to be shaped by a clear vision of the circumscribed role of the State. Cromer welcomed increased state expenditure on education, but earmarked it primarily for technical training; in general, he felt that liberal and higher education should be provided only on a fee for service basis. He endorsed the nationalist demand for an Egyptian university in terms which further underscored his vision of education as a pillar of the prevailing social order. He wished to see the university organized "in such a way as to attract the sons of wealthy Egyptians – now a rapidly increasing body – who will come to regard the time spent in study at the University as a necessary part of their intellectual equipment for life, in the same way as, in Europe, the training at the great Universities is regarded by the sons of the higher classes."[71] Such ideas limiting the scope of public education continued to predominate in official circles. By 1913, the Egyptian Ministry of Education directly administered only 198 schools: 142 *kuttābs*, 4 technical training schools, 2 normal schools, 34 primary schools, 6 secondary schools, and 10 technical and professional colleges; the majority of schools, particularly the *kuttābs* and primary schools, were run by provincial councils and private societies under Ministry inspection.[72] While the educational system continued to expand slowly, the official commitment to public instruction originally made in the early nineteenth century wavered.

The scope and quality of female education were greatly affected by shifts in government policy. In the traditional system, girls, particularly the daughters of literate parents, commonly studied with boys, at least until they reached age ten or twelve, in many of the *kuttābs* scattered throughout the country, or, if their parents could afford it, with private tutors at home.[73] Although boys were far more likely to be sent to the *kuttāb* for at least an elementary education, girls were not strangers to the system: we lack figures for the earlier period, but girls represented, in 1898, a little under 10 per cent of the students in th *kuttābs* under government inspection.[74] During the Muḥammad ʿAlī period, the cause of female education was publicly championed by an Azhar-educated *shaykh*, Rifaʿt Bey Rafīʿī, who accompanied the scholastic mission to France in 1826 as spiritual advisor. In his book *Kitāb al-murshid al-amīn fil-bināt wa al-banīn* (*Official Instruction for Girls and Boys*), he argued the case for equal education for women, citing numerous *ḥadīths* as evidence of the Prophet's approval.[75]

Debates over women's education continued to erupt from time to time in religious circles. As late as 1904, Rashīd Riḍā, one of the leading al-Azhar reformers, felt the need to address the basic issue of women's education in several of his *fatāwā* (legal opinions), also citing specific *ḥadīths* to counter religious attacks on the concept of female education.[76] The opposition remained a minority: throughout the nineteenth century, the attitude of official ʿulamāʾ was generally favorable to some form of education for women.

Most undoubtedly took their cue from a state power anxious to mobilize its population, female as well as male. Muḥammad ʿAlī's policies included, as we have seen, the training of women as doctors. In addition, he consciously encouraged the general education of women: the women of his *ḥarīm* were enlisted in his first experiment in female education, a palace school for girls where reading, writing, geography, and drawing were taught.[77] After the relative neglect of education under ʿAbbās and Saʿīd, Ismāʿīl renewed official encouragement of women's education by ordering the *waqf* administration to open a school for girls. A princess of the royal family founded another female institution for daughters of the elite, and yet a third school was in the planning stages when the government's fiscal crisis led to the closing of the *waqf* school and the conversion of the princess's into an institution for orphans and the indigent.[78] Official sponsorship of female education, like that of education in general, was stymied by lack of funds and, ultimately, power.

After the British occupation in 1882, state policy on female education was formulated in contradictory terms. When Anglo-Egyptian officials turned their attention to education in the second decade of rule, female training was the object of special solicitude: Cromer himself had tapped female education as particularly important as early as his Annual Report of 1891, and continued to press the case as central to his "civilizing mission": "I wish to state my very strong conviction, based on some thirty years of sympathetic intercourse with Orientals, that the East can never really advance unless some thorough – but, of course, gradual – change be made in the position of women. Education is, I need hardly say, only a part – albeit an important part – of the general question."[79] Achievements in this field remained a source of pride for Cromer and one of his strongest defenses against criticism from nationalist sympathizers. He claimed that they overlooked progress made in female education, which was one of his "own particular pet hobbies"; in the face of local lack of interest in educating women, Cromer had persisted in his goals so that "it is entirely due to my own initiative that a complete change had taken place."[80] In order to promote female attendance at government schools, a large number of students were indeed admitted free; by 1905, however, gratis education for girls had been almost entirely eliminated because it was no longer deemed necessary to attract students.[81] In brief, Cromer seemed satisfied if the desire for basic education of women appeared firmly implanted in the upper classes: female education was not necessarily aimed at increasing broad participation in economic and social life.

Indeed, the uses of female education gradually came to be defined in a restrictive fashion. Beyond the basic literacy skills which would help raise the marriage age and make women better mothers, Cromer's vision encompassed the training of "native governesses" to fill a growing demand.[82] As the number of schools and students increased in the first years of the twentieth century, the tracking of females into certain courses of study grew pronounced. The Ministry of Education began to convert some of the *kuttābs* under its control, most of which had been coeducational, into girls' schools: seventeen had been made into girls-only institutions by 1913. The *kuttāb* curriculum for girls now included needlework, elementary hygiene, child care, cookery, and laundry work, all "practical subjects" which "aim at preparing them for the duties of the home-life." Domestic science was also introduced into the two girls' primary schools under direct state administration; the Ministry of Education further guaranteed that provincial council and private schools would follow suit by instituting a special primary school certificate examination for girls which included "practical tests in cookery, laundry work, and needlework, as well as written tests in hygiene and housewifery." The Būlāq Normal School for training women teachers added a new section in domestic science, and another was planned for Alexandria.[83] It was female education of a very particular kind, oriented toward the role of wife, mother, and servant, not productive worker or professional.

The success of these official policies, measured in terms of the educational levels of women, is difficult to gauge. During the colonial period, responsibility for female education was transferred from family and religious establishments, where it went largely untabulated, to state auspices where successes were carefully recorded. Within the educational institutions supervised by the government, the focus of women's education did seem to bear fruit. At the most elementary level, the Department of Education commenced direct supervisions of 46 *kuttābs*, transferred from the *waqf* administration, in 1895: out of 2,307 students, 139, or 6 per cent, were girls. As the State slowly extended its control over a number of other *kuttābs* (142 by 1913), the proportion of female students tended to rise, reaching 24 per cent in 1903 and 37 per cent in 1913, when the numbers of students in government *kuttābs* had risen to 14,027. Many more *kuttābs* came under state inspection through the system of grants-in-aid. Increases in female students, however, were less dramatic: in 1903, the 2,623 *kuttābs* under inspection were educating 76,228 students, of whom 7 per cent were female. By 1913, the number of students, in state-inspected schools had grown to 229,156, but females still constituted under 10 per cent of the student body. The proportion of girls in all *kuttābs* under state control or inspection reached a high of 12 per cent in 1913.[84]

The State clearly made headway with elementary level female education, at least within its own system. Progress can be in part ascribed to an active program in government schools – the recruiting of women teachers and the establishment of special *kuttābs* for females opened places for girls at a time when many parents were seeking education for their children. Indeed, the challenge for the Egyptian school system in the 1900s and 1910s was not so much one of attracting girl students as of making room for them.[85] In the 1890s, the government had pursued specific policies designed to encourage female attendance in the elementary schools it inspected, such as doubling the per capita state subsidy for girls; by the 1900s, however, the State was more concerned with the type of education offered, and strove to develop basic literacy and domestic skills in girl students while guarding against too much education of an impractical nature which would divert them from "their natural avocation."[86] Opportunities for female elementary education undoubtedly expanded under British rule, but at a modest pace and a relatively simple level.

Sexual differentiation in education developed more blatantly at higher levels. The Department of Education operated, by 1913, 34 "higher primary" schools, the necessary stepping stone to higher education; they were sex-segregated, however, and only two, the Sanīyyah and the ʿAbbās schools in Cairo, admitted girls. Already by 1904, a critical shortage of places for potential female students had developed, a problem only partly solved by the establishment of coeducational and girls' primary schools under the auspices of provincial councils and other private groups. As of 1913, the combined total of students in government-directed or -inspected higher primary schools had reached 21,853, of whom some 2,600, or 12 per cent, were female. Girls who completed school and sat for the primary certificate examination formed a much lower percentage: in 1909, for example, the 4,750 examination candidates included only 40 girls. As in the government-controlled *kuttābs*, students were increasingly expected to pay tuition, effectively curtailing the attendance of all but the daughters of comfortable families. Yet despite the financial burden, the higher primary system continued to accommodate greater numbers of females; the same was not true for secondary schools: up to 1914, neither state-run, nor provincial council, nor private secondary schools admitted any girls at all.[87]

A similar form of exclusion arose in the embryonic system of technical education. By 1912, the three state-run industrial schools and the fifteen trades and agricultural schools under state inspection boasted all-male student bodies; women were not being trained in the new skills required by an increasingly mechanized and irrigated agricultural system and a nascent industry based on cotton. Even when the Asyūṭ Trades School sought to encourage "native crafts," some of which, like carpet hooking and rug weaving, had been commonly performed by women, it enlisted male students only. The Department of Technical Education did eventually turn its attention to female training, but tended to view it as appropriate only in limited fields. As of 1909:

> A school of practical housewifery has been instituted at Boulak, in addition to the trades school for boys. It will provide practical training for domestic service and for the duties of wife and mother, a matter of especial importance in Egypt, where among the poorer classes the laws of household economy and hygiene are unknown and infant mortality is very high.[88]

The State also encouraged the establishment of private and provincial council schools of "domestic economy" in Cairo, Beni-Suef, Damietta, and Gīzah which were oriented toward the training of servants. The only institution designed to train girls in an actual trade or craft was a dressmaking and needlework school in Cairo, privately founded but subsidized by the Technical Education Department as of 1913.[89] Far from opening new skills to women, technical education of girls up to 1914 actually restricted them to fields of personal service divorced from the realm of production, thereby reinforcing sexual divisions of labor.

The one female profession permitted, and indeed promoted, under the new state school system was that of *kuttāb* and higher primary school teachers. As Cromer saw it: "It is obvious that, in a country where custom demands the seclusion of women, schools for girls can enjoy no large measure of popularity or prosperity, nor can the growing practice of extending to girls the benefits of private tuition in their homes be carried on to any great extent, until women are trained for the profession of teaching."[90] The Sanīyyah school first opened a section for teacher training in 1900 with four students enrolled in a course designed to train them as primary school teachers. In the following years, the majority of girls who completed the higher primary curriculum entered the teachers' training program, and could be subsequently employed as teachers at the Sanīyyah and ʿAbbās schools, or even as headmistresses at private schools. Although the number of girls in teacher training at Sanīyyah had increased to 36 by 1912, the higher primary schools still suffered from a shortage of teachers, and Europeans tended to hold the better teaching positions. A normal school for training *kuttāb* teachers was also opened in Būlāq in 1903, complete with a model *kuttāb* for practical training. Within two years, the Būlāq school had graduated thirteen teachers, twelve of whom were immediately employed in state-run *kuttābs*. The opening of all-female *kuttābs* continued to heighten the demand for female teachers, and the Būlāq school steadily expanded, to 69 students by 1911. The provincial councils also founded training schools for *kuttāb* teachers, so that by 1913 some 308 girls were enrolled in courses of teacher training for the elementary or higher primary level.[91] The development of separate and special forms of education for women did help swell the ranks of female teachers who were deemed necessary to the system.

Preparatory education for other professions was not, however, generally made available to women. Although some families apparently wanted the higher primary schools to equip their daughters for other endeavors, the government curriculum remained firmly grounded in preparation for teachers' training college. The singular exception lay in the training of nurses and midwives. Admission criteria to the Nurses' and Midwives' School were upgraded in 1898 to require a primary certificate of candidates, and the school continued to produce trained personnel to staff the government's Sanitary Service. The number of students, however, remained small: by 1913, 45 women were enrolled. The Medical School, as well as the professional schools of agriculture, engineering, law, and veterinary sciences, on the other hand, did not admit women. When the first Egyptian university opened its doors in 1908, offering courses in Arabic literature, mathematics, physical science, Arab astronomy and science, English literature, French literature, and political economy, a special series of "Lectures for Ladies" was organized which women students could attend. While the sciences and Arabic literature courses for men were given in Arabic, all the Ladies' Lectures were offered only in French; the 35 Egyptians and 23 Europeans who attended in 1909 were enrolled in the university but confined in a female ghetto outside of the regular course of degree study. A handful of women students were sent abroad, primarily to England, for teachers' training; by 1913, five women participated in the Egyptian Educational Mission to Europe and another female was sent at her family's expense.[92]

Despite Cromer's claims, there is little evidence that British policies much advanced the cause of female education; on the contrary, the overall effect may have been to retard and siderail women's schooling. Progress in the field of literacy remained almost imperceptible: between 1907 and 1917, the female literacy rate rose from 1 to 2 per cent of the population, while the male rate rose from 13 to 15 per cent, rates not to be much improved until the 1930s. Such modest advances are understandable in light of the limitations of the educational system: in 1913, some 280,000 students were enrolled in public and private schools at all levels, just 2 per cent of a population of roughly 12,000,000.[93] Because of changes in the school system and the dearth of figures on school attendance or literacy from the earlier part of the century, we do not have figures for comparison, but it remains highly doubtful that the situation improved under colonial rule. Certainly, the education of women was not a novel idea: upper class women, as we have seen, had often received basic education in the past. Well placed ladies, such as ʿAishah Hānem Ismāʿīl and Sittī Rosa, published poetry, plays, and collections of folktales in the nineteenth century.[94] In addition, the emerging Egyptian State, particularly during the reigns of Muḥammad ʿAlī and Ismāʿīl, had undertaken women's education at public expense as part of its task. When British officials took the helm, they tended to reproduce, with variations, the educational system they knew at home, including an emphasis on private education, sexual segregation, and the tracking of girls into domestic labor, whether as unpaid wifes or paid servants. As such, their claims to the furthering of female education ring rather hollow.

Conclusion

The development of a powerful and centralized state apparatus in nineteenth century Egypt had only a limited impact on the traditional social institutions of family, quarter, guild, and order. While a certain number of official programs and edicts sought to reduce the authority of these institutions, the effect was minimal in lieu of the State actually assuming responsibility for the range of services and security provided by informal or voluntary associations. Most inroads made on the integrity and activities of "traditional" institutions can be attributed, primarily, to economic changes in which state formation and policies played only a marginal role. It was the process of integration of Egypt into a European economic system that weakened some guilds, especially those connected with textiles, and strained family and quarter organization by increasing landlessness and urbanization.

Indeed, the State, when confronted with the intricate organization, allegiances, customary and judicial supports, and array of services offered by traditional institutions, tampered little with them. Instead of attempting to penetrate existing institutions, the government turned its attention to the creation of new ones under its direct control: the modern city of Cairo, the public health care system, and the system of public education were all state initiatives that bypassed customary arrangements buttressed by kinship, neighborhood ties, or the religious establishment. While the city of Cairo represented a tangible and permanent official accomplishment, the health and education systems remained limited in scope and supplied services to only a small section of the population: the State lacked the power, resources, and will to take full control. Nevertheless, even limited state intervention in the spheres of health and education, for example, influenced the development of these services of such central importance to women.

The nineteenth century Egyptian State was two distinct state formations: the emerging absolutist State of Muḥammad ʿAlī and his successors, and the colonial State under informal, but very effective, British control after 1882. Prior to the British occupation, the Egyptian government was involved in a race against time and European encroachment. The policies of Muḥammad ʿAlī and Ismāʿīl encompassed the care and training of the population in order to strengthen and develop the country; by promoting health services and education, the absolutist State set out to involve the maximum number of its subjects in the country's revival. Customary sexual segregation in Egypt, at least in a number of traditional institutions, led officials to the conclusion that women must be enlisted in the new campaigns. They were educated, and trained as health care workers and doctors, so that they could minister to their sex. The absolutist State could also, in many of its practices, be blind to gender: women were drafted for corvée and factory labor, just as they were candidates for training as professionals. Here we see that sexual segregation could be a double-edged sword: while it closed certain areas to women it also drew them into a greater variety of pursuits.

The establishment of a State firmly ruled by colonial interests altered the *raison d'être* of the central power. The narrow goals of fiscal solvency and agricultural development represented a departure from former priorities. The State was now content to transfer responsibility for the care and training of the population to the uncertain sphere of private interests; the laissez-faire philosophy of statecraft held almost complete sway until the early 1900s, when a growing nationalist movement began to agitate, with at least some success, for government programs in health and education. The state initiatives that followed, however, tended to offer women minimal services and exclude them from higher education: training in modern professions, for example, was closed to women altogether.

British officials generally justified their policies toward women, or the lack of same, by citing Islamic opposition to women's entrance into the public sphere. The available evidence suggests, however, that women could and did enter public space freely as long as interaction with unrelated men was controlled. Nineteenth century *ʿulamāʾ* generally weighed in positively on the issue of female education, and the absolutist State developed its programs without encountering opposition on the woman question. Under the colonial State, the places in schools and training programs open to girls were actually oversubscribed. Colonial views were more likely influenced by the implicit model of the home country – British education was sex-segregated and women's professional opportunities were greatly circumscribed – coupled with the commitment to minimum state expenditure on social services.

Although the government finally turned its attention, at least in part, to social welfare in the early 1900s, and undertook the statistical surveying and recording of socio-economic conditions essential to the modern State, it did not attempt to recapture the momentum of state development in the precolonial period. When the absolutist State had attempted to mobilize its population, it had inadvertently promoted the training and education of women as well as men. The blocked development of the late nineteenth century, however, and colonial imposition of European models represented a break in Egyptian state formation which adversely affected women's educational and professional opportunities, and slowed the evolution of social institutions which would serve their needs.

Chapter 4

Women, resistance, and repression

Life is like a *ghāziyah*: she dances just briefly for each.

Egyptian proverb (Taymūr, 1244, p. 214)

She went forth to avenge her father but returned pregnant.

Egyptian proverb (Taymūr, 1281, p. 220)

The growth of the state apparatus in the nineteenth century, which encouraged and enabled the government to intervene on a modest scale in social institutions, also expanded the repressive means wielded by the State and its officials. Control of the population had long been a central concern of the prior Mamluke government: tranquil conditions were a prerequisite for the collection of tax revenues in the countryside. The aspirations of the developing absolutist State under Muḥammad ʿAlī, however, went beyond the mere preservation of public order to encompass the direct exploitation of its subjects in agricultural and industrial labor, as well as military service. Much heavier corvée demands, and the introduction of drafts for soldiers and laborers in state industry, invariably raised the level of state intervention in the countryside and prompted greater recourse to coercion as popular resistance grew. Government officials, present in greater numbers and employing heightened powers, formed an integral part of the new order: servants of the State collected taxes, corralled men and women for labor, drafted men for military service, and even issued directives about the cultivation and marketing of crops.

These novel interventions spawned revolt and resistance among Egypt's people. The more dramatic challenges to state power, urban unrest and peasant revolts, were mirrored during more "peaceful" times by countless individual acts of resistance which shaded into common crime. Under the reign of the absolutist state, such resistance took the form of protest against, or attacks on, local officials trespassing on territory customarily reserved for the family or community. After the introduction of colonial government in 1882, popular resistance to the State took on a distinctly anti-British tone, and protest could be aimed at any foreign presence, as well as at those closely associated with the state apparatus, regardless of nationality. In a large-scale peasant revolt, the political and class character of the event, even if couched in religious terms, is incontrovertible; more common, however, were a variety of acts which fused protest against the State with a desire for gain or revenge. Much of what British

5 "Fellaheen women carrying baskets of manure to be used as fuel," late nineteenth century

officials labeled "brigandage" or listed as simple rural crime can just as accurately be described as community or individual protest against the state power and the rural classes most closely associated with it.

The rise in unrest and acts of defiance, however categorized, helped promote, in turn, the further development of the means of state repression: the judiciary, the police, and the prison system all underwent considerable expansion in the course of the nineteenth century. Penal law, the enforcement of which had long been reserved to the state power, was codified, and methods of enforcement and punishment were systematized with the establishment of new courts operating with clearly defined jurisdictions and new rules of procedure. The local gendarmeries, village watchmen, and other guardians of public order were reformed and professionalized, and, in the later part of the century, penal institutions were expanded and new methods of "rehabilitation" introduced. In brief, the development of the State, in its absolutist and colonial forms, entailed confrontation between the newly empowered State and its subjects, and, consequently, a refining of the repressive arm of the state apparatus.

Did women experience these developments any differently from men? As members of society enjoying somewhat weaker rights and lower social status, women were potentially more vulnerable to oppression by state officials, particularly if they found themselves without family protection. On the other hand, menfolk more often represented the family in the public sphere and official exactions, as well as punishments, fell most directly on them. We can expect, therefore, to find men as the principal participants in acts of resistance to state power, be they mass uprisings or more subtle forms of sabotage or non-cooperation. The extent to which women also played a role in these events serves as a powerful reflection of their own vulnerability to state repression as well as the level of their access to the public sphere. It is important to note that women's individual defiance of law or custom, including such crimes as robbery, the abandonment of children, and prostitution, can be interpreted as a form of resistance in some cases and a badge of deprivation and despair in others. Some women's "crimes" were committed against the state power and others, perhaps the majority, were aimed at a source of oppression much closer to home, the family with its specific rules for women. As we shall see below, female criminality differed, in frequency and kind, from male: struggling against social handicaps in addition to state incursions, women reacted in ways which demonstrated their narrower sphere of activity and the boundaries of their social power, for many of their criminal acts were turned against themselves, not others.

Finally, the police, judiciary, and penal system tended to develop, over time, special ways of treating women. Particularly under the colonial State, European-inspired penal practices were introduced which made neat distinctions between male and female prisoners, segregating them and devising appropriate treatment for each group. Such differentiation not only clarified the attitudes toward women then prevailing among government officials, but also formed part of a larger pattern of institutional segregation by sex. Women were certainly involved in the acts of revolt, protest, and malaise common in the nineteenth century, but the degree and character of this involvement reflected, as we shall see below, their particular roles in the family and society as well as the attitudes of state officials toward them.

The growth of repression

During the Muḥammad ʿAlī period, the emerging absolutist State made new demands on its population in the form of drafts for corvée and military service. Confronted with the prospect of losing their men to state service, some families chose instead to flee. Syria was one refuge: groups of families fled across the desert to begin a new life as tillers in the region of Mount Lebanon. By 1830, an estimated 5,000 to 6,000 peasants from the province of al-Sharqīyah had moved to Syria where ʿAbd Allāh Pāshā of ʿAkkā granted them land and temporary tax exemptions. Muḥammad ʿAlī, concerned by the shortage of agricultural laborers, demanded their return in vain. Others swelled the populations of urban areas. Some 6,000 to 7,000 men, women, and children squatted in three- to four-foot-high mud huts on the outskirts of Alexandria, living off the sale of garden produce or casual labor. In Cairo, numerous peasant families eked out their precarious living by turning to domestic service or crafts. Flight to neighboring villages in order to escape tax payments and conscription was also common.[1]

Faced with depopulation of the rural areas, the State responded with draconian measures. In 1829, Muḥammad ʿAlī, noting that "some of the indolent *fallāḥīn* had left their villages, homeland and fields, and had taken up residence in Cairo and its environs, and were becoming beggars," instructed the *mudīr* (director) of the Diwān al-Khidīwī (Ministry of the Interior) to find the missing *fallāḥīn* and return them at once to their natal villages.[2] Peasant refugees in Cairo were seized and forcibly returned to their villages or taken in chains to work on state-controlled lands. In Alexandria, government troops encircled the peasant shantytown and herded its inhabitants onto boats which would transport them home. Blows from whips and sticks hastened the evacuation of men, women, children, and the aged.[3] The State also instructed the *ma'mūrs* (provincial officials) to "gather up the peasants who have fled with efficiency and dispatch, and return them to their place of origin . . . if this cannot be done [efficiently], then jail the children of the missing *fallāḥ* or those who are taking care of his property, until the *fallāḥ* returns."[4] At least one *ma'mūr* suggested, however, that the policy of taking peasant families hostage against the return of the missing member was counterproductive: the *fallāḥ* would only return and work well and willingly if his life were made more "comfortable."[5] Indeed, the measures taken to return peasants to the land, and specifically to their native villages, were not entirely successful. In 1845, the State was still sending government troops to round up peasants not in their place of origin. They were gathered together and marched with their families under military escort back to the village they had originally left.[6]

The perennial problem of peasant flight was exacerbated by the tendency of women and children to leave the village to follow drafted males. Weeping women and children would follow the recruiting party taking their men off to the army until they were forced to return to their villages.[7] The British consul commented on the response to recruitment: "Men are raised from villages by an arbitrary conscription which is extremely obnoxious to the feelings of the people; and always creates a momentary insurrection among female inhabitants when they are doomed to witness the affecting sight of their relatives carried off in irons."[8]

Whenever possible, as long as the man was not posted abroad, wives and children would follow the drafted male from garrison to garrison, and set up housekeeping in a shantytown nearby, to live as best as they could, sharing the soldier's ration. An estimated 22,000 women and children camped outside the Hankah garrison. The large numbers and wretched conditions of army, navy, and arsenal workers' families in Alexandria caused consternation as epidemics of plague swept the city in the late 1830s and early 1840s: some 30,000 women and children were living near the military barracks in tiny huts, cisterns, and catacombs where the plague was taking a heavy toll.[9] An assembly of military and health officials, meeting in 1844 to consider measures to combat the plague, raised the problem of military families: "it has been established that the vast majority of plague cases are found, this year, among the land and sea forces and the arsenal workers, and that it is possible to attribute these circumstances principally to their cohabitation with their families, lodged in the quarters, consisting of huts, which more than anywhere else are the principal seats of plague infection."[10] The assembly then recommended that all troops and workers be separated from their families for thirty days, and that the men, the families, and all their effects be sterilized in an effort to eliminate infection.

Some evidence exists that the State undertook to provide subsistence to military families. Bowring stated that the arsenal workers and their families received food rations but the actual wages of the men were very low and usually in arrears. Another report claimed that Muḥammad ʿAlī, recognizing that the ration and pay of the soldier could not stretch to feed his family, assigned every soldier's male children an equal ration, thereby covering the food needs of the entire family. In the late 1840s, some 14,000 male children were supposedly receiving these rations.[11] The State thought of providing shelter as well, but a project for the construction of housing for the families of sailors and arsenal workers in Alexandria was apparently never implemented.[12] Partial state accommodation to the presence of soldiers' families was discontinued under Ibrāhīm. In 1848, the families of 14,000 new conscripts were forbidden to follow their menfolk to camps and campaigns. In the following year, under ʿAbbās, the practice of providing rations for male children was abruptly terminated.[13] Despite such measures, the State was unable to keep soldiers' families in the countryside. Over ten years later, the Egyptian army retained its familial character:

When the soldiers are camped, a camp of women is established at some distance; when they are in the barracks, a village of women is constructed as quickly as the barracks of the men; finally in the cities, the families live in the houses closest to the barracks . . . always I have seen the women arrive at any destination at about the same time as the men.[14]

As meager as the family income might have been when it consisted solely of the soldier's wage and ration, troop movement abroad deprived these military families of support altogether. Some observers cite the presence of soldiers' families on campaigns abroad, even in Arabia and Greece, but it seems more likely that posting overseas meant leaving the family in Egypt. The family, already removed from the land and living near army camps and barracks, was suddenly bereft of all support. The wives might receive small sums from the State or directly from their husbands, but soldiers were paid little if at all. War widows continually crowded the doors of the War Ministry, asking for their absent husbands' pay. ʿAbbās' agreement to send 1,000 sailors to join the Turkish fleet in Istanbul caused alarm among navy families in Alexandria, who faced total impoverishment without the sailor's wage and ration. With the departure of the troops, women were thrown back on their own or their extended families' resources. Some were said to have turned to prostitution to feed their families.[15]

The demands made by the government on its population lightened considerably under the colonial State: curtailment of military aspirations and the greater rationalization of the state apparatus meant far fewer drafts of laborers and soldiers. The primary agent of dislocation in the countryside during the latter part of the nineteenth century was the process of land consolidation and the growing problem of peasant debt: peasant families were pushed off the land by the commercialization of agriculture. The absence of state intervention to establish credit facilities or otherwise halt foreclosure for debt, hardly surprising given the ties between the state power and landed interests, can be singled out as a cause of peasant migration. The era of active recruitment and harnessing of peasant labor to official ends, however, was past.

During the nineteenth century, an expanding state apparatus also made its presence known in the form of local officials whose power waxed with that of the central government. The *shaykh al-balad* (village head), formerly the *multazim*'s representative in the village, became a local government official under Muḥammad ʿAlī. While administrative reforms initially deprived the local *shaykhs* of much of their power, by mid-century their role in peasant recruitment and tax collection had raised their power over the villagers to heights unknown before.[16] They represented, on the local level, the newly acquired economic and political might of the central government. The despotic control they came to exercise over the peasantry extended beyond matters of taxes and the appropriation of labor to actual interference in peasant social regulation and land rights.

Women proved particularly vulnerable to a *shaykh al-balad*'s power and often complained to the courts of arbitrary confiscation of property or even coercion of person. In one case where the *shaykh al-balad* simply took a piece of *mīrī* land for his own use, the *muftī* insisted that the land be returned to the rightful cultivator. In cases where *shaykhs* wrested houses, trees, or goods from female owners, the court issued equally clear injunctions.[17] Elsewhere, the village *shaykh* took advantage of the fact that a young woman was working as a servant in his village, at some distance away from her own home and family, to marry her under duress to one of his slaves. The court ruled such a marriage legally defective, citing the use of force and the unsuitability of the match. Even when the woman was still within a family unit, a *shaykh* might force her male relatives to agree to a marriage, using beatings or imprisonment to secure their consent.[18] The court firmly opposed any such interference in family control of marriage arrangements, affirming the authority of the family's male *wālī* and the woman's right of refusal; at the same time, however, judges were usually careful to reaffirm the legitimacy of the political power.

While the authority of the *shaykhs* declined somewhat in the 1850s, they acquired expanded powers over the corvée and land taxation under Ismāʿīl, powers which enabled them to accumulate considerable land and retain their positions of dominance well into the twentieth century.[19] Although British officials feared, in the 1880s, that outlawing the rough justice of the *kurbāj*, usually administered by the *shaykhs*, might undermine their ability to police the village and preserve order, the *shaykhs* survived and soon found their power buttressed by the upgrading of the corps of village watchmen (*ghafīrs*) who functioned as local police. The erosion of the office, so often discussed by various concerned officials, was belied by the political importance of the village *shaykh* or *ʿumdah* up through the mid-twentieth century.[20]

The State, in both its absolutist and colonial forms, thus signaled its presence to the population. Corvée and military drafts during the first part of the century elicited the most dramatic and negative response, but the expansion of the state apparatus, particularly of its repressive arm, continued on a local level throughout the period. That people perceived the government as an oppressive power against which they needs must mobilize the resources at their command, was clearly demonstrated by the seeking of redress from the religious courts. As the State became a more rationalized and identifiable institution, the idea of pressing legal claims against it for its failure to recompense for services took form. The existence of the *sharīʿah* court system, associated as it was with the *ʿulamāʾ* whose allegiance to the new State was tenuous, and with the concept of social justice, was a logical forum for the presentation of grievances against the State. Widows or women whose husbands were absent went to the *sharīʿah* court to demand payment of their husbands' wages from the State.[21]

The appearance of these cases in 1830 coincides with the dramatic rise in military recruitment and corvée drafts that occurred between 1820 and 1830, but it is not satisfactorily explained solely by the increase in scope and intensity of the State's direct exploitation of its population. Injustice attributable to the central power was clearly no novelty, and Egyptians had raised complaints against administrative practices in the past. The institution of *maẓālim* tribunals had provided a place for the presentation of such grievances: these extraordinary courts enabled a wronged subject to present his or her case directly before the sovereign power or its representative.[22] Another practice which continued throughout the period was that of direct recourse to the offending Ministry or department: soldiers' wives reportedly thronged the entrance to the War Ministry in Cairo, waiting to present their petitions for their absent husbands' pay.[23] Presentation of such claims in the *sharī ʿah* courts, however, while it may have precedent in earlier judicial history, was revived or introduced in the 1820s. Such claims tell us much about popular perceptions of both the *maḥkamah* and the State, suggesting that women credited court decisions with efficacy as well as a certain freedom from state control, while they held the State accountable for the loss of their husbands' support or lives.

Popular revolt

Protest against the emerging state power was by no means limited to court petitions. Women as well as men participated in the rural revolts and urban uprisings endemic to the period of state consolidation. Throughout the nineteenth century, rebellions which challenged the authority of the central government had their roots, or at least found fertile ground, in the Egyptian countryside. Corvée labor, military levies, direct taxation, and the whimsical exercise of authority by government officials represented, at the local level, the growth and penetration of state power. In addition, in many of the other developments most resented by peasants and rural artisans alike, such as land loss and the erosion of textile crafts, the fine hand of the State and its rural class allies could be easily discerned; official means of coercion made possible consolidation of land and the creation of a wage labor force.

One response to state intervention in the countryside was revolt. Muḥammad ʿAlī's seizure of the grain crop in 1812 precipitated the first major revolt of this reign when the peasants in Upper Egypt rebelled and were violently suppressed.[24] In 1820–1821, some 40,000 peasants in the province of Qīnah rallied behind one Shaykh Aḥmad and established an independent government in the province until a military expedition crushed them two months later.[25] The most serious revolt of the era broke out in the same area of Upper Egypt in 1822–1823 under the leadership of another Shaykh Aḥmad, who called for the overthrow of Muḥammad ʿAlī. The rebellion extended from Isnā to Aswān, lasting for over six weeks. Many of the *fallāḥ* soldiers, sent to quell the revolt, deserted to the rebels so that the government had to use

Turkish and Bedouin troops to calm the area.[26] Whether this revolt focused primarily on grievances related to conscription and the corvée, or reflected opposition to broader shifts in political power at the expense of rural artisans, as has been convincingly argued, intervention by a rising state power had, in either event, bred rural discontent and outright rebellion.[27]

The following few years saw revolts in al-Minūfīyah and al-Sharqīyah; sporadic revolts against conscription policies continued throughout the 1830s.[28] Disorders stemming from resistance to conscription were reported in Upper Egypt in 1848, and the governor of the region, Salīm Pāshā, was assassinated, although it is not clear whether personal affairs or opposition to conscription and a "general hatred for his governorship" served as the motive.[29] In 1865, one Aḥmad al-Ṭayyib led yet another revolt in Qīnah which contested state power and the religious establishment which had increasingly come to serve it. He reportedly wanted to "divide all property equally and to kill all the Ulema and destroy all theological teaching by learned men and to preach a sort of revelation or interpretation of the Koran of his own."[30] Although the revolt apparently never progressed beyond the stage of mass gatherings and one ambush of a Greek boat on the Nile, the expanded power of the State allowed for immediate and brutal repression: some 1,600 to 2,000 men, women, and children were thought to have been killed in retribution by army troops.[31] Rural areas later supported the ʿUrābī revolt in 1881–1882 by attacking tax collectors and refusing to cooperate with the corvée. Public opinion in the provinces of Upper Egypt also applauded the revolt of the Mahdi in Sudan in the 1880s, and the Egyptian government could trust neither the local population nor native soldiers in its campaign against the Mahdist movement.[32]

Throughout this turbulent course of events, rural women made their presence felt. In disturbances in the province of al-Sharqīyah during the French occupation, a group of seventy men, women, and children, all "marauders," were captured and brought to jail in Cairo.[33] At times, the role of women seemed pivotal, as witnessed in Muḥammad ʿAlī's plans for the inhabitants of a village outside Cairo where he constructed a new palace. His scheme of moving the villagers from near the site to a new spot under the pretext of promoting their health and well being may have had quite different motivations: "By moving this village the Pasha will obtain another result which very probably contributes heavily to this decision: he moves away from his palace a swarm of women and children very disposed to revolt – *which I have already once witnessed* – and which, in certain circumstances, would form an obstacle to his secret plans."[34] During the repression of the 1865 revolt, officials held women as responsible as men, and stories of rape, massacre, and the ripping open of pregnant women's wombs by soldiers circulated in the area.[35] In the wake of the ʿUrābī revolt, women were jailed in prisons at Maḥallah al-Kūbrā and Ṭanṭah for "rioting" and "looting."[36]

Women also played a role in the urban uprisings of the time which brought the population into direct confrontation with its rulers. As part of their activities in the urban life of neighborhood and order, women became involved in the moments of urban revolt that accompanied the erosion of the old order and the establishment of the new State. While Egyptian cities, and particularly the administrative capital of Cairo, had long been under relatively firm control by the ruling group, economic crisis coupled with shifts in the balance of political forces could breed urban unrest and even rebellion. In the late eighteenth century, economic and political crisis greatly affected the life of the artisanal and working classes of Cairo. Poor harvests in the early 1790s brought famine and epidemics to the countryside, disrupting the supply of agricultural products to the city. High inflation in the post-1780 period hit hardest those on fixed wages, especially the humbler artisans and day laborers. Political anarchy wreaked havoc as warring Mamluke factions clashed repeatedly and increased their exactions. For the majority of the urban population, the standard of living declined as economic and social conditions fell to a level, according to Raymond, inferior to that of the seventeenth century.[37]

In a situation of crisis, lower classes took to the streets and the city witnessed a series of urban revolts beginning in the 1780s and lasting until Muḥammad ʿAlī was firmly ensconced as ruler. The guild organizations and *ṣūfī* orders associated with the poorer sections of the population took on a distinctly insurrectionary cast: the vegetable sellers' guild and the Bayyūmīyah order, for example, were implicated in demonstrations and street fighting against the beys and their retainers.[38] As in the countryside, protest was often couched in religious terms which helped established members of the *ʿulamā'*, upon occasion, to assume leadership roles and shape the course of popular political action. ʿUmar Makram, the *naqīb al-ashrāf* (official head of the group of descendants of the Prophet) played a signal part in Cairene resistance to the French occupation in 1798.[39] Forced to flee when the French consolidated control, he returned after their withdrawal, resumed his official position in 1802, and continued his career as a popular leader of urban revolt. During the disorders of 1804, when rival factions struggled for power in Cairo, the French consul, after musing about the difficulties of keeping an artisanal population under arms for any length of time, noted the surprisingly belligerent nature of Cairo's inhabitants: "The same enthusiasm reigns here as in France during the first moments of the revolution. Everyone buys arms, the children also follow the example of their elders . . . The population made reprisals today against the soldiers, every day there are some people killed. It is the Cheik-Sied-Omar-el-Makrem who directs everything."[40]

As the population battled Mamluke soldiers in Cairo, women played a role in street fighting by stoning soldiers from their perches on top of the barricades as the men attacked.[41] In a similar scene in Damanhūr in 1806, they joined with the other inhabitants of the town to resist the Mamluke attack led by Alfī Bey: "The inhabitants pushed their boldness to the point of making sorties on the Mamluke batteries. The women as well took part in the fight, and, in the evening, from atop the knolls which functioned as the ramparts of their town, they sang couplets which they had composed about the cowardice and effeminate conduct of Alfī."[42] Mamluke soldiers certainly regarded women as active members of the insurrectionary population: in Cairo, women on the street were stopped, stripped, and even killed during mop-up operations.[43]

The proclivities of lower class women for restiveness and revolt were recognized by state officials and could become a special source of concern. In 1840, when conflict with Istanbul loomed on the horizon, the police sent disguised agents into the city's quarters to arrest women who were spreading false information or agitating against the government.[44] Similarly, in 1863, a visit by the Ottoman Sultan to Egypt prompted the Khedive to take precautionary measures, which included ordering all women "of the lower orders" to stay indoors during his visit, for "Arab women are outspoken and might shout out their greivances."[45]

Although much of the street agitation and fighting was waged by the urban poor, more affluent women could also take public political action when their interests were threatened. Women were among those who demonstrated in Cairo in 1801 in front of the *wazīr*'s house against official changes in *iltizām* regulations.[46] It was also the women, not the men, of the bourgeois class of Cairo who publicly protested Muḥammad ʿAlī's abolition of the *iltizāms* and interference in *waqf* affairs in an 1814 demonstration: "[The women] repaired in large numbers to the mosque of al-Azhar, dislodged the students, and accused the Sheikh of pusillanimity and cowardice. Late in the evening, however, they were prevailed upon, by evasive promises, to return to their homes. This female tumult being regarded by the Kihaya Bey as the forerunner of a general insurrection, the Sheikhs, suspected of fomenting the disturbance, were convoked, and overawed by indistinct menaces."[47] Despite the assumption on the part of the male observer, and perhaps male officials alike, that the fine hand of the *ʿulamāʾ* pulled the strings of the demonstration, many of these women, as *multazims*, traders, and *waqf* administrators, had ample reasons of their own to protest against the new policies.

After the consolidation of the repressive apparatus of the absolutist State under Muḥammad ʿAlī and his successors put an end to large-scale urban uprisings, Cairo was to remain fairly quiet apart from the occasional quarter fracas. The urban population could still be mobilized at times of political crisis – the ʿUrābī revolt of 1881–1882 and the national revolution of 1919 brought large numbers of men and women into the streets – but the protracted struggles of the early nineteenth century which pitted urban masses against a ruling elite no longer occurred.[48] Opposition to the consolidation of rule in general tended to take place on an individual or family level, and increasingly assumed the character of passive resistance to official policies and personnel.

Local and individual resistance

Most popular opposition to the rising state power, other than mass rebellion, took one of two forms: individual protest against or evasion of official policies, and, in the later part of the century, attacks on soldiers and officials who represented the colonial government. Most of these activities were defined as crimes by the State, and were not differentiated from acts of aggression or hostility directed against neighbors or family members. As long as the target of an illegal act was an official policy, a state employee, or even someone closely associated with the central government in the eyes of the perpetrator, however, we can understand the logic and motivation of the crime only in the political context of popular resistance to growing state power.

The policies of military and corvée drafts of the Muḥammad ʿAlī period were one major object of resistance. By the 1830s, they were taking a heavy toll: critical drains of labor ruined crops and impoverished the countryside, leading to scenes of "frightening depopulation" and "great wretchedness."[49] Towns and industrial centers fared little better. Census data from the towns of Manṣūrah and Maḥallah showed a net loss of population as deaths greatly outstripped births. The people's fear of taxes and corvée recruitment based on population figures, which made them reluctant to register births, renders such data unreliable. Still, a European doctor in Maḥallah thought that some discrepancy between births and deaths existed, and attributed it "more to the want of men in the vigour of life than to any other general cause."[50] Women whose husbands were conscripted might watch them disappear without a trace. Some waited for a report of their husbands' deaths during military service, often many years in coming, before petitioning the court to declare their husbands legally dead so that they might remarry. The woman who stayed in her village for fifteen years until two men returned to inform her of her husband's death, and then asked the court if she could remarry, was but one case of many.[51]

Sometimes direct action was taken to evade the draft. In 1851, the heirs of one al-Sayyid ʿAmr ʿAmr from the village of Kafr Zein accused a man named Hawās of shooting and killing ʿAmr because he was a military recruiter. The heirs were unable to find witnesses willing to testify on their behalf, probably owing to peasant approval of Hawās' extralegal action, so that the village as a whole had to assume responsibility for the *diyah* (blood money).[52] The heirs of a woman from Qalyūb accused the local military recruiter of killing her after she refused to hand over her son for military service. The recruiter dragged her to his house and beat her to death in a vain attempt to learn her son's whereabouts.[53] Later, when draft levies grew less onerous, women still went to extraordinary lengths to protect their menfolk. In 1864, a woman from Luxor went to Qīnah to complain to the *mudīr* that her only son had been drafted while many others had bribed their way out; if the *mudīr* failed to help her, she intended to travel to Cairo and present her complaint in person to the Khedive.[54]

With the lessening of demand for soldiers under the colonial State and overall rationalization of the state apparatus, new rules and regulations alleviated some of the worst abuses of the draft system. A new draft law in 1901 exempted the families of evaders or deserters from punishment as had hitherto been the case: the village as a whole was now to be fined if the number of evaders exceeded a certain percentage of those called up, and the burden of punishment was to fall, whenever possible, on the evaders themselves. The system of exemptions was also expanded, so that by 1905 almost 40 per cent of the potential pool of draftees proved exempt: 16 per cent for family reasons, 11 per cent for physical defects, 2 per cent for religious study, and 9 per cent upon payment for an exemption fee.[55]

The system, developed under Muḥammad ʿAlī, of drafting people for labor in state industry, met similar forms of opposition. Some observers were impressed by the high level of skill and tractability of the new labor force. In one report cited by Hekekyan, a French visitor extolled the virtues of textile workers with barely disguised envy:

> I must admit that the worker, whom I consider in France to be one of the greatest obstacles to the prosperity of these establishments, amazed me when I found him so docile, hardworking, and sober; his skill attracted my attention and I observed that workers in spinning and carding do not yield their place in anything to the most skilled workers in Europe; in general, most are good, and one can find a good number with deep knowledge of spinning; I would say the same about the weavers who would make excellent cloth if they had good materials.[56]

A further and signal advantage of Egyptian labor, according to the same source, was its price: wages could be fixed at about one fifth of the going rate in Europe.

At the same time, however, protests, flight, and sabotage testified to generalized discontent and grievances over pay and conditions. With the government as employer, workers sometimes attempted to lodge their complaints with Muḥammad ʿAlī himself. Arsenal workers surrounded the Pāshā one day as he rode past the factory, seized hold of his horse's reins, and demanded their back pay.[57] Desertions were common as well: of 180 men employed in a rice mill in Lower Egypt, 70 sneaked away at one time to work on their own land.[58] Several factories were burnt to the ground in fires of suspicious origin, and Hekekyan, one of Muḥammad ʿAlī's advisors, felt it necessary to dismiss all impressed skilled laborers from one factory because of the high incidence of sabotage.[59]

As in the case of military recruitment, opposition to impressment undoubtedly helped lead to the eventual demise of state industry. Such worker sabotage and flight not only spoke to distaste for the hours and discipline of factory labor, but also underlined the basic contradictions in the policies of recruitment and organization of the work force. The new workers had been removed from their land and their shops, and thus from the source of their livelihood, yet wages in the factories did not adequately compensate for this loss. Whereas occasional wage labor formerly had supplemented the family income, now the impressed wage laborer was removed from family production and received sub-subsistence pay. Family support, as well as the partial support of the worker, devolved on family members who had escaped the recruitment net. Such evidence suggests, however, that military, corvée, and industrial recruitment weakened family resources to such an extent that the State was actually devouring its population in the first half of the nineteenth century before the various draft and corvée systems were rationalized. Later, we still find evidence of occasional evasion of military or corvée service, such as complaints from large landholders that their *fallāḥ* work force ran away when called up for corvée duty, but the levies were far smaller and less burdensome.[60]

As we have seen above, peasants also resisted, when possible, the interventions and bullying of local officials. Never enthusiastic tax-payers, the rural population took advantage of any lull in state control to withhold payment. In 1849, for example, after the Khedive ʿAbbās revoked many of the land grants whose beneficiaries had been responsible for tax collection, army units had to be sent to many parts of the country to insist that the peasants pay up.[61] The *shaykh al-balad* or *ʿumdah* also faced opposition from his village flock. The numerous complaints made in village courts against shaykhly high-handedness reappear throughout the century, although they were generally brought to the newly constituted civil courts under the authority of the central government in the second half of the century. In the year 1901, for instance, some 3,427 *ʿumdahs* held office in Egypt; 592, or a full 17 per cent of them, were accused of some kind of wrongdoing, although only 60 were ultimately convicted.[62] In the litigious climate of nineteenth century Egypt, personal opposition to, or complaints about, state officials constituted an important part of the court's business.

The British occupation focused attention on the new rulers, embodied on an immediate and local level in the person of the British soldier. During the 1880s, before the Egyptian army had been reconstructed under the aegis of the new government, British troops were stationed throughout the country. When circumstances permitted, the local population were known to harass individual soldiers. In 1884, for example, two "donkey boys" beat an English soldier with their sticks in Cairo one evening; the Egyptian police, summoned to the scene by a Janissary in the employ of a British consul, intervened only with palpable reluctance and tried to discourage witnesses from testifying against the boys, all of which prompted the British consul Borg to remark: "I have been able, moreover, of late, to convince myself that a feeling of undisguised hostility towards us exists among the lower classes, which feeling is cordially shared by the men who are supposed to maintain order."[63] British soldiers complained that groups threw clods of earth at the trains or boats in which they travelled, and shouted insults from afar.[64] After two British officers, hunting near a village in Gīzah, shot, presumably by accident, a passing Bedouin, a fight broke out in which a member of the Bedouin's party was killed by the officers. They were then taken to the village and "roughed up" by the Bedouin and the *fallāḥīn*; one officer reported that "women threw dirty water, which smelt of urine, over his face." Official concern over such incidents was reflected in the severity of punishment for what amounted to manhandling of those responsible for a death: lashes and imprisonment were prescribed for seven of the Bedouin and six peasants, some of whom were tribal or village leaders punished for failure to halt the proceedings.[65]

Women as well as men were accused of many petty offenses against the army of occupation. Out of a total of 108 "crimes" (felonies) committed against British soldiers and heard in the Native Courts between April 1885 and February 1886, twelve involved women who had stolen small amounts of money from individual soldiers. In some cases, such as that of "Zemzem, daughter of Hassan," a "woman of ill repute" who stole 2s 6d from a soldier, we can assume that the proximate and predatory nature of prostitution played a role. The other eleven women are not identified as prostitutes, however, and in at least one case, that of a woman named Zaynab, the perpetrator and two male accomplices had ambushed and robbed a soldier. For such thefts, women found guilty were sentenced to anywhere from ten days to one month in jail. The thirty "contraventions" (misdemeanors) recorded for the same period included five cases of women using provocative or indecent language with soldiers. Although the charges are worded in ways which might include sexual proposition, it seems far more likely that soldiers would report and take action against hostile and insulting behavior; indeed, in one case, five women were accused as a group of "provocation in addressing an English soldier." Given the established reputation of Egyptian women in the realm of public taunt, we can assume that most of these women were verbally abusing the soldiers, an act of aggression for which they were usually fined 5 piasters each and court costs. Such infractions were peculiar to females; men were generally accused of refusing to transport soldiers or perform other services rather than of insult.[66]

Crime

Acts of resistance to the State or occupying forces are not always distinguished, and certainly not by the State itself, from common crime. Although we lack statistics from the earlier part of the century, there is little evidence of excessive concern about common crime or insecurity in the country until the 1880s. In 1884, however, special "Brigandage Commissions" were established to deal with a perceived rural crime wave of robbery and murder, perpetrated at least upon occasion by organized bands. Whatever the effects of the extensive but temporary repressive powers wielded by the Brigandage Commissions, to which we shall return later, by the early twentieth century official statistics began once again to register alarming increases in crime. According to the Annual Reports of the Consul-General, between 1900 and 1905 for instance, the number of "crimes" or felonies, a category which included murder, robbery, destruction of crops, poisoning of cattle, arson, rape and indecent assault, rose from 1,290 to 3,011; by 1913, 4,096 such crimes were recorded. While the number of such offenses relative to a population of some 10,000,000 to 12,000,000 remained modest, an upsurge in murder, robbery, and especially the typically rural crime of arson is well documented.

To what was this increase in criminality attributed? British officials argued that it was, in part, exaggerated: improvement in the collection of statistics had inflated the increase in crimes. Still, problems relating to security were generally acknowledged to have multiplied, and various explanations were offered. Analysts often cast formal blame on the judicial system, citing excessive leniency and lack of sufficiently deterring punishment. According to Cromer, crime increases sprang primarily from the fact that "the law does not inspire sufficient terror to evil-doers," a regrettable but unavoidable consequence of the abolition of torture and the *kurbāj* under British rule, the price of bringing an end to arbitrary government.[67] When extraordinary measures against crime were allowed to be taken, such as the summary justice of the Brigandage Commissions in the 1880s or the Law of Relegation in 1909 which exiled "dangerous characters" to the Khargah Oasis before they could commit a crime, officials claimed immediate and salutary effects.[68] In addition to the insufficiency of means of repression, the lack of full cooperation from the local population was also cited. A general reluctance among people to report crimes or act as witnesses at trials impeded state prosecution and allowed criminals to escape punishment. Cromer and his successor Gorst attributed such reticence to a culture gap: "natives" did not understand the concept of "public duty," and the mores of the "oriental community" militated against their participation in the formal judicial process.[69] The fact that Egyptians had been willingly participating in the *sharī'ah* court system for many generations went unexplained.

Problems in procedure and punishment gave free rein, in Cromer's view, to a natural proclivity for crime found among Egyptians: "The people insist on fighting out their feuds and grievances among themselves and slay and rob each other with deplorable freedom."[70] Crime was being further encouraged, interestingly enough, by the growing prosperity of the country. As large numbers of Egyptians "tasted the enjoyment of wealth," they aspired to further enrichment, competed amongst themselves, clashed over land or other business, and then turned to crime to settle the score. Beset by envy of another's material success, an Egyptian peasant: "with the foreknowledge that, under existing institutions, he cannot be punished unless his guilt is proved and, further, that proof will be difficult to obtain, his wayward character and undisciplined mind at once turn to thoughts of vengeance. He then either tears up his rival's crops, or buys some paraffin oil and sets fire to his water-wheel."[71] The upsurge in crime, according to Cromer, could thus be traced to internecine squabbling among the peasant class.

Although he supported his analysis by arguing that most crime occurred in districts where small peasant proprietors, not large landholders, predominated, other pieces of evidence suggest that impoverishment and peasant resistance to landed interests underlay many of the attacks on people and property. The brigandage of the 1880s was most commonly attributed to want, which drove groups of men to robbery of the well-to-do.[72] Wealthy merchants and landholders often made requests for protection from hostile *fallāḥīn* prone to harassment and sabotage. After the repression of the ʿUrābī revolt, its leader remained a folk hero for many: four European merchants residing in the Egyptian countryside described how they had been "surrounded by a wild crowd of fellaheen, some of them armed with naboots . . . [who] had the impudence to say that Arabi has dishonoured their mothers and that these fellaheen, his faithful followers, will shortly dishonour their sisters." Such incidents, they complained, had become common occurrences in their district.[73] Foreign land purchase could also galvanize resistance among villagers. In 1898, after the firm of John Lagonico bought an extensive piece of land in the province of al-Gharbīyah over local protest, the company's workers became the object of a systematic campaign of harassment waged by neighboring peasants who prevented them from opening canals and even, at one point, launched a coordinated attack of 300 strong.[74]

Pressure on the land and the problems of debt endemic to the late 1800s and early 1900s undoubtedly exacerbated conflict among peasants as well. Quarrels over access to land, water, and irrigation devices were sure to grow in number and severity when destitution threatened, and such quarrels did lead, upon occasion, to assaults on the property or person of one's fellow peasant. In general, the crimes of the period, regardless of who was the victim, owed much to the generalized demoralization and dislocation of rural areas bred by economic insecurity and land loss. The impact of this crime on rural consciousness must have been striking. As late as 1867, Lady Duff Gordon could report that a single murder in the Luxor region, the first in the district in eight years, had "generated excessive horror and consternation."[75] While the 869 murders committed nationwide in the peak year of 1909 may not strike modern sensibilities as so alarming, they represented a doubling of the murder rate since the early 1890s.

How did the rise in crime affect women? While lacking complete statistics broken down by the sex of perpetrator and victim, we can still draw some conclusions about the scope and type of crimes committed by and against women. Women were far more likely to be victimized by, than to commit, violent crimes. In a series of 134 claims for compensation for murder or injury referred to the *muftī* between 1848 and 1882, women appeared in only eighteen cases, fourteen times as victim and four times as assailant.[76] The victims of male assailants, thirteen of whom were killed and one who miscarried after being hit, had been attacked with clubs or hoes, strangled, or, in one late case, shot. Nine had been the victims of men unrelated to them, often thieves or unknown assailants, except in the case of one woman who intervened in a fight among five men and was accidentally hit by a club. The other five victims had been murdered by male relatives: one by her brother because she was pregnant, two by their husbands for unspecified reasons, and two by nephews and grand-nephews in circumstances which suggest that gain was the motive. Women might be murdered in the course of the thefts and quarrels of village life, but they were vulnerable as well to attacks from family members for reasons of honor, greed, or simple anger. Many murders of women by family members probably went unrecorded, since the *sharīʿah* courts only heard claims for compensation which would neither be requested nor awarded in cases where the woman had transgressed sexual mores. The man who killed his pregnant sister by beating her to death with a club (*nabūt*) was exempted from paying any compensation (*qiṣaāṣ*), although some form of expiation (*kafārah*) was required.[77]

As crime in general rose, we can safely assume that the number of women victims increased also. In the southern provinces of Asyūṭ, al-Gharbīyah, Minyā, Buhayrah, Minūfīyah, Fayyūm, Gīzah, and Banī-Suwayf, 101 of the 447 murders committed in 1912 involved "questions of women," and females usually bore the brunt of punishment for sexual misbehavior. Furthermore, attempts to murder women often ended in success: while the numbers of "murders" and "attempted murders" were roughly equal in other categories of motive such as feuds, robberies, and quarrels, in the case of "women," unsuccessful attempts amounted to only a third of the actual killings.[78]

Women, on the other hand, did not often resort to murder. The four female assailants in al-Mahdī's *fatāwā* all inflicted injury, not death. In three cases, their victims were other women, two of whom miscarried and one of whom was blinded as the result of fights; the fourth victim, a male, claimed that a woman intervened in a quarrel between him and another man, and struck him on the mouth, knocking his teeth out.[79] In no case was it reported that women used weapons or were attempting to commit murder. Data on prisoners in the later part of the century, who had been or were being tried in the newly established civil courts of the village police or district, confirm the pattern of female criminality. Women prisoners, accused or convicted of felonies and misdemeanors, constituted a fairly constant 2 or 3 per cent of the prison population, surprisingly low when compared to the 20 per cent of nineteenth century England.[80] Furthermore, the prisoners included prostitutes who had fallen on the wrong side of local authorities, and women accused of various misdemeanors, including petty theft. Women's response to the turbulence and hard times of the period did not, apparently, often include recourse to crime; the endurance of family structure and the honoring of central obligations of material support to womenfolk may have acted to discourage it.

The signal exception to women's adherence to the dictates of law and custom lay in the practice of prostitution, which invariably flourished in hard times. Although legal, strictly speaking, in the nineteenth century, the trade of prostitution was held to be so contrary to normal and accepted behavior as to render it criminal in the eyes of society. Women who plied the trades of public entertainment and prostitution inhabited a world where the bonds of family and custom were loosened; their distinctive occupations colored their status and made family life and connections a very secondary consideration. This world remains veiled in obscurity, for the stigma attached to such activities militated against official recognition of these women in the court records or elsewhere. Information on the organization of occupations acknowledged as "shameful" is thus sparse, and we are thrown back upon the observations of European travellers whose fascination with the exotic and sensual produced detailed descriptions of the activities of this class of women. However unreliable much of this material may be, tinged as it was by prevailing notions about the exotic East and sifted through male imaginings, some of the stories and encounters do help to clarify the various categories of these professions and changes in status and definition that may have occurred over time.

Women who performed in public places or in front of men were exposed to social opprobrium and heavy taxation by the State. They danced at festivals and in front of houses to mark special events, or they could be hired to entertain at private parties attended exclusively by men. Lane asserted, without much support, that the title *ghazīyah*, used in a generic sense to mean public dancer, actually referred to a common origin, shared by many of these women, in the Ghawāzī tribe.[81] Most observers agreed that at least some of the dancers were prostitutes as well, although others seemed to function as the *ʿawālim* of the poor, performing songs and dances in the more popular quarters.[82] In Cairo, from the sixteenth century, public dancers, both male and female, were under the fiscal control of a tax farm, the *muqāṭaʿah* of the *khurdah*, along with others involved in entertainment such as snake charmers, jugglers, and hashish sellers. In the early nineteenth century, the entertainment trades were still being taxed by the State.[83] Although groups of public dancers marched in guild processions, there is little to suggest that the dancers' guild amounted to anything more than a government-controlled administrative unit, constituted to the sole end of collecting these taxes.

The line between public dancers and prostitutes proper cannot be drawn with any precision. Administrative differences seemed to exist, at least in the eighteenth century, when prostitutes in Cairo fell under the control of the *wālī*, whose policing function entailed the regulation of prostitutes as well as thieves, beggars, and other professions considered shameful.[84] The *wālī* kept a register of all known prostitutes in Cairo, collected a monthly payment from each, and acted as both judge and administrator of punishment in the case of any supposed crime or transgression. He could earn profits above his share of taxes collected by threatening to register a woman discovered in a compromising situation as a prostitute unless she paid a handsome bribe.[85] Although public dancers were not formally under his jurisdiction, those suspected of prostitution could be registered and thus become subject to his authority. Such state control of prostitution furnished a precedent for further regulation during the period of the French occupation. In 1799, for example, measures taken to combat an epidemic of plague (*ṭāʿūn*) included the banning of all prostitutes from Cairo for a period of thirty days: women of ill repute (*al-nisāʾ al-mashurāt*), thought to be potential transmitters of the disease, were forbidden to enter the city, and all inhabitants were expressly prohibited from providing them shelter on pain of death.[86]

This kind of government control, which extended to dancers and prostitutes alike, encouraged many women to establish themselves outside of Cairo at some distance from the heavy hand of the State. In the period preceding Muḥammad ʿAlī, Maḥallah al-Kūbrā in the Delta was known as a center for prostitution: the women there were reputed to run their own affairs without state interference, safe from police control and taxation. Savary encountered a village on the road from Rosetta to Cairo where a community of prostitutes occupied a *khān* and offered their services to travellers. Lane claimed, in the days of Muḥammad ʿAlī, that Minūf, a small town in the Delta, was "generally said" to be such a center of prostitution, and other towns such as Asyūṭ and Qīnah in Upper Egypt boasted quarters of ill repute.[87]

In June of 1834, the government went a step further and outlawed all prostitution and public dancing performed by women in Cairo, and deported the better known prostitutes to Upper Egypt. The ostensible cause of such an unprecedented act lay in the corruption and excesses of the State's own system of control. Collection of prostitute taxes was a profitable tax farm, but scandal erupted when the current tax-farmer, a Copt named Antūn Tūmā, began to register "honorable women" as prostitutes in order to increase his revenues; some of these women, it was rumored, were the wives and daughters of his personal enemies. Public protest, led by the *'ulamā'*, apparently convinced Muḥammad 'Alī to ban all prostitution in Cairo, thereby assuaging public opinion and adding another feather to his cap of reform. The outlawing of prostitution and public dancing closed Cairo brothels and rendered female street dancers a thing of the past, but underground prostitution apparently continued.[88] Information is lacking on how delegalization of the trade in Cairo increased the vulnerability of these women; the role of pimps and protectors must have expanded as the threat of punishment or jail increased. The preference for residence in provincial towns where travellers and visitors to religious fairs and other gatherings provided a steady, although reduced, clientele was probably intensified by the increased dificulties of doing business in Cairo.

A blanket ban on female entertainers may have also helped to blur distinctions between women with accomplished entertainment skills and those pushed into plain prostitution by reverses of fortune. Although Muḥammad 'Alī's ban applied, in theory, only to women engaged in public performances or prostitution, some of the women exiled from Cairo to Upper Egypt were clearly performers of considerable talent and training. On Flaubert's Egyptian journey, during which he sought out these women of the night following his own proclivities and particular brand of romantic misogyny, the young poet met some of these exiles. He described at length his encounter in Isnā with the famed Kuchuk Hānem who danced, played, and sang with a grace and skill bespeaking a past with the *'awālim*. Deportation from Cairo had reduced her income, standard of living, and security: ensconced in a simple house in a backwater town, she lived in fear of thieves stealing her precious jewelry, a memento of a better time, and eked out a living by providing entertainment and sexual services to travellers of some means, such as Flaubert.[89] At least some of the "women of learning" were thus classed with the public dancers of the popular quarters and exiled, a development which had repercussions on the status of the occupation as a whole. The inability of later travellers to distinguish the *'awālim* from public dancers and prostitutes may reflect a similar lack of distinction by the State with a resulting dip in status and material standing for the *'awālim*.

The intervention of the State in 1834 and the subsequent banishment of women from the public sphere of entertainment in Cairo thus condemned many women of special training to languish in the Upper Egyptian towns of Qīnah, Isnā, and Aswān; these "courtesans," far from their original milieu, left Flaubert with an impression of lethargy and hopelessness in their attempts to attract the occasional visitor. Many of the public entertainers were also rendered penurious outcasts. Female dancers in Cairo were replaced by young men who affected the dress and movements of women in their performances.[90] Although groups of prostitutes, such as the one joined by the divorced woman in one of al-Mahdi's *fatāwā*, still operated in other parts of the country, Cairo was off limits to open prostitution.

The ban did not, however, long survive Muḥammad ʿAlī's government. By the 1860s, we find the State back in the business of permitting, and profiting from, prostitution. In 1866, a new tax was instituted on "dancing girls" which left the amount to be garnered from each woman, based presumably on earning power, to the discretion of the tax-farming official who actually collected the money; at least one *fallāḥ* jested that the ruler, by instituting this tax, had earned himself the title of "Pimp Pasha."[91] The Egyptian government also promulgated a series of regulations designed to limit the transmission of disease: prostitutes were required to undergo regular medical examinations and possess valid health certificates. Local police regulations might further define the area of town in which brothels could be established or even set standards for the public behavior of prostitutes. In 1883 in Port Said, for example, prostitutes were forbidden to solicit on public streets or from the doors of their houses; nor were they allowed to lean out of the window, "trying to attract passersby and causing a scandal."[92] Under British rule, the military and civil police enforced such regulations, at least in all major cities and ports. The officially licensed prostitutes who clustered in the Wasaʿah area of Cairo, for example, were firmly under the control of a network of pimps and procurers who bought and sold women in Cairo and the rest of the country. The chilling portrait of "painted harlots sitting like beasts of prey behind the iron grilles of their ground-floor brothels" subject to the autocratic rule of a self-proclaimed "king" of Wasaʿah suggests the degradation of the trade.[93] State regulation of Egyptian prostitutes focused, almost exclusively, on the protection of their clients from disease; the conditions under which the women worked – sometimes as virtual prisoners of their pimps – lay outside the concerns of the State.

The government exercised even less control over prostitutes who were foreign nationals and therefore came under the putative protection of their respective consuls. As the mercantile boom in the later part of the century turned Egyptian ports into beehives of activity which, together with the presence of large numbers of soldiers far from home, encouraged prostitution, the government found that it lacked the legal and practical basis to regulate the trade where foreigners were concerned. Brothels owned by Europeans operated largely outside the law, subject to neither licensing nor health regulations, and occasional attempts to close them down proved largely ineffective.[94] At least one English police officer bemoaned the situation which arose from the protection afforded prostitutes and particularly pimps by the Capitulations. The European-run prostitution which flourished in the Wish al-Birkah section of Cairo could entail abuse:

> The native bully was subject to Egyptian criminal law and could be brought to book if he went too far in a profession that had to be recognized in a country where prostitution was legal and licensed, but the European souteneur had little to fear from Egyptian law, being subject only to his consular jurisdiction with its feeble legislation and often indifferent officials. These lieutenants of the white-slave traffic were well organized with their headquarter offices in many ports and cities of Europe, and our police attempts to control them were made still more difficult by the refusal of their women to complain against them for fear of vitriol or the razor.[95]

It was, indeed, this "white-slave traffic," the then current euphemism for internationalized prostitution, that most disturbed British officials and residents. Alarm generated by reports that Alexandria and Port Said served as major depots for the trade in prostitutes, most of whom were Europeans being sent to the Middle or Far East, led to the founding of a "Société pour la Suppression de la Traite des Blanches" in 1905 in Alexandria. The Société mounted watches in the Alexandrian port in an attempt to intercept girls and steer them to "honest" hotels; in the first seven months of operation it also released from brothels and repatriated eleven young women: three Russians, two Romanians, a Greek, a Turk, a Frenchwoman, a Moroccan, a Japanese, and an American. In 1911, the number of "children of minor age" met in the port by the Société and handed over to religious and consular authorities, or to an "International Home," had reached 2,253. Branches of the Société were also founded in Cairo and Port Said where their activities included receiving passengers from boats or trains, "rescuing" young women from "vice," and denouncing "traffickers" who were then subject to deportation.[96] While not a governmental body, the Société received annual subsidies from the Egyptian State and the local municipality, and one or two British officials were members enjoying "special influence" but not official position.[97] The success of its activities rested, primarily, on its powers of persuasion, for prostitution remained a legal, although restricted, activity under the colonial State. Individual prostitutes did run afoul of the law more often than other women: one report from a jail in Upper Egypt in 1899, for example, listed five women prisoners of whom three were prostitutes.[98] Still, official licenses to practice the trade were contingent upon a health examination, and extralegal prostitution was generally tolerated.

Muḥammad ʿAlī's ban on prostitution and the later insistence of the absolutist and colonial state apparatuses on some forms of regulation transformed the structure of the trade. When prostitution was tolerated by the government but not regulated in any systematic fashion, as in the early 1800s, women had exercised considerable control: we find little evidence of men living off prostitutes' earnings. When the State decided to intervene in the trade, however, the absence of any legal protection or status made prostitutes vulnerable to official bans and regulations; the development of a shadowy network of pimps and procurers, so often discussed in the late 1800s and early 1900s, represented an effective, if oftentimes unpleasant and dangerous, form of protection from state incursion. Criminalization and regulation also contributed to the development of a prostitution underworld in which the women themselves surrendered much of their power to male guardians. Gone were the bands of prostitutes of former times: whether native Egyptians or imported foreigners, the prostitutes of the early twentieth century were often "in the hands of professional bullies, to whom they are bound by marriage, debts, or fear."[99]

Information on the origins and eventual fate of prostitutes is sparse and contradictory. Some observers, including Lane, stressed the common tribal origins of both dancers and prostitutes.[100] Clot-Bey, on the contrary, thought adverse circumstances rather than birth pushed women into the trade: unilateral repudiation by a husband could bring destitution and drive a woman unable to remarry to prostitution.[101] One of al-Mahdī's opinions in a dispute over child custody describes one such situation. A divorced woman, who wanted to retain custody of her three-year-old daughter, was accused by her former husband of intending to take the child to a place which was "neither her homeland nor the place where she was married," but where she belonged to a "group of fornicators" (*al-jamā'ah al-zina*). The *muftī* agreed with her ex-husband that her involvement in prostitution constituted an absolute impediment to giving the child proper care.[102] The case suggests that divorced women in financial predicaments might indeed resort to prostitution, but such a course robbed them of the few familial rights which remained from their marriage. The possible advantages of such a choice, insofar as some prostitutes were apparently organized in semi-autonomous communities, included financial independence and security within a social group that substituted for the family bonds which had been severed by divorce. Given the nature of the trade, however, such security was fragile at best, liable to erosion by illness or the onset of aging, which diminished a woman's physical charm, and the perils of falling prey to the tyranny of pimps. We occasionally get glimpses, however, of a solidarity within prostitute circles which tempered this insecurity: in Isnā in 1850, for example, Flaubert observed older and infirm women acting as procurers, musicians, and domestic servants for prostitutes still in their prime.[103] Nor was it entirely impossible for a reformed prostitute to rejoin the world of family life. Lady Duff Gordon received such a visitor, a woman who had formerly been a prostitute in Asyūṭ: "She had repented, and married a converted Copt. They are a droll pair of penitents, so very smart in their dress and manner."[104]

Another typically female transgression, often although not necessarily related to prostitution, was that of child abandonment or infanticide. The foundlings recovered alive in Cairo in the early 1900s, anywhere from 76 to 131 every year, were generally presumed to be illegitimate children born to prostitutes or women who had been raped or had illicit love affairs. The mothers abandoned their babies soon after birth, leaving them to their fate in a deserted building or lot where they might or might not be found by a passer-by. If discovered, the mother faced charges of criminal prosecution, so that the act of abandonment reflected a real desperation arising from the total absence of material support and the heavy social opprobrium leveled at any unwed mother. The abandonment or neglect of older children, whose presence on Cairo and Alexandria streets as "vagrants" raised concern in the early 1900s, is better attributed to simple material scarcity and the strain on families of rapid and forced urbanization. The problem of untended children had grown acute enough by 1908 to prompt the passage of a special law empowering the courts to consign vagrant children to state reformatories until they reached age eighteen.[105] In the case of both of these crimes, women perpetrators appear more as victims of strict social mores and the erosion of family support than as criminals.

During the nineteenth century in Egypt, then, women formed a very low percentage of accused and condemned criminals, and many of their crimes – petty theft, prostitution, child abandonment – bore the marks of a poverty and social strain exacerbated by rapid urbanization and economic pressures of the latter part of the century. As crime in general increased, women's postion of political marginality and social weakness was underscored by the fact that they were far more likely to be victims than perpetrators, and the crimes of which they were most commonly accused pitted them against standards of social and moral conduct they could no longer afford to uphold.

The means of repression

Resistance, unrest, and the increase in crime prompted the elaboration and refinement of the state apparatus responsible for internal security. Under the colonial government, the State developed a far more effective and pervasive security system which put particular emphasis on rural and urban police, the administration of swift and summary justice, and reform of the prison system.

The establishment of effective security forces which could guarantee public order was an immediate concern of the colonial State. In the first years of rule, the government found it necessary to import English police officers and employ relatively large numbers of them, especially in Cairo and Alexandria, to preserve order. The expense of maintaining many foreigners in the police force, however, soon encouraged the exploration of alternate approaches; the idea of transforming the village and quarter watchmen, the *ghafīrs*, into a professional police force was seriously proposed in the late 1880s. During the 1890s and 1900s, the corps of *ghafīrs* was winnowed and regular pay and discipline was introduced; by 1896, the *ghafīrs* in both rural and urban areas were deemed well selected and sufficiently paid, although further reductions in numbers and upgrading in salary continued well into the 1900s.[106] By all accounts, the corps came to form an adequate first line of defense against routine crime and minor disruptions of public order.

While the slow process of transformation of the *ghafīrs* proceeded, the State took more extraordinary measures to rein in a restive population. Beginning in 1884, the Brigandage Commissions were established under the Ministry of the Interior and entrusted with the investigation and trial of the rural crime of "brigandage." For the next five years, these extraordinary tribunals handled almost all justice in the countryside, acting as investigator, judge, and jury, and operating with a completely free hand. The regular courts and rules of procedure were held in abeyance while the Commissions summoned, tortured, tried, and sentenced without recourse to any fixed set of regulations. Only in 1889, after a report by the Procureur-Général Legrelle showed the "irregularities, the injustice, and the cruelty of these quasi-tribunals in the most startling light," were their broad powers publicly questioned and the Commissions disbanded.[107]

When later faced with high levels of crime in the 1900s, however, the State proved ready to adopt equally stern measures. The Relegation Law No. 15 of 1909 provided for investigations to ferret out "habitual" or "potential" criminals who could then be placed under surveillance or even sent to a penal settlement in order to prevent them from committing crimes. Between 1909 and 1911, some 300 people were sent each year to the Khargah Oasis by special commissions, not for perpetrating crimes, but merely for being thought likely to do so. Once at Khargah, the exiles, most of whom took their families with them, worked in agriculture. Although in most cases the suspects were allowed to pay a substantial security in lieu of exile, the vast majority could not afford to ransom themselves.[108]

Alongside such temporary Draconian measures, the colonial State also undertook the longer term project of prison reform. The Egyptian absolutist State had, like its European counterparts, relied primarily on exemplary execution, exile of those who disturbed public security, and limited imprisonment of those who could not pay fines or indemnities for minor offenses. In nineteenth century Europe, however, a wave of penal reform transformed the criminal justice system, replacing the ritual of public hanging with private execution and substituting long prison terms calculated to rehabilitate for the numerous executions and transportations of the eighteenth century.[109] Before the British occupation, the Egyptian State stood aloof from these developments: prisons remained crude buildings or sheds designed to hold offenders until executions could be carried out or pecuniary restitution made. During the early years of colonial administration, few changes were made in prison conditions: some buildings were cleaned and whitewashed but overcrowding, insufficient food and bedding, and endemic disease characterized most jails which still functioned as holding cells, not reformatory institutions.

With the appointment of a new Inspector-General of Prisons, Charles Coles, in 1897, the Egyptian government acquired an enthusiastic advocate of prison reform. Coles was a close student of European and American penal institutions, and used his summer leaves during the sixteen years he headed the Egyptian prison system to visit prisons in England, France, Belgium, Germany, and Austria. He was particularly impressed by what he heard about American experiments in reformatory treatment, and pressed for the introduction of their main features into Egypt. His efforts culminated in the establishment of a model Reformatory which incorporated state of the art reforms: the prisoners underwent nine months to one year of solitary cell confinement, lived a daily rigid schedule of school, exercise, and work under a complex system of financial reward, and wore a prison uniform complete with stars on the cap to indicate class in school, stripes on the arm for good conduct and crafts, and stripes on the breast for number of years in the Reformatory. The institution was plagued, however, by disruptions and the absence of full official commitment. A serious prison riot in its second year of operation and the discovery of a counterfeiting ring being run out of the Reformatory tarnished its image, and the appointment of Kitchener as Consul-General in 1911 brought to power a man who had no use for either the theory or practice of penal reform. After a visit to the Reformatory, Kitchener opined that prisoners would be better employed building roads. Coles soon lost the necessary support for his projects and was "assisted out of the country" in 1913.[110]

Although the most experimental aspects of Coles' reforms, such as the Reformatory, did not survive him, basic changes in the prison system did endure. The problem of severe overcrowding, which made discipline difficult and disease endemic – some seventy prisoners died of cholera in the summer of 1896 – was addressed through a program of prison construction. Some ten new prisons were built by the end of 1905 which, insofar as finances permitted, incorporated structural features of reform such as cellular block design, ventilated lavatories, and a central workshop. At the same time, efforts were being made to impose some form of discipline. Although prison sentences had become the standard punishment by the 1890s, the prisons were still being run on a haphazard basis: there was little classification or separation of prisoners, either by offense or age; the prisoners' families were responsible for providing food and bedding; and decrees sanctioning labor inside or outside the prison remained a dead letter. Officials worried that incarceration in Egypt was totally ineffectual:

> The great difficulty in Egypt is to make imprisonment a real punishment. The disgrace of being put in prison – a factor of considerable efficacy in more advanced countries – is scarcely felt by the mass of the population here. The mere confinement in the society of their fellow prisoners, with frequent opportunities of seeing and conversing with their relations when bringing their supply of food, is hardly felt as a punishment. Isolation, which would have a most salutary deterrent effect, and the maintenance of a severe prison discipline, are impossible without properly constructed prisons.[111]

In the early 1900s, the Prison Department undertook to provide most condemned prisoners with clothing, bedding, and food, thereby obviating the need for family visits and allowing prison officials to exert more control over the prison population. Chronic overcrowding, however, frustrated attempts to impose solitary confinement as the standard initiation into prison discipline as well as the most common form of punishment; officials remained concerned that prison life was too pleasant to be an effective deterrent.[112]

The perceived need to make sentences harsher and the ever present desire to save money gradually led to an emphasis on hard labor. Labor camps were established in each province and convicts were set to work cutting and cleaning canals and constructing roads. Although the popularity of the camps among prisoners led Coles to question the effectiveness of camp discipline, the program was a success insofar as it paid for the prisoners' subsistence and relieved prison overcrowding. After Kitchener assumed office, hard labor was used more frequently: he personally demonstrated his enthusiasm for this method of punishment by ordering prisoners to build an eighteen mile road from Cairo to Helwan within six months. Labor was also instituted in lieu of imprisonment for those who could not pay fines. At the same time, execution was transformed from a public ritual of retribution to quiet punishment within prison walls; the old-style public hanging on a primitive gallows which brought slow death through strangulation was replaced by private and instantaneous death on a gallows with a drop.[113]

A final enduring legacy of the reform period involved the separate and special treatment of juvenile offenders. Here the reformatory system took firmer root, and European institutions, particularly the County Council School for Waifs and Strays near London and the Belgian Reformatory at Ypres, provided clear and detailed models. Boys under age eighteen were separated from adult prisoners and sent to the Reformatory, originally located in Alexandria and later moved to Cairo, where they were integrated into a system of complete supervision. They spent the day in classes, workshops, drill and gymnastics, cleaning, meals, and supervised recreation. At no time were they to be left to their own devices: even the lavatories were equipped with only half doors so that there was "no hole or corner where the boys could get out of sight of their guardians or of each other."[114] A number of rewards and punishments – whipping, pocket money for sweets, outings – were given or taken away depending on the acquisition or loss of good conduct stripes. While in the Reformatory, the boys could be taught a number of crafts, including carpentry, fitting, tailoring, whitesmithery, shoemaking, printing, or bookbinding, which up to 70 per cent of them pursued after release. Coles claimed that the system worked well: within two years of release only 15 per cent of former inmates were reconvicted.

Whether or not Coles' positive assessment of the juvenile Reformatory can be credited, only very modest success can be granted to adult institutions. The overall thrust of prison reform aimed at bringing the inmate population under the strict control of prison officials by bending their will to that of their keepers as part of a process of rehabilitation; prisoners were to leave their old life, with all its criminal associations, behind. A critical precondition of this process was the elimination of the prison subculture, with its independent forms of organization and allegiance, which flourished whenever official control relaxed. The various attempts at reform, including the partial introduction of the "solitary system" in the model Reformatory, failed to secure this objective. Indeed, Coles himself records the case of a prisoner, Muḥammad al-Manshāwī, who ruled a prison subculture during some twenty years of incarceration. With ample money and the status of "Bey," Muḥammad procured the material goods he wanted, evaded all forms of punishment, and even married the daughter of the Deputy Governor of the prison while serving his sentence. The internal solidarity and willfulness bred by the prison subculture could also find expression in violent uprisings. During Coles' tenure as Inspector, the major prison at Tūrah saw three large-scale revolts. The third was triggered by inmates' protests over the substitution of corn bread for wheat, and was put down only by opening fire on the prisoners.[115] Lacking both official backing and the money necessary to institute a full-blown European-style penitentiary system, Egyptian penal institutions continued to house subcultures and enjoy a range of connections with the world outside the prison walls.

Women in prison

As we have seen above, Egyptian women committed far fewer crimes than men, and constituted, therefore, a relatively small percentage of the prison population. According to the Annual Reports of the Consul-General made to the British government between 1885 and 1913, women composed some 2 to 5 per cent of the 10,000 to 15,000 prisoners housed in Egyptian jails at any one time. Under the absolutist State, women prisoners had not received any special or separate treatment. They were held in the same prisons as men, although a room or two were usually set aside for them. Conditions were harsh: female prisoners could be crowded into a damp small space and allowed no exercise; the prisons in Maḥallah al-Kūbrā, Zaqāzīq, and Manṣūrah did not include separate latrines for women so that the female prisoners had to use the same exposed facilities as the men. Because many of the most common female crimes, such as prostitution or child abandonment, alienated them from their families, women were likely to suffer special deprivations in prison since their families might not readily supply their material needs. Indeed, when Herbert Chermside toured Egyptian prisons in 1882, he found women detainees in particular complained of hunger, and lacked sufficient bedding and clothing. In some cases, women kept their younger children with them in prison, straining further an already insufficient ration.[116]

The absence of separate facilities for women in a society which practiced a high level of sexual segregation suggests a special hostility toward women prisoners who had, in many cases, broken with the accepted norms of family life and proper female behavior, thereby alienating their right to special treatment as women. Similar attitudes, Estelle Freedman has argued, were at work in nineteenth century America where women criminals were viewed as betrayers of their female nature and subjected to particularly harsh treatment and abuse by their keepers.[117] In most respects, however, women shared the experience of their male counterparts: they were simply incarcerated with no attempts to rehabilitate and reequip them for release.

The reforms subsequently introduced by the colonial government, modeled on parallel developments in England, were primarily concerned with the segregation of female prisoners, the special needs of mothers, and the development of some form of training program. That women prisoners should be entirely separated from men and lodged in their own ward with separate courtyard and latrines was a first and basic plank of reform. By 1884, a separate prison for women was operating in Cairo, although elsewhere in the country female prisoners still inhabited small rooms under substandard conditions within the male prisons. Finally, in 1891, an entirely female prison was built in Būlāq; designed to house 200 inmates, the prison could absorb about half the female prison population of the entire country. A detached female prison was also constructed next to the new male prison at Shabīn al-Kōm. Some women, however, remained in wards in the male prisons; as of 1894, more than a dozen female prisoners were still being kept in the women's ward of the Asyūṭ prison.

The special role of women as childbearers and -rearers was also recognized: women in the ninth month of pregnancy or those who had recently delivered were not received in prison, and a woman could keep any of her children under age seven in jail with her if she so desired. Observers reported that many women inmates indeed did so: in some prisons, most women appeared to have babes in arms. The occupational program for females also stressed "womanly" activities. While the Cairo prison opened workshops in carpentry and mat-making for men in the 1880s, women were set to sewing, charged with making clothes for the male inmates. The women's prison in Būlāq also employed inmates in sewing: the only workshop in the prison was engaged in the cutting out and sewing of underclothing for the employees and inmates of the prison system. The Juvenile Reformatory in Gīzah initially employed girl inmates, who composed some 12 per cent of the population, in all domestic tasks – cooking, washing, general cleaning – for themselves and the boy inmates, while the boys were being trained in industrial crafts. Coles eventually revised the system because the girls were spending all their time in activities which did not prepare them well for standard housework; they were still to be trained, however, in housewifery, not in skills designed for the marketplace.[118]

Overall, the thrust of prison reform for women was to separate them from men and provide for ways in which they could continue to shoulder their child-care responsibilities. One is struck, otherwise, by the absence of interest in female prisoners: Coles, for example, barely mentions women in the course of his extensive discussions of reform. Admittedly, women formed a very small percentage of the inmate population, but their near invisibility, at least as far as the reformers were concerned, calls for explanation: once relegated to separate facilities and set a few household tasks, the problems posed by female criminality appear to have been considered solved. We are left to conclude that British officials in Egypt, like their predecessors among the officials of the absolutist State, viewed women criminals as such pariahs and misfits as to stand outside the pale of reform. In western Europe and North America, the late nineteenth century reform of female prisons was, according to Freedman, carried out by middle and upper class women reformers who viewed female criminality as part of broader social problems and pressed for feminization of the penal environment. In Egypt, on the other hand, prison reform remained part of the program of rationalization of the state apparatus imposed by colonial officials; there was no group of independent women reformers who raised the issues of women's special problems and needs. Up through 1914, then, women were segregated but not particularly served by the reforms of the prison system.

Conclusion

Attention to the nineteenth century cycle of the emergence of a powerful and repressive State, followed by popular resistance and then renewed efforts to streamline and heighten the efficacy of official means of repression, helps define the situation of women in Egypt. Active in peasant uprisings and urban revolts, women demonstrated their familiarity with the politics of the square and street, and their willingness and ability to play a supporting, or even occasionally central, role in protest in the public sphere. Social acceptance of their activity underscores the extent to which women were perceived as legitimate participants in the political, economic, and social life of the public sphere.

In the latter part of the century, as the State grew more powerful and its repression more effective, popular protest tended to take increasingly individualized and local forms. While we continue to find women among those who resisted draft levies or harassed soldiers of the Occupation, their individual acts reflect social weakness: they often used the strategy, passive resistance, and the weapon, the taunt, of the weak. When resistance took place on a mass scale, women could play an important supporting role; when attacks by small groups or individuals replaced popular mobilization as the main form of resistance to the State or the British, however, women were far less visible, reflecting the limits of their ability to engage in political activity on their own. Mass protest meant the involvement and mobilization of women, but effective repression in the post-1882 period spelled their removal from the political stage.

The reverses women suffered as the result of repression of mass political movements were further exacerbated by the rise of common crime and pervasive insecurity in the late nineteenth century. As the economic dislocations and social pressures of the period promoted the growth of a wide variety of serious crimes, women were far more apt to be victims than perpetrators. The crimes women commonly committed in hard times – prostitution, child abandonment – inflicted injury most often on the woman herself and further eroded already weak ties with the family that had once sustained her. Ironically, state action, particularly in the regulation of prostitution, had the effect of undermining whatever tenuous control and power professional women prostitutes and entertainers had come to exercise, and instead encouraged the growth of an illicit underworld of pimps and procurers. In general, rises in the rates of common crime victimized those in society with the least social power and resources – the women of the poor – and repressive measures imposed by the State tended to increase, rather than alleviate, their problems.

Finally, the development of the state apparatus of repression under the British entailed the adoption of European methods. The imposition of penal measures developed outside the country on a society with a different history and set of institutions led to a patchwork quilt of establishments, old and new, as well as partial and selective reform. The impact on women, whose rate of incarceration remained exceptionally low, was limited: prison officials did segregate women and confine them to domestic tasks, but showed no particular interest in other forms of special treatment or advocacy. Women were neglected by male officials, and their invisibility suggests a much larger problem in the conception of policy. Women were simply to be segregated and treated in ways befitting their place as women. The prevailing definition of womanhood, as demonstrated in the emphasis on sewing and housewifery, owed more, however, to Victorian ideals than to any close study of Egyptian society. Progressive "reform" could mean, for women, restriction to ever narrower spheres of activity.

Chapter 5

The practice of slavery: women as property

The lady's secrets are in the vault, but those of the slave woman are in the marketplace.

Egyptian proverb (Taymūr, 1008, p. 173)

The daughter of a great family is precious even if she be a slave.

Egyptian proverb (Taymūr, 828, p. 140)

Slavery has never been a uniform, absolute condition of bondage defying historical variation. The North American experience of that peculiar institution, marked by racial prejudice and a lifetime of unremitting hard labor for the majority of the enslaved, has fostered a vision of slavery which often serves as the point of comparison for other forms of unfree servitude. The plight of slaves in Egypt has been described, for example, as "much better than that of American slaves."[1] Apologists for Egyptian slavery pointed to the greater comfort of the slave, less subject as he or she was to the lash and hard labor; critics of the institution were more prone to see slavery as a monolithic system and Egyptian slaves as little different from their counterparts engaged in slave labor on the plantations of the American South. In both cases, however, the institution of slavery as well as the status of the slaves were assumed to partake of a unitary juridical and social definition, subject only to variation in degree, not in kind.

The dangers of such an approach, which ignores the differences in legal and social status and variations in social and economic roles among slaves in the many societies where some form of unfree servitude has been practiced, have been aptly discussed in the context of slavery in ancient Greece.[2] In any consideration of slavery in Egypt, similar caution is required, for Islamic laws and exhortations, coupled with the social and economic roles of the juridically unfree, render simple comparison with American slavery misleading. With American slavery as the touchstone, we are ill prepared for the multiplicity of social roles and status among manumitted slaves who blended into Egyptian society often at the apex of the social system, entering the ranks of high officialdom and the wealthy merchant class. The roles and status of female slaves and women of slave origin were shaped by the activities assigned them during the period of enslavement, the legal framework of slavery, and social perceptions of their status within slavery and after manumission; only from within this economic, social, and religious complex does the meaning of slavery in Egypt emerge.

As Frederick Cooper has noted in his study of the East African coast, slavery does not necessarily develop from the need for, or even entail, menial labor; on a social and political level it can signify, primarily, an extreme dependence or loyalty, a drive to create artificial ties which carry the weight of kinship. Cooper's work traces changes in slavery in East Africa when transformations in the economy of the region occasioned a move from slavery as this kind of social subordination to slavery as unfree labor on agricultural plantations. He cautions, however, against a social/economic dichotomy: it is not that slavery was sometimes culturally determined and other times economically determined, but rather that slavery was a social *and* economic institution.[3] Similarly, in the case of nineteenth century Egypt, the institution of slavery was shaped by the economic role of slaves together with the social and political function of servitude as expressed, often, in the legal rules and social customs which governed the relations of master or mistress and slave. The ways in which the demands of economic production and reproduction meshed with the prevailing definitions of slavery under Islamic law and social practice affected the daily conditions, and future prospects, of slaves.

Unlike the East African coast, the institution of slavery in Egypt did not undergo any dramatic changes in the course of the nineteenth century. While the growth of plantation agriculture and the increasing importance of cash crops to the economy were certainly marked features of development in both areas, the implications for slavery could not have been more different. In East Africa, demands for plantation labor revitalized slavery as an institution and changed its character; in Egypt, slaves remained marginal, if not irrelevant, to the plantation system, and the institution of slavery atrophied. Egyptian slavery ended in the early twentieth century with a whimper, not a bang, largely because the quintessential slave, the woman who served as concubine or domestic, had become an anachronism. The lives of women enslaved in Egypt, as well as the institution as a whole, belonged to a world which would not survive the transformations of the nineteenth century.

Slavery in nineteenth century Egypt

Slavery did not play a key economic role in Egypt. In simple numerical terms, slaves remained marginal to the economic system. On the basis of figures available for the years 1838–1840, there were some 22,000 to 30,000 slaves in the country: given an estimated total population of over 5,000,000, the enslaved composed less than 0.5 per cent of all inhabitants, far too few to form a critical part of the labor force.[4] Moreover, the influx of black slaves during the period

1828 to 1845 may have been unusually high because of heavy demand for military service, a rise reflected in the upsurge of legal disputes about slave sales.[5] Approximately half of the slave population lived in Cairo: in 1839, Bowring estimated that 6,000 Cairene households owned an average of two female slaves with an additional 2,000 male slaves distributed throughout the city.[6] Even so clustered in one urban area, the slave population of Cairo did not rise much above 5 per cent of the total population of 250,000.

Over the course of the nineteenth century, the slave population declined; available manumission figures for the 1880s, 1890s and early 1900s, however, can provide only a rough estimate of its size. We do have some numbers: between 1877 and 1889, approximately 18,000 slaves, or 1,500 on the average each year, passed through the newly opened manumissions bureaux; thereafter, the number of manumissions shrank almost steadily each year, from 1,400 in 1890 to 153 in 1905. Between 1890 and 1905, an estimated 7,000 slaves were manumitted so that a rough total of 25,000 were processed by officials between 1877 and 1905.[7] Although no significant supplies of new slaves were available after the late 1870s, and almost all Egyptian slaves had been liberated by 1905, we cannot assume that 25,000 represents an accurate estimate of the Egyptian slave population before the official drive for manumission began in 1877. On the one hand, the figures, at least for some years, were inflated by the counting of slaves set free outside the boundaries of Egypt proper, in Sudan or in Egyptian ports where they had been discovered in transit or in the process of being smuggled into Egypt. On the other hand, manumission, long a common practice among the slave-owning classes, as we shall see below, did not necessarily take effect in the official bureaux set up for the purpose; masters and mistresses had been manumitting their slaves throughout the period simply by pronouncing them free in the presence of witnesses, leaving no written records in state offices or *sharī ʿah* courts. Although many slaves undoubtedly sought out the manumission bureaux to equip themselves with a document which might prove of use, we have no guarantee that all of them did so; official manumission figures, therefore, do not include those slaves quietly set free in the traditional manner.

British sources tend, naturally enough, to see the English-sponsored campaign of abolition as the turning point in Egyptian slavery. In the absence of any reliable census of the slave population, we still get the impression from observers that the number of enslaved had been reduced to insignificance by the early to mid 1890s.[8] It is much more difficult to establish when and why a massive erosion of the institution took place; there is some evidence to suggest that the 1860s and early 1870s, i.e. the period before the much trumpeted official reforms, actually witnessed the most dramatic inroads on the institution.[9] In any event, with the outlawing of the slave trade and changes in manumission procedures, numbers were surely further diminished, and the slave population, never large enough to make a critical contribution to production in Egypt, dwindled still further, well on the way to complete extinction.

The nature of Egyptian slavery and the tenuousness of its position within Egyptian society were reflected in the demographic structure of the slave population. The majority of slaves were female: throughout the first half of the nineteenth century, observers noted that slave caravans and markets transported and sold more women and girls than men and boys; everywhere female slaves were in the clear majority and were estimated to be, in Cairo at least, up to six times as common as males.[10] Later manumission figures show the same disproportion of men and women: females were a distinct majority (57.3 per cent) of those officially freed between 1877 and 1882. By the 1890s, manumission lists from within the boundaries of Egypt suggest even greater sex discrepancies: from January to May of 1892, for instance, 88 women and 20 men were manumitted in Egypt.[11]

Many of these slaves, bond or freed, carried a *nisab* denoting their color which also implied, roughly speaking, their place of origin. Four varieties of female slaves appear in the court records: *al-baiḍā'* (white), *al-samrā'* (brown or light colored), *al-ḥabashīyyah* (light colored), and *al-saudā'* (black). White slaves were traditionally imported from the Caucasus, but during the Muḥammad ʿAlī period the war in Greece netted numbers of Greek women captives who soon formed an important part of the white slave population.[12] Although the term *samrā'* seems purely descriptive, *ḥabashīyyah* was apparently applied to female slaves from Ethiopia who were differentiated from those called *saudā'* of sub-Saharan African origin. In the slave market and later in life, the slave rarely carried any *nisab* designating a precise place of origin, tribal affiliation, or any of the other common *nisab* of the free-born; some black slaves did carry the names of the trade routes they had travelled into slavery which could affect a buyer's assessment of their qualities and value.[13]

The slaves were sold at prices which varied widely but were influenced, in part, by their race, sex, health, age, and skills, in addition to less easily delineated qualities such as physical beauty and overall demeanor. Racial consideration underlay a range of prices with white slaves at the upper end of the scale, Ethiopians in the middle, and blacks at the bottom: white females, for example, fetched from four to six times more than black females, and Ethiopians, male or female, were valued 20 to 30 per cent higher than their black counterparts. Female slaves within each racial category were consistently more expensive than males although black eunuchs, perhaps as a function of supply given the high mortality rates associated with castration, were valued above black males and females alike. Illness invariably depressed the selling price to anywhere from one quarter to one tenth of the customary value, but pregnancy, while considered a defect which could invalidate a sale if not made known to the purchaser, did not affect market prices significantly. Despite an apparent preference for young slaves who were considered more malleable, children were sold at lower prices than adults; advanced age had the same effect as infirmity in severely depreciating a slave's value. Special skills did not usually boost the price, although some black males with military training or females accomplished in the culinary arts were more valuable as a result.[14] Over the course of the nineteenth century, the prices of slaves tended to rise – almost doubling between the 1830s and the 1860s – as a result, no doubt, of new difficulties in supply and the imposition of government taxes.[15]

Selling prices of different types of slaves, apart from those with obvious defects which lowered their value, can also be understood by reference to the roles various slaves were destined to play within society and the vast gradations of status that occurred among members of the slave population. From the outset of bondage, some female slaves were accorded a privacy in keeping with their ultimate destination, the women's quarters of an elite household. In the Cairo markets, white females, for example, were seldom displayed in public; prospective buyers were invited to private apartments where the women were lodged, or the slaves were presented for inspection at home.[16] Although some were bought by wealthy women for service within the *ḥarīm*, many were purchased by members of the royal family, high Turkish officials, and rich merchants as concubines. In time, they merged into the family as permanent members of the *ḥarīm*, or even as wives of relatives or retainers.[17]

Few barriers were raised to bonds of marriage or the development of other sorts of familial ties. One case presented to al-Mahdī underscores the rapid assimilation of the daughter of a white slave:

Question: There is a *sayyidah* named Khadījah, and the aforementioned *sayyidah* bought a pregnant white slave who gave birth to a girl, and after the delivery the aforementioned slave died and left the girl who was seven days old. And the aforementioned *sayyidah* was nursing the children of the decreased ʿAlī Bek and so she nursed the girl along with the children of the deceased ʿAlī Bek. And the *sayyidah* married a man named *al-shaykh* Khaḍir and gave birth to a girl by him, and the daughter of the slave was nursing and she [the natural daughter] nursed with her [the slave's daughter] from her [the *sayyidah*], and from the wetnurse who was nursing her girl until the weaning of the aforementioned girl. Then the *shaykh* Khaḍir, after a certain period, said to his wife: "Come with me to the country," and she said to him: "The girl is small and I can't come. You have a black slave to serve you, and I have been asking you to marry, and so I will give you Ḥasanah, the daughter of the white slave, in marriage." And so he said: "All right," and so she married her to him. And after that, she mentioned that she had nursed her and some of the *muslimīn* learned of that. And is the marriage of the aforementioned girl to the aforementioned *shaykh* Khaḍir permissible?

Answer: If there is fair legal proof or Khaḍir agrees that the aforementioned Ḥasanah nursed from the *sayyidah* Khadījah, the wife of the aforementioned Khaḍir, with his daughter by her, it is not permissible for the *shaykh* Khaḍir to marry her because she is his daughter's foster sister.[18]

Khadījah's project, apparently conceived in order to evade her responsibility of accompanying her husband, thus foundered on the shoals of the prohibition against marriage between close relatives which applied to those related through the sharing of a wetnurse. Although she was forbidden to marry the young slave to her husband, the case illustrates that slavery did not preclude the establishment of relations, as foster daughter or as wife, between a slave and her owner's family. Even as consorts outside of legal marriage, slaves acquired certain rights and privileges upon the birth of a child to their master. As we shall see below, the ability of slaves to insist on these rights and the prevalence of recognized concubinage bolstered their position during the period of enslavement and after manumission.

As attendants, concubines, or wives, most white slaves were found in the wealthiest of households. Some, as in the case above, were purchased to serve the ladies of the household; others, who appear in various transactions in the courts, had been owned by male Turkish officials serving the State, such as the former *wālī* of ʿAkkah under Muḥammad ʿAlī or other members of the Turkish *efendī* class.[19] Muḥammad ʿAlī's own palace establishment housed a number of white slaves in the *ḥarīms*, probably both concubines and ladies' attendants. The women of his *ḥarīm* who were enlisted in his first experiment in female education, a palace school for girls where reading, writing, geography, and drawing were taught, were forty white slave recruits.[20] Affluent members of the European community, often to their respective consuls' dismay, also acquired white slave concubines to act as wives and bear them children.[21] The possession of a white slave, entailing a considerable initial outlay and the ongoing expense of providing the amenities of the *ḥarīm* due to these women, probably restricted demand for white slaves and led, in a period of changing fortunes, to an overall decrease in demand. Although figures are lacking on the proportion of white slaves in the slave population, observers thought that, as early as the Muḥammad ʿAlī period, the number was in rapid decline.[22]

The assimilation of these women into a luxurious establishment, often on terms not so different from free women of the upper class, helps to explain the difficulties which beset European officials attempting to free Greek slaves after the termination of the war in Greece in keeping with the terms imposed after the battle of Navarino in October 1827. While a number of Greek women were liberated, the French consul reported that his efforts to buy the freedom of many were stymied by their absorption into upper class society: "Greek women are no longer in Egypt. Those which are still found have almost all been married to Muslims after having been converted to Islam, and it is almost impossible to liberate them."[23] Lane went further in asserting that many of the Greek women refused liberation, apparently preferring elegant bondage to impoverished freedom in their homeland.[24] Although conditions of servitude must have varied in accordance with the temperament of different masters, the size of the household, etc., most evidence points to a life of relative ease and comfort for an albeit small, and continually diminishing, number of white slaves.

Focus on the obvious privileges and status accorded to white slaves has led writers in the past to make an absolute correlation between race and roles and status within the slave community. Racial difference did indeed influence the purchase price of female slaves, on a spectrum of white to black with the "dark-skinned" or brown occupying an intermediate position, but the generalization of price differentials to absolute role or status categories can be very misleading.[25] Although white slaves were, on the basis of the court evidence, commonly found among the upper classes, the *ḥabashīyyah*, *samrā'*, and *saudā'* slaves did not always occupy positions of lower status or live a life of drudgery and menial service. Lighter-skinned slaves, some of whom retained the *nisab al-ḥabashīyyah*, which had apparently come to denote color rather than simply Ethiopian origin, were much prized as concubines.[26] Lane's assertion that they were the poor man's concubine, inasmuch as Egyptians of the middle classes purchased them while white females were monopolized by wealthy Turks, is not well borne out by legal records. Just as some white slaves were found in Egyptian households, so were some *ḥabashīyyah* slaves owned by Turkish officials.[27] In both Turkish and Egyptian households, brown-skinned slaves could be concubines or attendants in the *ḥarīm*; in some instances, concubinage led to freedom and marriage into elite households without any noticeable distinction from white slaves.[28]

The roles and status of black female slaves display considerably more variation, but menial domestic service was not the lot of all, and the status of black women during servitude and after manumission was not always so different from that of the fairer-skinned. Construction of a strict hierarchy of slaves, with black slaves at the bottom doing the "coarse work" of the household, comes into conflict with numerous examples in the legal records of black slaves who were well integrated into upper class families.[29] Blacks, making up the bulk of the slave population, were found throughout society. Most observers noted their presence in domestic service in upper and middle class households where the degree of drudgery depended, in large part, on the wealth of the family: in large *ḥarīms*, many slaves and servants served as a buffer against hard household labor.[30] This *ḥarīm* service was not necessarily very exciting or exotic. As one close observer of the Khedive's household noted in the early twentieth century, the *ḥarīm* slave was usually "a maidservant with no power to give notice," dressed in long-sleeved cotton overalls covering her well from neck to ankle, "clean and practical but . . . not seductive." Caught up in an elaborate routine of household tasks, a miniature Versailles where the pouring of coffee took on a sacramental air, the daily monotony of the *ḥarīm* slaves stands in marked contrast to visions of wanton luxury.[31] The court records confirm that some black slaves were indeed owned by freed white slave women of Turkish *ḥarīms* where they acted as ladies' attendants.

Many of the unfree domestic servants, however, were probably found in more modest households where work would be less of a ritual and more of a burden. The prevalence of slaves as maids in Egyptian households was noted by one observer for the Anti-Slavery Society, who thought a significant number of households possessed one or two slaves of all work as late as 1881. Other correspondence, in 1882, claimed exactly the contrary: in the houses of government officials and others of the "comfortable" classes in Cairo and the cities of Lower Egypt, domestic chores were being performed by hired servants, not slaves.[32] Still, the records of the Home for Freed Female Slaves in Cairo in the 1880s make it clear that many of the recently freed slaves had been domestic servants in middle or upper class households.[33]

Black women were also bought as concubines by officers of the Turkish military or viceregal class, a stepping stone to marriage and assimilation into elite circles.[34] Lady Duff Gordon reported in 1864 that the magistrate stationed in Luxor, an official of some standing named Salīm Efendī, had bought two black slave women, mother and daughter, for his kitchen and bedroom respectively. Local society apparently accepted the presence of a black concubine in one of the best houses with equanimity; indeed, Salīm discussed publicly how he had wanted only the girl but had bought the mother as well at his future concubine's insistence. With his lawful wife in Cairo where their sons could be schooled, these slave women provided him with physical companionship and housekeeping services in an arrangement of complete respectability.[35] While white slaves were commonly purchased as concubines, then, black slaves could be found in more diverse situations, including service and concubinage in elite households.

The extent to which black slaves were employed in agricultural labor remains a subject of debate. The dearth of agricultural slaves of any kind in the court records is not conclusive evidence, for slave agricultural labor is usually discussed in reference to Upper Egypt.[36] Most observers were firmly convinced that slaves were rarely employed in the fields, being reserved for household service or purposes of sensuality.[37] In a review of slave occupations, written in 1881, slaves of Upper, Middle, and Lower Egypt, owned by various classes, were all thought to be engaged in domestic service; in the 1890s, the Home for Freed Female Slaves in Cairo reported receiving women who had been, almost exclusively, domestic servants.[38] Although the presence of a few slaves in agricultural pursuits in Upper Egypt should not be discounted, there is little to suggest that slaves were employed in significant numbers. Moreover, some of the blacks, men and women alike, sighted in the earlier part of the century in Upper Egyptian fields may not have been, properly speaking, enslaved at all. In response to labor shortages arising from decimation of the population in the 1820s, Muḥammad ʿAlī hit upon the solution of importing a new population:

In order to correct these enormous losses, the Pasha brought, from Ethiopia and Nubia, caravans of blacks of both sexes whom he installed on the land and accorded privileges for three years. This project began three months ago, it appears to have succeeded. The black population of these meridional parts of Africa is around 3,000,000 according to what the Pasha told me. He has them gathered up by force, and intends to have them people this country in order to recoup the losses he has had, and those which he will be forced to have in order to satisfy his ambition and all his projects.[39]

Whatever the final outcome of this scheme, some of the blacks engaged in agriculture in later times may have their origins in this juridically free, although not necessarily willing, population transferred from their territory further south.

A major and significant exception to the absence of slaves from the fields appears in the exploitation of slave labor in the Upper Egyptian province of Isnā during the second half of the nineteenth century. Colonel Schaefer, head of the Service for the Abolition of Slavery, reported the presence of "many" slaves in the fields near Aswān in 1883.[40] By 1887, however, he could state that: "The very few slaves there are in the provinces are nearly all free, and most of them born in the country, and are like the ordinary fellah." Isnā remained the anomaly, for there "slavery has some analogy with American slavery . . . There were landowners who possessed a number of slaves, and the condition . . . was not so good as is commonly the case in Egypt." In his report on manumissions by province for the year 1885, Isnā furnished the majority with 1,424 manumissions out of a countrywide total of 2,628 for twenty provinces: 54 per cent of all slaves had been freed in one province alone that year.[41] Although these black slaves were employed in agriculture, the dearth of earlier references to any substantial numbers of agricultural slaves suggests that the situation in Isnā was a temporary aberration, the result, perhaps, of the availability of slaves because of proximity to slave trading centres, and an acute labor shortage. In the greater part of Egyptian territory, however, the employment of slaves in menial occupations, both rural and urban alike, remained a rarity.

The typical slave in nineteenth century Egypt, then, was a female of foreign origin but no particular race, employed in the owner's household as a domestic servant or concubine. As a subordinate family member, the fate of this slave was deeply affected over the course of the century, not only by the development of state policies dealing with the slave trade and the institution itself, but also by the ways in which longstanding ideological definitions of bondage and the customary roles of slaves in the economic and social life of the household lost much of their rationale and resonance with the broader transformations of the period.

Slavery and the State

The State under Muḥammad ʿAlī, while it might undertake forced transfers of black populations or recruit slaves for military service, interfered little in the trading practices or treatment of slaves. Certain regulations were in effect for the Cairo slave market: male slaves could be examined only above the navel and below the knee, and the inspection of female slaves was limited to their hands and feet if the prospective buyer were male.[42] Suggestions made by European consuls to Muḥammad ʿAlī that the State step in to regulate the punishment meted out to slaves, for example, were received with good grace but never implemented; nor did Muḥammad ʿAlī's professed personal desire to regulate or even abolish slavery bear fruit during his lifetime.[43]

Neither the Egyptian state nor the British government, increasingly involved in the affairs of the country, took effective action against slavery and the slave trade until the 1870s. When official measures were first introduced, it was the slave trade, the supply, rather than slavery as an institution, the demand, that served as the focus of their efforts. Although the major trade routes of slave supply are well documented, the actual numbers of slaves brought by caravan from Darfūr, Sennār, Khartūm, Bornū and Walāy, and from the East African coast via the Red Sea and Red Sea ports, remain shrouded in obscurity, with estimates of the annual import figures ranging anywhere from 1,200 to over 15,000 slaves between 1800 and 1877.[44] In the absence of agreement among contemporary observers and reliable statistics, we can only assume that the number of slaves imported fluctuated from year to year in relation, perhaps, to external disruptions in the trade routes or internal changes in demand. The 1877 British and Egyptian Convention for the Suppression of the Slave Trade, a product of British anti-slavery agitation and Egyptian government cooperation, laid the first firm basis for official restriction of importation, and the numbers underwent an appreciable decline in the following years.

Anti-slavery organizations had been active on the British political scene for over a century, winning significant victories in 1807 when all British subjects were required to abstain from the slave trade, and in 1833 when slaves in British territories were emancipated. After the abolition of slavery in the United States in 1863, the attention of abolitionists turned increasingly toward Africa, particularly the East African coast trade centered in Zanzibar. A British treaty with the Sultan of Zanzibar in 1873, abolishing the trade within his dominions, was followed by a bilateral agreement between Britain and Egypt in 1877.[45] By prohibiting the import and export of Sudanese and Abyssinian slaves, and specifying punishment for slave traders, this Convention did hasten the ultimate demise of the slave trade. Slaving, however, was not to be suppressed overnight: in 1895, almost twenty years later, a second Convention between Great Britain and Egypt was signed which prohibited the import and export of all kinds of slaves and tightened procedures for punishment of violators. The inevitability and severity of penalties for any infringements of the Convention guaranteed it final success in the elimination of the trade.[46]

During the same period, the Egyptian government took unilateral steps to halt the trade. In 1854, the Khedive Saʿīd banned the import of slaves from Sudan, and in 1858 he gave new orders instructing his officials to liquidate the trade immediately.[47] Although a number of measures outlawing the import or export of slaves were thus in place well before the 1877 Convention, their efficacy was questionable. Khedive Ismāʾīl's speech in Paris in 1867 denouncing the slave trade was derided, for example, by Lady Duff Gordon as "absurd":

> With 3,000 [slaves] in his hareem, several slave regiments, and lots of gangs on all his sugar plantations, his impudence is wonderful. He is himself the greatest living slave trader as well as owner. My lads [her two black slaves] are afraid to go out alone for fear of being snapped up by *cawasses* and taken to the army or the sugar works.[48]

Not until the early 1880s did the more systematic organization of state agencies dealing with the slave trade lend substance to these official pronouncements.

First, a Service for the Abolition of Slavery headed by Count della Scala was charged, in 1880, with the prevention of the importation of slaves into Egypt; using an army corps assigned for the purpose, it watched over desert roads and stopped and searched caravans. After the British occupation in 1882, the Slave Trade Service was incorporated into the police and placed under Colonel Schaefer. In addition to stopping caravans en route, Schaefer arrested slave traders and merchants in Cairo and oversaw their courts-martial, which could result in sentences of up to three years at hard labor.[49] Local Egyptian officials in the provinces were also put on the alert and held responsible for the detection of slaves who might be newly imported into Egypt under the guise of being wives or freed slaves. A series of government directives and the well publicized punishments of traders apparently achieved the desired effect and customary slave sources began to dry up.

The land routes from the south over which the majority of slaves had formerly travelled to bondage were the object of particular vigilance. While sizeable caravans could still be sighted in 1881, the trade was greatly reduced by the Service over the next few years.[50] Cromer claimed that this trade was "extinct" by 1890 and, indeed, most cases after that date appear to involve very limited numbers of slaves.[51] The route from the East African coast to Egypt via the coast of the Arabian peninsula presented more difficulties because of pilgrimage traffic. In 1886, Schaefer reported on the problems of checking returning pilgrims to make certain they were not importing slaves with them: of 119 blacks and Abyssinians who passed through the police station in Suez, 41 were slaves, newly bought in Jeddah; 36 of these, however, carried papers of manumission from the *qāḍī* in Mecca and therefore could not be stopped and sent to the Slave Home. Schaefer noted that some of these slaves did not even know they had been manumitted – a rather theoretical freedom at best. Although the issue of new slaves returning with pilgrims continued to arise through the rest of the century, compounded by the difficulty of distinguishing a slave from a black wife or freed servant as well as the potential for fraud in manumission documents, only a handful of slaves were involved each year.[52] At the same time, while primarily concerned with the policing of the slave trade in and out of Egypt, the Egyptian government also made inroads on cutting down transit trade in slaves through the Suez Canal.[53]

Since sales and purchases of slaves of all kinds were formally prohibited in 1884 by a Khedivial Decree annexed to the 1877 Convention, the Slavery Service, which became an independent department under the Ministry of the Interior in 1887, also took responsibility for the arrest and trials of slave dealers and any individuals engaged in private sales. Although Schaefer reported some obstacles to obtaining evidence for the courts-martial of dealers, a sufficient number of "important convictions" were made to discourage, he thought, the pursuit of the profession. By 1887, almost all professional slave trading had ceased and private sales, never very common, had been driven well underground. He was able to report to Cromer with some satisfaction that most present sales were: "fraudulent sales, by which a freed slave, in connivance with a dealer, allows herself to be sold and runs away the next day to share the profits of the sale with her associate. This has rather helped us; it has been practiced to an extent sufficient to make people doubt whether there were any *bona fide* slaves to be bought."[54] The following year, Schaefer assured the Anti-Slavery Society in England that the Service for the Abolition of Slavery would soon find itself out of business.[55]

Despite a few minor problems of enforcement in the mid and late 1880s, arising primarily from the involvement of Khedivial boats in slave running and the absence of clear procedures for the trial of those accused of private sales, the slave trade was effectively banned by 1890. British commitment to a ban combined with increasingly effective measures taken by the Egyptian government had eliminated, for all intents and purposes, the slave trade within Egyptian borders.[56]

Abolition of the trade did not mean the legal end of slavery as an institution. Various proposals by European consuls that the State outlaw or at least regulate the practice had no practical effect during the Muḥammad ʿAlī period.[57] As the issue of slavery came to the fore in the 1870s and 1880s, British officials in Egypt had to be reminded that the institution itself was not affected by the various international conventions dealing with the trade. In 1884, British government instructions to consular officers, first drafted in 1873, were still in effect and strictly circumscribed the role of officials as emancipators:

> The abolition of the status of domestic slavery in Egypt must be brought about in the opinion of Her Majesty's Government, through the agency of measures to be taken by the

Egyptian Government rather than through the interference of the British Consular Officers, who should not encourage slaves to apply to them to procure their emancipation except in cases of ill-treatment.[58]

Furthermore, unless the officer felt prepared to establish the existence of ill-treatment before local authorities who alone would judge such a claim, he should not intervene at all. Only the trade, not the emancipation of those already enslaved, fell legally within the province of the British consular staff.

In his own reflections on the problem, Cromer was less inclined to maintain the fine distinction between the Egyptian government and its British advisors. He never doubted that the abolition of slavery in Egypt lay within his power, but sought a procedure which would not alienate the upper classes of slave owners who provided, after all, some of the main allies of the informal British rule. Indeed, in his first years as Consul-General, Cromer tended to stress the dangers inherent in a policy of abolition which would contravene social custom and religious law; the idea of taxing slaves was dropped because it would necessitate violating the *ḥarīm*, and any move toward legal abolition was avoided since it would fly in the face of Islamic law and inflame the "religious party."[59] He was wont to cite the successes of the Maḥdī in Sudan and a more general popular attachment to "Mohammedan law" as warnings against any precipitous moves on the slavery question; while he admired the Indian Act of 1843 which effectively abolished slavery there, he argued that the introduction of anything similar into Egypt would "put every Mahommedan in the country against us."[60] As late as 1894, Cromer still objected to complete abolition on the grounds that the Khedive and the Legislative Council had no authority to tamper with the Islamic laws recognizing and regulating the practice.[61]

Cromer's position, sometimes at loggerheads with the anti-slavery forces, was probably based on a pragmatic assessment of the British interests at stake. Samuel Baker, an English official who had served with the Egyptian army, outlined a similar stance, but with a frankness Cromer could ill afford, in a letter to the head of the Anti-Slavery Society. Having voiced disagreement with "neck-or-nothing philanthropists who declare that all slaves should be immediately liberated by a stroke of the pen," he noted that "our fathers" were slave owners and were paid some £20 million in compensation at the time of abolition. Baker held it both unjust and impossible to "rob the Egyptians of their slaves that were purchased according to their laws and customs"; and the required compensation could not but cut into Egypt's interest payments on the foreign debt which were, after all, the clear priority of the British government and its people.[62] Such class identification and fiscal caution on the part of colonial officials created tensions with the anti-slavery groups which could erupt into open charges of misgovernance. The British and Foreign Anti-Slavery Society published a pamphlet in 1885, *Scandals at Cairo in Connection with Slavery*, highly critical of Lord Cromer: it claimed that slave dealers were not always punished, and that some slave owners used their influence to block manumission of their own slaves – all charges which, Cromer himself acknowledged, had basis in fact.[63] Although Cromer publicly stated his opposition to the institution, he continued to believe that it could be abolished through indirect means – cutting off the supply and minimizing a master's coercive powers – and bemoaned the "misdirected zeal of the anti-slavery people" that imperiled the chosen sane and steady course.[64]

Significant inroads were indeed made in this fashion: the institution of slavery was not abolished between 1877 and 1895, but an owner's control of his or her slave was so undermined as to render ownership a legal fiction. Although the 1877 Convention did not outlaw the possession of slaves, an annex to the Convention established a number of manumission bureaux which issued certificates of freedom and placed former slaves, mostly women, in "respectable" work such as domestic service. While slavery remained legal, the bureaux came increasingly to manumit all slaves who requested freedom: in May 1881, the Cairo Bureau, for example, was instructed by the Minister of the Interior to issue certificates to all applicants regardless of circumstances.[65] In 1885, the number of bureaux was greatly increased and all were placed under the authority of Colonel Schaefer in the Service, thus centralizing and strengthening control of manumission procedures. The combined effect of such measures was the *de facto* abolition of slavery, since all slaves who desired freedom appeared able to obtain it.[66] The sole remaining difficulty, that of removing all legal disabilities of slaves whose owners refused formal manumission, was addressed through a new Convention between Great Britain and Egypt for the Suppression of Slavery and the Slave Trade in 1895. In addition to tightening the penalties for trading in slaves, the Convention specified punishment for "those who have obstructed a free person from enjoying full liberty and disposal of own person."[67] Since the State could free any slave it chose, owners formally lost the power to interfere with any activity, be it employment, marriage, or residence, of their slaves.

Did the much anticipated reaction of the "Islamic party" materialize in the course of these twenty years of gradual abolition? The *sharī'ah* courts, when asked in the early 1880s, followed a policy of enforcing Islamic laws concerning slavery. A slave was only manumitted, under the religious law, by an express act of the owner (or by *umm walad* status, as we shall see below); otherwise, the owner or his heirs remained the slave's legal guardians. When a police officer requested the *muftī*'s opinion on a woman slave who married over the objection of her legal owner, for instance, the *muftī* found the marriage legally invalid (*bāṭil*).[68] A concubine, whose master had died, was thwarted in her desire to marry one of his relatives by his son, who claimed the right of *walāyah* (guardianship) over her as the heir of her master.[69] Whether or not these slaves had received manumission papers from the State was not a concern of the court: rights of guardianship persisted until the master himself freed the slave. Islamic law remained crystal clear on this point and the *muftī*, when pressed for a ruling, had little flexibility; there is no evidence from the courts to suggest, however, that the *qāḍīs* ever played a more aggressive role by actually demanding proof of manumission before writing a marriage contract, as several British officials had reported.[70] The *muftī*'s decisions were limited to cases where the master actively protested against a slave's marriage and insisted upon strict application of the *sharīʿah*.

Indeed, Wilfred Blunt claimed that at least one highly placed religious leader, Muḥammad al-Anbābī, *shaykh al-Azhar* at the time of the ʿUrābī revolt, condemned slavery as practiced in Egypt as a perversion of the institution. The Qur'ān, according to this interpretation, permitted the enslavement of idolators only in wartime and, even then, solely for the purpose of converting them. ʿUrābī himself, according to the same source, gave orders for the suppression of the trade and swore not to rest until the "stigma of slavery is entirely removed from the Egyptian community."[71] Although we have only Blunt's testimony on this point, and as self-appointed liaison between the National Party and the British he surely wished to present the Party in the best possible light, other evidence on the degree of Egyptian attachment to slavery generally supports the view that the institution was not deeply embedded in the society by the late nineteenth century. On the contrary, Cromer noted that, far from raising obstacles, "native public opinion" had acquiesced gracefully to the freeing of slaves.[72] After the 1895 Convention imposed penalties for any owner who refused a slave a certificate of freedom upon request, the threat of punishment had to be invoked only nine times over the course of the next year and a half.[73] In brief, the hue and cry anticipated by Cromer while he had earlier dragged his feet was nowhere raised.

Undoubtedly, Cromer had employed the spectre of the feared "Muslim reaction" as a method of silencing his anti-slavery critics, claiming a delicate balance of internal political forces which British rule must take into consideration. In addition to increasing his own maneuverability, however, Cromer as a colonial official imbued with the prejudices of the age, was predisposed to view Islam and Islamic law as the primary supports of slavery, and to assume that believing Muslims were the foremost opponents of abolition. Most western consular officials followed this lead, and the institution of slavery was generally perceived to be a part of the Islamic tradition of Egypt which must be treated with the utmost caution. Such an attitude tended to cloud the nature of slavery in Egypt, and disguise the very important fact that the institution was in a state of rapid decline as a result of broad social transformations. Islamic law, embodying many of the customary views of the institution and the status of slaves, did help shape the lives and prospects of slave women in Egypt; it operated, however, in ways far more complex than simple advocacy of the institution. Slavery, and its abolition, were governed during the nineteenth century by the economic and social roles played by slaves, as well as the popular perceptions, legal status, and moral sentiments defining the institution. Women slaves were almost always attached to a household and engaged in the rendering of personal service. Relations with the family of ownership thus determined their lot during the period of enslavement; these relations, in turn, were influenced by prevailing judicial and customary attitudes toward those in bondage.

Islam and slavery

Slave status under Islamic law was governed by a set of scattered opinions which blended identities of the slave as thing and the slave as person. Legal status as the property of an owner was tempered, to a certain degree, by judicial recognition of the special quality, the humanity, of this form of property. In terms of religious status, a slave was fully equal to his or her co-religionists, although the lack of freedom could absolve a slave from strict observance of religious duties which might prove difficult to undertake. On the level of legal competence, the incompetence (*hadjr*) of a slave was modified in several respects: slaves could contract marriages and, when authorized by an owner, engage in business dealings of a legally binding nature. Generally speaking, the rights a slave did share with a free person were halved: a slave woman's *ʿiddah*, for example, was normally one half that of a free woman. Legal rules defining the status of the enslaved were elaborated and expanded in the context of exhortations found in the Qur'ān and the *ḥadīth*. While slavery was accepted as a legitimate institution, the Qur'ān lauded emancipation as a meritorious act, banned the prostitution of female slaves, and held up legal marriage and the giving of a dowry as pious acts on the part of slave owners. Numerous *ḥadīths* enjoined masters to treat their slaves with kindness and compassion.[74]

In assessing the status of female slaves, we must ask to what extent the limited legal rights accorded to slaves and the vaguer and more sweeping religious exhortations actually influenced the lot of the enslaved woman: on a spectrum going from slave to free, from thing to person, how often were the rules and perceptions undergirding slaves' rights and personhood asserted over against the basic fact that these women were property? Were slaves allowed or encouraged to marry? Were the legal stipulations protecting a concubine and her offspring adhered to? Was the call for just and compassionate treatment heard and translated into action? Although the sample from the courts in Cairo and Manṣūrah and al-Mahdī's *Fatāwā* is small, there is sufficient evidence of a diverse nature to provide at least a fragmentary picture of the life and status of slave women.[75]

Owners, in their capacity as the legal *wālī* (marriage guardian) of their slaves, did undertake to arrange marriages while slaves were still within their households. The path fraught with least difficulty was that of marrying a female slave to a male slave of the same household: the new couple could then embark on marital life without causing any disruption in the owner's household.[76] As long as they remained slaves, however, the rights and duties of marriage were subject to modification at the owner's whim: one of them could be sold to another family, effectively throwing the marriage into abeyance for the duration of servitude and separation. Al-Mahdī handled two such cases, one of which follows:

Question: There is a female slave whose owner conditionally freed her (*dabbaraha*)[77] and married her to a male slave he also owned, and he left them in his house and journeyed; and when he returned he found that the male slave had misbehaved and he got angry with him and sold him, and kept his *mudabbarah* wife from him. And several years after the sale, the slave's buyer raided and took the female slave from her master's house on the pretext that she was married to the male slave. And can the owner of the female slave take her back from he who took her, and the buyer of the male not object to her return?

Answer: The *mudabbarah* will be freed after the death of her master, and she is not free before his death without the effectuation of the manumission, and the owner of her husband cannot remove her from the possession of her master, her emancipator, solely on the abovementioned pretext, and God is exalted in knowledge.[78]

If the owner manumitted one of the couple, as he did in three other cases where he owned both husband and wife, the freed person could not leave the master's house with his or her mate; a slave, regardless of whether or not the spouse had been freed, remained under the master's authority. For a female slave, the house of her master, not that of her husband, constituted the "house of obedience" (*bayt al-ṭāʿah*) which she could not lawfully desert; a slave wife thus owed her master, not her husband, ultimate loyalty and obedience.[79] Similarly, the rights of marriage were reduced by slave status: the slave woman who wanted a separate house so that she could enjoy nuptial privacy was told by the *muftī* that a master had no obligation to provide special lodging for a married slave.[80] Perhaps the most dramatic disability of slave marriage concerned the children of the union: if a woman were a slave, her children, regardless of the father's status, were born into slavery as the property of her master; when the mother was free, however, the children inherited her status even if their father remained in bondage. The freedom of any child born to a marriage between a slave woman and a free man could be stipulated, however, as a condition in the marriage contract, a possibility known and practiced during the nineteenth century according to al-Mahdī's opinions. Arranging marriages for female slaves could be not only a virtuous but also a profitable act on the part of the master: female slaves, not commonly employed in material production in this period in Egypt, did upon occasion produce children whom their masters could successfully claim as new slaves.[81] The freedom of a female to refuse such a marriage was limited: the legal schools agreed that a master could coerce his female slaves to marry while some divergence of opinion continued regarding the right of legally major males to refuse a marriage.[82] The court records are silent on the coercion of slaves, so that it may have been an uncommon practice.

This issue of coerced marriage arose, however, in a somewhat different context. No legal barrier was raised to marriage between slave and free. Numerous manumitted slave women were married to men who had never been slaves, marriages which may have taken place before the act of manumission. As we have seen above, an owner might marry a female slave to a free relative or friend, an occurrence witnessed as well by contemporary observers.[83] Objections were raised, however, when attempts were made to marry a free woman against her will to a male slave: it was here that the issue of "suitability" arose, for a woman cannot marry a man of "unsuitable" status, that is, a man considered beneath her in terms of social standing, without the express permission of her *wālī*. A mistress who wanted to marry her free servant to one of her male slaves was forbidden to do so over the refusal of the servant and her relatives.[84] A *shaykh al-balad* was similarly reprimanded for forcing a free servant girl to marry his slave without her agreement or that of her *wālī*.[85] In both instances, the proposed marriages suffered from a dual impediment in the eyes of the *muftī*: lack of consent from a legally major woman, and the absence of the *wālī*'s approval for an unsuitable marriage. In a somewhat stickier case, the *muftī* grappled with the problem posed by a father, acting as *wālī*, who wanted to marry his minor daughter to one of his own slaves despite the exhortation to marry minor girls only to "suitable" men. The *muftī* ruled the marriage valid only in the unlikely event that the *wālī* had been ignorant of the groom's lack of suitability.[86] Although the question of suitability never arose with marriages between slave women and free men who were, by definition, of higher social status, the incidence of other kinds of cases suggests that marital alliances of slave and free were by no means uncommon, and the owners of slave women, as well as men, often made such arrangements.[87]

A number of slave women, as we have seen, were bought as concubines for their masters and performed wifely duties without the bond of legal matrimony. Concubinage was defined and regulated by legal rules which, at least in the period under consideration, appear to have been fairly well observed. Men could only cohabit with slaves they personally owned: slaves of a wife or other relatives were forbidden to them, as were any women of natural or acquired kinship, or women married to others. Co owners were not permitted to use a slave as concubine, and "prostitution" of the slave, which included any giving of her to others for sexual purposes, was prohibited.[88] Women slaves, however, were sometimes vulnerable to sexual abuse and violation of the law at their expense. It was not unheard of, for example, for a man to have sexual intercourse with a slave owned by his wife who was, under the law, forbidden to him. The three cases referred to the *muftī* which dealt with such a situation were more concerned, however, with the status of children born of this illegal union than with castigation of the responsible male. In every case, the *muftī* ruled that the slave and her children had not acquired the special rights they would have if the sire had been the master; the mistress's husband, in the meantime, suffered not even a reprimand. Another slave, made pregnant by her master's brother, was left no legal recourse after his death.[89] Although more apt to be sexually accessible to the relatives of her owner, a slave might also have illicit relations with men outside of the master's household. An unusual case, submitted to the *muftī*, demonstrates the limited benefits to the woman:

Question: A Sudanese man owns male and female slaves and a man made one of them pregnant; he used to keep company with her because the people of that region customarily did not prevent their slaves from going out to work in agriculture or to gather firewood, etc. And the slave woman (*jāriyah*) had children and the man who had violated her claimed that he was the father and the slave confirmed that. Then the aforementioned owner of the slave took the children by force and put them under his guardianship without legal proceedings. If it is proven that the aforementioned slave woman is enslaved (*mamlūkah*) to her master, are the children enslaved to the woman's master following their mother's status, and he can take the children of the slave, and the man who violated her has no rights to them because they take the slave status of their mother?

Answer: Yes, the children of the aforementioned slave (*amah*) by a "stranger" are slaves who take their mother's status. The owner of the mother has the right of disposal (*taṣarruf*) of her and of her children, and such is the case. And the aforementioned "fornicator" cannot take possession of her nor of her children without legal proceedings, and God knows best.[90]

Although no restrictions were placed on the number of concubines a man could keep in addition to his four legal wives, there is little evidence to suggest that, outside the large *ḥarīms* of the ruling family, multiple concubines were commonplace. Indeed, the keeping of a single concubine could become a source of friction in a household. One case submitted to the *muftī* described the domestic strife between a couple arising from the presence of a concubine unwanted by the legal wife. The husband complained that his wife's relatives, legion in number, frequently visited the house and created discord by insisting that this concubine was a "source of evil" and should be sold. The only solution, in his opinion, was the cancellation of the relatives' visiting privileges, with the exception of her parents; he refused to accept their argument that his sexual relationship with the slave required her sale. The *muftī* decided that neither party to the quarrel had the force of law on its side: the husband could not, legally speaking, prevent his wife's relatives from paying calls, and neither the wife, nor her relatives, could force the husband to sell a slave solely because she was his consort.[91]

Although a concubine received some legal protection, she could be sold or married off at the whim of her master. Only when she achieved the status of *umm walad* by bearing children recognized as the master's offspring was she not only safe from sale, but also promised her freedom upon the death of her owner. Her children, as the progeny of their master, were born free and enjoyed full inheritance rights in their father's estate.[92] Through childbearing she also realized the *raison d'être* implicit in the common appellation of a concubine in the court records as the *mustauladdah*, or "one by whom one wants to have children."

During the Muḥammad ʿAlī period, such guarantees had the force of law: of the 58 cases in the Cairo court sample concerning slaves, 5 cases outlined the shares of children of concubines in their deceased father's estate, shares equal to those offspring born to a legal wife.[93] When in Luxor in the 1860s, Lady Duff Gordon, after helping the local magistrate find olives to satisfy a yen of his pregnant black concubine, wryly observed "how shocked a white Christian gentleman of our colonies would be at our conduct to make all this fuss about a black girl." According to local practice, the concubine would surely be offered her freedom and have all expenses paid for an advantageous marriage should she so wish after the birth of the child; as for the baby, it could expect to enjoy rights equal to those of the other children of the magistrate.[94] Concubinage continued to be practiced in the highest social circles throughout the century: in 1894, Cromer reported that the young Khedive ʿAbbās Ḥilmī planned to marry his pregnant Circassian slave. Although the marriage apparently never took place, the woman gave birth, a few months later, to a child who received a clear welcome into the royal family.[95]

In humbler circles, *umm walad* status did bring immunity from sale. The *muftī* always upheld the ban on sales of an *umm walad*: he forbade the sale of a *ḥabashīyyah* slave in one case who, although a non-Muslim (*dhimmī*), had borne a son to her master, and also ruled that an *umm walad*, even if her children had died, could not be put on the market. Nor could an *umm walad* serve as the pledge in a business transaction since, by law, she could not be transferred to a new owner.[96] Even with these protections, an *umm walad*'s life, blending the roles of wife and slave, was marked by the absolute obedience she owed her master. Until the time of his death and her freedom, slave status deprived her of most rights free women exercised under law. The *umm walad* who contracted a marriage without her master's permission after her son by him had died was informed by the *muftī* that her master's disapproval invalidated the marriage.[97] Women with *umm walad* status were required to obey their masters' request to accompany them on journeys: a free wife could have exercised the right of refusal.[98]

Nevertheless, the safety from sale, eventual freedom, and material security that an *umm walad* could hope to achieve through her children rendered that status truly desirable. The difficulty, for many concubines, lay in proving a child's legitimacy, that is, in securing legal recognition of a master's paternity. The Ḥanafī school of law diverged from other schools on the issue: Ḥanafīs required an explicit acknowledgment on the part of the father, and allowed him to disavow the child even in the face of legal presumptions in favor of paternity, such as the fact that the woman had previously borne children to him. Other schools presumed a master's paternity in the case of a pregnant concubine, although he could deny the child by swearing he had not cohabited with his concubine for six months prior to birth.[99] In the courts in 1800, the stricter Ḥanafī interpretation held sway: Maryām, a slave woman, was refused her petition for *umm walad* status when her master denied he had sexual relations with her and refused to acknowledge paternity of her child.[100] Al-Mahdī, the *muftī*, took a similar position at mid-century:

Question: There is a man who owned a slave woman (*jāriyah*) for a period of two years and it became apparent that she was pregnant and she miscarried. And her master said to her: "By whom is this pregnancy?" And she said to him: "By you, my master." And he said to her: "This pregnancy is not by me." And if she claimed that the pregnancy is by her master and the aforementioned master denies her claim, can he sell her, and does he have the final word?

Answer: A slave cannot prove the legitimacy of a child by her master unless he claims it, and the aforementioned slave does not become an *umm walad* of her master, and such is the situation. And her master can sell her, and God is exalted in knowgedge.[101]

Slave women apparently met with no more success in cases where their masters had died during a pregnancy. Several women raised claims to estates on the grounds that they were impregnated by their masters before death. In each of these cases, the pregnancy of the slaves was not at issue but other heirs disputed paternity. Although the courts demonstrated a greater willingness to consider presumptive evidence, such as the fact that these women had previously had children by their masters, only clear acknowledgment of the child by the master before death guaranteed that the mother would be an *umm walad* and the child a free and equal heir.[102] Indeed, al-Mahdī took the position that proof of a sexual relationship between a man and his concubine, even with his own conscious avowal of sexual relations, did not legitimize the child; intimacy alone was no proof of paternity. In order to be legitimate, a child must be acknowledged by the master; children born after one legally avowed (*istilḥāq*) would be considered legitimate, however, as long as they were not denied by the master.[103] Thus, although *umm walad* status did confer benefits and security, designation as an *umm walad* depended, almost entirely, on the will of the owner.

The stakes were high even if the courts were not very encouraging, so a significant number of women tried to claim *umm walad* status. Out of the 51 cases referred to al-Mahdī dealing with manumission, 11 were brought by women who sought such status; without the explicit acknowledgment of their masters, however, the courts refused to recognize them as *umm walad*.[104] On the other hand, we have many instances of women acquiring *umm walad* status, receiving their freedom upon their owners' deaths, and raising children who were acknowledged descendants of their masters.[105] The fact that a number of concubines and their children did share in masters' estates means that owners were sometimes willing to acknowledge paternity and integrate a slave and her children into their family. Whether such a man was anxious to assure the continuity of his line, sincerely attached to his concubine, or moved by a sense of social justice cannot be determined. Other concubines, however, were not so fortunate: as long as a master refused to acknowledge paternity, a concubine and her children remained in slavery without any promise of freedom or inheritance. The control an owner exercised over his concubine, including the final say on the legitimacy of her children, was absolute.

In areas touching on the reproductive functions of a female slave, on her marriage or her status as the mother of her master's children, law and custom conferred rights which, while not identical with those of a free woman, did underscore the human qualities of the enslaved. In a society where slavery remained marginal to economic production, and most slave women played the role of servant or concubine, these rights were protected by the logic of the female slave's situation: functioning as housekeeper or sexual partner, her activities, at least in the sphere of the household, were not that different from those of a free wife. Her status, within slavery, tended to rise as her role in reproduction approached that of other women. The presence of slave women in wifely roles may have resulted, on the other hand, in a devaluation of the status of free wives as suggested by the occasional but fervent opposition on the part of wives and their families to the introduction of concubines into the household. That such devaluation became generalized over time in the slave-possessing upper classes as a whole and contributed to the greater restrictions placed upon free wives among the more affluent sectors of society is hinted at by the precarious status of these women relative to those of more modest households.

Despite a certain overlap in the status of slave and free, however, slave women were often treated as things, undifferentiated from other forms of property. Although an owner's control was tempered by legal rules and moral prescriptions, the fundamental identity of a slave as possession was clearly manifested in the court data. In the Cairo records, eight of the nine cases concerning women still in bondage were disputes over slave sales, usually concerning whether or not the ill health or pregnancy of a slave invalidated a sale, or weighing various claims to legal possession resting on the validity of prior transactions.[106] In al-Maḥdī's opinions, slaves were pledged as security (*rahn*) for loans, treated as part of the goods composing a bridal gift (*mahr*), inherited, and jointly owned by business partners.[107] In all these cases, the human quality of the slave disappears in the overwhelmingly commercial character of the transactions; slaves were a form of property with high market value, and struggles for possession were colored by a keen appreciation of their value as property, not as human beings.

Treatment of the murder of a slave combined, in legal theory, perceptions of the slave as person and as thing. Although all schools recognized retaliation (*qiṣāṣ*), or the death of the murderer, as a legitimate penalty should a slave kill another slave or free person, only the Ḥanafīs held that a free person could be put to death for slaying a slave.[108] In practice, however, in the sole case involving the murder of a slave in the sample, the route of monetary compensation (*diyah*) to the slave's owner was chosen by the court: the murderer was required to pay the value of the slave "as appraised by known experts" to the owner.[109] Although this method of dealing with homicide also prevailed when the victim was free, the preference, even among Ḥanafīs, for *diyah* rather than *qiṣāṣ* when the victim was a slave emphasizes the identity of a slave as a commodity rather than a person. Evidence is lacking on the legal or social response to the killing of a slave by an owner in this period, but the logic of the law suggests that no penalty would be forthcoming since an owner could not pay a *diyah* to himself. Neither the court records nor contemporary observers mentioned such an event; the status of slaves as members, albeit inferior ones, of the family unit and their high market value undoubtedly discouraged precipitous punishment and severe treatment of a slave by her master or mistress.

Although we have no detailed accounts of the conditions and status of women slaves in the period, the court evidence, silent on cruelty or abuse other than the cases of sexual abuse mentioned above, suggests that domestic slaves were protected from the worst excesses of treatment. The rare mistreatment of a slave carried a certain social stigma strong enough, apparently, for at least one woman to report her own brother-in-law to the authorities for the beating of his slave.[110] Recognized as human beings and not strictly differentiated from their owners by race or religion, slave women exercised the limited rights accorded them by law. An important measure of their status lay in their future, in the potentiality of manumission and full participation in society as freed persons.

Manumission and freedom

Many owners observed the religious exhortation to free slaves after a period of service. Manumissions were rarely recorded, however, in the courts: the Cairo sample included only one case, that of a mistress freeing her female slave. On the other hand, among the women appearing as principals in legal transactions of various kinds in the 1800 to 1860 sample of 2,054 cases, 42, or about 2 per cent, were manumitted slaves. Available testimony on the number of slaves imported each year up through the late 1870s varies so widely that any attempt to estimate the number of freed slaves by comparing importation figures with slave population figures yields unreliable results. Since the importation of slaves continued apace, however, and the slave population did not undergo any discernible increase, the number of manumitted must have been significant.[111] While no data are available on the rate of manumission *per se*, the freed slave woman was clearly no rarity in Cairo society. The strong positive moral sanction which underlay high manumission rates was reflected in the view of manumission as a form of religious expiation. A religious *shaykh*, for example, might exhort a sick or dying owner to free slaves as a final pious act.[112] Manumission as a commonplace occurrence also tended to be self-perpetuating: many slaves must have come to expect freedom as a reward for loyal service if not as the normal outcome of a period of enslavement.

The three paths to enfranchisement recognized by Islamic law, outright manumission with immediate effect (*ʿitq*), manumission with effect from the owner's death (*tadbīr*), and contractual enfranchisement (*mukātabah*), were all known to the courts, although we have evidence for the practice of the first two only during this period.[113] The absence of contractual enfranchisement is best understood in terms of the slave's position in Egyptian society: as a member of a private household engaged in personal service, the Egyptian slave lacked direct access to money: the typical woman slave was neither a trader nor a wage-earner and thus had not the means to purchase her freedom. *Tadbīr*, which enabled an owner to perform the pious act of manumission without losing the slave's services, was more popular. The courts insisted, however, that a slave freed in this conditional fashion (the *mudabbarah*) could not be sold and must be fully liberated upon the owner's death; slaves who tried to secure their freedom before the master's death were always informed by the court that they remained, legally, in bondage.[114] Most former slaves had been freed outright (*ʿitq*) and the courts zealously protected their rights: neither a former owner nor his heirs could reclaim a slave who had been freed as long as the slave possessed some legal proof, in the form of written or oral testimony, of her manumission. When the heirs of owners pressed such claims, the former slaves took the matter to the courts where they could be sure of a favorable hearing.[115]

The deep roots, in tradition and religious law, of the practice of manumission undoubtedly contributed to the success of the major manumission drive of the late 1870s and 1880s. After the opening of government manumission bureaux, as specified in an annex to the 1877 Convention, slaves obtained their freedom with apparent ease. During the next few years, manumission procedures were streamlined and methods of enforcement improved: the bureaux, initially controlled by various provincial officials, were brought under the central authority of the Service of the Abolition of Slavery in Cairo and, as of 1885, run by the police. By 1887, Colonel Schaefer could report that "almost every slave" now knew of the manumission bureaux because of a thorough publicity campaign making use of the Arabic press; indeed, the bureaux had been so successful that Schaefer reported a surplus of freed slaves in Upper Egypt who "bothered" the military authorities. There were no reports of problems in locating slaves who wished to be freed or in wresting them away from their owners; on the contrary, Schaefer himself was loath to free all those who presented themselves in the Aswān region out of a concern for the stability of the area.[116]

While we have figures for the number of slaves manumitted after 1877 (see above), we lack any comparable information on those freed before that date. Did the institution of manumission bureaux and the government campaign for liberation dramatically increase manumission activity? We cannot be sure. After 1877, all slaves who wished to be free could apply to government offices, and we may safely assume that this multiplied the number of formal manumissions. On the other hand, the practice of manumission had long been a well established part of the institution of slavery; as we have seen, few owners obstructed or even protested against the loss of their slaves. While Cromer cited a few examples of owners who attempted to stop their slaves from reaching the manumission office or opposed a freed slave's marriage as a form of harassment, such incidents occurred rarely.[117] The tempo of manumission may well have quickened in the post-1877 period, but the practice enjoyed long precedent and strong ethical and legal sanctions.

Once freed, the slave retained a certain attachment to her emancipator and emancipator's family as a client: a slave freed by a member of the elite often carried the magic name of her manumitter to her death. ʿAishah, the *maʿtūqah* (freed slave) of the deceased Ismāʿīl Bāshā, or Fāṭimah, the *maʿtūqah* of the deceased ʿAbd Allāh Bāshā, were ladies of the elite in their own right who bore the names of their manumitters along with the honorific titles of *sitt*, *khātūn*, and *maṣūnah*.[118] The doors to marriage and property were opened by intimate association and an ongoing client relationship with families of money and power; the many slaves of the larger *ḥarīms* and other privileged households could expect a future in freedom that matched the lifestyle of their past. Although not all slaves had these expectations fulfilled, neither race nor a past in bondage impeded assimilation as freed women into the very classes that had formerly possessed them. In some cases, the patronage bond involved ongoing pecuniary advantage: the Khedive Ismāʿīl's former *ḥarīm* slaves were still collecting a monthly allowance under his grandson, the Khedive ʿAbbās Ḥilmī.[119] Other freed slaves, particularly those who had borne children to the master, might remain in the household of the emancipator and be treated as family members long after the owner's death.[120]

The client relationship could also be a source of friction, however, and of incursions upon the slave's newly found freedom. In lieu of her own natural agnates, the emancipator's family exercised tutelage in matrimony and stood as her heir. In response to complaints from freed slaves, the courts agreed that such guardianship was to be exercised within legally prescribed bounds: if the family failed to arrange a marriage for the freed slave, she could appoint her own marriage agent; once freed, no one, not even her emancipator, could prevent her from marrying whomsoever she chose and living where she wished.[121] If she were unmarried, her estate devolved on her former owner or owner's family. Disputes could also arise when the former owner refused to cede this right, as legally required, to the heirs she acquired through marriage. On two separate occasions, a man protested to the court that his deceased wife's former mistress had taken money or jewels possessed by the former slave which rightfully should go to the husband.[122] The transition from bondage to a new status as freed wife was thus not always accomplished smoothly but social practice seemed to support the laws equating the rights of a former slave with those of a free-born woman. Once freed, a woman acquired inheritance rights and protection from coercion by her ex-owner: the Cairo court ruled that a man could not force his freed slave to marry against her will.[123] These rights were buttressed by the slave's proven potential for marriage and property holding among upper and middle class circles.

Marriage into elite households gave some former slaves access to substantial wealth. As a *sitt*, *maṣūnah*, or *khātūn*, all of which denoted high social standing, freed slaves purchased sizeable properties through their agents in the courts. In the five cases of elite purchase recorded, three of the ladies were white, one was brown (*ḥabashīyyah*), and one was black. In three additional cases of purchase, freed slave women of humbler status, addressed as *ḥurmah*, bought more modest properties on their own account.[124] Freed slaves, then, as wives and mothers with inheritance rights or as independent producers and traders, possessed property and conducted business: slave origins did not exclude these women from participation in economic life. Former slave women also acquired landed interests like other women of the elite: in Manṣūrah, three black slaves, formerly owned by the same mistress, appointed an agent to represent them in Cairo in the Dīwān al-Rūznāmah.[125]

Patterns of inheritance help to clarify the social and economic standing women achieved after gaining their freedom. Out of eight successions of former female slaves, four left the bulk of the estate to the woman's husband or children, while another two involved disputes between the woman's husband and the family of the former owner; in the remaining two cases, the owner or owner's family inherited the freed slave without contest.[126] Six of the eight women, therefore, were married with husbands or children surviving them. The impression that freed women often became part of the marital family is further strengthened by the fact that former female slaves were frequently mentioned as heirs to their husbands or children.[127] As in the case of sales and purchases, these women had, in the wake of enfranchisement, been absorbed into different classes. Some were married to members of the official elite, *bāshās* and *efendīs*, or to wealthy traders and members of the *'ulamā'*; others, inheriting smaller estates, were the wives of shopkeepers and artisans. Some had wed men who themselves had been slaves, usually in the service of the palace or state officials. Although most of these women appear to have been sole wife, in three cases they were co-wives in an elite household: in two families a free woman was first wife, and in the third family all three wives had been slaves.

A freed slave woman, at least one from an elite household, was apparently in considerable matrimonial demand. Her own master might propose or, if from the royal *ḥarīm*, her hand might be sought by ministers, *bāshās*, or beys, all of whom sought to strengthen their alliance with the Khedive's household through a connection with his *ḥarīm*.[128] Nor was race an impediment: we have ample evidence that black slave women married into well placed families. When Colonel Schaefer instructed his staff on the inspection of ships in the Suez Canal in the 1880s, he found it necessary to point out that some of the Muslim pilgrims traveled with wives who "might be taken for slaves."[129] Marriage to free Egyptians or Turco-Circassians continued to be the quickest and surest form of assimilation in the nineteenth century.

Because the bulk of the information used here comes from the Cairo courts, caution is called for in generalizing these findings to the other half of the slave population scattered throughout the provinces. At least one report noted the existence of a small village in Lower Egypt in the 1830s, inhabited exclusively by freed black slaves who had married amongst themselves, and freed slave families were hired as a unit for wage labor in Upper Egypt in the 1880s.[130] Such physical and social isolation, perhaps exceptional even in the countryside, appears to have been unknown in Cairo. The Home for Freed Female Slaves was established in Cairo in 1884 to receive manumitted slaves and place them in employment, usually as domestic servants. In the 1890s, the Home received some thirty to forty women a year, representing only one fifth of the total who passed through the official manumission office and undoubtedly much less of those actually enfranchised. The fate of the vast majority of freed slaves is not discussed, but they were apparently integrated into society without recourse to the Home's services. By the Home's own account, it had no trouble finding domestic positions for the women who turned to it, and others left the Home to marry: we may assume that the majority of freed female slaves secured their own situations without the Home's assistance, marrying and embarking on family life as freed women.[131]

The Home was likely to be the last refuge of the "domestic drudges," the slaves owned by more modest households where coarse household work and ties to a family without wealth and power left them ill-equipped for a freedom differing to any great extent from their bondage. It was on this, largely black, group that the fears of European observers focused: any precipitous manumission campaign would contribute to the increase of immorality in society since they perceived blacks as "dominated by morbid sexual desire," and headed for "idleness, ignorance, want, and vice" upon liberation.[132] The vision of large numbers of slave women thrown headlong into prostitution by their lack of skills, knowledge, and ambition simply failed to materialize; we have no evidence that the fate of freed slave women took a turn for the worse in the late nineteenth century. On the contrary, even the occupants of the Home were smoothly integrated into society. The court records, of course, surely over-represent the other sector of the slave population, those enjoying the relative privilege arising from association with the official and merchant elite who could look forward to a life of luxury after manumission.

The actual conditions of servitude and life after manumission thus varied according to the class of owner, the duties expected of the slave, and the tenor of the individual household. In a society, however, where female slaves were almost exclusively domestic servants and concubines, marginal to economic production, the ties between owner and owned assumed a character distinct from that of pure economic exploitation. The legal rules of Islam, which addressed the slave as both thing and person, neatly intersected, in the Egyptian case, with the prevailing uses of slave labor. Although the property of her owner, the female slave was also a woman whose reproductive role and right to a family life were acknowledged. During slavery she did lack the rights and protections that free women enjoyed within the family unless she established herself as the mother of her master's children. With manumission, however, she gained or regained *in toto* her personhood and acquired all the rights and privileges of a free woman. Although ill-treatment and sexual abuse may have been the lot of some, women were not stigmatized by a past in slavery and, indeed, some gained entrance to elite circles through this peculiar passage. For female slaves, engaged in household labor and sexual service little differentiated from the "woman's work" of the free, the transition to freedom could be accomplished smoothly and without barriers raised by racial prejudice and other forms of social discrimination.

Conclusion

As a household institution, Egyptian slavery was not tied to a particular system of economic production; indeed, at the time the plantation system was gaining ground in Egypt, slavery was in full retreat. Never of signal importance in the country, the institution slowly crumbled in the course of the nineteenth century as the political and social reality of which it had been part lost its former coherence.

The prototypical Egyptian slave, a female concubine or personal servant, belonged to a household of social prominence and political importance where she helped swell the number of retainers, a fully loyal following which lacked competing ties of kin or community. The entire system was rooted in an earlier time, exemplified in the eighteenth century Egypt of great Mamluke houses where not only the *ḥarīm* but also household troops depended on slave recruits for their vitality. The rise of the State under Muḥammad ʿAlī put an end to the warring of these private militias, and male military slaves faded from the scene except for a few brief and unsuccessful attempts to use slave labor in the State's army. Female slaves in the *ḥarīm*, however, retained an albeit shrinking significance as the hallmark of affluence and social power.

Over the course of the nineteenth century, this significance grew ever more symbolic. Their economic role, as producers of a few household goods or even as reproducers of slaves, was never very extensive: the *ḥarīms* tended to be consumers of handicrafts, not the reverse, and the common practice of manumitting slaves while still of marriageable childbearing age limited their role as mothers of a new slave generation. In the political sphere, the consolidation of a bureaucratic State, first under Muḥammad ʿAlī and later under the aegis of the British occupation, lessened the weight of the private household and therefore its need of additional members whose primary contribution was loyalty and dependence. The penetration of capitalism reinforced such trends and further eroded the social system of patronage: as wage labor increased and the internal and external market expanded, the "traditional" relationship of clientage was often bypassed, replaced by relations mediated directly through economic ties. Slavery, at least in its Egyptian form, swiftly became an anachronism, preserved, finally, only in the museum-like surroundings of the household of the Khedive and the like.

We can easily comprehend the ease with which slavery was abolished in Egypt. The State outlawed the slave trade without any serious opposition: outside of a few slave dealers, the society lacked a group or class whose basic interests were intertwined with the institution of slavery, for slaves had been a source of comfort and pleasure in the nineteenth century but little else. Once the supply was cut off, and slaves could seek manumission freely, the institution in Egypt died a painless death. The British campaign merely accelerated a process which was well under way before the 1877 Convention.

The impact of abolition on the society as a whole was probably not very dramatic. For most classes of Egyptian society, slavery remained an institution of the elite and its passing would hardly have been noticed. In the circles where slavery was more common, among the upper classes, the practice may well have undermined the status of women, especially when the vast majority of slaves were females in female roles. The similarities between the roles of slave and free would tend to elevate the status of the slave and depress the status of the free as their activities and conditions of life converged. As domestic servants and concubines, many slaves became quasi-wives, fulfilling functions of nurturance and reproduction; indeed, some were eventually recognized as legitimate mothers with rights to family wealth. Their wifely roles surely encouraged the narrowing of distinctions between free wives and slaves. Female slaves themselves were able to blur this distinction further by mobilizing the rights afforded them by law, by fighting in court for the recognition of their children or for *umm walad* status. On the other hand, female slavery may have outlived its political and social usefulness precisely because its vision of female subservience meshed so well with prevailing views of women, be they slave or free. Here we have seen the patriarchal nature of social consciousness in its starkest form.

Conclusion

Women of the peasant and urban lower classes in Egypt lived through a period, from 1800 to 1914, of economic, political, and social transformation. The integration of Egypt into a European economic system, entailing the conversion of a significant part of Egyptian agriculture to cotton exports and the erosion of the indigenous craft industry, was accomplished in these years despite the abortive attempt of the Egyptian State under Muḥammad ʿAlī to harness production to its own ends. Consolidation of land, the establishment and subsequent diminution of large-scale industry, and the migration of significant sections of the population were actually abetted by the policies of a centralized and bureaucratic State under Muḥammad ʿAlī and his successors, and, after 1882, by British colonial rule.

The four dimensions of women's roles and status – access to property, family relations, participation in social production and the public sphere, and ideological definitions – both reflected and structured the impact of these changes on women and the family. First, women's access to property was buttressed by Islamic laws which acknowledged women as heirs to family property and by marriage customs which bestowed the *mahr* (bridal gift) upon the bride. These claims to family property rested on the woman's identity as a family member, an identity ostensibly based on bonds of blood or marriage; in the actual determination of women's rights to property, however, the family and courts also weighed the woman's contribution to family production. Daughters of peasant families who had married into other households found that their rights to the property of their natal family might be restricted or bypassed altogether, while their claims to property in the marital household were mediated through their husbands. Among urban lower class families, women also commonly shared property and business ventures with their husbands. Women's formal rights to family property were not altogether ignored, but they were subject to erosion or outright attack when perceived as harmful to the coherence of the family unit. From 1800 to 1914, when the family as an economic unit felt pressure from the loss of land and contraction of home crafts, the struggle to maintain the integrity of property and shared production could mean encroachment upon women's individual rights to property. While the contributions of women to production, be they in the form of labor on the family plot, crafts, petty trade, or services, were in no way diminished over this period, the ability of women to draw on these activities to buttress property rights declined as other forms of production expanded.

Secondly, patrilocal marriage and the ease of divorce made women transient members of a family unit. In the peasant family, usually composed of husband, wife, and children, or brothers, their wives, and children, women were viewed as adjuncts, strangers to the *sharikah* that defined the family unit. Similarly, women in Cairo were largely excluded from the guilds that organized male economic life. In both cases, however, other forces operated to combat female dependence: women could use their claims to property and their status as independent legal persons to wield power within the family. With the money and goods acquired from the inheritance, *mahr*, or independent labor, they formed economic associations with other family members, usually although not always their husbands, based on joint purchase or lending.

A woman's capacity to ameliorate her family situation lay primarily, however, in the third dimension of her existence, the realm of social production and the public sphere. It was as an independent peasant producer of textiles for a local market or as a petty trader in Cairo that a woman could earn an income distinct from that gained through shared family production. These types of economic activities underscored her contribution to the family economy, and lent her experience and skill in dealing with the world of affairs outside the household. The protection such activities afforded against disinheritance at the hand of male relatives or loss of family position upon the death of, or divorce by, her husband arose from her ability to use the money and knowledge acquired to increase her weight in family economic arrangements and to struggle, if necessary, for her rights in court. Between 1800 and 1914, however, with the disruption of textile crafts in the rural areas, peasant women grew increasingly dependent on family support and ever more vulnerable to inroads by male relatives on their property rights. In Cairo, this trend was less marked since the most common female trades – itinerant peddling, services to other women, and casual labor of various kinds – were little affected by changes in the organization of agriculture and industry. In addition, the informal institutions that underlay the social and economic life of women defied state control; women's "public" activities remained, by and large, under their own direction.

At the same time, however, the rapid expansion of the public sphere under the aegis of a growing state apparatus took its toll on women. As the State began to provide, if only in a tentative and partial fashion, for the health and education of its population, it established patterns of sexual discrimination that were to long endure. The particular nature of the colonial state, its imposition of institutions controlled by foreigners and ideologies alien to local custom, further worked to marginalize women. Women bore the burden of two forms of discrimination – imported and home grown – while the possibilities for a woman-based reform or self-improvement movement were stunted by the exclusion of "natives" in general, both men and women, from the institutions of colonial government. The rise of the modern State held special consequences for women, as popular movements, such as the peasant revolts and urban uprisings of early nineteenth century Egypt, were definitively repressed and women were less well equipped than men to resist state power in other ways. The colonial situation had particularly negative effects on the majority of women since they were completely alienated – by language, culture, and experience as well as gender – from the state apparatus.

Lastly, the centrality of women's activities in social production and the public sphere to their power within the family and larger society should not blind us to the powerful role that social perceptions of women played in shaping their lives. Women's access to property and activities in family and public life were conditioned by a set of values and customs which underwent only subtle modification in this period. The ideology defining women's social and economic life was not a fully autonomous structure impervious to change; it adapted, nevertheless, to a shifting social reality without any evidence of radical breaks with past perceptions and practices. The proceedings and judgments of the *sharīʿah* court were deeply colored by the dominant perception of women as family members whose rights, obligations, and behavior were defined by their identity as daughters, sisters, wives, or mothers. Although the identity of men was also that of family members, relations within the family were based on unequal reciprocity: women were to be protected and policed by male relatives to whom they owed obedience and submission. This relationship was expressed in various forms in the courts: women, for example, were entitled to material support (*nafaqah*) only as long as they reciprocated with submission; the disobedient wife lost all claim to protection.

The judges of the period, imbued with these perceptions, invariably acted to reinforce traditional patterns of male dominance. By championing male–female relations of protection and control within the family, the courts sided with the woman who sought to secure her rights to protection but looked askance at the woman, who, through divorce or impropriety, had weakened or lost her family ties. In a period when the family as an economic unit was under considerable strain, the religious courts continued to shore up customs that had bonded the family in less troubled times. In their defense of traditional definitions of family relations, the courts were actually aided by women pressing claims to family support in court; female reliance on the material protection provided by the family had increased as some of the sources of income earned outside the household dried up, and the family, as a productive unit, was subject to the exigencies of state intervention.

While defense of traditional family arrangements spelled security for many, the darker side of prevailing ideology was all too apparent to women who found themselves outside a familial circle. Divorced women who failed to join another family unit were apt to lose custody of their children and often experienced real material hardship; the courts of the time tended to disregard the particular circumstances of these women, and required them to conform, for example, to the standards of a "fit mother" only possible to achieve within a family setting. The status of women without families shaded into that of prostitutes, whose legal rights were nonexistent. They, and other women of ill-reputed trades, were exempt from the obligations of obedience and lived free of familial control; the absence of obligations also meant the absence of rights and protections, so that their freedom, the freedom of the outlaw, could be trespassed at will and they were easy prey for official harassment and underworld exploitation. Women slaves, on the other hand, owed a heightened obedience to their owners without enjoying the rights of free women. The ease with which freed slaves were integrated into society suggests that their background of total subservience was an acceptable womanly attribute with little or no stigma attached. The submission required from women thus appears equally as central to social definitions of their role as the rights conferred by law and custom.

Although such perceptions of women, as found in the *sharī'ah* court records, were couched in terms of interpretations of Islamic law, the specifically "Islamic" nature of social consciousness cannot be assumed. Insofar as religious law assigned women the role of dependence and men the role of protector, it sanctified prevailing family structure in which women joined a family as adjuncts to men. Other aspects of the law, however, such as female rights to inheritance or choice of marriage partner, introduced countervailing tendencies which could actually threaten the integrity of the male-centred family. Islamic family law was certainly weighted toward the preservation of male dominance and bore the values of the patriarchal society in which it evolved. To credit Islamic law or the Islamic "environment" with total power over the definition of social relations, however, would be to ignore the wide range of variation in women's roles, across time, class, and geography, that we have seen in Egypt of 1800 to 1914 alone. The law was subject to selective choice and interpretation in response to social needs of the time; judges, and the people who used the court system, chose to adhere strictly to certain rules and ignore others altogether.

Nevertheless, Islamic laws and mores were neither neutral in, nor irrelevant to, the ongoing process of social definition of women's roles. In buttressing the family as a patriarchal institution and lending this institution legitimacy of a religious, and thus transcendent, character, Islamic law and the court system placed very real constraints on women. Although many women might manage to improve their situation through participation in family production or independent economic activities, social perceptions of them as dependent and subservient were undergirded not only by custom, but also by religious authority. The strength of such authority may well help account for the fact that the disruptions of the nineteenth century, especially the undermining of family coherence based on shared production, did not lead to a radical transformation in family structure.

Of greater importance to the preservation of family structure and the role of women therein, however, was the specific character of social change between 1800 and 1914. Increases in wage labor, internal migrations, and the acceleration of state intervention in daily life did not entail the development of social institutions which relieved the family of its role in subsistence production and the reproduction of the conditions of existence. The family, whether rural or urban, still functioned as a unit of production, albeit on a reduced scale, and as the uncontested regulator of social life. The inability and unwillingness of the State to assume such responsibilities dovetailed with the desire of the family to retain its traditional functions, especially in a period of economic dislocation. Preservation of family structure at a time when women's activities were on the decline, however, meant an accentuation of female dependence and stiffer penalties for women estranged from the family. The contours of a woman's life in nineteenth century Egypt were thus shaped by the interplay of economic factors of access to property and participation in social production, the social factors of family reproduction, and the political factors of an evolving state power, all strongly undergirded by the dominant social consciousness expressed in Islamic law and customs. Through their active participation in the street politics, court battles, and social networks of the time, however, women themselves also contributed much to the shaping of their history.

Appendix: The court records, overview and sample

I. The courts[1]

Extant records from the nineteenth century *sharī'ah* courts of Egypt fall into two main categories: minutes from the proceedings of the courts of Cairo, housed in the Maḥkamah al-shar'īyyah archives in Cairo, and minutes from various provincial courts, housed in the Dār al-Maḥfuẓāt in Cairo.

A. Cairo courts

The following list, based on indexes in the Maḥkamah al-shar'īyyah archives, includes courts with extant records from the nineteenth century. Each *sijill* (register) is 300 to 500 pages in length and contains anywhere from 600 to several thousand cases.

Court	*Dates*	*Number of sijillāt*
Miṣr al-Qadīmah	934–1225 AH 1527–1810 AD	31
Ṣalāhīyyah al-Najmīyyah	934–1226 1527–1811	99
Bāb al-'Alī	937–1326 1530–1910	559
Tulūn	937–1226 1530–1811	80
Būlāq	943–1226 1536–1811	83
Jāmi' al-Ḥākim	945–1225 1538–1810	44
al-Ṣalih	953–1226 1546–1811	64
Bāb al-Sha'rīyyah	955–1226 1548–1811	74
Qanātir al-Sibā'	957–1226 1550–1811	45
al-Qismah al-'Askarīyyah	961–1292 1554–1875	418

Court	*Dates*	*Number of sijillāt*
Qusūn	963–1225 1556–1810	67
al-Qismah al-ʿArabīyyah	970–1298 1562–1881	157
al-Zahid	972–1226 1564–1811	47
Taqarīr al-Nazār	1138–1292 1725–1875	42
Isqatāt al-Qūra	1141–1283 1728–1866	46
al-Dīwān al-ʿAlī	1154–1307 1741–1889	16
al-Iʿlanāt	1253–1292 1837–1875	52
Tirkāt	1253–1292 1837–1875	32
Waqfiyyāt	1253–1292 1837–1875	19

B. Provincial courts

The provincial court records are less complete; the Dār al-Maḥfuẓāt holds the minutes of scattered provincial courts, by no means a consistent or systematic collection of provincial records. The following list, based on the holdings of the Dār al-Maḥfuẓāt, is composed of courts with extant records from the nineteenth century. Each *sijill* from the provincial courts is roughly 200 pages in length and contains from 400 to 800 cases.

Court	*Dates*	*Number of sijillāt*
Dumyāṭ (Damietta)	1021–1272 AH* 1612–1861 AD	60
Manṣūrah	1119–1282** 1707–1865	17
Iskandariyyah (Alex.)	1130–1279 1717–1862	224
Mīt Ghamr	1251–1279 1835–1862	17
Rashīd (Rosetta)	1264–1290* 1848–1873	7

* Some later years preserved as well.
** Records missing from 1263–1281 AH.

II. The sample

A. Cairo sample

1. The Bāb al-ʿAlī: The Bāb al-ʿAlī registers were chosen because they record cases continuously throughout the period under study and appear to be complete. One year per decade for the first seven decades of the nineteenth century was arbitrarily selected for study:

Year	*Dates*	*Sijill number*	*No. of cases surveyed*	*No. of cases with women litigants*
1216 AH 1801–1802 AD	7 Rabīʿ I 1216– 4 Ramaḍān 1216	323	846	260
1226–1227 1812	28 Dhū al-hijjah –1 Rabīʿ I 1227	345	619	325
1236–1237 1821–1822	27 Ramaḍān 1236 –11 Rabīʿ I 1237	366		
	16 Dhū al-hijjah 1236–25 Jumādā I 1237	370	632	300
1246 1830	(?) Rabīʿ I 1246 –(?) Rajab 1246	387		
	12 Rajab 1246 –26 Ramaḍān 1246	388	560	270
1255–1256 1839–1840	5 Shawwāl 1255 –1 Rabīʿ I 1256	413	240	153
1266 1850	10 Jumādā II 1266 –19 Shaʿbān 1266	440	270	160
1276 1859–1860	24 Rabīʿ II 1276 –26 Rajab 1276	476	280	151

Up through the sample year of 1246, the MBA registers recorded a wide variety of cases, including: registration of inheritance, debt and guardianship, proxy appointments, conversion to Islam, property sales, divorce agreements and decrees, family support, marriage and *mahr* agreements, *waqf* arrangements, and money payments of all kinds. Beginning with the sample year of 1255–1256, the MBA registers record, almost exclusively, property sales and *waqf* arrangements. Inheritance settlements, and the wide range of demands for, and settlement of, money payments, which involved issues of family support, wifely duties, child custody, thefts, and business and personal relations of many kinds are thereafter recorded in the Iʿlanāt registers. The following Iʿlanāt registers were sampled in order to include these types of cases in the period from 1255 to 1276.

2. al-Iʿlanāt

Year	Dates	Sijill number	No. of cases surveyed	No. of cases with women litigants
1255–1256 AH	1 Shawwāl 1255	5	200	158
1839–1840 AD	–16 Rabīʿ I 1256			
1266	1 Muḥarram 1266	23		
1849–1850	–27 Jumādā 1266			
	1 Rajab 1266	24	200	156
	–15 Dhū al-qaʿdah 1266			
1276	2 Muḥarram 1276	37	175	152
1859–1860	–19 Dhū al-hijjah 1276			

The Cairo court registers number the cases consecutively within each register, but pagination is frequently lacking. All references to Cairo court records are by number of case, not by page.

B. Provincial sample

The court records for Manṣūrah were chosen for the rural sample because they are the most complete available for the period under consideration, and Manṣūrah is located in an important agricultural region in the Delta. The records from Alexandria and Damietta are also complete, but both these courts were located in port towns.

One year per decade for six decades was selected for arbitrary sample. The break in the Manṣūrah records in 1263 precluded any sample from the 1270s.

Year	Dates	Sijill number	No. of cases surveyed	No. of cases with women litigants
1216 AH	1 Rajab 1216–(?)	47/138/37	70	25
1801 AD				
1226–1228	6 Shawwāl 1226–20	47/138/44	50	27
1811–1813	Rabīʿ I 1228			
1235–1238	16 Rajab 1235	47/138/49	55	25
1820–1823	–end Jumādā I 1238			
1245–1247	23 Shaʿbān 1245	47/138/51	40	27
1830–1831	–13 Jumādā I 1247			
1257–1259	19 Ramaḍān 1257	47/138/57	40	26
1841–1843	–end Jumādā I 1259			
1261–1263	26 Muḥarram 1261	47/138/59	40	26
1845–1847	–29 Shawwāl 1263			

The Manṣūrah records contain minutes from a wide variety of cases; property sales constitute the overwhelming majority of entries, but the court heard, now and again, almost all types of cases we found in the Bāb al-ʿAlī and Iʿlanāt registers.

Cases in the Manṣūrah records are not numbered. References to Manṣūrah cases are by page number only; most pages contain two or three cases.

III. Form of cases

The registers contain minutes of court cases in summarized form. The ʿudūl (notaries) who wrote up the cases apparently exercised considerable discretion as to how detailed a record they would leave. Some cases are reported in a terse style without much detail beyond the names of plaintiff and defendant, the issue at hand, and the judgment of the *qāḍī*. Elsewhere, however, detailed testimony might be recorded complete with a blow by blow account of complex arrangements or quarrels as told by the parties involved. In the latter case, the story may be related in a quasi-colloquial language which stands in marked contrast to the legal language employed in the rest of the case.

Standard legal formulae structure most cases, and the order of presentation of witnesses, plaintiff and defendant, and complaint proceeds in a predictable fashion. Many abbreviations, also standard, are employed. The handwriting of the *ʿudūl* in this period, however, often verges on the undecipherable, a problem compounded by laxity in grammar and syntax.

Notes

Introduction

1 See Edward Said, *Orientalism.*

2 For example, Nadia Youssef, *Women and Work in Developing Societies*; and Fatima Mernissi, *Beyond the Veil, Male–Female Dynamics in a Modern Muslim Society.*

3 See Frederick Engels, *The Origin of the Family, Private Property and the State,* pp. 94–146.

4 See Eli Zaretsky, *Capitalism, the Family and Personal Life*, p. 93; and Karen Sacks, "Engels Revisted: Women, the Organization of Production, and Private Property," in Rayna Reiter (ed.), *Toward an Anthropology of Women*, pp. 211–234.

5 See Eric Wolf, *Peasants*, pp. 65–72.

6 See Jane Humphries, "The Working Class Family, Women's Liberation, and Class Struggle: The Case of Nineteenth Century British History," *RRPE*, IX, 3 (Fall 1977), 25–41; also Zillah Eisenstein, "Developing a Theory of Capitalist Patriarchy," in Z. Eisenstein (ed.), *Capitalist Patriarchy and the Case for Socialist Feminism*, pp. 5–40.

7 Engels, *Origin*, pp. 137–139, 221.

8 See Viana Muller, "The Formation of the State and the Oppression of Women: Some Theoretical Considerations and a Case Study in England and Wales," *RRPE*, IX, 3 (Fall 1977), 7–21; Michelle Zimbalist Rosaldo, "A Theoretical Overview," in M. Z. Rosaldo and Louise Lamphere (eds.), *Women, Culture, and Society*, p. 36; and Sacks, "Engels Revisted," in Reiter (ed.), *Toward an Anthropology*, pp. 211–234.

9 See Ronald C. Jenning, "Women in Early Seventeenth Century Ottoman Judicial Records," *JESHME*, 18 (January 1975), 53–114.

10 André Raymond, *Artisans et commerçants au Caire au XVIII*[e] siècle; Terence Walz has also relied heavily on court records for his study of the slave trade in the eighteenth and early nineteenth centuries; see Terence Walz, *Trade between Egypt and Bilād as-Sudān, 1700–1820.*

11 See Emile Tyan, *Histoire de l'organization judiciaire en pays d'Islam*, pp. 11–12.

12 See Raymond, *Artisans*, p. 418; and also *Déscription de l'Egypte, état moderne*, vol. 2, part 2, p. 475.

13 Chafik Chehata, *Droit Musulman*, p. 28; ʿAbd al-Mujīd Muḥammad al-Ḥifnāwī, *Ta'rīkh al-qanūn al-maṣrī*, pp. 466–467; Gabriel Baer, *Studies in the Social History of Modern Egypt*, pp. 130–131.

14 Aḥmad Fathī Zaghlūl, *al-Muḥāmāt*, pp. 159–165, 185–187; al-Ḥifnāwī, *Ta'rīkh*, pp. 463–464; Farhat Ziadeh, *Lawyers and the Rule of Law and Liberalism in Modern Egypt*, pp. 12–15.

15 Muḥammad al-ʿAbbāsī al-Mahdī, *al-Fatāwā al-mahdīyah fī al-waqāʾi al-miṣrīyah*, vol. 1, 8 Dhū al-qaʿdah 1265/1849, p. 22.

16 *Ibid.*, vol. 1, 20 Rabīʿ II 1265/1849, p. 154.

17 Zaghlūl, *al-Muḥāmāt*, pp. 249–266.

1 Ploughs and shares: women, agricultural production, and property

1 See E. R. J. Owen, *The Middle East in the World Economy, 1800–1914*, pp. 24, 216–217, for an overview of Egypt's population growth.

2 Basil Kerblay, "Chayanov and the Theory of Peasantry as a Specific Type of Economy," in Teodor Shanin (ed.), *Peasants and Peasant Societies*, p. 159. As Kerblay notes, Chayanov's theory of the "peasant economy" works better for thinly populated areas where peasants can buy or take in more land, thus making the decision to expand labor a meaningful one. In the Egyptian context, periods of agricultural labor shortage might give the peasant a similar choice as long as there was no competition for land from other quarters. With the rise of extensive cotton cultivation, however, little good agricultural land was available to peasant farmers.

3 The concept of a "peasant economy" as proposed by Daniel Thorner, "Peasant Economy as a Category in Economic History," in Shanin (ed.), *Peasants*, allows for the existence of larger economic units – landlords' demesnes, haciendas employing peasants, and even capitalist farms – "alongside peasant producers." The model is reminiscent of a dual economy in which various sectors in society exist alongside one another without effective or mutually transformative links. Claude Meillassoux, in *Femmes, greniers et capitaux, passim*, argues to the contrary that the "domestic mode of production," which shares the focus of the "peasant economy" model on the peasant producer/consumer unit, ceases to exist with the rise of exploitation by a dominant class.

4 Baer, *Studies*, p. 212. Although Baer freely acknowledges that changes occurred in the socio-economic structure of Egypt, and that there was "considerable economic development," as the former "subsistence economy" was replaced by an "export-oriented economy," he remains firmly convinced that basic social institutions, including the family, were not affected. This thesis is difficult to reconcile with his own discussion of changes in rural society: peasant land expropriation, the rise of a class of landless peasants, the emergence of a market economy, and the growth of social differentiation among the village population. How peasant social and productive relations, especially within the family, remained totally unaltered by such sweeping developments is difficult to fathom.

5 Charles Issawi, "Egypt since 1800: A Study in Lopsided Development," in Charles Issawi (ed.), *The Economic History of the Middle East, 1800–1914*, p. 361.

6 Roger Owen, "The Management of Large Estates in Nineteenth Century Egypt," unpublished paper, p. 15.

7 Anouar Abdel-Malek, *Egypt: Military Society, the Army Regime, the Left, and Social Change under Nasser*, p. 401. The concept of "backward colonial capitalism," first applied to developments in Egyptian agriculture by Abdel-Malek, has been further discussed in Owen, "The Management of Large Estates," and Alan Richards, "Primitive Accumulation in Egypt, 1798–1882," *Review*, I, 1 (Fall 1977), 3–49.

8 For periodization of Egyptian agriculture in the nineteenth century, see Owen, *The Middle East*, chs. 5 and 9; and Alan Richards, *Egypt's Agricultural Development*,

1800–1980. Technical and Social Change, chs. 2 and 3. The following overview owes much to both these readable and illuminating surveys of the nineteenth century.

9 Kenneth M. Cuno, "The Origins of Private Ownership of Land in Egypt: A Reappraisal," *IJMES*, 12 (1980), 245–275.

10 See ʿAbd al-Raḥīm ʿAbd al-Raḥmān ʿAbd al-Raḥīm, *al-Rīf al-maṣrī fī al-qarn al-thāmin ʿashir*, pp. 178–181.

11 Owen, *The Middle East*, p. 17.

12 See Richards, "Primitive Accumulation," pp. 15–16. Richards bases his figures on Girard's estimates.

13 ʿAbd al-Raḥīm, *al-Rīf al-maṣrī*, p. 186.

14 See Raymond, *Artisans*, vol. 1, pp. 98–106.

15 ʿAbd al-Raḥmān al-Jabartī, *ʿAjāʾib al-āthār fī al-tarājim waal-akhbar*, vol. 1, Dhū al-hijjah 1198/1784, pp. 582–583.

16 ʿAbd al-Raḥīm, *al-Rīf al-maṣrī*, pp. 172–177.

17 See Helen Anne B. Rivlin, *The Agricultural Policy of Muḥammad ʿAlī in Egypt*, ch. 2, for a discussion of the *iltizām* system. See also Gabriel Baer, *A History of Landownership in Modern Egypt*, pp. 1–2; and Richards, "Primitive Accumulation," p. 10.

18 Alongside *iltizām* land, some 600,000 *faddāns* in Upper Egypt and the Cairo vicinity were held as agricultural *waqf* land (*al-rizāq al-aḥbasīyah*) created by land grants made by former Sultāns or by *multazims* out of their *usyah* holdings. This *waqf* land was free of tax in the seventeenth and eighteenth centuries. See Baer, *A History*, p. 3.

19 Rivlin, *Agricultural Policy*, p. 23.

20 ʿAbd al-Raḥīm, *al-Rīf al-maṣrī*, p. 184.

21 Owen, *The Middle East*, p. 17. The *shaykh al-balad* was often granted portions of village land exempt from taxes by the *multazim* in partial payment for his administrative duties. This land, the *masmūḥ al-shaykh*, was passed down to the heir who became the new *shaykh al-balad*; see Richard, "Primitive Accumulation," p. 10, and Rivlin, *Agricultural Policy*, p. 24.

22 For a helpful description of Egyptian trade in the eighteenth century, see Raymond, *Artisans*, vol. 1, pp. 129–149, 174–191.

23 ʿAbd al-Raḥīm, *al-Rīf al-maṣrī*, pp. 201–202.

24 Vincennes, MR 534, "Memoires et reconnaissances," Jacotin, "Notes sur la province de Menouf."

25 Vincennes, B^6 80, "Noms des villages de la province de Syout avec quelques notes."

26 ʿAbd al-Raḥīm, *al-Rīf al-maṣrī*, pp. 194–195.

27 *Déscription de l'Egypte, état moderne*, vol. 2, part 2, Jallois, "Notice sur la ville de Rosette," p. 353.

28 Members of the French Expedition listed local village industry in several provinces; most villages, even those of modest size, manufactured oil, bricks, and textiles. Information on industry and local markets was recorded in Vincennes, B^6 80, "Noms des villages de la province de Syout avec quelques notes," and "Noms des villages de la province de Faioum avec quelques notes." Similar patterns of industry and trade were detailed in Vincennes, MR 581, Theviotte, "Memoires, Description de la ville de Belbeis et de ses environs."

29 See Raymond, *Artisans*, vol. 1, p. 229.

30 *Déscription, état moderne*, vol. 2, part 2, "Mémoire sur l'agriculture, l'industrie et le commerce de l'Egypte," p. 601.

31 Vincennes, B[6] 80, "Noms des villages de la province de Syout avec quelques notes." See also C. E. Savary, *Lettres sur l'Egypte*, vol. 1, p. 322.

32 *Déscription, état moderne*, vol. 2, part 2, Jomard, "Description abregée de la ville et de la citadelle du Kaire," p. 717.

33 See ʿAbd al-Raḥīm, *al-Rīf al-maṣrī*, pp. 191–192.

34 See Raymond, *Artisans*, vol. 1, pp. 78–80. The French consul made a similar observation in 1812, noting that a marked preference for English textiles had forced the closing of many local textile workshops, MAE, Correspondence consulaire et commercial, Alexandrie XVIII, Marcel à ministre, 20 July 1812.

35 Muḥammad ʿAlī's policies and goals have been variously interpreted. See Mustafa Fahmy, *La révolution de l'industrie en Egypte et ses conséquences sociales au 19e siècle*; ʿAbd al-Raḥmān al-Rāfiʿī, *ʿAsr Muḥammad ʿAlī*; and Rivlin, *Agricultural Policy*, for three divergent views.

36 See Rivlin, *Agricultural Policy*, pp. 112–113. Rivlin describes yet other hardships of the system of agricultural monopolies: the peasants received tax credits (which were calculated in undervalued paper currency) instead of payment for the crop; they had to pay the costs of transport to the local depot; they were often cheated out of the little they were entitled to by corrupt government officials.

37 FO 142/3, Barker to Earl of Aberdeen, 8 March 1830.

38 Rivlin, *Agricultural Policy*, pp. 114–115.

39 FO 78/381, Bowring Report, March 1839.

40 Richards, "Primitive Accumulation," p. 25.

41 MAE, Correspondence politique des consuls, Turquie: Alexandrie et Caire, XVII, Barrot à ministre, 10 January 1845.

42 Ibrāhīm ʿAmr, *al-Arḍ wa al-fallāḥ*, p. 81.

43 James Augustus St John, *Egypt and Mohammed Ali*, vol. 2, p. 349; ʿAbd al-Raḥman al-Rāfiʿī, *Taʾrīkh al-ḥarakah al-qawmīyah*, vol. 3, p. 573.

44 MAE, Correspond. pol. des consuls, Turq: Alex. et Caire, XIV, Labot à ministre, 29 December 1841.

45 FO 142/15, Murray to Wellesley, 13 May 1847.

46 See Rivlin, *Agricultural Policy*, p. 201. Rivlin also suggests that the move to peasant recruitment was influenced by the new conscription policy introduced into France at the time of the revolution.

47 MAE, Correspond. pol. des consuls, Turq: Alex. et Caire, I, "Notes sur les barbareques," September 1829, gives the following figures according to Drovetti's estimates: regular troops at 53,000 and irregulars at 15,000 for a total of 68,000. MAE, Correspond. pol. des consuls, Turq: Alex. et Caire, I, "Huder Report," March 1830, revised these estimates upwards to 54,100 regular troops, 24,000 irregulars, and 9,400 navy, for a total of 87,500. These numbers were subject to fluctuation as a result of military demand and population supply. See also Rivlin, *Agricultural Policy*, p. 209.

48 MAE, Correspond. pol. des consuls, Turq: Alex. et Caire, I, Mimaut à ministre, 3 April 1830.

49 *Ibid.*, II, Mimaut à ministre, 20 February 1831.

50 *Ibid.*, II, Mimaut à secretaire, 18 June 1832.
51 Rivlin, *Agricultural Policy*, pp. 209–210.
52 MAE, Correspond. con. et com., Alex. XXXII, Barrot à ministre, 28 April 1848; MAE, Correspond. pol. des consuls, Turq: Alex. et Caire XX, Barrot à ministre, 16 May 1848.
53 Rivlin, *Agricultural Policy*, p. 199.
54 FO 142/13, Barnett to Foreign Secretary, 17 August 1842.
55 Hekekyan Papers, British Museum 37449, vol. 2, 1844, fo. 391.
56 *Ibid.*, fo. 393.
57 MAE, Correspond. pol. des consuls, Turq: Alex. et Caire, XIV, Labot à ministre, 29 December 1841.
58 *Ibid.*, XVI, Lavalette à ministre, 6 May 1844.
59 FO 78/257, Campbell to Duke of Wellington, 15 April 1835. Campbell discounts an official's claim that there is no population deficiency in Upper Egypt, noting that "This is contrary to the reports generally given by all travellers with whom I have conversed on the subject." In FO 78/282, Campbell to Palmerston, 24 January 1836, he gives similar information on Lower Egypt.
60 FO 78/381, Bowring Report, March 1838, fo. 6. The population of Egypt at mid-century can only be estimated given the widely divergent figures issued by the Egyptian State and contemporary observers. The most reliable accounts place the total population at around 5,500,000. Cairo, the largest urban center, contained roughly 260,000 inhabitants; the overwhelming majority of the population – some 5,000,000 people – lived in the countryside. See Daniel Panzac, "La population de l'Egypte," in M. C. Aulas, *l'Egypte d'aujourd'hui*, pp. 157–158; and André Raymond, "Le Caire," in *ibid.*, pp. 216–217.
61 *al-Waqāʾiʿ al-miṣrīyah*, n.v., n.d., 1245/1829–1830.
62 FO 142/16, Murray to Palmerston, 1 June 1848.
63 Baer, *A History*, p. 3.
64 Rivlin, *Agricultural Policy*, pp. 47–55.
65 *Ibid.*, p. 58.
66 See Richards, "Primitive Accumulation," p. 14.
67 See Rivlin, *Agricultural Policy*, ch. 5.
68 Richards, "Primitive Accumulation," p. 23.
69 Baer, *A History*, p. 15.
70 For various peasant land transactions, see al-Mahdī, *Fatāwā*, vol. 2, 28 Dhū al-hijjah 1264/1848, p. 36; vol. 2, 12 Jumādā II, 1265/1849, p. 44; vol. 2, 27 Shaʿbān 1265/1849, p. 49; vol. 5, 28 Dhū al-hijjah, 1264/1848, p. 369.
71 Owen, "The Management of Large Estates," p. 10. It was proposed that the peasants working on *chifliks* farm a few *faddāns* on their own account, using animals belonging to the estate to supplement their income. We cannot be sure, however, if this proposal was ever implemented.
72 Richards, "Primitive Accumulation," p. 25; and Rivlin, *Agricultural Policy*, p. 236.
73 MAE, Correspond. pol. des consuls, Turq: Alex. et Caire, V, Mimaut à ministre, 25 April 1835.
74 Baer, *A History*, p. 29.
75 See Richards, *Egypt's Agricultural*, p. 31.

76 See Owen, *The Middle East*, pp. 135–139.
77 See *ibid.*, pp. 129–130; and Richards, *Egypt's Agricultural*, p. 38.
78 Lady Duff Gordon, *Letters from Egypt (1862–1869)*, pp. 301–302, 319.
79 "Further Correspondence Respecting Reorganization in Egypt," "Reports by Mr. Villiers Stewart," *PP*, 1883, LXXXIII, 147.
80 Owen, *The Middle East*, pp. 129–130.
81 "Despatch from Sir E. Baring, Enclosing a Report on the Conditions of the Agricultural Population in Egypt," *PP*, 1888, CX, 191; Owen, *The Middle East*, p. 143; Richards, *Egypt's Agricultural*, pp. 31–34.
82 Owen, *The Middle East*, pp. 135–137.
83 Duff Gordon, *Letters*, pp. 230, 243–244, 317–318.
84 MAE, Correspond. con. et com., Le Caire, XXIX, Delaporte à ministre, 16 June 1851, p. 123.
85 Vincennes, MR 1678, J. Lambert, "Memoire sur le percement de l'Isthme de Suez," 1 May 1863.
86 "Correspondence Respecting Reorganization in Egypt," *PP*, 1883, LXXXIII, 147.
87 Hekekyan Papers, BM 37454, vol. 7, 1855, fo. 347.
88 FO 142/16, Murray to Palmerston, 5 May 1849.
89 All reports I have seen on corvée labor in the 1860s and 1870s concur on these issues. See, for example, Duff Gordon, *Letters*, p. 243; Stanley Lane-Poole, *Social Life in Egypt, A Description of the Country and its People*, p. 49; "Reports by Mr. Villiers Stewart – Interview with Sheikh of Deyrouth," *PP*, 1883, LXXXIII, 147.
90 "Reports by Mr. Villiers Stewart, Upper Egypt Series – Statements of Natives," *PP*, 1883, LXXXIII, 147.
91 FO 142/16, Murray to Palmerston, 5 May 1849; MAE, Correspond. pol. des Consuls, Turq: Alex, et Caire, XX, Sabatier à ministre, 16 March 1854.
92 Baer, *Studies*, pp. 25–26.
93 For examples of all these practices in the 1860s and 1870s, see al-Mahdī, *Fatāwā*, vol. 2, 1 Dhū al-hijjah 1275/1859, p. 261; vol. 2, 2 Ṣafar 1276/1859, p. 403; vol. 2, 28 Muḥarram 1281/1864, pp. 416–417; vol. 2, 13 Muḥarram 1295/1878, pp. 439–440.
94 See Owen, *The Middle East*, p. 140.
95 Richards, *Egypt's Agricultural*, p. 28.
96 Many observers described this process of land loss. FO 141/183, "Report of Ibrahim Abou Yoones, Omdeh of Talka," 12 Ṣafar 1300/1882; FO 141/183, "Ministère des Finances memo on problems of peasants," 31 May 1883; FO 141/203, Mustafa Aga to Baring, Luxor, 2 October 1884.
97 "Further Correspondence, Reports by Mr. Villiers Stewart, Statements of Natives – Upper Egypt, Province of Keneh," *PP*, 1883, LXXXIII, 147.
98 See Owen, *The Middle East*, pp. 146–147.
99 "Further Correspondence, Reports by Mr. Villiers Stewart, Statements of Natives – Delta Series," *PP*, 1883, LXXXIII, 147; "Further Correspondence Respecting Reorganization in Egypt," Report by M. Suares, "De l'agriculture en Egypte telle qu'elle est pratiquée de nos jours," *PP*, 1883, LXXXIII, 197.
100 See Richards, *Egypt's Agricultural*, p. 34; "Further Correspondence," Report by M. Suares, "De l'agriculture," *PP*, 1883, LXXXIII, 197.

101 For a discussion of British agricultural policy, see Owen, *The Middle East*, pp. 221–224.
102 Boyle Papers, Middle East Centre, St Antony's College, Oxford University, Box B, Boyle to Mother, 12 April 1900.
103 See Richards, *Egypt's Agricultural*, pp. 69–78.
104 PRO 30/57, Kitchener Papers, 9, NN 3, 8, 9a.
105 See Richards, *Egypt's Agricultural*, pp. 82–91.
106 For the history of land tax rates, see Sir William Willcocks and J. I. Craig, *Egyptian Irrigation*, vol. 2, pp. 802–808; FO 141/206, Roussell, "Memo: On Taxation in Upper and Lower Egypt," 1 June 1884.
107 "Reports . . . Egypt and the Soudan in 1912," *PP*, 1913, LXXXI, 207, p. 4.
108 Owen, *The Middle East*, pp. 241–243.
109 FO 633/5, Cromer Papers, 203, E. Baring to Mrs Vincent, Cairo, 29 May 1887; FO 633/6, Cromer Papers, 39, E. Baring to Lord Granville, 25 March 1883; FO 633/7, Cromer Papers, 313, 314, 315, 317, 318, C. E. Scott Moncrieff to E. Baring, Cairo, 5–8 February 1887; "Reports . . . Egypt and the Progress of Reforms," Col. Scott Moncrieff to Nūbar Pāshā, 31 January 1885, *PP*, 1884–1885, LXXXIX, 1.
110 For various estimates of corvée numbers, see "Despatch from Sir E. Baring," *PP*, 1888, CX, 191; "Report . . . Egypt and the Progress of Reforms in 1896," *PP*, 1897, CII, 505, pp. 13–14; Milner, *England in Egypt*, p. 201.
111 "Report by Mr. Villiers Stewart . . . 1882" (May 1895), *PP*, 1895, CIX, 941.
112 "Despatch from Sir E. Baring," *PP*, 1888, CX, 191; FO 633/10, Cromer Papers, Sir E. Baring to Marquis of Salisbury, 19 March 1891.
113 FO 141/228, Col. Parr to Egerton, 16 September 1885; "Despatch from Sir E. Baring," *PP*, 1888, CX, 191; "Report . . . on Egypt and the Soudan in 1902," *PP*, 1903, LXXXVII, 953, pp. 37–38.
114 FO 633/15, Cromer Papers, fo. 29; Owen, *The Middle East*, pp. 216–218.
115 "Reports by Mr. Villiers Stewart" (May 1895), *PP*, 1895, CIX, 941.
116 "Reports . . . Egypt and the Soudan in 1903," Inclosure 1: "Statements Showing the Condition of the Fellaheen," *PP*, 1904, CXI, 203.
117 FO 141/170, W. Rowsell to Cherif Pasha, 4 April 1883; Owen, *The Middle East*, pp. 229–230.
118 See Richards, *Egypt's Agricultural*, pp. 66–68.
119 "Report . . . Egypt and the Soudan in 1903," Inclosure 1: "Statements Showing the Condition of the Fellaheen," *PP*, 1904, CXI, 203.
120 See Owen, *The Middle East*, pp. 231–232; also Richards, *Egypt's Agricultural*, pp. 93–98.
121 See Chabrol de Volvic, *Essai sur les moeurs des habitants modernes de l'Egypte*, pp. 49–59, who stresses the laborious existence of peasant women. In Vincennes, MR 543, "Notes sur l'Egypte," Dugua observed with shock large numbers of scantily clad peasant women in the fields.
122 See C. E. Savary, *Lettres sur l'Egypte*, vol. 1, p. 54, who observed many females in rice cultivation near Rosetta. Also MAE, Correspond. con. et com., Alex. XX, Menouine à ministre, 22 September 1820, includes the observation that women and children made up the bulk of the cotton harvest labor force.

123 See Gerard de Nerval, *Scènes de la vie orientale*, *passim*; also Hekekyan Papers, BM 37450, vol. 3. fo. 254.
124 Hekekyan Papers, BM 37450, vol. 3, fo. 85.
125 MAE, Correspond. pol. des consuls, Turq: Alex. et Caire, XXIII, Le Moyne à ministre, 28 April 1851.
126 Hekekyan Papers, BM 37452, vol. 5, fo. 413; 37454, vol. 7, fo. 365.
127 Augustus St John, *Egypt and Mohammed Ali*, vol. 2, p. 349.
128 Hekekyan Papers, BM 37454, vol. 7, p. 365.
129 Nerval, *Scènes*, p. 87.
130 Hekekyan Papers, BM 37450, vol. 3, p. 34.
131 Lane-Poole, *Social Life*, p. 49.
132 "Reports by Mr. Villiers Stewart . . ., Statements of Natives – Delta Series," *PP*, 1883, LXXXIII, 147.
133 "Report . . . Egypt and the Soudan in 1909," *PP*, 1910, CXII, 347, p. 18.
134 "Reports by Mr. Villiers Stewart, Statements of Natives – Upper Egypt," *PP*, 1883, LXXXIII, 147.
135 P. N. Hamont, *l'Egypte sous Mehemet Ali*, vol. 1, pp. 109–110. See also C. Rochfort Scott, *Rambles in Egypt and Candia*, vol. 2, p. 221; St John, *Egypt*, vol. 1, p. 158; R. R. Madden, *Egypt and Mohammed Ali*, p. 32; Hekekyan Papers, *BM* 37450, vol. 3, fo. 198.
136 "Report . . . Egypt and the Soudan in 1903," Inclosure 1: "Statements Showing the Condition of the Fellaheen," *PP*, 1904, CXI, 203.
137 "Reports by Mr. Villiers Stewart, Statements of Natives – Delta Series," *PP*, 1883, LXXXXIII, 147.
138 The number of children recorded as surviving a parent in 14 sample families in the Manṣūrah records, MM sample 1800 to 1820:

No. of families	No. of children
2	0
4	1
2	2
4	3
0	4
2	5

139 Registers consulted in the archives of the Manṣurah court between 1800 and 1820 included: 46/138/37, 46/138/44, and 46/138/49.
140 MM 46/138/49, 29 Shawwāl 1236/1821, fo. 9.
141 MM 46/138/37, 15 Shaʿbān 1216/1801, fo. 22; MM 46/138/49, 12 Rajab 1235/1820, fo. 7.
142 The Manṣūrah sample included two cases in which the deceased's son was required to pay the deceased's wife the balance of her *mahr* and debts owed her by her husband: MM 46/138/37, 15 Shaʿbān 1216/1801, fo. 22; MM 46/138/44, 12 Dhū al-hijjah, 1226/1811, fo. 14.
143 MM 46/138/57, 9 Dhū al-qaʿdah 1257/1841, fo. 12; al-Mahdī, *Fatāwā*, Dhū al-qaʿdah 1270/1854, pp. 189–190.
144 MM 46/138/51, 16 Ramaḍān 1245/1830, fo. 7.

145 "Report. . . Egypt and the Soudan in 1903," Inclosure 1: "Statements Showing the Condition of the Fellaheen," *PP*, 1904, CXI, 203; see Families 1 and 2.
146 MM 46/138/44, n.d. (assume 1226/1810–1881), fo. 13.
147 al-Maḥdī, *Fatāwā*, vol. 1, 18 Dhū al-hijjah 1269/1853, p. 109; vol. 2, 22 Jumādā I 1268/1852, p. 329; vol. 2, 27 Rabīʿ II 1266/1850, p. 303.
148 *Ibid.*, vol. 2, 12 Shaʿbān 1266/1850, p. 306.
149 *Ibid.*, vol. 2, 23 Jumādā II 1267/1851, p. 91; vol. 2, 27 Shaʿbān 1265/1849, p. 49; vol. 2, 9 Dhū al-hijjah 1269/1853, p. 168; vol. 2, 14 Ṣafar 1268/1851, p. 109.
150 *Ibid.*, vol. 2, 18 Dhū al-qaʿdah 1264/1848, p. 33.
151 *Ibid.*, vol. 2, 12 Shaʿbān 1265/1849, p. 48.
152 *Ibid.*, vol. 2, 17 Ramaḍān 1265/1849, p. 50.
153 *Ibid.*, vol. 2, 18 Dhū al-qaʿdah 1264/1848, p. 33.
154 *Ibid.*, vol. 2, 9 Dhū al-hijjah 1269/1853, p. 168.
155 *Ibid.*, vol. 2, 1 Shaʿbān 1267/1851, p. 92; vol. 2, 12 Ṣafar 1268/1851, p. 108; vol. 2, 14 Ṣafar 1268/1851, p. 109; vol. 2, 16 Jumādā II 1267/1851, p. 91; vol. 2, 11 Ṣafar 1266/1849, p. 62; vol. 2, 1 Dhū al-qaʿdah 1267/1851, p. 98.
156 Numbers of children per family as recorded in the Manṣūrah sample between 1829 and 1846:

No. of families	No. of children
3	1
2	2
3	3

157 al-Maḥdī, *Fatāwā*, vol. 1, 3 Shaʿbān 1267/1851, p. 248.
158 *Ibid.*, vol. 5, 28 Rajab 1266/1850, p. 230; vol. 5, 12 Shawwāl 1268/1852, p. 238.
159 *Ibid.*, vol. 5, 30 Jumādā II 1270/1854, p. 243.
160 *Ibid.*, vol. 5, 1 Jumādā I 1266/1850, p. 229; vol. 2, 6 Dhū al-hijjah 1264/1848, p. 35.
161 *Ibid.*, vol. 2, 6 Dhū al-hijjah 1264/1848, p. 35.
162 *Ibid.*, vol. 2, 11 Rajab 1265/1849, p. 293; vol. 2, 24 Rabīʿ I 1267/1851, p. 316.
163 *Ibid.*, vol. 2, 24 Rabīʿ II 1266/1849, p. 67; vol. 1, 21 Dhū al-qaʿdah 1265/1849, p. 143.
164 MM 46/138/51, 26 Shaʿbān 1245/1830, fo. 2.
165 al-Maḥdī, *Fatāwā*, vol. 5, 24 Jumādā II 1270/1854, p. 125; vol. 2, 21 Ṣafar 1267/1850, p. 313.
166 *Ibid.*, vol. 2, 25 Rabīʿ II 1266/1850, p. 303; vol. 2, 7 Jumādā I 1265/1849, p. 288.
167 Examples of this type of testimony include: MM 46/138/57, 26 Shawwāl 1257/1841, fo. 8; MM 46/138/57, 10 Dhū al-qaʿdah 1257/1841, fo. 10; MM 46/138/57, 2 Dhū al-qaʿdah 1257/1841, fo. 10; MM 46/138/57, 5 Dhū al-qaʿdah 1257/1841, fo. 10; MM 46/138/57, 7 Dhū al-qaʿdah 1257/1841, fo. 11; MM 46/138/57, 18 Dhū al-qaʿdah 1257/1842, fo. 12; MM 46/138/59, 1 Rabīʿ I 1261/1845, fo. 10.
168 For example: al-Maḥdī, *Fatāwā*, vol. 2, 19 Muḥarram 1270/1853, p. 174; vol. 2, 1 Rabīʿ I 1270/1853, p. 176; vol. 2, 16 Rabīʿ I 1270/1853, p. 177; vol. 2, 8 Rabīʿ II 1270/1854, pp. 178–179; vol. 2, 30 Jumādā II 1270/1854, p. 183; vol. 2, 2 Ramaḍān 1270/1854, pp. 184–185.
169 *Ibid.*, vol. 2, 2 Muḥarram 1270/1853, p. 172; vol. 2, 10 Shawwāl 1270/1854, p. 186.
170 *Ibid.*, vol. 2, 10 Jumādā I 1275/1858, p. 260.

171 *Ibid.*, vol. 2, 28 Muḥarram 1281/1864, pp. 416–417; vol. 2, 13 Muḥarram 1295/1878, pp. 439–440.

172 *Ibid.*, vol. 2, 2 Ṣafar 1276/1859, p. 403; vol. 2, 21 Rabīʿ I 1276/1859, pp. 403–404; vol. 2, 6 Ṣafar 1296/1879, p. 441.

173 *Isqāṭ*, the alienation of rights to the usufruct, remained the legal device for the sale of *kharājīyah* land. For examples of women selling their rights of usufruct, see: al-Mahdī, *Fatāwā*, vol. 2, 28 Dhū al-hijjah 1264/1848, p. 36; vol. 2, 14 Muḥarram 1270/1853, p. 173; vol. 2, 29 Muḥarram 1270/1853, p. 175; vol. 2, 25 Ramaḍān 1270/1854, pp. 185–186; vol. 2, 1 Dhū al-hijjah 1275/1859, p. 261.

174 For examples of women receiving land upon the death of a male holder, see al-Mahdī, *Fatāwā*, vol. 2, 28 Jumādā I, 1270/1854, p. 182; vol. 2, 16 Shaʿbān 1270/1854, p. 184; vol. 2, 3 Ramaḍān 1270/1854, p. 185. For examples of women receiving land from a living male relative, see *ibid.*, vol. 2, 4 Ṣafar 1270/1853, p. 175; vol. 2, 23 Rabīʿ I 1270/1853, p. 178; vol. 2, 17 Rabīʿ II 1270/1854, p. 180.

175 See John L. Esposito, *Women in Muslim Family Law*, pp. 16–22, for a discussion of marriage in Islamic law.

176 al-Mahdī, *Fatāwā*, vol. 1, 2 Rajab 1270/1854, p. 52; vol. 1, 18 Ṣafar 1274/1857, p. 70.

177 *Ibid.*, vol. 1, 19 Rabīʿ II 1265/1849, p. 18; see also vol. 1, 4 Jumādā I 1265/1849, p. 18.

178 MM 46/138/49, 7 Shaʿbān 1235/1820, fo. 5.

179 "Report. . . Egypt and the Soudan in 1903," Inclosure 1: "Statements Showing the Condition of the Fellaheen," *PP*, 1904, CXI, 203, Family 3. The 1917 Egyptian Census attempted to include information on polygamy, but the results were found to be unsatisfactory: see Maṣlaḥat al-iḥṣā' wa al-taʿdād, *The Census of Egypt Taken in 1917*, vol. 1, p. xlvii.

180 al-Mahdī, *Fatāwā*, vol. 1, 10 Shawwāl 1272/1856, pp. 206–207; vol. 1, 30 Dhū al-hijjah 1290/1874, pp. 84–85.

181 *Ibid.*, vol. 1, 1 Ṣafar 1265/1848, p. 153; vol. 1, Dhū al-qaʿdah 1265/1849, p. 22.

182 *Ibid.*, vol. 1, 24 Shaʿbān 1267/1851, p. 179.

183 Among the numerous cases of *khulʿ*, we mention the following: MM 46/138/37, 5 Rajab 1216/1801, fo. 5; MM 46/138/44, 14 Dhū al-qaʿdah 1226/1811, fo. 12; al-Mahdī, *Fatāwā*, vol. 1, 25 Muḥarram 1270/1853, pp. 197–198; vol. 1, 4 Rabīʿ II 1270/1854, p. 198; vol. 1, 25 Ramaḍān 1270/1854, p. 200; vol. 1, 17 Rabīʿ II 1271/1855, pp. 201–202; vol. 1, 27 Rajab 1271/1855, p. 202; vol. 1, 9 Ṣafar 1272/1855, p. 205; vol. 1, 3 Rabīʿ I, 1272/1855, p. 205; vol. 1, 11 Ramaḍān 1272/1856, p. 206; vol. 1, 22 Shaʿbān 1273/1857, p. 210.

184 MM 46/138/44, 14 Dhū al-qaʿdah 1226/1811, fo. 12; MM 46/138/44, 18 Dhū al-qaʿdah 1226/1811, fo. 16.

185 al-Mahdī, *Fatāwā*, vol. 1, 19 Jumādā I 1271/1855, p. 202; vol. 1, 16 Ramaḍān 1271/1855, p. 203.

186 *Ibid.*, vol. 1, 25 Dhū al-hijjah 1270/1854, p. 201; vol. 1, 22 Jumādā II 1272/1856, p. 206.

187 *Ibid.*, vol. 1, 19 Jumādā II 1270/1854, p. 199; vol. 1, 26 Dhū al-qaʿdah 1270/1854, p. 200; vol. 1, 22 Muḥarram 1272/1855, pp. 204–205.

188 See Joseph Schacht, *An Introduction to Islamic Law*, p. 120, on the right of males in the father's line to act as *wālī*.
189 MM 46/138/37, n.d. (assume Rajab 1216/1801), fo. 13.
190 MM 46/138/49, 20 Shawwāl 1235/1820, fo. 19.
191 al-Mahdī, *Fatāwā*, vol. 1, 11 Rabiʿ II 1265/1849, p. 243. For other female *wālīs*, see *ibid.*, vol. 1, 6 Ramaḍān 1272/1856, p. 64; vol. 1, 4 Rabīʿ II 1273/1856, p. 65; vol. 1, 19 Rabī II 1274/1857, p. 70.
192 MM 46/138/59, 9 Rabīʿ II 1261/1845, fo. 22.
193 MM 46/138/37, 13 Shaʿbān 1216/1801, fo. 20.
194 al-Mahdī, *Fatāwā*, vol. 1, 16 Shaʿban 1269/1853, p. 302; vol. 1, 25 Jumādā II 1267/1851, p. 283.
195 *Ibid.*, vol. 1, 2 Ṣafar 1267/1850, p. 283; vol. 1, 13 Rabīʿ II 1265/1849, p. 264.
196 *Ibid.*, vol. 1, 5 Jumādā II 1265/1849, p. 266; vol. 1, 8 Jumādā II 1265/1849, p. 266; vol. 1, 30 Shawwāl 1266/1850, p. 279; vol. 1, 7 Jumādā II 1268/1852, p. 293.
197 There are numerous cases of this kind. See, for example, *ibid.*, vol. 1, 16 Jumādā I 1265/1849, p. 266.
198 There are many examples of intricate inheritance arrangements, including MM 46/138/37, 2 Shaʿbān 1216/1801, fo. 23; MM 46/138/49, 15 Dhū al-qaʿdah 1235/1820, fo. 14; MM 46/138/44, 16 Dhū al-qaʿdah 1226/1811, fo. 15. The last is a sale which demonstrates a complex transfer of property. The deceased woman, Raqīyah, had acquired certain property by way of purchase and inheritance from her first husband. The son of her second marriage, her principal heir, thus inherited, through her, part of the property of her first husband.
199 MM 46/138/49, 11 Rajab 1235/1820, fo. 5.
200 MM 46/138/44, 20 Dhū al-qaʿdah 1226/1811, fo. 15.
201 al-Mahdī, *Fatāwā*, vol. 1, 15 Shaʿbān 1266/1850, p. 389; vol. 1, 4 Dhū al-hijjah 1264/1848, p. 378.
202 *Ibid.*, vol. 1, 16 Muḥarram 1266/1849, p. 386.

2 Spindles and songs: women in urban occupations

1 See Issawi, "Egypt since 1800: A Study in Lopsided Development," in Issawi (ed.), *The Economic History*, p. 364; Baer, *Studies*, p. 154; and Owen, *The Middle East*, pp. 149, 237–238.
2 See Issawi, "Egypt since 1800," in Issawi (ed.), *The Economic History*, pp. 365–366; and Rivlin, *Agricultural Policy*, pp. 197–199.
3 See Fahmy, *La révolution*, pp. 98–107, for arguments in favor of the European sabotage explanation. Owen, *The Middle East*, pp. 73–76, contests this explanation on the grounds of timing (industry continued to expand well after 1838) and the lack of necessity for a high external tariff to protect the largely internal demand for manufactured goods; internal administrative protection, he argues, was far more critical to the health of industrial enterprise.
4 See Raymond, *Artisans*, vol. 2, p. 813.
5 See Peter Gran, *Islamic Roots of Capitalism, Egypt 1760–1840*, pp. 6–10; and Raymond, *Artisans*, vol. 2, p. 813.

6 MAE, Correspond. con. et com., Caire XXV, Les Français résidant au Caire à ministère, 17 May 1793.
7 See Raymond, *Artisans*, vol. 1, pp. 162, 171, 199–201, 240–241.
8 *Ibid.*, pp. 249–250, 273–279.
9 *Ibid.*, vol. 1, pp. 174, 209–210.
10 MAE, Correspond. con. et com., Alex. XVIII, Marcel à ministre, 20 July 1812.
11 See Raymond, *Artisans*, vol. 1, pp. 207–224.
12 *Ibid.*, vol. 1, pp. 213, 221.
13 *Ibid.*, vol. 1, pp. 229–234.
14 *Ibid.*, vol. 1, pp. 317–319; *Déscription de l'Egypte, état moderne*, Jomard, "Déscription abregée," vol. 2, part 2, pp. 2, 587, 699, 703, 717.
15 FO 78/170, Barker to Foreign Office, 10 March 1828.
16 Gabriel Baer, *Egyptian Guilds in Modern Times*, pp. 131–132; Fahmy, *La révolution*, pp. 12–13.
17 FO 78/147, Salt to Foreign Office, 4 April 1826.
18 MAE, Correspond. consulaire, Alex., 1828–1830, G. Douin, 107, "Memoire presenté à M. Mimaut sur la position du commerce français en Egypte," n.d.
19 MAE, Correspond. pol. des consuls, Turq: Alex. et Caire IV, Mimaut à ministre, 20 May 1834; MAE, Correspond. pol. des consuls, Turq: Alex. et Caire VII, Note par de Lesseps, 22 September 1838.
20 FO 78/245, Campbell to Palmerston, 27 April 1834.
21 Hekekyan claims there were 31 cotton mills; Fahmy lists 30; and Rivlin settles on the figure of 29. Hekekyan Papers, BM 37450, vol. 3, fo. 253; Fahmy, *La révolution*, p. 24; Rivlin, *Agricultural Policy*, p. 197.
22 FO 78/381, Bowring Report, March 1839, fo. 55. Bowring's inventory of the Khurūnfīsh factory apparently lists all machinery in the building in the early 1830s. Hekekyan, surveying the same factory in 1835, and listing only the equipment in actual operation at the time, arrived at the very different figure of 84 carding machines, 20 mule-jennies, and 320 looms. Hekekyan Papers, BM 37461, vol. 14, fo. 34. Clot-Bey, on the other hand, agrees with Bowring's figure of 100 mules. See Antoine Clot-Bey, *Aperçu général sur l'Egypte*, vol. 2, pp. 271–272.
23 MAE, Correspond. con. et com., Alex. XX, Menouine à ministre, 22 September 1820; FO 78/246, Campbell to Palmerston, 7 August 1834.
24 Clot-Bey, *Aperçu*, vol. 2, pp. 273–275; FO 78/381, Bowring Report, March 1839, fos. 61–62.
25 MAE, Correspond. con. et com., Caire XXVI, Roussel à ministre, 19 December 1817.
26 MAE, Correspond. con. et com., Alex. XXI, Drovetti à ministre, 10 July 1822; MAE, Correspond. con. et com., Caire XXVI, Malivoire à ministre, 6 November 1825 and 10 November 1825.
27 FO 78/170, Barker to Foreign Office, 10 March 1828.
28 FO 78/342, Campbell to Bowring, 18 January 1838.
29 MAE, Correspond. con. et com., Alex. XXIX, Benedetti à ministre, "Rapport sur la situation du commerce français en Egypte," 29 May 1841.
30 MAE, Correspond. pol. des consuls, Turq: Alex. et Caire XVII, Barrot à ministre, 10

January 1845; MAE, Correspond. con. et com., Alex. XXXIII, Dunoyer à ministre, 4 June 1849.

31 Rivlin, *Agricultural Policy*, p. 199; Fahmy, *La révolution*, pp. 84–85. Rivlin thinks the maximum number of people in the factory system was 40,000. Fahmy offers a detailed breakdown of his estimated 260,000-person working class, which includes, among others, women spinning at home.

32 Clot-Bey, for example, estimated that Egypt boasted some 3,000 linen weavers and some 4,000 wool weavers. It seems highly unlikely that there were an additional 73,000 cotton weavers, the number necessary to reach Fahmy's total of 80,000. See Clot-Bey, *Aperçu*, vol. 2, pp. 273–274.

33 Hekekyan Papers, BM 37450, vol. 3, fo. 253; FO 78/381, Bowring Report, March 1839, fos. 62–63.

34 Campbell estimated that the Alexandria arsenal employed about 4,350 people. FO 142/6, Campbell to Palmerston, April 1833.

35 MAE, Correspond. con. et com., Caire XXVI, Roussel à ministre, 19 December 1817; Clot-Bey, *Aperçu*, vol. 2, p. 273.

36 MAE, Correspond. con. et com., Caire XXVI, Malivoire à ministre, 20 January 1827. Malivoire earlier included a translation of the letter from Bughos Yusif to Drovetti which explained the government's decision to make European workers' continued presence in Egypt contingent upon their willingness to forgo protection under the Capitulations. MAE, Correspond. con. et com., Caire XXVI, Malivoire à ministre, 8 June 1826.

37 MAE, Correspond. pol. des consuls, Turq: Alex. et Caire, Mimaut à ministre, 8 February 1835.

38 St John, *Egypt*, vol. 2, p. 410.

39 Many observers stressed the force employed to round up unwilling factory personnel. Hekekyan Papers, BM 37449, vol. 2, fo. 148; St John, *Egypt*, vol. 2, p. 412; MAE, Correspond. pol. des consuls, Alex. et Caire II, Coeborn, n.d.

40 FO 78/381, Bowring Report, March 1839, fo. 213.

41 FO 142/6, Campbell to Palmerston, 24 April 1833.

42 Hekekyan included several lists of wage rates in cotton and linen factories. Hekekyan Papers, BM 37450, vol. 3, fo. 233, and 37466, vol. 19, fo. 178. See also C. Rochfort Scott, *Rambles in Egypt and Candia*, vol. 1, p. 63; FO 78/381, Bowring Report, March 1839, fo. 62.

43 MAE, Correspond. con. et com., Alex. XXII, Drovetti à ministre, February 1825; Hekekyan Papers, BM 37499, vol. 2, fos. 92, 148; FO 78/381, Bowring Report, March 1839, fo. 119.

44 Factory wages were reportedly in arrears throughout the course of the industrial experiment. FO 78/160, Salt to Foreign Office, 12 August 1827; FO 142/13, Barnett to Sec. of State, 18 September 1841, 15; St John, *Egypt*, vol. 2, p. 418.

45 See St John's description, for example, of the horrors of factory life. St John, *Egypt*, vol. 2, p. 412.

46 Fahmy, while arguing that working conditions in Egyptian factories were superior to those in Europe, still admits to a working day of sunrise to sunset and practices which included deducting food costs from an already meager wage. Fahmy, *La révolution*, pp. 87–92.

47 The planned mobilization of factory workers reportedly included 38,000 workers from Alexandria, 25,000 from Maḥallah, and 72,000 from Cairo. The figures appear exaggerated. MAE, Correspond. pol. des consuls, Turq: Alex. et Caire IX, Cochelet à ministre, 16 January 1840; *ibid.*, Cochelet à ministre, 26 February 1840.

48 See Issawi, "Egypt since 1800," in Issawi (ed.), *The Economic History*, p. 363; Baer, *Studies*, p. 154; Robert Mabro and Samir Radwan, *The Industrialization of Egypt, 1939–1973*, pp. 19–20.

49 David S. Landes, *Bankers and Pashas*, pp. 68, 87–88, 95–99.

50 Owen, *The Middle East*, pp. 123–129; "Report by Mr. Cave on the Financial Condition of Egypt," in Issawi (ed.), *The Economic History*, pp. 435–436.

51 See Raūf ʿAbbās Ḥāmid Muḥammad, *al-Ḥarakah al-ʿummālīyah fī Miṣr: 1899–1952*, p. 39; Baer, *Studies*, pp. 212–213; Owen, *The Middle East*, pp. 150–152.

52 FO 141/170, F. Goldsmid, "Brief Report on Certain Questions to be Solved at Ermint and Mitana," 16 March 1883.

53 Stanley Lane-Poole, *Cairo. Sketches of its History, Monuments, and Social Life*, pp. 66–68.

54 Owen, *The Middle East*, pp. 76, 148–149.

55 See Ann Elizabeth Mayer, "ʿAbbās Ḥilmī II: The Khedive and Egypt's Struggle for Independence," unpublished PhD dissertation, pp. 82–87; Robert L. Tignor, *Modernization and British Colonial Rule in Egypt, 1882–1914*, pp. 50–57.

56 Gladstone Papers, BM 44634, "Report by the Earl of Northbrook on the Financial Situation in Egypt: November 1884."

57 See Owen, *The Middle East*, pp. 224–225.

58 See *ibid.*, pp. 219–220, 225, 235–239; also Mabro and Radwan, *The Industrialization of Egypt*, pp. 22–25.

59 "Rapport de la Commission du Commerce et de l'Industrie," in Issawi (ed.), *The Economic History*, p. 453; see also Joel Beinin, "Formation of the Egyptian Working Class," *MERIP Reports*, 94 (February 1981), 15–16.

60 Raūf ʿAbbās Muḥammad, *al-Ḥarakah al-ʿummālīyah*, p. 48.

61 FO 141/307, Charles Galloway to Lord Cromer, Manchester, 11 June 1894.

62 See Raūf ʿAbbās Muḥammad, *al-Ḥarakah al-ʿummālīyah*, pp. 51–65; and Beinin, "Formation," pp. 17–18.

63 "Report . . . Egypt and the Soudan in 1908," *PP*, 1909, CV, 33, p. 10.

64 "Report . . . Egypt and the Soudan in 1905," *PP*, 1906, CXXXVII, 475.

65 J. W. A. Young, "A Little to the East, Experience of an Anglo-Egyptian Official 1899–1925," unpublished MS, St Antony's Private Papers, Oxford University, ch. 7, fos. 5–6.

66 W. de Morgan, "Pottery Manufacture in Egypt," BM, Egerton 3293, fo. 38.

67 Young, "A Little to the East," ch. 7, fos. 5–6.

68 St John, *Egypt*, vol. 1, pp. 216–217, 339, and vol. 2, p. 279; Edward Lane, *An Account of the Manners and Customers of the Modern Egyptians*, p. 9; Hekekyan Papers, BM 37450, vol. 3, fo. 231, and 37451, vol. 4, fo. 46.

69 al-Maḥdī, *Fatāwā*, vol. 5, 24 Shaʿbān 1267/1851, p. 335. This case settled an argument between two women, debtor and lender, over goods pledged as security for a loan of 564 piasters.

70 *Ibid.*, vol. 5, 21 Ṣafar 1267/1850, p. 93.

71 *Ibid.*, vol. 1, 7 Jumādā I 1268/1852, p. 293, and vol. 1, 28 Dhū al-hijjah 1264/1848, p. 261.

72 See M. L. Whately, *Child-Life in Egypt*, pp. 25–34.

73 Baer, *Egyptian Guilds*, p. 33. Baer cites the 1889 administrative order exempting certain female professions from the professional tax.

74 See Raymond, *Artisans*, vol. 1, p. 275, who comments on this occupation in Cairo.

75 One Ottoman piaster equals 40 *parahs*.

76 MM 46/138/49, 17 Rajab 1235/1820, fo. 7.

77 MBA, s. 323, no. 523, 1216/1801–1802; s. 366, no. 262, 1235–1236/1820–1821.

78 See al-Mahdī, *Fatāwā*, vol. 3, 4 Rabīʿ I 1292/1875, pp. 187–188; vol. 3, 7 Rajab 1275/1859, p. 151; vol. 3, 7 Shawwāl 1275/1859, p. 153.

79 *Ibid.*, vol. 4, 30 Dhū al-hijjah, 1272/1856, p. 511.

80 There are many such cases. See *ibid.*, vol. 4, 23 Muḥarram 1267/1850, p. 498; vol. 4, 15 Muḥarram 1268/1851, p. 499; vol. 4, 16 Ṣafar 1272/1855, p. 509; vol. 4, 19 Muḥarram 1274/1857, p. 514; vol. 4, 27 Muḥarram 1274/1857, p. 514.

81 *Ibid.*, vol. 4, 18 Rajab 1272/1856, p. 509.

82 For example, MBA, s. 323, no. 628, 1216/1801–1802; s. 345, no. 196, 1226–1227/1811–1812.

83 See ʿAbd al-Raḥīm, *al-Rīf al-maṣrī*, pp. 192–193; *Déscription de l'Egypte, état moderne*, vol. 2, part 2, Chabrol de Volvic, "Essai sur les moeurs des habitants modernes de l'Egypte," p. 507.

84 See ʿAbd al-Raḥīm, *al-Rīf al-maṣrī*, pp. 192–193; *Déscription, état moderne*, vol. 2, part 2, Girard, "Memoire sur l'agriculture, l'industrie et le commerce de l'Egypte," pp. 596–599.

85 Vincennes, MR 1677, Truguet, "Memoire sur l'Egypte," 1784.

86 *Déscription, état moderne*, vol. 2, part 2, Girard, "Memoire sur l'agriculture," pp. 596–598.

87 See M. de Chabrol de Volvic, *Essai*, p. 142; and *Déscription, état moderne*, vol. 2, part 2, Coutelle, "Observations sur la topographie de la Presqu'ile de Sinai," p. 298. Vincennes, MR 1677, Dubois-Ayme, "Memoires sur les tribus arabes des deserts de l'Egypte," August 1811, contains the same observation.

88 See Clot-Bey, *Aperçu*, vol. 2, p. 289. Clot-Bey stresses the importance of home spinning in the period preceding Muḥammad ʿAlī's industrialization of textiles. See also *Déscription, état moderne*, Jomard, "Déscription abregée," vol. 2, part 2, pp. 702–703.

89 MBA, s. 323, nos. 319, 385, 1216/1801–1802; s. 345, nos. 11, 292, 1226–1227/1811–1812; s. 366, no. 419, 1235–1236/1820–1821.

90 See Fahmy, *La révolution*, pp. 32–33, 93, for ordinances and regulations governing the state-run cottage industry.

91 MAE, Correspond. con. et com., Alex. XXIV, Mimaut à ministre, 22 June 1831. Mimaut reported that linen cloth was still being produced in quantity, but production was hampered by government control and the recruitment of many skilled weavers into the army.

92 MAE, Correspond. con. et com., Alex. XXXIV, Labatier à ministre, 27 February 1855; Baer, *Egyptian Guilds*, p. 131.

93 See Whately, *Child-Life*, pp. 84–92; and Jean Vallet, *Conditions des ouvriers de la grande industrie au Caire*, p. 128.
94 al-Mahdī, *Fatāwā*, vol. 1, 27 Dhū al-qaʿdah 1265/1849, p. 384.
95 *Ibid.*, vol. 1, 5 Jumādā II 1265/1849, p. 266.
96 *Ibid.*, vol. 1, 18 Jumādā I 1266/1850, p. 175.
97 See Vallet, *Conditions*, pp. 30, 63, 108.
98 Fahmy, *La révolution*, pp. 64–65; Hamont, *L'Egypte*, vol. 2, p. 249; St John, *Egypt*, vol. 1, pp. 84–85.
99 FO 142/6, Campbell to Palmerston, 28 April 1833.
100 Hekekyan Papers, BM 37450, vol. 3, fo. 36.
101 Hamont, *L'Egypte*, vol. 2, p. 356; Scott, *Rambles*, vol. 1, p. 93; FO 78/381, Bowring Report, March 1839, fos. 68–69.
102 Hekekyan Papers, BM 37450, vol. 3, fos. 233, 258.
103 FO 78/381, Bowring Report, March 1839, fos. 57–58, 74; Hekekyan Papers, BM 37450, vol. 3, fos. 31, 36.
104 Hekekyan Papers, BM 37450, vol. 3, fos. 31, 36.
105 *Ibid.*, 37449, vol. 2, fo. 78, and 37466, vol. 19, fo. 178.
106 *Ibid.*, 37449, vol. 2, fo. 74.
107 Scott, *Rambles* vol. 2, p. 180.
108 Hekekyan Papers, BM 37466, vol. 19, Poulain Report, fo. 87.
109 See Vallet, *Conditions*, pp. 90–125.
110 *Ibid.*, pp. 2, 96, 118–119.
111 "Report . . . Egypt and the Soudan in 1899," Inclosure: "Memorandum by M. H. H. Pinching, Director General of the Sanitary Department, on the Outbreak of Plague at Alexandria," *PP*, 1900, CV, 995, p. 40; "Report . . . Egypt and the Soudan in 1900," Inclosure: "Report by M. H. Pinching, Plague," *PP*, 1901, XCI, 1057, pp. 62–64.
112 "Report . . . Egypt and the Soudan in 1909," *PP*, 1910, CXII, 347, pp. 30–31.
113 Baer, *Egyptian Guilds*, p. 33. Baer cites the 1889 administrative order; the full list includes: domestic servants, cotton workers, greengrocers, bakers, *bashakirah* (bakery workers), sellers of milk, soothsayers, pastry cooks, midwives, and other women "except those who had shops like men." The 1897 Census listed a number of female occupations, including domestic servant, petty trader of an unspecified nature, peddler of butter and oil, fruit, milk, fish, and drugs and spices, laundress, baker, embroiderer, singer, cook, seamstress, funeral attendant, teacher, ceramics worker, bath attendant, sweeper, and midwife: Egypt, Direction du recensement, *Recensement général de l'Egypte*, vol. 1, p. 50.
114 MBA, s. 345, no. 604, 1226–1227/1811–1812. A bath attendant buys a small property with her own money.
115 See Lane-Poole, *Social Life*, p. 31.
116 MBA, s. 323, no. 695, 1216/1801–1802; s. 366, no. 255, 1235–1236/1820–1821.
117 Savary, *Lettres*, vol. 1, p. 149.
118 Edward Lane, *An Account of the Manners and Customs of the Modern Egyptians*, p. 355; Edward W. Lane, "Description of Egypt," BM 34080, vol. 1, fo. 111; Clot-Bey, *Aperçu*, p. 80.

119 Duff Gordon, *Letters*, p. 46.
120 al-Mahḍī, *Fatāwā*, vol. 1, 21 Dhū al-hijjah 1264/1848, pp. 15–16.
121 FO 78/344, Campbell to Palmerston, 21 April 1838.
122 Hekekyan Papers, BM 37450, vol. 3, fo. 335.
123 Consular reports list numerous foreign subjects employed as servants in Egypt, usually in specialized service as ladies' maids, nursemaids, cooks, etc. MAE, Correspond. con. et com., Alex. XXIV, Mimaut à ministre, 5 January 1831, p. 163; *ibid.*, XXVIII, Duvigneau à Cochelet, 2 January 1839; MAE, Correspond. pol. des consuls, Turq: Alex. et Caire XXII, Lorette à Lemoyne, 29 April 1851; FO 78/162, Barker to Bidwell, 31 December 1831.
124 al-Mahdī, *Fatāwā*, vol. 1, 13 Rabī' II 1265/1849, p. 264; vol. 1, 2 Ṣafar 1267/1850, p. 283; vol. 1, 25 Jumādā II 1267/1851, p. 283.
125 *Ibid.*, vol. 1, 21 Ramaḍān 1267/1851, p. 34.
126 MBA, s. 387, no. 141, 1246/1830–1831; I, s. 5, no. 487, 1255–1256/1839–1840; al-Maḥdī, *Fatāwā*, vol. 1, 1 Rabī' I 1271/1854, p. 55.
127 See Raymond, *Artisans*, vol. 2, pp. 720–724.
128 MBA, s. 323, no. 387, 450, 488, 614, 641, 650, 682, 702, 731, 743, 1216/1801–1802; s. 345, nos. 12, 82, 145, 178, 1226–1227/1811–1812; s. 366, nos. 230, 241, 1235–1236/1820–1821.
129 al-Maḥdī, *Fatāwā*, vol. 3, 14 Jumādā II 1265/1949, p. 17; vol. 3, 19 Dhū al-hijjah 1265/1849, p. 26; vol. 3, 23 Dhū al-hijjah 1265/1849, p. 200; vol. 3, 6 Dhū al-qa'dah 1275/1859, p. 153; vol. 3, 22 Sha'bān 1281/1865, p. 168.
130 FO 141/183, Charif Pasha to Malet, 4 September 1883.
131 Legal theory recognized two separate types of *waqf* endowments: the *waqf khayrī*, or "charitable *waqf*," and the *waqf ahlī*, or "family *waqf*." The former assigned the property's revenue immediately to a charitable cause, while the latter specified benefits for the founder's descendants as long as the family line survived. In practice, we find many *waqfs* with mixed purposes and various ways of dividing up the revenue, obviating any pristine distinction between the two. See Baer, *Studies*, pp. 79–83.
132 al-Maḥdī, *Fatāwā*, vol. 2, 28 Rajab 1270/1854, p. 547; vol. 2, 25 Shawwāl 1270/1854, p. 578; vol. 2, 30 Rajab 1275/1859, pp. 652–653.
133 *Ibid.*, vol. 2, 13 Jumādā II 1265/1849, pp. 457–458.
134 *Ibid.*, vol. 2, 5 Ṣafar 1265/1849, p. 447; vol. 2, 2 Jumādā I 1265/1849, pp. 451–452; vol. 2, 13 Ṣafar 1275/1858, p. 643; vol. 2, 28 Rajab 1275/1859, p. 651.
135 *Ibid.*, vol. 2, 11 Shawwāl 1270/1854, p. 454; also vol. 2, 28 Jumādā II 1275/1859, pp. 650–651.
136 *Ibid.*, vol. 2, 6 Jumādā I 1265/1849, p. 454; vol. 2, 9 Jumādā II 1265/1849, p. 455. In an arbitrary sample of 2,051 Cairo court cases between 1801 and 1860, we found 180 cases of female *waqf* administrators.
137 MBA, s. 323, no. 375, 1216/1801–1802. *Istibdāl* is the sale of a *waqf* in order to replace it with another property. Such sale is admissible only when the original *waqf* property produces no revenue and/or is in ruins, and a judge must oversee the transaction. See Emile Tyan, *Histoire de l'organization judiciaire en pays d'Islam*, p. 378.
138 In our samples from MBA and I, 1801–1860, we found 27 succession disputes

concerning women: the first occurred in 1820–1821, and 26 of the 27 occurred between 1830 and 1860. The sample is too small, however, to constitute compelling evidence for an absolute rise in female disinheritance.

139 MBA, s. 387, nos. 15, 213, 218, 1246/1830; I, s. 23, nos. 35, 80, 1266/1849–1850.

140 MBA, s. 323, no. 22, 1216/1801–1802.

141 MBA, s. 323, no. 326, 1216/1801–1802.

3 Private and public life: women and the growth of the State

1 See Janet Abu-Lughod, *Cairo: 1001 Years of the City Victorious*, pp. 64–65, 71.

2 MBA, s. 323, no. 698, 1216/1801–1802.

3 See Raymond, *Artisans*, vol. 2, pp. 383–387.

4 *Ibid.*, vol. 1, p. 205; vol. 2, pp. 506–507.

5 Baer, *Egyptian guilds*, pp. 27–30.

6 *Ibid.*, pp. 8–11, Baer's thesis of absolute decline of the guild structure is based on the assumption that guild documents of the seventeenth century described ceremonies and structures that were in actual use; it seems just as likely, however, that they depicted an ideal rather than a reality.

7 See Gran, *Islamic Roots*, pp. 6–10.

8 See Baer, *Egyptian Guilds*, pp. 23–24. Baer's suggestion that the number of guilds remained more or less constant during the nineteenth century is based on the French list of guilds used by Raymond in "Une liste des corporations de métiers au Caire en 1801," *Arabica*, IV, part 2 (1957), 151–163. Raymond later termed this list partial and revised his estimates upward: see Raymond, *Artisans*, vol. 2, p. 511.

9 See Raymond, *Artisans*, vol. 2, pp. 527–528.

10 Lane, *Manners and Customs*, p. 191; Chabrol de Volvic, *Essai*, p. 156; Rouchdi Fakkar, *Aspects de la vie quotidienne en Egypte*, pp. 63–67.

11 See F. De Jong, *Ṭuruq*, ch. 1, for a survey of *ṣūfī* orders at the time of Muḥammad ʿAlī's accession to power.

12 See *ibid.*, pp. 37, 98 n. 13. See also Gran, *Islamic Roots*, pp. 47–49.

13 De Jong, *Ṭuruq*, p. 8; Gran, *Islamic Roots*, pp. 47–49.

14 The *dhikr*, strictly speaking, is the repetition of the names of God often accompanied by rhythmic body movements. It is usually preceded by a communal reading, and the entire ritual is called *ḥadra*. In colloquial usage, the term *dhikr* designates the entire ceremony. See De Jong, *Ṭuruq*, p. 196 n. 1.

15 *Ibid.*, pp. 196–200.

16 al-Jabartī, *Ajāʾib*, vol. 2, p. 306.

17 Gran, *Islamic Roots*, p. 129; Chabrol de Volvic, *Essai*, p. 22. Gran notes that not all *ʿulamāʾ* were receptive to women students. While al-Zabīdī had female pupils, his own student, al-ʿAṭṭār, apparently never taught women and, indeed, held them in very low esteem.

18 "Report . . . Egypt and the Soudan in 1906," *PP*, 1907, C, 617, p. 50.

19 St John, *Egypt*, vol. 2, p. 335.

20 See Abu-Lughod, *Cairo*, pp. 85–97, for a detailed account of urban reform under Muḥammad ʿAlī.

21 *Ibid.*, pp. 110–113.

22 *Ibid.*, pp. 118–131.
23 See André Raymond, "Problemes urbains et urbanisme au Caire au XVIIe et XVIIIe siècles," in *Colloque international sur l'histoire du Caire*, pp. 358–359.
24 MAE, Correspond. pol. des consuls, Turq: Alex. et Caire XIX, Barrot à ministre, 16 January 1848; FO 142/16, Murray to Palmerston, 27 October 1848.
25 See Fahmy, *La révolution*, p. 74.
26 See Baer, *Egyptian Guilds*, p. 131; for a brief but penetrating discussion which questions the appropriateness of the term "guild" in the Middle Eastern context, see Clifford Geertz, "Suq: The Bazaar Economy in Sefrou," in Clifford Geertz, Hildred Geertz, and Lawrence Rosen, *Meaning and Order in Moroccan Society*, p. 244 n. 53.
27 For a discussion of the expansion of the *shaykh al-sajjādah al-Bakrīyyah*'s authority, see De Jong, *Ṭuruq*, pp. 9–12, 20–23.
28 *Ibid.*, Appendix III, pp. 196–200.
29 Gran, *Islamic Roots*, p. 122.
30 Rivlin, *Agricultural Policy*, p. 352 n. 35; Baer, *Studies*, p. 137.
31 Laverne Kuhnke, "The 'Doctoress' on a Donkey: Women Health Officers in Nineteenth Century Egypt," *Clio Medica*, IX, 3 (1974), 201.
32 "Report . . . Egypt and the Soudan in 1908," *PP*, 1909, CV, 333, p. 32.
33 "Report . . . Egypt and the Progress of Reforms," *PP*, 1897, CII, 505, pp. 20–21.
34 D'Abernon Papers, BM 48961A, fos. 77–80; FO 633/14, Cromer Papers, P. G. Graham to Lord Cromer, 6 November 1910, fos. 94a–94d.
35 "Report . . . Egypt and the Soudan in 1904," *PP*, 1905, CIII, 1087, p. 70; "Report . . . Egypt and the Soudan in 1909," *PP*, 1910, CXII, 347, p. 34.
36 See Abu-Lughod, *Cairo*, pp. 91–92.
37 FO 141/186, W. G. Hunter to Malet, 6 August 1883; FO 141/187, Clifford Lloyd to Baring, 21 November 1883.
38 "Report . . . Egypt and the Progress of Reforms, 1890," *PP*, 1890–1891, XCVII, 717, pp. 31–32.
39 FO 633/8, *Cromer Papers*, Lord Cromer to Lord Lansdowne, Cairo, 8 June 1897, fos. 121–122.
40 "Report . . . Egypt and the Progress of Reforms, 1891," *PP*, 1892, XCVI, 399.
41 Kuhnke, "The 'Doctoress,'" pp. 201–202.
42 FO 633/14, Cromer Papers, Cromer to P. G. Graham, 14 October 1910, fo. 128.
43 "Report . . . Egypt and the Soudan in 1906," *PP*, 1907, C, 617, p. 45.
44 "Report . . . Egypt and the Soudan in 1909," *PP*, 1910, CXII, 347, p. 34.
45 "Report . . . Egypt and the Soudan in 1911," *PP*, 1912–1913, CXXXI, 635, p. 37.
46 FO 141/241, Inspector General, Administration of Service Sanitaire to Sirdar, Egyptian Army, 25 September 1886.
47 FO 141/176, Malet to Earl of Granville, 28 August 1883; "Report . . . Egypt and the Progress of Reforms, 1897," CII, 505, pp. 20–21.
48 "Report . . . Egypt and the Soudan in 1905," *PP*, 1906, CXXXVII, 475, p. 73; "Report . . . Egypt and the Soudan in 1906," *PP*, 1907, C, 617, p. 46.
49 "Report . . . Egypt and the Soudan in 1908," *PP*, 1909, CV, 333, p. 32; "Report . . . Egypt and the Soudan in 1913," *PP*, 1914, CI, 327, pp. 45, 50–51.
50 FO 141/176, MacDonald to Malet, 13 August 1883.

51 *Ibid.*; FO 141/187, Clifford Lloyd to Baring, 14 November 1883; FO 141/226, Nubar to Baring, 11 June 1885; "Report . . . Egypt and the Progress of Reforms, 1897," *PP*, 1898, CVII, 621, pp. 36–37.

52 "Report . . . Egypt and the Progress of Reforms, 1897," *PP*, 1898, CVII, 621, pp. 36–37; "Report . . . Egypt and the Soudan in 1900," *PP*, 1901, XCI, 1057, pp. 42–43; "Report . . . Egypt and the Soudan in 1906," *PP*, 1907, C, 617, p. 44; "Report . . . Egypt and the Soudan in 1908," *PP*, 1909, CV, 333, p. 31.

53 "Report . . . Egypt and the Soudan in 1902," *PP*, 1903, LXXXVII, 953, p. 44.

54 Charles Coles, *Recollections and Reflections*, pp. 63–64.

55 "Report . . . Egypt and the Soudan in 1900," Inclosure: "Report by M. H. Pinching, Plague," *PP*, 1901, XCI, 1057, p. 60.

56 For Clot-Bey's narrative of the school's history, see Antoine Clot-Bey, *Mémoires de A. B. Clot-Bey*, pp. 107–108, 158–161.

57 MAE, Correspond, con. et. com., Alex. XXXI, Lavalette à ministre, 22 May 1844; *ibid.*, Alex. XXXII, Benedetti à ministre, 19 May 1847; *ibid.*, Le Caire XXVIII, Benedetti à ministre, 10 December 1847.

58 FO 141/180, Osman Orfi to Cookson, 14 August 1883; "Report by H. R. Greene, Surgeon Major, Medical Staff, Sous-Director of Sanitary Services of Egypt," *PP*, 1884–1885, LXXXIX, 1.

59 As of 1883, the Midwifery School curriculum was as follows: Year I: Arabic grammar, reading, calligraphy, arithmetic. Year II: Anatomy, minor surgery, calligraphy, arithmetic. Year III: Normal delivery, "matière médicale," calligraphy. Year IV: Abnormal delivery, "matière médicale," diseases of women and hygiene, calligraphy. FO 140/186, "Programmes des études actuellement suives aux écoles de Medicine, de Pharmacie, et de Maternité," 1883.

60 "Report by H. R. Greene, Surgeon Major, Medical Staff, Sous-Director of Sanitary Services of Egypt" and "Draft Decree organizing Sanitary Service," *PP*, 1884–1885, LXXXIX, 1.

61 "Report . . . Egypt and the Soudan in 1904," *PP*, 1905, CIII, 1087, p. 68.

62 "Report . . . Egypt and the Soudan in 1912," *PP*, 1913, LXXXI, 207, p. 43; "Report . . . Egypt and the Soudan in 1913," *PP*, 1914, CI, 327, p. 10.

63 FO 141/186, "List of Doctors Sent to Affected Districts," n.d. (assume July 1883); d'Abernon Papers, BM Add. 48961A, fos. 265–268.

64 "Report . . . Egypt and the Progress of Reforms, 1890," *PP*, 1890–1891, XCVII, 717, pp. 30–31; "Report . . . Egypt and the Soudan in 1913," *PP*, 1914, CI, 327, p. 40.

65 FO 633/8, Cromer Papers, Lord Cromer to Mr Davidson, Cairo, 23 January 1900, fo. 252.

66 For discussion of Muḥammad ʿAlī's educational policies, see Yacoub Artin Pasha, *L'instruction publique en Egypte*, pp. 75–79; and James Heyworth-Dunne, *An Introduction to the History of Education in Modern Egypt, passim.*

67 See Artin Pasha, *L'instruction*, pp. 89–98; and Robert Tignor, *Modernization and British Colonial Rule in Egypt, 1882–1914*, p. 341.

68 "Report . . . Egypt and the Progress of Reforms, 1892," *PP*, 1893–4, CXI, 1127; "Report . . . Egypt and the Progress of Reforms, 1895," *PP*,1896, XCVII, 989; "Report . . . Egypt and the Soudan in 1906," *PP*, 1907, C, 617, pp. 49–51.

69 Young, "A Little to the East," fo. 3.
70 FO 633/13, Cromer Papers, Cromer to Sir Edward Grey, 8 March 1907. Here Cromer responds to criticism from Blunt and Robertson.
71 "Report . . . Egypt and the Soudan in 1906," *PP*, 1907, C, 617, p. 51.
72 "Report . . . Egypt and the Soudan in 1913," *PP*, 1914, CI, 327, p. 34.
73 See Artin Pasha, *L'instruction*, pp. 124–128, 132–134; and Duff Gordon, *Letters*, p. 130.
74 "Report . . . Egypt and the Soudan in 1906," *PP*, 1907, C, 617, p. 50.
75 See Artin Pasha, *L'instruction*, pp. 116–123.
76 See Muḥammad Rashīd Riḍā, *Fatāwā al-Imām Muḥammad Rashīd Riḍā*, vol. 1, no. 12, pp. 43–44; vol. 1, no. 24, pp. 66–67.
77 Hamont, *L'Egypte*, pp. 423–424.
78 Artin Pasha, *L'instruction*, pp. 135–136.
79 "Report . . . Egypt and the Soudan in 1900," *PP*, 1901, XCI, 1057, pp. 50–51.
80 "Report . . . Egypt and the Soudan in 1906," *PP*, 1907, C, 617, p. 57.
81 "Report . . . Egypt and the Soudan in 1905," *PP*, 1906, CXXXVII, 475, p. 88.
82 "Report . . . Egypt and the Progress of Reforms, 1891," *PP*, 1892, XCVI, 399.
83 "Report . . . Egypt and the Soudan in 1913," *PP*, 1914, CI, 327, p. 37.
84 "Report . . . Egypt and the Progress of Reforms, 1895," *PP*, 1896, XCVII, 989; "Report . . . Egypt and the Soudan in 1903," *PP*, 1904, CXI, 203, p. 61; "Report . . . Egypt and the Soudan in 1913," *PP*, 1914, CI, 327, pp. 34–35.
85 "Report . . . Egypt and the Soudan in 1908," *PP*, 1909, CV, 333, p. 41.
86 "Report . . . Egypt and the Soudan in 1904," *PP*, 1905, CIII, 1087, p. 73.
87 *Ibid.*, p. 77; "Report . . . Egypt and the Soudan in 1909," *PP*, 1910, CXII, 347, p. 45; "Report . . . Egypt and the Soudan in 1913," *PP*, 1914, CI, 327, pp. 34–35.
88 "Report . . . Egypt and the Soudan in 1909," *PP*, CXII, 347, p. 49.
89 "Report . . . Egypt and the Soudan in 1912," *PP*, 1913, LXXXI, 207, p. 30; "Report . . . Egypt and the Soudan in 1913," *PP*, 1914, CI, 327, p. 39.
90 "Report . . . Egypt and the Progress of Reforms, 1898," *PP*, 1899, CXII, 961, p. 44.
91 "Report . . . Egypt and the Soudan in 1903," *PP*, 1904, CXI, 203, p. 65; "Report . . . Egypt and the Soudan in 1905," *PP*, 1906, CXXXVII, 475, p. 92; "Report . . . Egypt and the Soudan in 1909," *PP*, 1910, CXII, 347, pp. 44–46; "Report . . . Egypt and the Soudan in 1912," *PP*, 1913, LXXXI, 207, p. 30; "Report . . . Egypt and the Soudan in 1913," *PP*, 1914, CI, 327, pp. 34, 40.
92 "Report . . . Egypt and the Progress of Reforms, 1898," *PP*, 1899, CXII, 961, p. 44; "Report . . . Egypt and the Soudan in 1906," *PP*, 1907, C, 617, pp. 50, 51; "Report . . . Egypt and the Soudan in 1909," *PP*, 1910, CXII, 347, pp. 47–48; "Report . . . Egypt and the Soudan in 1913," *PP*, 1914, CI, 327, p. 34.
93 See Panzac, "La population de l'Egypte à l'époque contemporaine," in Aulas *et al.*, *L'Egypte d'aujourd'hui*, p. 173.
94 See Artin Pasha, *L'instruction*, p. 124.

4 Women, resistance, and repression

1 Vincennes, MR 1677, "Etat militaire de l'Egypte en 1825," 8 September 1825; MAE, Correspond. pol. des consuls, Turq: Alex. et Caire I, Mimaut à ministre, 26

April 1830; MAE, Correspond. con. et com., Alex XXIV, Mimaut à ministre, 1 August 1831; Hekekyan Papers, BM 37449, vol. 2, fo. 130.

2 *al-Waqā'i' al-miṣrīyah*, n.v., n.d., 1245/1829–1830.

3 Hekekyan Papers, BM 37449, vol. 2, fo 130; MAE, Correspond, con. et com., Alex. XXIV, Mimaut à ministre, 1 August 1831.

4 *al-Waqā'i' al-miṣrīyah*, n.v., n.d., 1245/1829–1830.

5 *Ibid.*, n.p.

6 FO 142/13, Barnett to Secretary, 16 March 1845.

7 St John, *Egypt*, vol. 1, p. 276.

8 FO 78/184, Barker to Malcolm, 8 July 1829.

9 Hamont, *L'Egypte*, vol. 2, pp. 19–20; Vincennes, MR 1678, Mathieu de Faviers, "Situation de l'armée regulière égyptienne," 30 May 1831; Scott, *Rambles*, vol. 2, p. 216; MAE, Correspond. con. et com., Alex. XXVII, de Lessups à ministre, 5 March 1837; MAE, Correspond. pol. des consuls, Turq: Alex. et Caire XV, Gallice à See, 6 June 1843.

10 MAE, Correspond. con. et com., Alex. XXXI, Lavalette à ministre, 1844.

11 FO 78/381, Bowring Report, March 1839, fo. 100; MAE, Correspond. pol. des consuls, Turq: Alex. et Caire XXI, Benedetti à ministre, 5 December 1849.

12 MAE, Correspond. con. et com., Alex. XXVII, de Lessups à ministre, 5 March 1837; FO 78/381, Bowring Report, March 1839, fo. 100.

13 MAE, Correspond. pol. des consuls, Turq: Alex. et Caire XX, Barrot à ministre, 19 June 1848; *ibid.*, XXI, Benedetti à ministre, 5 December 1849.

14 Vincennes, MR 1678, Motel, "L'armée égyptienne," 27 June 1861.

15 MAE, Correspond. con. et com., Alex. XXIX, Benedetti à ministre, 29 May 1841; *ibid.*, XXXIII, Benedetti à ministre, 18 April 1849; MAE, Correspond. pol. des consuls, Turq: Alex. et Caire XX, Barrot à ministre, 19 June 1848; Hamont, *L'Egypte*, vol. 2, pp. 19–20, 57; St John, *Egypt*, vol. 2, p. 176.

16 See Baer, *Studies*, ch. 3, for a discussion of the evolution of the political and economic power of the village *shaykh*.

17 al-Mahdī, *Fatāwā*, vol. 2, 6 Shawwāl 1267/1851, p. 96; vol. 5, 29 Jumādā II 1265/1849, p. 110; vol. 5, 19 Jumādā I 1267/1851, p. 117.

18 *Ibid.*, vol. 1, 8 Rabī' I 1268/1852, p. 38; vol. 1, 4 Jumādā I 1265/1849, p. 18.

19 See Richards, *Egypt's Agricultural Development*, pp. 36–37.

20 FO 141/203, Kent to Baring, Maḥallah, 11 October 1884; 1884; "Report . . . Egypt and the Progress of Reforms, 1890," *PP*, 1891, XCVI, 399, pp. 22–23; "Report . . . Egypt and the Soudan in 1906," *PP*, 1907, C, 617, p. 40. See also Baer, *Studies*, ch. 3.

21 In our sample from MBA and I between 1830 and 1860, we found sixteen cases of women placing claims against the State for wages or benefits owed to a deceased husband.

22 See Tyan, *L'organization*, pp. 438–441.

23 Hamont, *L'Egypte*, vol. 2, p. 57.

24 Richards, "Primitive Accumulation," p. 22.

25 Baer, *Studies*, p. 96.

26 Rivlin, *Agricultural Policy*, pp. 201–202.

27 For a discussion of the Qīnah revolt as an artisan-based rebellion, see Fred H.

Lawson, "Rural Revolt and Provincial Society in Egypt, 1820–1824," *IJMES*, 13 (1981), 131–153.

28 Richards, "Primitive Accumulation," p. 22.

29 MAE, Correspond. pol. des consuls, Turq: Alex. et Caire xx, Barrot à ministre, 16 May 1848.

30 Duff Gordon, *Letters*, p. 209.

31 *Ibid.*, pp. 214–215.

32 Richards, *Egypt's Agricultural*, p. 42; FO 141/192, Memo, Clifford Lloyd, 23 February 1884; FO 141/201, Mustapha Shahir to Baring, 3 April 1884.

33 al-Jabartī, *'Ajā'ib*, vol. 2, Rabī' I 1214/1799, p. 304.

34 MAE, Correspond. pol. des consuls, Turq: Alex. et Caire XIV, Gallice à ministre, 23 March 1841, p. 263.

35 Duff Gordon, *Letters*, pp. 212–215.

36 FO 141/170, H. Chermside to Earl of Dufferin, 6 December 1882.

37 See Gran, *Islamic Roots*, pp. 18–24; Raymond, *Artisans*, vol. 1, pp. 103–106.

38 See André Raymond, "Quartiers et mouvements populaires au Caire au XVIIIème siècle," in P. M. Holt (ed.), *Political and Social Change in Modern Egypt*, pp. 104–116; André Raymond, "Deux leaders populaires au Caire à la fin du XVIIIe et au début du XIXe siècle," *La Nouvelle Revue du Caire*, 1 (1975), 281–398; Gran, *Islamic Roots*, pp. 24–26.

39 The *naqīb al-ashrāf* held considerable power over the highly respected community of the descendants of the Prophet, including the exclusive right to punish members of the *ashrāf*, supervise their *awqāf*, and distribute the revenues. See De Jong, *Ṭuruq*, p. 12.

40 MAE, Correspond. con. et com., Alex. XVII, Drovetti à ministre, 12 Prairial an 13 (1804).

41 *Ibid.*, 18 Prairial an 13 (1804).

42 MAE, Correspond. con. et com., Alex. XVIII, Drovetti à ministre, 20 April 1806.

43 MAE, Correspond. con. et com., Alex. XVII, Drovetti à ministre, 14 Floréal an 13 (1804); *ibid.*, Drovetti à ministre, 19 Floréal an 13 (1804).

44 MAE, Correspond. pol. des consuls, Turq: Alex. et Caire XI, Bourville à ministre, 13 September 1840.

45 Duff Gordon, *Letters*, pp. 72–73.

46 al-Jarbartī, *'Ajā'ib*, vol. 2, Jumādā I 1216/1801, p. 494.

47 St John, *Egypt*, vol. 2, p. 461.

48 For women's participation in the 1919 revolution, see Thomas Philipp, "Feminism and Feminist Politics in Egypt," in Lois Beck and Nikki Keddie (eds.), *Women in the Muslim World*, pp. 277–294.

49 MAE, Correspond. pol. des consuls, Turq: Alex. et Caire v, Mimaut à ministre, 25 April 1835; FO 78/282, Campbell to Palmerston, 24 January 1836; Hekekyan Papers, BM 37450, vol. 3, fos. 62–63.

50 Hekekyan Papers, BM 37450, vol. 3, fo. 247. Hekekyan also recorded census data for Manṣūrah and the province of al-Daqhalīyyah, as collected by Antonio Colucci, in which the number of deaths far exceeded the number of births: Hekekyan Papers, BM 37466, vol. 9, fos. 97–100.

51 al-Mahdī, *Fatāwā*, vol. 1, 11 Rabī' II, 1265/1849, p. 243.

52 *Ibid.*, vol. 5, 16 Rajab 1267/1851, p. 426.
53 *Ibid.*, vol. 5, 30 Dhū al-hijjah 1267/1851, p. 429.
54 Duff Gordon, *Letters*, p. 153.
55 "Report . . . Egypt and the Soudan in 1901," *PP*, 1902, CXXX, 703, p. 29; "Report . . . Egypt and the Soudan in 1905," *PP*, 1906, CXXXVII, 475, p. 68.
56 Hekekyan Papers, BM 37466, vol. 19, fo. 86. The British consul, Campbell, although generally critical of the industrialization project, was equally impressed by the "dexterity and ability" and "skill and despatch" of the "Arab" workers: FO 142/7, Campbell to Dawkins, 7 April 1833; FO 142/6, Campbell to Palmerston, 24 April 1833.
57 FO 142/13, Barnett to Secretary, 18 September 1841, no. 15.
58 Hekekyan Papers, BM 37450, vol. 3, fo. 152.
59 St John, *Egypt*, vol. 2, p. 413; Hekekyan Papers, BM 37449, vol. 2, fo. 174.
60 FO 141/179, Felice to Borg, 6 February 1883.
61 MAE, Correspond. pol. des consuls, Turq: Alex. et Caire XXI, Benedetti à ministre, 8 January 1850.
62 "Report . . . Egypt and the Soudan in 1902," *PP*, 1903, LXXXVII, 953, p. 43.
63 FO 141/202, Borg to Egerton, 9 July 1884.
64 FO 141/228, Stephenson to Baring, 4 July 1885.
65 "Correspondence Respecting the Attack made on Two Officers of her Majesty's Army at Keneseh, in Egypt," *PP*, 1887, XCII, 671.
66 FO 141/240, Nūbar Pāshā to Baring, 6 March 1886.
67 "Report . . . Egypt and the Soudan in 1906," *PP*, 1907, C, 617, p. 47; "Report . . . Egypt and the Soudan in 1907," *PP*, 1908, CXXV, 183, pp. 59–60.
68 "Report . . . Egypt and the Soudan in 1910," *PP*, 1911, CIII, 241, p. 33.
69 "Report . . . Egypt and the Progress of Reforms, 1890," *PP*, 1891, XCVI, 399, pp. 22–23; "Report . . . Egypt and the Soudan in 1908," *PP*, 1909, CV, 333, pp. 34–35.
70 "Report . . . Egypt and the Soudan in 1908," *PP*, 1909, CV, 333, p. 35.
71 "Report . . . Egypt and the Soudan in 1904," *PP*, 1905, CIII, 1087, p. 45.
72 Milner, *England in Egypt*, pp. 278–279; "Reports by Colonel Johnson on Brigandage (so called) in Egypt," *PP*, 1884–1885, LXXXIX, 1.
73 "Further Correspondence Respecting the Affairs of Egypt," Malet to Granville, Letter from four European merchants, 2 November 1882, *PP*, 1883, LXXXIII, 375.
74 FO 141/337, A. J. and E. Argenti to Borg, Alex., 6 August 1898.
75 Duff Gordon, *Letters*, p. 295.
76 al-Mahdī, *Fatāwā*, vol. 5, pp. 404–464.
77 *Ibid.*, vol. 5, 19 Dhū al-qaʿdah 1265/1849, pp. 404–405.
78 "Report . . . Egypt and the Soudan in 1912," *PP*, 1913, LXXXI, 207, p. 35.
79 al-Mahdī, *Fatāwā*, vol. 5, 23 Jumādā II 1266/1850, p. 413; vol. 5, 23 Shawwāl 1266/1850, p. 415; vol. 5, 30 Jumādā II 1269/1853, p. 444; vol. 5, 11 Shaʿbān 1272/1856, p. 454.
80 See Estelle Freedman, "Their Sisters' Keepers: The Origins of Female Corrections in America," unpublished PhD dissertation, pp. 13–14.
81 See Clot-Bey, *Aperçu*, vol. 2, p. 84; and Lane, *Manners and Customs*, pp. 189, 377–381.
82 Savary, *Lettres*, vol. 1, p. 155; St John, *Egypt*, vol. 2, p. 374.

83 Raymond, *Artisans*, vol. 2, p. 607; St John, *Egypt*, vol. 2, pp. 374, 468.
84 Raymond, *Artisans*, vol. 2, p. 609.
85 Vincennes, MR 543, Degua, "Notes sur l'Egypte."
86 al-Jabartī, *ʿAjāʾib*, vol. 2, Dhū al-qaʿdah 1213/1799, pp. 272–273.
87 See *Déscription, état moderne*, vol. 2, part 2, DuBois-Aymé et Jallois, "Voyage dans l'intérieur du Delta," p. 109; Savary, *Lettres*, p. 66; Lane, "Description of Egypt," BM 34081, vol. 2, fo. 152.
88 Lane, *Manners and Customs*, p. 377n; Hamont, *L'Egypte*, vol. 1, pp. 316–317; St John, *Egypt*, vol. 1, p. 115.
89 See Francis Steegmuller, *Flaubert in Egypt: A Sensibility on Tour*, pp. 113, 158.
90 Hamont, *L'Egypte*, vol. 1, pp. 319–320.
91 Duff Gordon, *Letters*, pp. 292–293.
92 FO 141/181, Wolf to Baring, 30 October 1883; "Letter from General Stephenson to the Secretary for War as to the Existence in Egypt of a System Similar to that which Prevailed under the Contagious Diseases Act," *PP*, 1887, LVII, 751.
93 See T. Russell, *Egyptian Service, 1902–1946*, pp. 178–180.
94 FO 141/337, Cameron to Cromer, Port Said, 10 June 1898: an Englishman in Port Said complained that a Frenchman had set up a brothel in the house next door and then refused the government's request to close it down.
95 Russell, *Egyptian Service*, p. 181.
96 FO 141/403, "Report of Société pour la Suppression de la Traite des Blanches," 30 December 1905.
97 Cheetham Papers, St Antony's Private Papers, Oxford University, Folder III, Cheetham to Kitchener, 1 September 1913.
98 Clara Boyle, *Boyle of Cairo, A Diplomatist's Adventures in the Middle East*, p. 68.
99 "Report . . . Egypt and the Soudan in 1904," *PP*, 1905, CIII, 1087, p. 56.
100 Lane, *Manners and Customs*, p. 377; R. R. Madden, *Travels in Turkey, Egypt, Nubia and Palestine*, vol. 1, pp. 300–302.
101 Clot-Bey, *Aperçu*, vol. 1, p. 402.
102 al-Mahdī, *Fatāwā*, vol. 1, 30 Shawwāl 1266/1850, p. 279.
103 Steegmuller, *Flaubert in Egypt*, p. 113.
104 Duff Gordon, *Letters*, p. 250.
105 "Report . . . Egypt and the Soudan in 1901," *PP*, 1902, CXXX, 703, pp. 29–30; "Report . . . Egypt and the Soudan in 1902," *PP*, 1903, LXXXVII, 953, pp. 49–50; "Report . . . Egypt and the Soudan in 1904," *PP*, 1905, CIII, 1087, p. 68; "Report . . . Egypt and the Soudan in 1905," *PP*, 1906, CXXXVII, 475, p. 70; "Report . . . Egypt and the Soudan in 1908," *PP*, 1909, CV, 333, p. 36.
106 FO 633/5, Cromer Papers, 191, Sir E. Baring to Mr Vincent, 16 May 1887; *ibid.*, 264, Sir E. Baring to Sir J. Ferguson, 24 March 1888; "Report . . . Egypt and the Progress of Reforms, 1896," *PP*, 1897, CII, 505, pp. 16–17; "Report . . . Egypt and the Soudan in 1906," *PP*, 1907, C, 617, p. 40; Coles, *Recollections*, pp. 61–62.
107 See Milner, *England in Egypt*, pp. 130–131, 278–279.
108 "Report . . . Egypt and the Soudan in 1909," *PP*, 1910, CXII, 347, pp. 24–25, 56–61; "Report . . . Egypt and the Soudan in 1910," *PP*, 1911, CIII, 241, pp. 33–34.
109 See Michel Foucault, *Discipline and Punish, The Birth of the Prison*; and Michael

Ignatief, *A Just Measure of Pain, The Penitentiary in the Industrial Revolution, 1750–1850*.

110 See Coles, *Recollections*, pp. 102–110, 121–141.

111 "Report . . . Egypt and the Progress of Reforms, 1897," *PP*, 1898, CVII, 621, pp. 25–26.

112 "Report . . . Egypt and the Progress of Reforms, 1893," annex by J. Scott, Judicial Adviser, *PP*, 1894, XCVI, 645; "Report . . . Egypt and the Progress of Reforms, 1896," *PP*, 1897, CII, 505, pp. 17–18; "Report . . . Egypt and the Soudan in 1903," *PP*, 1904, CXI, 203, p. 40.

113 Coles, *Recollections*, pp. 23, 101–105.

114 *Ibid.*, p. 115.

115 *Ibid.*, pp. 129–135.

116 FO 141/170, H. Chermside to Earl of Dufferin, 6 December 1882.

117 Freedman, "Their Sisters' Keepers," pp. 44–49.

118 FO 141/170, C. W. Wilson to Earl of Dufferin, 7 December 1882; FO 141/205, Crookshank, "Report – Cairo Prison," and "General Rules for Prisons," 16 March 1884; "Report . . . Egypt and the Progress of Reforms, 1891," *PP*, 1892, XCVI, 399; "Report . . . Egypt and the Progress of Reforms, 1894," *PP*, 1895, CIX, 941; Coles, *Recollections* p. 115.

5 The practice of slavery: women as property

1 Baer, *Studies*, p. 166. Baer implicity accepts the comparison between slaves in Egypt and the American south.

2 See M. J. Finley, "Between Slavery and Freedom," *Comparative Studies in Society and History*, VI, 3 (April 1964), 233–249. Finley argues that status in many ancient societies cannot be fully understood as a slave-free antinomy, but rather as a continuum of statuses in which subtle gradations proved more significant than any absolute classification of "slave" and "free."

3 Frederick Cooper, *Planatation Slavery on the East Coast of Africa*, pp. 2–9, 153–155.

4 Baer, *Studies*, pp. 136, 167–168. Baer's figures are based on Menguin, Bowring, and Campbell.

5 Walz, *Trade between*, p. 174.

6 FO 78/381, Bowring Report, March 1839, fo. 14.

7 "Despatch from Sir E. Baring Respecting Slavery in Egypt," *PP*, 1884, LXXV, 509; "Correspondence Respecting Slavery in Egypt," *PP*, 1887, XCII, 679; "Report . . . Egypt and the Progress of Reforms, 1892," *PP*, 1893–1894, CXI, 1127; "Report . . . Egypt and the Progress of Reforms, 1896," *PP*, 1897, CII, 505; "Report . . . Egypt and the Progress of Reforms, 1898," *PP*, 1899, CXII, 961; "Report . . . Egypt and the Soudan in 1900," *PP*, 1901, XCI, 1057; "Report . . . Egypt and the Soudan in 1902," *PP*, 1903, LXXXVII, 953; "Report . . . Egypt and the Soudan in 1903," *PP*, 1904, CXI, 203; "Report . . . Egypt and the Soudan in 1905," *PP*, 1906, CXXXVII, 475; Baer, *Studies*, pp. 167–168.

8 BFAAPS, Correspondence, Rhodes House S22 G26, Cromer to Allen, 24 March 1894.

9 al-Maḥdī, *Fatāwā*, vol. 2, pp. 2–16. Seventy-seven various kinds of disputes about manumission (*'ataq*) were referred to the *muftī* for an opinion between 1848 and 1884. Of these, 73 arose in the 1850s, and only 4 were handled in the 1860s and 1870s. Since al-Maḥdī continued to deliver opinions on other matters, we can assume that far fewer cases of slavery were being raised after the 1850s.

10 FO 24/1, Gen. Consul George Baldwin, 21 June 1789; Chabrol de Volvic, *Essai*, p. 28; St John, *Egypt*, vol. 2, p. 321; FO 78/381, Bowring Report, March 1839, fo. 14.

11 FO 141/170, Borg to Earl of Dufferin, 23 December 1882; BFAAPS, Correspond., Rhodes House, s16 g25, "List of Freed Slaves," 1892.

12 Lane, *Manners and Customs*, p. 184; MAE, Correspond. con. et com., Alex. XXIII, Gros à ministre, 29 April 1828; *ibid.*, 20 January 1829.

13 Walz, *Trade between*, pp. 176–179.

14 For a discussion of slave prices on the basis of extensive research into Cairo court reocrds, see Walz, *Trade between*, pp. 207–210. Walz stresses that slave prices were variable because many "imponderables," such as appearance, reputation, etc., affected the price of an individual slave. His findings on the relative values of slaves of different race, gender, and age are borne out by contemporary observers. In Bowring's list of prices in Khartoum, females outvalued males, and Ethiopians were significantly more expensive than sub-Saharan blacks: FO 78/381, Bowring Report, March 1839, fo. 154. Among Greek captives of war, girls were considerably more valuable than boys, and women in their teens and twenties fetched the highest prices: MAE, Correspond. con. et com., Alex. XXIII, Gros à ministre, 29 April 1829.

15 MAE, Correspond, con. et com., Caire XXIX, Delaporte à ministre, 5 August 1852; Duff Gordon, *Letters*, p. 306.

16 Baer, *Studies*, p. 169; FO 78/381, Bowring Report, March 1839, fo. 166.

17 The privileged position of white female slaves, owned, as they were, almost exclusively by affluent households and oftentimes acquiring the position of sole consort or even legal wife of members of high officials, was noted at the time. See Clot-Bey, *Aperçu*, vol. 1, p. 342; and Lane, *Manners and Customs*, pp. 84–85.

18 al-Maḥdī, *Fatāwā*, vol. 1, 6 Dhū al-hijjah, 1267/1851, pp. 35–36.

19 I, s. 37, nos. 89, 519, 1276/1859–1860; MBA, s. 440, no. 223, 225, 1266/1850.

20 Hamont, *l'Egypte*, pp. 423–424.

21 al-Maḥdī, *Fatāwā*, vol. 1, 27 Shawwāl 1266/1850, pp. 246–247.

22 R. Brunschvig, "'Abd," in *EI*, 2nd rev. edn. vol. 1, p. 35; Lane, *Manners and Customs*, p. 184.

23 MAE, Correspond. con. et com., Alex. XXIII, Gros à ministre, 29 April 1828.

24 Lane, *Manners and Customs*, p. 185.

25 Baer, relying heavily on Lane's observations, divides slaves into three almost airtight categories according to race: Baer, *Studies*, p. 163.

26 See Walz, *Trade between*, p. 179.

27 MBA, s. 440, 243, 1266/1849–1850.

28 MBA, s. 323, 565, 1216/1801–1802; I, s. 24, 78, 1266/1849–1850; al-Maḥdī, *Fatāwā*, vol. 2, 20 Rabī' II 1266/1850, p. 3; vol. 2, 23 Sha'bān 1270/1854, p. 11.

29 Baer, in *Studies*, pp. 163–164, develops this view of black slaves on the basis of reports from contemporary European observers.

30 *Déscription de l'Egypte, état moderne*, vol. 2, part 2, M. Jomard, "Déscription abregée

de la ville et de la citadelle du Kaire," p. 695; FO 78/381, Bowring Report, March 1839, fo. 162; R. R. Madden, *Egypt and Mohammed Ali*, pp. 118–119.

31 Hanum Djavidan, *Harem Life*, pp. 87–90.

32 BFAAPS, Correspond., Rhodes House, S16 G25, "N" to Allen, 18 July 1881; *ibid.*, Schweinfurth to –, 23 October 1882.

33 BFAAPS, Correspond., Rhodes House, S22 G26, Moncrieff Report, 18 April 1886.

34 MBA, s. 323, no. 326, 1216/1801–1802; I, 2.37, nos. 85, 511, 1276/1859–1860.

35 Duff Gordon, *Letters*, pp. 133–134.

36 See Baer, *Studies*, pp. 165–166. Baer relies, for this period, exclusively on Hekekyan's testimony that black slaves were employed as agricultural laborers on viceregal estates in Upper Egypt.

37 FO 78/381, Bowring Report, March 1839, fo. 162; Madden, *Egypt*, p. 118.

38 BFAAPS, Correspond., Rhodes House, S22 G25, "N" to Allen, 18 July 1881; *ibid.*, S22 G26, Moncrieff Report, 18 April 1886.

39 Vincennes, MR 1677, "Etat militaire actuel de l'Egypte," 5 May 1825, fo. 18.

40 FO 141/187, Schaefer to Baring, 22 September 1883.

41 "Correspondence Respecting Slavery in Egypt," *PP*, 1887, XCII, 679.

42 Walz, *Trade between*, p. 180.

43 FO 78/284, Campbell to Palmerston, 24 December 1836, p. 179; MAE, Correspond. pol. des consuls, Turq: Alex. et Caire VI, de Lessups à ministre, 7 September 1837.

44 Baer, *Studies*, p. 169; Walz, *Trade between*, pp. 177–179; Vincennes, MR 543, Degua, "Notes sur l'Egypte"; FO 141/170, Borg to Earl of Dufferin, 23 December 1882.

45 See Moses Nwulia, *Britain and Slavery in East Africa*, pp. 11, 86–87, 136–139.

46 Baer, *Studies*, pp. 179–181.

47 *Ibid.*, pp. 176–177.

48 Duff Gordon, *Letters*, p. 330.

49 FO 141/177, Malet to Granville, 19 February 1883, 5 March 1883, 23 October 1883; "Report . . . Egypt and the Progress of Reforms, 1890," *PP*, 1891, XCVI, 399, pp. 35–36.

50 BFAAPS, Correspond., Rhodes House, S16 G25, Gotfried Roth to Allen, 20 March 1881; FO 141/170, Borg to Earl of Dufferin, 23 December 1882.

51 "Report . . . Egypt and the Progress of Reforms, 1890," *PP*, 1891, XCVI, 399, pp. 35–36; "Report . . . Egypt and the Soudan in 1899," *PP*, 1900, CV, 995, p. 24: an Egyptian soldier, for example, who had been held captive in Sudan for fifteen years, returned to his village in Lower Egypt in 1899 with seven women slaves in tow. He was charged with importing and dealing in slaves.

52 FO 141/241, Schaefer to Baring, 16 December 1886.

53 FO 633/5, Cromer Papers, 127, Sir E. Baring to Mrs Amos, 25 February 1887.

54 "Correspondence Respecting Slavery in Egypt," Schaefer to Baring, 10 February 1887, *PP*, 1887, XCII, 679.

55 BFAAPS, Correspond., Rhodes House, S16 G25, Schaefer to Allen, 28 May 1888.

56 FO 141/202, Borg to Bowring, 7 October 1884; FO 141/217, Borg, "Memo on the Sale of Slaves from Family to Family," 31 August 1885; FO 633/5, Cromer Papers, 136, Sir E. Baring to Col. Kitchener, 5 March 1885; BFAAPS, Correspond.,

Rhodes House, s16 G25, Schaefer to Allen, 23 July 1888, includes Schaefer's report on a circular sent by Riyād Pāshā to all Egyptian *mudīrs* and governors exhorting them to enforce prohibitions on the slave trade.

57 FO 78/284, Campbell to Palmerston, 24 December 1836.

58 FO 141/203, Borg, "Draft of Memorandum for the Guidance of British Consular Officers," 12 December 1884.

59 FO 633/5, Cromer Papers, 1, Baring to Marquess of Ripon, 26 September 1883; FO 633/6, Cromer Papers, 21, Baring to Lord Granville, 14 January 1884.

60 "Despatch from Sir E. Baring Respecting Slavery in Egypt," 25 February 1884, *PP*, 1884, LXXV, 509.

61 FO 141/304, Cromer to Lord Kimberly, 15 November 1894.

62 BFAAPS, Correspond., Rhodes House, s16 G25, S. W. Baker to Allen, 20 December 1882.

63 FO 141/217, Baring to Salisbury, 31 August 1885.

64 FO 633/6, Cromer Papers, 70, Baring to Lord Iddesleigh, 14 November 1886.

65 FO 141/170, Borg to Earl to Dufferin, 23 December 1882.

66 "Report . . . Egypt and the Progress of Reforms, 1891," *PP*, 1892, XCVI, 399.

67 "Report . . . Egypt and the Progress of Reforms, 1895," *PP*, 1896, XCVII, 989; "Report . . . Egypt and the Progress of Reforms, 1896," *PP*, 1897, CII, 505.

68 al-Maḥdī, *Fatāwā*, vol. 1, 10 Rabīʿ 1 1296/1879, p. 89.

69 *Ibid.*, vol. 1, 12 Muḥarram 1295/1878, p. 88.

70 See Baer, *Studies*, pp. 183–184.

71 BFAAPS, Correspond., Rhodes House, s16 G25, W. S. Blunt to Allen, 17 March 1882.

72 "Report. . . Egypt and the Progress of Reforms, 1891," *PP*, 1892, XCVI, 399, p. 36.

73 "Report . . . Egypt and the Progress of Reforms, 1896," *PP*, 1897, CII, 505, p. 25.

74 See Brunschvig, "ʿAbd," in *EI*, pp. 25–30; and Schacht, *An Introduction*, pp. 127–129.

75 The sample includes 58 cases involving slaves from MBA and I, three cases from MM, and 70 opinions delivered by al-Maḥdī.

76 There were seven cases of owner-arranged marriage between slaves of the same household, out of a total of sixteen cases of owner-arranged marriage: I, s. 37, no. 511, 1276/1859–1860; al-Maḥdī, *Fatāwā*, vol. 1, 20 Ṣafar 1271/1854, p. 55 (two cases); vol. 2, 28 Rabīʿ II 1267/1851, p. 5; vol. 2, 13 Shawwāl 1269/1853, p. 9; vol. 2, 14 Jumādā I 1270/1854, p. 10; vol. 2, 5 Rajab 1270/1854, p. 11.

77 *Tadbīr (dabbara)* is the promise of manumission to take effect upon the death of the owner.

78 al-Maḥdī, *Fatāwā*, vol. 2, 28 Rabīʿ II, 1267/1851, p. 5.

79 *Ibid.*, vol. 1, 20 Ṣafar 1271/1854, p. 55 (two cases); vol. 2, 14 Jumādā I 1270/1854, p. 10.

80 *Ibid.*, vol. 2, 13 Shawwāl 1269/1853, p. 9.

81 *Ibid.*, vol. 2, 14 Jumādā I 1270/1854, p. 10; vol. 2, 24 Jumādā II, 1270/1854, p. 10; vol. 2, 24 Shawwāl 1270/1854, p. 11; vol. 2, 23 Muḥarram 1271/1854, p. 11; vol. 2, 25 Dhū al-hijjah 1271/1855, pp. 12–13; vol. 2, 11 Muḥarram 1272/1855, p. 13.

82 Brunschvig, "ʿAbd," in *EI*, p. 27.

83 Clot-Bey, *Aperçu*, vol. 1, p. 342; MAE, Correspond. con. et com., Alex. XXIII, Gros à ministre, 19 April 1828, p. 100.
84 al-Maḥdī, *Fatāwā*, vol. 1, 21 Dhū al-hijjah 1264/1848, pp. 15–16.
85 *Ibid.*, vol. 1, 8 Rabīʿ I 1268/1848, p. 16.
86 *Ibid.*, vol. 1, 23 Dhū al-hijjah 1264/1848, p. 16.
87 In al-Maḥdī's *Fatāwā*, we find many examples of marriage between slave and free. See vol. 1, 21 Rabīʿ I 1271/1854, p. 56; vol. 1, 20 Ṣafar 1273/1856, p. 65; vol 1, 22 Shaʿbān 1273/1857, p. 67; vol. 1, 10 Rabīʿ I 1296/1879, p. 89; vol. 2, 24 Rabīʿ I 1269/1853, pp. 7–8; vol. 2, 24 Jumādā II 1270/1854, p. 10; vol. 2, 24 Shawwāl 1270/1854, p. 11; vol. 2, 23 Muḥarram 1271/1854, p. 11; vol. 2, 25 Dhū al-hijjah 1271/1855, pp. 12–13; vol. 2, 11 Muḥarram 1271/1855, p. 13.
88 See Brunschvig, "'Abd," in *EI*, p. 28; and Schacht, *An Introduction*, p. 127.
89 al-Maḥdī, *Fatāwā*, vol. 2, 30 Dhū al-hijjah 1265/1849, p. 2; vol. 2, 24 Ramaḍān 1267/1851, p. 5; vol. 2, 23 Dhū al-qaʿdah 1269/1853, p. 9; vol. 2, 22 Jumādā I 1270/1854, p. 10.
90 *Ibid.*, vol. 2, 4 Jumādā 1268/1852, p. 6.
91 *Ibid.*, vol. 1, 6 Rajab 1266/1850, p. 389.
92 See Brunschvig, "'Abd," in *EI*, p. 28; and Schacht, *An Introduction*, p. 129.
93 I, s. 5, no. 603, 1255–1256/1839–1840; s. 23, no. 26, 1266/1849–1850; s. 24, nos. 60, 61, 1266/1849–1850; s. 37, no. 83, 1276/1859–1860.
94 Duff Gordon, *Letters*, pp. 174–175.
95 FO 633/6, Cromer Papers, 229, Cromer to Lord Kimberly, 9 December 1894.
96 al-Maḥdī, *Fatāwā*, vol. 2, 20 Rabīʿ/ II 1266/1850, p. 3; vol. 2, 23 Dhū al-hijjah 1267/1851, p. 5; vol. 2, 15 Jumādā II 1271/1855, p. 12.
97 *Ibid.*, vol. 1, 8 Rabīʿ II 1269/1853, p. 47.
98 *Ibid.*, vol. 2, 27 Shawwāl 1266/1850, p. 2; vol. 2, 10 Jumādā I 1271/1855, p. 12.
99 Brunschvig, "'Abd," in *EI*, p. 28.
100 MBA, s. 323, no. 565, 1216/1801–1802.
101 al-Maḥdī, *Fatāwā*, vol. 2, 25 Shaʿbān 1269/1853, p. 8.
102 For example, MBA, s. 387, no. 186, 1246/1830–1831; al-Maḥdī, *Fatāwā*, vol. 1, 29 Shawwāl 1265/1849, pp. 254–255; vol. 2, 4 Dhū al-hijjah 1269/1853, p. 9 (two cases).
103 al-Maḥdī, *Fatāwā*, vol. 2, 20 Muḥarram 1268/1851, p. 6; vol. 2, 26 Dhū al-hijjah 1269/1853, p. 10.
104 *Ibid.*, vol. 2, 20 Muḥarram 1268/1851, p. 6; vol. 2, 5 Rabīʿ II 1269/1853, p. 8; vol. 2, 24 Jumādā I 1269/1853, p. 8; vol. 2, 25 Shaʿbān 1269/1853, pp. 8 9; vol. 2, 4 Dhū al-hijjah 1269/1853, p. 9 (two cases); vol. 2, 26 Dhū al-hijjah 1269/1853, p. 10; vol. 2, 10 Rabīʿ I 1270/1853, p. 10; vol. 2, 10 Rabīʿ II 1272/1855, p. 13; vol. 2, 5 Dhū al-qaʿdah 1274/1858, p. 15; vol. 2, 19 Rajab 1279/1863, p. 15.
105 *Ibid.*, vol. 1, 27 Shawwāl 1266/1850, pp. 246–247; vol. 2, 6 Rabīʿ II 1268/1852, p. 6; vol. 2, 29 Shaʿbān 1268/1852, p. 7; vol. 2, 2 Rajab 1270/1854, pp. 10–11; vol. 2, 25 Rabīʿ II 1272/1856, p. 13; vol. 2, 24 Muḥarram 1273/1856, p. 14; vol. 2, 22 Jumādā II 1282/1865, p. 16; vol. 2, 9 Jumādā II 1290/1873, p. 16.
106 I, s. 5, nos. 468, 475, 484, 571, 1255–1256/1839–1840; s. 23, no. 42, 1266/1849–

1850; MBA, s. 345, nos. 289, 368, 584, 1226–1227/1811–1812; s. 366, no. 242, 1235–1236/1820–1821.

107 See, for example, al-Maḥdī, *Fatāwā*, vol. 1, 14 Rajab 1273/1857, pp. 66–67; vol. 2, 17 Jumādā I 1266/1850, p. 3; vol. 5, 12 Shaʿbān 1266/1850, p. 373.

108 Brunschvig, "ʿAbd," in *EI*, p. 29.

109 al-Maḥdī, *Fatāwā*, vol. 5, 7 Muḥarram 1265/1848, p. 71.

110 FO 141/205, Beaman to Baring, Cairo, 3 April 1884. Beaman, in his capacity as the *wakīl* of Yacūb Pāshā Sāmī, conveyed Yacūb's daughter's complaint against her brother-in-law.

111 On the unreliability of slave trade statistics, see Walz, *Trade between*, pp. 211–212. For a widely divergent list of importation figures, see Baer, *Studies*, pp. 171–172.

112 al-Maḥdī, *Fatāwā*, vol. 2, 25 Rabīʿ I 1267/1851, p. 4.

113 MBA, s. 345, no. 450, 1226–1227/1811–1812; or see, for example, al-Maḥdī, *Fatāwā*, vol. 1, 12 Muḥarram 1295/1878, p. 88; vol. 2, 28 Rabīʿ II 1267/1851, p. 5.

114 al-Maḥdī, *Fatāwā*, vol. 2, 25 Dhū al-hijjah 1271/1885, p. 12; vol. 2, 20 Shawwāl 1272/1856, pp. 13–14.

115 *Ibid.*,vol. 2, 4 Jumādā II 1269/1853, p. 8; vol. 2, 24 Rabīʿ II 1272/1856, p. 13; vol. 2, 8 Dhū al-qaʿdah 1272/1856, p. 14.

116 FO 141/179, Borg to Cartwright, 12 April 1883; FO 141/187, Schaefer to Baring, 22 September 1883; FO 141/226, Baring to Nūbar Pāshā, 16 May 1885; FO 141/235, Baring to Lord Rosebery, 9 May 1886; "Correspondence Respecting Slavery in Egypt," Schaefer to Baring, 10 February 1887, *PP*, 1887, XCII, 679; BFAAPS, Correspond., Rhodes House, S16 G25, Schaefer to Allen, 9 December 1888.

117 FO 141/217, Baring to Earl of Granville, 12 February 1885: concerning the case of a black female slave, Mabrūkah, whose former owner protested that he had not been consulted about her marriage; and FO 141/278, Cromer to Lord Salisbury, 30 April 1890: concerning a Circassian slave woman whose owner, a relative of Fakhrī Pāshā, current Minister of Justice, had sent Fakhrī Pāshā himself to fetch her from the manumission bureau and prevent her from obtaining a certificate.

118 MBA, s. 440, no. 243, 1266/1849–1850; I, s. 37, no. 519, 1276/1859–1860.

119 Djavidan, *Harem Life*, p. 106.

120 al-Maḥdī, *Fatāwā*, vol. 1, 26 Shaʿbān 1281/1865, p. 76; vol. 2, 22 Jumādā II 1282/1865, p. 16.

121 For the legal theory of clientage, see Brunschvig, "ʿAbd," in *EI*, pp. 30–31. For examples of nineteenth century practice, see al-Maḥdī, *Fatāwā*, vol. 1, 26 Shaʿbān 1281/1865, p. 76; vol. 2, 24 Muḥarram 1273/1856, p. 14; vol. 2, 22 Jumādā II 1282/1865, p. 16.

122 I, s. 24, no. 78, 1266/1849–1850; s. 37, no. 20, 1276/1859–1860.

123 MBA, s. 345, no. 551, 1226–1227/1811–1812.

124 MBA, s. 323, no. 326, 1216/1801–1802; s. 345, no. 492, 1226–1227/1811–1812; s. 388, no. 1168, 1246/1830–1831; s. 440, nos. 223, 225, 240, 243, 1266/1849–1850; s. 476, no. 257, 1276/1859–1860.

125 MM 46/138/59, 11 Rabīʿ I 1261/1845, fo. 17. The Dīwān al-Rūznāmah, under the Ministry of Finance, was responsible for land registration and the collection of the *mīrī*.

126 I, s. 5, no. 505, 1255–1256/1839–1840; s. 24, nos. 78, 86, 1266/1849–1850; s. 37, nos. 20, 33, 48, 80, 1276/1859–1860.

127 MBA, s. 388, no. 1092, 1246/1830–1831; I, s. 23, nos. 8, 46, 61, 97, 98, 1266/1849–1850; s. 24, nos. 67, 73, 1266/1849–1850; s. 37, nos. 63, 85, 508, 511, 519, 525, 573, 580, 582, 1276/1859–1860.

128 al-Maḥdī, *Fatāwā*, vol. 2, 9 Rabīʿ I, 1271/1854, p. 12; Djavidan, *Harem Life*, pp. 106–107.

129 MM 46/38/51, 6 Shawwāl 1245/1830, fo. 12; "Correspondence Respecting Slavery in Egypt," Schaefer to Baring, 10 February 1887, *PP*, 1887, XCII, 679.

130 MAE, Correspond. con. et com., Alex. XXV, de Lessups à ministre, 22 December 1834; BFAAPS, Correspond., Rhodes House, S16 G25, Schaefer to Allen, 11 September 1888.

131 BFAAPS, Correspond., Rhodes House, S22 G26 Moncrieff Report, 18 April 1886.

132 FO 141/170, Borg to Earl of Dufferin, 23 December 1882; BFAAPS, Correspond., Rhodes House, S16 G25, Dutrieux, 22 June 1883.

Appendix

1 For a detailed description of the Cairo courts in the seventeenth century, see Galal H. El-Nahal, *The Judicial Administration of Ottoman Egypt in the Seventeenth Century*; for a study of the contents of the Bāb al-ʿAlī registers, see Salwā Mīlād, "Sijallāt Maḥkamat al-Bāb al-ʿAlī: dirāsh arshīfiyyah diplūmatiyyah," unpublished PhD dissertation.

Glossary

afandī (*efendī*): respectful title for a man of the upper or middle classes
aghā: a Turkish official
ʿālim, *ʿulamāʾ* (pl.): a "learned man"; member of the religious elite
ʿālimah, *ʿawālim* (pl.): a "learned woman"; a trained female singer
amah: a slave woman
ʿarḍ al-fallāh: portion of the *iltizām* assigned to peasants
ʿarḍ al-wasīyah: portion of the *iltizām* assigned to *multazim*
ardabb: a dry measure equal to from 5 to 8 English bushels
awqāf: see *waqf*
balad: village
bāshā or *pāshā*: honorific title for male members of royal family or high officials
bey: title of an Ottoman official
chiflik: farm; royal estate
dallālah: a woman peddler, purveyor of consumer goods to the *ḥarīm*
dirham: a small silver coin
dīwān: council; ministry
diyah: blood money, the legal monetary compensation for causing a death
faddān: surface measure fixed at 4,416.533 square meters during Muḥammad ʿAlī's reign
fāʾiẓ: portion of land tax *multazim* entitled to retain
fallāh, *fallāḥīn* (pl.): a peasant
faskh or *tafrīq*: judicial decree of anulment of marriage
fatwā, *fatāwā* (pl.): legal opinion
firmān: decree or edict in the Ottoman Empire
ghafīr: guard, watchman
ghrūsh rūmī, *ghūrsh* (pl.): Ottoman piaster = 40 *parahs*
ḥadīth: a saying of the Prophet
ḥākim: governor; *ḥākim al-khuṭṭ*: governor in charge of a district (*khutt*); *ḥākim siyāsī*: civil judge
ḥarah: quarter of a city
ḥarīm: women's quarters
ḥiḍānah: legal rights to custody of a young child
ḥurmah: "woman"; common title for a woman of the lower classes
ʿiddah: the legal waiting period before a widow or divorcée can remarry
iltizām: tax farm

ʿizbah: a landed estate worked by resident peasants
jāriyah: a female slave
kharāj: land tax; *kharājīyah* land: category of land whose revenues accrue to the State
khātūn: "lady"; title of an upper class woman
khulʿ: divorce agreement by mutual consent of husband and wife
kurbāj: a whip or lash
madhhab: orthodox legal tradition; "school" of law
maḥkamah: Islamic court
mahr: bridal gift, paid by groom's family to the bride
maʾmūr: provincial administrator
marʾah: "woman"; title for woman of the peasant or urban lower classes
maṣūnah: "virtuous"; polite title for a woman of the middle or upper classes
maʿtūqah: a freed slave woman
maulid: an annual religious celebration commemorating a birth date – often of the Prophet or other revered people
maẓālim: council functioning as a court of appeal under civil authority
mīrī: the state land tax; *mīrī* land: land whose revenues accrue to State, used interchangeably with *kharājīyah* land
muftī: *ʿālim* empowered to issue *fatāwā*, usually acknowledged head of one of the four recognized *madhhabs*
multazim, *multazimah* (f.): a tax-farmer
nafaqah: legally required material maintenance based on bonds of kinship
nāʾib: an assistant; authorized representative of a *qāḍī*
nāshizah: a disobedient or rebellious wife, legally defined
nāẓir, *nāẓirah* (f.); a superintendent of *awqāf*
nisab: indication of lineage, origin, or kinship as part of a person's name
nisf fiḍḍah: Egyptian coin, same as *parah*; 90 *nisf fiḍḍah* = 1 *riyāl*
parah: unit of money; 40 *parahs* = 1 piaster or *ghrūsh rūmī*
qāḍī: a judge in an Islamic court
qāʾimmaqām: lieutenant-colonel; an official representing the *multazim* in the *iltizām*; a local administrator in Muḥammad ʿAlī's time
qiṣāṣ: "retaliation"; the death penalty for a murderer
riyāl: unit of money; 1 *riyāl* = 90 *parahs*
ṣadāq: the bridal gift, *mahr*
saʿīd: the region of Upper Egypt
sayyid, *sayyidah* (f.): "master" or "mistress"; respectful title for one of the *ashrāf*, direct descendants of the Prophet
shadūf: device to raise water for irrigation
sharīʿah: Islamic law
sharikah: legal partnership, association in Islamic law
shaykh: an instructor in a mosque; a tribal chief; a village leader or official, i.e. the *shaykh al-balad*
sitt: a "lady"; polite title for a woman of the upper classes
ṭāʾifah: troop; people; guild
ṭalāq: divorce by unilateral repudiation of wife by husband
ṭarbūsh: head gear

ṭarīqah: a mystical fraternity, a *ṣūfī* order
taṣarruf: right of usufruct
ʿulamāʾ: see ʿālim
ʿumdah: a village leader or head official
usyah land: land belonging to the *ʿarḍ al-wasīyah*
wakīl: assistant; agent in the court
walāyah: legal guardianship
wālī: governor of an Ottoman province; a legal guardian
waqf, *awqāf* (pl.): pious foundation endowed to benefit religious or charitable purpose
wazīr: vizier, assistant to the ruler; a cabinet minister

Bibliography

I. Archival sources

Egypt, Archives of the Maḥkamah shar ʿīyyah, Cairo. Bāb al-ʿAlī, registers 323, 345, 366, 370, 387, 388, 413, 440, 476; al-Iʿlanat, registers 5, 23, 24, 37 (see Appendix)

Egypt, Dār al-Maḥfuẓāt al-ʿumūiyyah, Cairo. Registers from the Maḥkamah Manṣūrah 47/138/37, 44, 49, 51, 57, 59

France, Les archives de la guerre, Vincennes. Two series were consulted: (1) B6: files 79–82, 96, 100, 102–109, 111, 118, 120, 121–127, 132, 135–137, 139–141, 161–162. Notes and correspondence from the French Expedition to Egypt (1798–1801); (2) MR (Memoires historiques): files 507–509, 511–516, 534, 538–539, 542–543, 546, 550, 553–555, 557, 565–566, 569, 571, 577–578, 581. Journals, reports, and memoirs from the period of the French Expedition. In addition, MR: files 1677–1678 contain information on military and related matters from 1770 to 1867

France, Les archives du ministère des affaires étrangères, Paris (MAE). Two series were consulted: (1) Correspondence consulaire et commerciale, Alexandrie, vols. XVI–XXXVI, 1792–1862, and le Caire, vols. XXV–XXX, 1786–1866; (2) Correspondence politique des consuls, Turquie: Alexandrie et le Caire, vols. I–XXIX, 1829–1861

United Kingdom, Public Record Office, London. The following series were consulted: (1) Egypt, FO 24/1–6 (1786–1818); (2) Turkey, FO 78/89–472, vols. on Egypt only (1817–1841), and FO 78/3319–4465, vols. on Egypt only (1881–1913); (3) Egypt, FO 141/36–590 (1840–1913); (4) Egypt, FO 142/1–16 (1805–1851); (5) FO 371/367, 368, 369, 372, 382, 383 (1906–1919); (6) FO 633, Cromer Papers; (7) PRO 30/57/9, Kitchener Papers

II. Unpublished papers

Boyle, Harry. Correspondence 1884–1923, St Antony's Private Papers, Oxford University

British and Foreign Anti-Slavery and Aborigines Protection Society. Nineteenth and twentieth century correspondence on slavery – North Africa and the Arab world. Rhodes House Library, Oxford, MSS British Empire S22: G25, G26, G30

Cheetham, Sir Milne. Private letters and telegrams to Sir A. Nicholson, Sir Louis Mallet, Sir Eldon Gorst, and Lord Kitchener on British policy in Egypt, 1910–1914. St Antony's Private Papers, Oxford University

D'Abernon Papers, British Museum, Department of Manuscripts, Add. 48961 A, B, vols. XLVI, XLVII, "Egypt in 1887"

deMorgan, William F. "Report on the Manufacture of Egyptian Glazed Pottery, 1892–1893," British Museum, Department of Manuscripts, Egerton 3293

Dilke Papers, British Museum, Department of Manuscripts, Add. 43923, vol. L, Parliamentary and other official papers of Sir C. Dilke, including memoranda prepared for the use of the Cabinet

Elmusa, Judith H. "Law, Social Change, and Political Order: Legal Reform in Egypt," PhD dissertation, Harvard University, May 1975
Freedman, Estelle Brenda. "Their Sisters' Keepers: The Origins of Female Corrections in America," Phd dissertation, Columbia University, 1976
Gladstone Papers, British Museum, Department of Manuscripts, Add. 44130, 44132, 44151, 44189, 44190, 44267, 44477, 44629, 44630, 44634, 44635, 44766, 44768, 44769, 44775
Hekekyan Papers, British Museum, Department of Manuscripts, Add. 37448–37471, 24 vols.
Lane, Edward W. "Description of Egypt," British Museum, Department of Manuscripts, Add. 34080–34088, 9 vols.
Mayer, Ann Elizabeth. "'Abbās Ḥilmī II: The Khedive and Egypt's Struggle for Independence," PhD dissertation, Michigan University, 1978
Mīlād, Salwā. "Sijallāt Maḥkamat al-Bāb al-ʿĀlī: dirāsah arshifīyyah diplūmatiyyah," PhD dissertation, Cairo University, 1975
Owen, Roger. "The Management of Large Estates in Nineteenth Century Egypt," mimeo
Seikaly, Samir Menas. "The Copts under British Rule, 1882–1914," D. Phil. thesis, London University, 1967
Young, J. W. A. "A Little to the East, Experiences of an Anglo-Egyptian Official, 1899–1925," unpublished MS, St Antony's Private Papers, Oxford University

III. Government publications

Egypt

Direction du recensement, *Recensement général de l'Egypte*, 2 vols., Cairo, Imprimerie nationale, 1898
La législation en matière immobilière en Egypte, Cairo, 1901 Maṣlaḥat al-iḥṣā' wa al-taʿdād. *The Census of Egypt Taken in 1917*, 2 vols., Cairo, Government Press, 1921

United Kingdom: Parliamentary Papers (*PP*)

"Convention between Great Britain and Egypt for the Suppression of Slavery," 1896, XCVII, 1047; 1896, XCVII, 1057
"Correspondence Respecting the Attack Made on Two Officers of Her Majesty's Army at Keneseh, in Egypt," 1887, XCII, 671
"Correspondence Respecting Condition of Egypt (1882 and 1889)," 1889, LXXXVII, 685
"Correspondence Respecting Execution of Provision of Convention with Egypt, 1877," 1884–85, LXXXIII, 475
"Correspondence Respecting Mixed Courts and Judicial Reforms," 1884, LXXXIX, 127
"Correspondence Respecting Re-organization in Egypt," 1883, LXXXIII, 1; 1883, LXXXIII, 43; 1883, LXXXIII, 197; 1883, LXXXIII, 147 (reports by Mr H. Villiers Stewart)
"Correspondence Respecting the Re-organization of the Egyptian Army," 1886, LXXIV, 159

"Correspondence Respecting Slavery in Egypt," 1887, XCII, 679
"Despatch from Sir E. Baring, Enclosing a Report on the Conditions of the Agricultural Population in Egypt," 1888, CX, 191
"Despatch from Sir E. Baring Respecting Slavery in Egypt," 1884, LXXV, 509
"Despatch Relative to the Efficiency and Gallantry of the Native Egyptian Troops," 1887, XCII, 425
"Further Correspondence Respecting the Affairs of Egypt," 1883, LXXXIII, 375
"Letter from General Stephenson to the Secretary of State for War as to the Existence in Egypt of a System similar to that which Prevailed under the Contagious Diseases Act," 1887, LVII, 751
"Reports by Colonel Johnson on Brigandage (so called) in Egypt," 1884–1885, LXXXIX, 1
"Reports by His Majesty's Agent and Consul-General on the Finances, Administration, and Condition of Egypt and the Soudan in 1899," 1900, CV, 995; "1900," 1901, XCI, 1057; "1901," 1902, CXXX, 703; "1902," 1903, LXXXVII, 953; "1903," 1904, CXI, 203; "1904," 1905, CIII, 1087; "1905," 1906, CXXXVII, 475; "1906," 1907, C, 617; "1907," 1908, CXXV, 183; "1908," 1909, CV, 333; "1909," 1910, CXII, 347; "1910," 1911, CIII, 241; "1911," 1912–1913, CXXXI, 635; "1912," 1913, LXXXI, 207; "1913," 1914, CI, 327.
"Reports by H. R. Greene, Surgeon Major, Medical Staff, Sous-Director of Sanitary Services of Egypt," 1884–1885, LXXXIX, 1
"Report by Mr. Villiers Stewart Respecting the Progress of Re-organization in Egypt since British Occupation in 1882," 1895, CIX, 941
"Reports by Sir Drummond Wolff on the Administration of Egypt," 1887, XCII, 431
"Report on the Administration and Condition of Egypt and the Progress of Reforms," 1890–1891, XCVII, 717
"Report on the Administration, Finances, and Conditions of Egypt and the Progress of Reforms," 1890–1891, XCVII, 717; 1891, XCVI, 399; 1892, XCVI, 399; 1893–1894, CXI, 1127; 1894, XCVI, 645; 1895, CIX, 895; 1896, XCVII, 989; 1897, CII, 505; 1898, CVII, 621; 1899, CXII, 961; 1900, CV, 995
"Reports on the State of Egypt and the Progress of Administrative Reforms," 1884–1885, LXXXIX, 1

IV. Published works, Arabic

ʿAbd al-Fatāḥ, Kāmīlyā. *Fī sīkulūjīyah al-mar'ah al-ʿāmilah*, Cairo, Maktabah al-qāhirah al-jadīdah, 1972
ʿAbd al-Raḥīm, ʿAbd al-Raḥīm ʿAbd al-Raḥman. *al-Rīf al-miṣrī fī al qarn al-thāmin ʿashr*, Cairo, Maṭbaʿah Jāmiʿah Jāmiʿah ʿAin Shams, 1974
Aḥmad, Aḥmad Ṭaha. *al-Mar'ah, kifāḥhā wa ʿamalhā*, Cairo, Dār al-jamāhīr, 1964
ʿAmr, Ibrāhīm. *al-Arḍ wa al-fallāḥ*, Cairo, Maṭbaʿah al-dār al-maṣrīyah, 1958
al-Ḥatta, Aḥmad Aḥmad. *Ta'rīkh al-zirāʿah al-miṣrīyah fī ʿahd Muḥammad ʿAlī al-kabīr*, Cairo, Dār al-maʿārif, 1369/1950
al-Ḥifnāwī, ʿAbd al-Mujīd Muḥammad. *Ta'rīkh al-qanūn al-maṣrī*, Cairo, Mu'assasah al-thaqāfah al jāmiʿīyah, 1972–1973
al-Jabartī, ʿAbd al-Raḥman. *ʿAjā'ib al-āthār fī al-tarājim wa al-akhbar*, 3 vols., Beirut, Dār al-Fāris, n.d.

al-Jiritlī, ʿAlī. *Taʾrīkh al-ṣināʿah fī misr fī al-nisf al-awwal min al-qarn al-tisʿa ʿasharah*, Cairo, Dār al-maʿārif, 1952

Khalīfa, Ijlāl. *al-Ḥarakah al-nasāʾīyah al-hadīthah*, Cairo, al-Maṭbaʿah al-ʿarabīyah al-jadīdah, 1973

al-Maḥdī, Muḥammad al-ʿAbbāsī. *al-Fatāwā al-maḥdīyah fī al-waqāʾi al-miṣrīyah*, 7 vols., Cairo, al-Maṭbaʿah al-Azharīyah, 1031–1304/1883–1886

Muḥammad, Raūf ʿAbbās Ḥāmid. *al-Ḥaraka al-ʿummālīyah fī Miṣr: 1899–1952*, Cairo, Dār al-kātib al-ʿarabī, 1968

al-Rāfiʿī, ʿAbd al-Raḥman. *ʿAsr Muḥammad ʿAlī*, Cairo, al-Nahḍah al-miṣrīyah, 1951

Taʾrīkh al-ḥarakah al-qawmīyah wa taṭawwur niẓām al-hukm fī miṣr, 3 vols., Cairo, Maṭbaʿah al-nahḍah, 1347–1348/1919–1930

Riḍā, Muḥammad Rashīd. *Fatāwā al-Imām Muḥammad Rashīd Riḍā*, 6 vols., Beirut, Dār al-kitāb al-jadīd, 1970

al-Saʿadāwī, Nawāl. *al-Marʾah wa al-jins*, Beirut, al-Muʾassasah al-ʿarabī lil-dirāsāt wa al-nashr, 1972

Shafīq, Dorīyah. *al-Marʾah al-miṣrīyah*, Cairo, Maṭbaʿah maṣr, 1955

Taymūr, Aḥmad. *al-Amthāl al ʿāmmīyah*, Cairo, Maṭabiʿ al-aḥrām al-tujarīyah, 1970

al-Waqāʾiʿ al-miṣrīyah, selected issues, Dār al-Kutab, Cairo

Zaghlūl, Aḥmad Fathī. *al-Muḥāmāt*, Cairo, Maṭbaʿah al-maʿārif, 1900

Zanātī, Maḥmūd Sallām. *Taʾrīkh al-qanūn al-miṣrī fī al-ʿusūr*, Cairo, Dār al-nahḍah al-ʿarabīyah, 1973

V. Published works, western language

Abdel-Malek, Anouar. *Egypt: Military Society, the Army Regime, the Left, and Social Change under Nasser*, Charles Lam Markmann (tr.), New York, Vintage Press, 1968

Abu-Lughod, Janet. *Cairo: 1001 Years of the City Victorious*, Princeton University Press, 1971

Anderson, J. N. D. "The Eclipse of the Patriarchal Family in Contemporary Islamic Law," in J. N. D. Anderson (ed.), *Family Law in Asia and Africa*, London, Allen and Unwin, 1968, pp. 221–234

Artin Pasha, Yacoub, *L'instruction publique en Egypte*, Paris, Ernest Leroux, 1890

Baer, Gabriel. *Egyptian Guilds in Modern Times*, Jerusalem, Israel Oriental Society, 1964

A History of Landownership in Modern Egypt, London, Oxford University Press, 1963

Population and Society in the Arab East, New York, Routledge and Kegan Paul, 1964

Studies in the Social History of Modern Egypt, Chicago University Press, 1969

Beck, Lois. "Women among the Qashqa'i Nomadic Pastoralists in Iran," in Lois Beck and Nikki Keddie (eds.), *Women in the Muslim World*, Cambridge, Mass., Harvard University Press, 1978, pp. 351–373

Beinin, Joel. "Formation of the Egyptian Working Class," *MERIP Reports*, 94 (February 1981), 13–23

Bloch, Marc. *Slavery and Serfdom in the Middle Ages*, William R. Beer (tr.), Berkeley, University of California Press, 1975

Boserup, Ester. *Women's Role in Economic Development*, New York, St Martin's Press, 1970

Boyle, Clara. *Boyle of Cairo, A Diplomatist's Adventures in the Middle East*, London, Titus Wilson and Son, 1965

Brunschvig, R., "'Abd," in *Encyclopaedia of Islam*, new edn, in process, 4 vols. to date, Leiden, E. J. Brill, 1960, vol. 1, part 1, pp. 24–40

Chabrol de Volvic, M. de. *Essai sur les moeurs des habitants modernes de l'Egypte*, Paris, n.p., n.d.

Chehata, Chafik. *Etudes de droit musulman*, Paris, Presses universitaires de France, 1971

Clot-Bey, Antoine. *Aperçu général sur l'Egypte*, 2 vols., Bruxelles, Meline, Cans, 1840

Mémoires de A. B. Clot-Bey, published and annotated by Jacques Tagher, Cairo, 1949

Cole, Juan Ricardo. "Feminism, Class, and Islam in Turn-of-the-Century Egypt," *IJMES*, 13 (1981), 387–407

Coles, Charles E. *Recollections and Reflections*, London, St Catherine Press, 1918

Cooper, Frederick. *Plantation Slavery on the East Coast of Africa*, New Haven, Yale University Press, 1977

Coulson, N. J. *Conflicts and Tensions in Islamic Jurisprudence*, Chicago University Press, 1969

A History of Islamic Law, Edinburgh University Press, 1964

Succession in the Muslim Family, Cambridge University Press, 1971

Cuno, Kenneth M. "The Origins of Private Ownership of Land in Egypt: A Reappraisal," *IJMES*, XII, 3 (1980), 245–275

Davidson, Basil. *The African Slave Trade. Precolonial History 1450–1850*, Boston, Little, Brown, 1961

De Jong, F. *Ṭuruq and Ṭuruq-linked Institutions in Nineteenth Century Egypt*, Leiden, E. J. Brill, 1978

Déscription de l'Egypte, état moderne, 4 vols., Paris, 1809–1812

Djavidan, Hanum. *Harem Life*, London, Noel Douglas, 1931

Duff Gordon, Lady. *Letters from Egypt (1862–1869)*, enlarged centenary edn, London, Routledge and Kegan Paul, 1969

Eisenstein, Zillah. "Developing a Theory of Capitalist Patriarchy," in Zillah Eisenstein (ed.), *Capitalist Patriarchy and the Case for Socialist Feminism*, New York, Monthly Review Press, 1979, pp. 5–40

Engels, Frederick. *The Origin of the Family, Private Property and the State*, ed. with intro. and notes by Eleanor Burke Leacock, New York, International Publishers, 1972

Esposito, John L. *Women in Muslim Family Law*, Syracuse University Press, 1982

Fahmy, Mustafa. *La révolution de l'industrie en Egypte et ses conséquences sociales au 19e siècle*, Leiden, E. J. Brill, 1954

Fakkar, Rushdi. *Aspects de la vie quotidienne en Egypte: à l'époque de Mehemet-Ali, première moitié du XIXe siècle, d'après les souvenirs d'une fille du peuple, en Egypte, 1834–1836, de Suzanne Voilquin*, Paris, G.-P. Maisonneuve et Larose, 1975

Fernea, E. W. *Guests of the Sheikh*, Garden City, NY, Doubleday, 1965

Finley, M. J. "Between Slavery and Freedom," *Comparative Studies in Society and History*, VI, 3 (April 1964), 233–249

Firestone, Yakov. "Production and Trade in an Islamic Context," *IJMES*, VI, 2 (April 1975), 185–209

"Production and Trade in an Islamic Context, Part Two," *IJMES*, VI, 3 (July 1975), 308–325

Foucault, Michel. *Discipline and Punish, The Birth of the Prison*, Alan Sheridan (tr.), New York, Pantheon Books, 1977

Fyzee, Asaf. *Outlines of Muhammedan Law*, 3rd edn, London, Oxford University Press, 1964

Geertz, Clifford. "Suq: The Bazaar Economy in Sefrou," in Clifford Geertz, Hildred Geertz, and Lawrence Rosen, *Meaning and Order in Moroccan Society*, Cambridge University Press, 1979, pp. 123–244

Gordon, Ann D., Mari Jo Buhle, and Nancy Schrom Dye, "The Problem of Women's History," in Berenice A. Carroll (ed.), *Liberating Women's History*, Urbana, University of Illinois Press, 1976, pp. 75–92

Gran, Peter. *Islamic Roots of Capitalism, Egypt 1760–1840*, Austin, University of Texas Press, 1979

Hamont, P. N. *L'Egypte sous Mehemet Ali*, 2 vols., Paris, Leautey et Lecointe, 1843

Heyd, Uriel. "The Ottoman ʿUlema and Westernization," in Uriel Heyd (ed.), *Studies in Islamic History and Civilization*, Scripta hierosolymitana, Jerusalem, Magnes Press, Hebrew University, 1961, vol. 9, pp. 63–96

Heyworth-Dunne, J. *An Introduction to the History of Education in Modern Egypt*, London, F. Cass, 1968

Hopkins, Keith. *Conquerors and Slaves, Sociological Studies in Roman History*, Cambridge University Press, 1978

Hourani, Albert. "History," in Leonard Binder (ed.), *The Study of the Middle East*, New York, Wiley, 1976, pp. 97–136

Humphries, Jane. "The Working Class Family, Women's Liberation, and Class Struggle: The Case of Nineteenth Century British History," *RRPE*, IX, 3 (Fall 1977), 25–41

Ignatief, Michael. *A Just Measure of Pain, The Penitentiary in the Industrial Revolution 1750–1850*, New York, Pantheon Books, 1978

Issawi, Charles. "Egypt since 1800: A Study in Lopsided Development," in Charles Issawi (ed.), *The Economic History of the Middle East, 1800–1914*, University of Chicago Press, 1966, pp. 359–374

Jennings, Ronald C., "Women in Early Seventeenth Century Ottoman Judicial Records," *Journal of the Economic and Social History of the Orient*, 18 (January 1975), 53–114

Keddie, Nikki. "Problems in the Study of Middle Eastern Women," *IJMES*, X, 2 (1979), 225–240

Kerblay, Basil. "Chayanov and the Theory of Peasantry as a Specific Type of Economy," in Theodor Shanin (ed.), *Peasants and Peasant Societies*, Harmondsworth, Penguin Books, 1971

Kuhnke, Laverne. "The 'Doctoress' on a Donkey: Women Health Officers in Nineteenth Century Egypt," *Clio Medica*, IX, 3 (1974), 193–205

Landes, David S. *Bankers and Pashas; International Finance and Economic Imperialism in Egypt*, London, Heinemann, 1958

Lane, Edward. *An Account of the Manners and Customs of the Modern Egyptians*, 5th edn, ed. Edward Stanley Poole, New York, Dover Publications, 1973

Lane-Poole, Stanley. *Cairo. Sketches of its History, Monuments, and Social Life*, 3rd edn, London, J. S. Virtue, 1898

Social Life in Egypt, A Description of the Country and its People, London, J. S. Virtue, 1884

Lawson, Fred H. "Rural Revolt and Provincial Society in Egypt, 1820–1824," *IJMES*, XIII, 2 (1981), 131–153

Lerner, Gerda. "Placing Women in History: A 1975 Perspective," in Berenice A. Carroll (ed.), *Liberating Women's History*, Urbana, University of Illinois Press, 1976, pp. 357–368

Linant de Bellefonds, Y. "Ḥaḍanah," in *Encyclopaedia of Islam*, new edn, in process, 4 vols. to date, Leiden, E. J. Brill, 1971, vol. 3

Traité de droit musulman comparé, Paris, n.p., 1965–1973

Mabro, Robert, and Samir Radwan. *The Industrialization of Egypt 1939–1973, Policy and Performance*, Oxford, Clarendon Press, 1976

Madden, R. R. *Egypt and Mohammed Ali*, 2nd edn, London, Hamilton, Adams, 1841

Travels in Turkey, Egypt, Nubia and Palestine in 1824, 1825, 1826, and 1827, 2 vols., London, H. Colburn, 1829

Maher, Vanessa. *Women and Property in Morocco: Their Changing Relation to the Process of Stratification in the Middle Atlas*, London, Cambridge University Press, 1974

"Women and Social Change in Morocco," in Lois Beck and Nikki Keddie (eds.), *Women in the Muslim World*, Cambridge, Mass., Harvard University Press, 1978, pp. 100–123

Marsot, Afaf Lufti al-Sayyid. "The Revolutionary Gentlewoman in Egypt," in Lois Beck and Nikki Keddie (eds.), *Women in the Muslim World*, Cambridge, Mass., Harvard University Press, 1978, pp. 261–276

al-Masry, Youssef. *Le drame sexuel de la femme dans l'Orient arabe*, Paris, Laffront, 1962

Meillassoux, Claude. *Femmes, greniers et capitaux*, Paris, François Maspero, 1975

Mernissi, Fatima. *Beyond the Veil, Male–Female Dynamics in a Modern Muslim Society*, Cambridge, Mass., Schenkman Publishing, 1975

Milner, Viscount. *England in Egypt*, 13th edn, New York, Howard Fertig, 1970

Montran, R. "L'empire ottoman et le commerce asiatique aux 16e et 17e siècles," in D. S. Richards (ed.), *Islam and the Trade of Asia*, Philadelphia, University of Pennsylvania Press, 1970, pp. 169–180

Muller, Viana. "The Formation of the State and the Oppression of Women: Some Theoretical Considerations and a Case Study in England and Wales," *RRPE*, IX, 3 (Fall 1977), 7–21

el-Nahal, Galal. *The Judicial Administration of Ottoman Egypt in the Seventeenth Century*, Minneapolis, Bibliotheca Islamica, 1979

Nerval, Gerard de. *Scènes de la vie orientale*, Paris, n.p., 1848

Nwulia, Moses D. E. *Britain and Slavery in East Africa*, Washington, DC, Three Continents Press, 1975

Owen, E. R. J. *Cotton in the Egyptian Economy 1820–1914*, Oxford, Clarendon Press, 1969

The Middle East in the World Economy 1800–1914, London, Methuen, 1981

Panzac, Daniel. "La population de l'Egypte à l'époque contemporaine," in M.-C. Aulas,

L'Egypte d'aujourd'hui, permamence et changement, Paris, Editions du Centre national de la recherche scientifique, 1977, pp. 157–178

Peters, Emrys L. "The Status of Women in four Middle Eastern Communities," in Lois Beck and Nikki Keddie (eds.), *Women in the Muslim World*, Cambridge, Mass., Harvard University Press, 1978, pp. 311–350

Philipp, Thomas. "Feminism and Nationalist Politics in Egypt," in Lois Beck and Nikki Keddie (eds.), *Women in the Muslim World*, Cambridge, Mass., Harvard University Press, 1978, pp. 277–294

"Rapport de la Commission du Commerce et de l'Industrie," in Charles Issawi (ed.), *The Economic History of the Middle East 1800–1914*, University of Chicago Press, 1966, pp. 452–460

Raymond, André. *Artisans et commerçants au Caire au XVIIIe siècle*, 2 vols., Damascus, Institut Français de Damas, 1973–1974

"Deux leaders populaires au Caire à la fin du XVIIIe et au début du XIXe siécle," *La Nouvelle Revue du Caire*, I (1975), 281–398

"Le Caire," in M.-C. Aulas, *L'Egypte d'aujourd'hui*, Paris, Editions du Centre national de la recherche scientifique, 1977, pp. 213–242

"Problèmes urbaines et urbanisme au Caire au XVIIe et XVIIIe siècles," in *Colloque international sur l'histoire du Caire*, Cairo, Ministère de la culture, 1972, pp. 353–372

"Quartiers et mouvements populaires au Caire au XVIIIème siècle," in P. M. Holt (ed.), *Political and Social Change in Modern Egypt*, London, Oxford University Press, 1968, pp. 104–116

"Une liste des corporations de métiers au Caire en 1801," *Arabica*, IV, part 2 (1957), 151–163

Reiter, Rayna. "Introduction," in Rayna Reiter (ed.), *Toward an Anthropology of Women*, New York, Monthly Review Press, 1975, pp. 11–19

"Report by Mr. Cave on the Financial Conditions of Egypt," in Charles Issawi (ed.), *The Economic History of the Middle East*, University of Chicago Press, 1966, pp. 430–438

Richards, Alan. *Egypt's Agricultural Development, 1800–1980. Technical and Social Change*, Boulder, Colo., Westview Press, 1982

"Primitive Accumulation in Egypt, 1798–1822," *Review*, I, I (Fall 1977), 3–49

Rivlin, Helen Anne B. *The Agricultural Policy of Muḥammad ʿAlī in Egypt*, Cambridge, Mass., Harvard University Press, 1961

Rosaldo, Michelle Zimbalist. "A Theoretical Overview," in Michelle Zimbalist Rosaldo and Louise Lamphere (eds.), *Women, Culture, and Society*, Stanford University Press, 1974

Russell, Thomas (Pasha). *Egyptian Service, 1902–1946*, London, John Murray, 1949

al-Saʿadawi, Nawal. *The Hidden Face of Eve*, London, Zed Press, 1980

Sacks, Karen. "Engels Revisited: Women, the Organization of Production, and Private Property," in Rayna Reiter (ed.), *Toward an Anthropology of Women*, New York, Monthly Review Press, 1975, pp. 211–234

Said, Edward. *Orientalism*, New York, Pantheon Books, 1978

St John, James Augustus. *Egypt and Mohammed Ali; or Travels in the Valley of the Nile*, 2 vols., London, Longman, Rees, Orme, Brown, Green and Longman, 1834

Savary, C. E. *Lettres sur l'Egypte*, 3 vols., Paris, an VII (1798)

Sayigh, Rosemary. "Roles and Functions of Arab Women: A Reappraisal,' *Arab Studies Quarterly*, III, 3 (Autumn 1981), 258–274
Schacht, Joseph. *An Introduction to Islamic Law*, Oxford University Press, 1964
Scott, C. Rochfort. *Rambles in Egypt and Candia*, 2 vols., London, H. Colburn, 1837
Shaw, Stanford J. *The Financial and Administrative Organization of Ottoman Egypt, 1517–1798*, Princeton University Press, 1962
Shukri, Ahmad. *Muhammedan Law of Marriage and Divorce*, New York, Columbia University Press, 1917
Steegmuller, Francis. *Flaubert in Egypt: A Sensibility on Tour*, London, Little, Brown, 1972
Sullerot, Evelyne. *Histoire et sociologie du travail feminin*, Paris, Gothier, 1968
Thorner, Daniel. "Peasant Economy as a Category in Economic History," in Teodor Shanin (ed.), *Peasants and Peasant Societies*, Harmondsworth, Penguin Books, 1971
Tignor, Robert L. *Modernization and British Colonial Rule in Egypt, 1882–1914*, Princeton University Press, 1966
Tillion, Germaine. *Le harem et les cousins*, Paris, Editions du Seuil, 1966
Tyan, Emile. *Histoire de l'organization judiciaire en pays d'Islam*, 2nd edn, Leiden, E. J. Brill, 1960
Vallet, Jean. *Contribution à l'étude de la condition des ouvriers de la grande industrie au Caire*, Valence, Imprimerie Valentinoise, 1911
Walz, Terence. *Trade between Egypt and Bilād as-Sudān, 1700–1820*, Cairo, Institut français d'archeologie orientale du Caire, 1978
Whately, M. L. *Child-Life in Egypt*, Philadelphia, American Sunday-Schools Union, 1866
Willcocks, Sir William, and J. I. Craig. *Egyptian Irrigation*, 3rd edn, 2 vols., London, E. and F. N. Spon, 1913
Wolf, Eric. *Peasants*, Englewood Cliffs, NJ, Prentice-Hall, 1966
Youssef, Nadia. *Women and Work in Developing Societies*, Berkeley, Institute of International Studies, University of California, 1974
Zaretsky, Eli. *Capitalism, the Family and Personal Life*, Winnipeg, Canadian Dimension, 1974
Ziadeh, Farhat. *Lawyers and the Rule of Law and Liberalism in Modern Egypt*, Stanford, Hoover Institute Publications, 1968

Index